What Readers Are Saying

"The most selfless and amazing book I have ever read. Thank you Annie Grace for your wisdom, intelligence, sense of humor, and love. I do believe you have saved my life. Today my youngest child got her final exam results and the next phase of her life begins. She will not be alone. Thank you, Annie Grace, for this gift." —*Bernie M., Dublin, Ireland*

"What an amazing book! *This Naked Mind* has been an eye-opener for me. I thought I could consciously decide to give up alcohol, and now I understand the necessity of informing the subconscious mind of the evils of drinking and then the cravings just disappear! I have also read and applied the work of Dr. John Sarno and knew the power of the subconscious mind but cannot believe how effective the book and method was for me. Thank you!" —*Theresa G., Chapel Hill, North Carolina*

"I loved this gentle, down-to-earth explanation of problems with alcohol use, and the clear, structured way to challenge your thinking and behaviors around drinking. It helped me pass from shame and guilt into real and positive action." —*Elizabeth R., Australia*

"Without sounding too extreme, this book has significantly—and I think permanently—changed me and my attitude toward drinking. I have used Annie's wisdom and done some things alcohol-free that I would never have thought I could do. I can't say enough good about it and advise those who are ambivalent about drinking and not drinking to read it. Thanks again, Annie Grace, you've given me my life back, seriously."

—*Katy F., Albuquerque, New Mexico*

"As a huge fan of Jason Vale, I was really interested to read *This Naked Mind*. It was so interesting to read more about the science behind addiction and the unconscious mind. It added a new level to my understanding of why I want to live a sober and happy life! I highly recommend this book to anyone, whether they are interested in cutting down or staying alcohol-free; there are so many practical tips and suggestions. I loved it!"

—*Sarah L., London, United Kingdom*

"Genuinely hopeful and realistic philosophy and practice. Thanks, Annie Grace." —*Louise P., Des Moines, Iowa*

"*This Naked Mind* brought clarity and focus on my drinking and ten-year struggle with sobriety that I had never paused to examine. Annie methodically brings the reader along a logical path of discovery. I felt she was speaking directly to me and that she knows exactly where I am mentally and physically. I continue to return to certain passages for reaffirmation. I highly recommend the excellent book to anyone seeking a refreshing approach to seeing alcohol in the full light of the day with eyes wide open."

—*Sam G., Sydney, Australia*

"*This Naked Mind* delves into the psychology and physiology behind addiction and addresses these exceedingly well with thoughtfully structured chapters and memorable analogies. You will realize how alcohol truly has no place in your life and the myths we use to justify its consumption. Really, really cannot recommend this neat little book enough."

—*Cheryl W., Melbourne, Australia*

"Reading *This Naked Mind* has been nothing short of a miracle. It has helped me to see alcohol for what it is and ended a twenty-five-year cycle of binge drinking and 'trying' to stop or moderate alcohol. I have not had a single craving since reading it, which is unheard of for me. I'm totally comfortable in situations where other people are drinking, and I don't feel the need to avoid temptation, because there isn't any! I feel happier, I'm regaining confidence, and my health is getting better every day. A must-read for anyone who wants to take control of their drinking but doesn't want a lifetime of struggle." —*Kay W., The Lake District, United Kingdom*

"Annie's book offers readers a unique and refreshing perspective on our relationship with alcohol and how that relationship can be changed. It exposes the false notion that alcohol is an essential feature of an interesting and happy life. The real gem in Annie's book is the idea that changing your relationship with alcohol need not be a life of endless suffering and deprivation, that a decision to change can in fact be quite simple and liberating. This book forces us to confront society's relationship with alcohol and will change lives." —*Tony S., Sydney, Australia*

"I never realized how powerless I was against alcohol until I got my power back. A moderate to heavy drinker in my twenties, I desired to drink less as I got older. To my surprise, the desire was not enough, and I struggled to stay in control of my cravings. After reading *This Naked Mind* I feel, for the first time in my life, an extraordinary sense of freedom and happiness about my relationship with alcohol. I am eternally grateful to Annie Grace for this amazing gift!" —*Mary P., Brooklyn, New York*

"This is an honest book. It is genuine. It is told in a simple manner that is cogent and memorable. It helped me, and I will likely read it again sometime. Thank you, Annie Grace." —*Steve G., Toronto, Ontario*

"It was unfathomable to consider moderating my alcohol intake that has been a daily habit for the last twenty-eight years. Unfathomable, that is, until I read Annie's book. In one week, I went from entrenched regular drinker to fully and happily alcohol-free—bypassing the moderation route entirely. I am so grateful to Annie Grace for her frank, compelling, and scientifically sound exposé on the insidious nature of alcohol. If you're considering freeing the hold that alcohol has over you, this is an inspiring and groundbreaking must-read. I am forever inspired and changed."
—*Kate S., Los Angeles, California*

"There is nothing but truth in your words. *This Naked Mind* is an awesome book that has filled my life with hope for the future."
—*Jacob K., Springvale, Minnesota*

"Awesome book. I've come to terms and it's time to end this destructive ride, but it came home this weekend . . . literally. While I digested your excellent book, my one and only child announced a weekend visit. This alcohol sickness slapped me senseless as I immediately felt panic at the idea of interrupting my drinking path. This book made me open my eyes, my heart and my soul to the grip this monster had on me when I was weighing my ability to drink vs. the few precious visits where I get to see my son who is my reason for living. Thank you, Annie. Simple words, but I am not able to express otherwise. Your words are a worthy sword, just the elixir I needed. Humbly yours." —*Victor L., Austin, Texas*

"Your voice in the book is clear as a bell and brings amazing clarity to the situation of drinking and drinkers and addiction, and the circularity of the substance itself causing the discomfort that we think the imbibing fixes. Skeptic that I am, your little book holds a big universe of hope."
—*Heidi M., Plymouth, Massachusetts*

"*This Naked Mind* has allowed me to view my drinking habits from a new perspective. Now I know the science behind my addictive tendencies, sobriety has become less of a struggle and more of a celebration because I am finally free to live life on my own terms rather than under the control of alcohol. The message in *This Naked Mind* is truly liberating."
—*Marcus J., London, United Kingdom*

"As a wife, parent, and counselor, I was increasingly distressed by my pattern of daily drinking and increasing dependence on alcohol. However, *This Naked Mind* gave me the critical insights into my own mind that I needed in order to overcome my problems. Now I have my energy, vitality, and health back. I highly recommend *This Naked Mind* for anyone concerned about their drinking." —*Rhiana N., Sydney, Australia*

"I stumbled upon *This Naked Mind* after another heavy relapse into alcohol misery, four weeks of nonstop boozing leading me near suicide. I have been a heavy drinker since eighteen and a severe alcoholic for the past ten years. With the one shred of myself left within me, I risked delirium tremens and instead of going to another detox facility (which never worked for me) or submitting to another higher power A.A. meeting (which also led to nothing), I came across a new, groundbreaking approach called *This Naked Mind*. I was three days into my severe withdrawals when I placed those headphones on and began listening to the audio version of Annie's book. I felt an instant connection with the words and experiences that Annie had gone through. Through the next three days and nights I furiously listened to the program, her words, backed by fact, and found myself coming to the realization that alcohol is poison, and all I needed was for this to be explained to me with facts and an understanding and compassionate heart. As of today, I still haven't had a drink, and I can only highly recommend this program to anyone who has a serious problem with alcohol. It just works." —*Wilder D., Melbourne, Australia*

"Prior to reading *This Naked Mind*, I was a moderate drinker with what I considered a very healthy relationship with alcohol. I figured that this probably wasn't targeted at me, but I decided to give it a try anyway. How wrong I was! By the time I was done reading the book, I had come to believe that there is no such thing as a healthy relationship with alcohol. The author's examples, analogies, and personal stories are incredibly compelling. My perspective changed entirely. I questioned why I drank at all, realizing that I received little if any value from drinking. Immediately upon reading this book, I lost the desire for my evening drinks, and I found the strength to have dinner with friends without drinking a couple of beers. Don't get me wrong—I haven't completely stopped drinking. I still have a drink or two occasionally. But it is far less frequent, and it is on my terms rather than out of habit or social pressure. If this book can have such a strong impact on somebody who didn't want to change, I can only imagine how powerful it can be for people who are truly looking for a change in their life." —*John D., New Jersey*

"Drinking levels that we once considered alcoholism are now the norm. Gourmet wines and boutique beers are marketed to us as an almost essential daily luxury. If you, like me, have found that alcohol has become more of a burden than a pleasure, Annie Grace's book is the key to regaining control. It's an honest, eloquent look at the dangerous realities of our drinking culture, which gives you all of the tools you need to take back control of your life and unlock the door to a new, happier life."

—*Victory W., Perth, Australia*

THIS NAKED MIND

Control Alcohol, Find Freedom,
Discover Happiness & Change Your Life

THIS NAKED MIND

Control Alcohol, Find Freedom,
Discover Happiness & Change Your Life

Annie Grace

AVERY

AN IMPRINT OF PENGUIN RANDOM HOUSE

NEW YORK

AVERY

an imprint of Penguin Random House LLC
penguinrandomhouse.com

Most Avery books are available at special quantity discounts for bulk purchase for sales promotions,
premiums, fund-raising, and educational needs. Special books or book excerpts also can be created
to fit specific needs. For details, write SpecialMarkets@penguinrandomhouse.com.

ISBN 9780525537236
ebook ISBN 9780996715010

Printed in the United States of America
19th Printing

Cover design and illustrations by DeAndre & Mary Purdie

Edited by Quill Pen Editorial Services

To He Who Is:

Because you loved me before I knew your name and taught me there is always room at the bottom.

Husband:

Thank you for your incredible strength and amazing grace.

Be in touch:

thisnakedmind.com
thisnakedmind.com/next
hello@thisnakedmind.com
Twitter: @thisnakedmind
Facebook: This Naked Mind

ACKNOWLEDGMENTS

"Here's to . . . The ones who see things differently. They're not fond of rules. And they have no respect for the status quo. You can quote them, disagree with them, glorify or vilify them. About the only thing you can't do is ignore them. Because they change things. They push the human race forward. And while some may see them as the crazy ones, we see genius. Because the people who are crazy enough to think they can change the world, are the ones who do."
—Apple Inc.

Above all others, I take great pleasure in acknowledging Dr. John Sarno and Mr. Allen Carr (1934–2006). Dr. Sarno is the father of The Mindbody Syndrome (TMS). He opened my mind to the power of the unconscious, and this book is my adaptation of his methods to the brain disease of addiction. Without Dr. Sarno's groundbreaking work this book would not have been possible.

Allen Carr is the author of *The Easy Way to Stop Smoking, Stop Drinking Now*, and many other Easyway™ books. Mr. Carr was an incredible source of inspiration and influence on the subject of drug addiction. I, and many other influential authors, learned from Allen's revolutionary ideas, discoveries, and understanding of addiction.

Dr. Sarno and Mr. Carr will forever have my sincerest admiration and gratitude.

I would like to also thank these brilliant minds whose ideas contributed extensively to this work:

- Thad A. Polk, professor of psychology and EECS at the University of Michigan and creator of the program *The Addictive Brain*, for his neurological insight into the reward circuit and the cycle of addiction;

- Dave Gray, author of *Liminal Thinking*, for his unique and methodical approach in changing beliefs we hold that may be based on flawed reality;

- Steve Ozanich, Mindbody healing author, who furthered Dr. Sarno's work and took the time to inspire me in the earliest days of this journey;

- Dan Harris, author of *10% Happier*, for bringing practicality and humor to the journey into the mind;

- Malcolm Gladwell, bestselling author, speaker, and journalist, for encouraging us all to challenge known ways of thinking;

- Charles Duhigg, *New York Times* staff writer and author of *The Power of Habit*, for his groundbreaking work on habit and willpower;

- Johann Hari, bestselling author of *Chasing the Scream,* for his new look at addiction and deep passion for changing the way society views and treats addicts;

- Carl Jung, founder of analytical psychology, for his insight into "the shadow" and his contribution to Bill Wilson's journey to sobriety;

- Bill Wilson, founder of Alcoholics Anonymous, not a doctor or psychologist, but a man who saved himself from addiction through seemingly unconventional methods. He changed the lives of millions by looking at the same old things in a different way.

TABLE OF CONTENTS

PREFACE

3:33 a.m. I wake up at the same time every night. I briefly wonder if that is supposed to mean something. Probably not, probably just a coincidence. I know what's coming, and I brace myself. The usual thoughts begin to surface. I try to piece the previous evening together, attempting to count my drinks. I count five glasses of wine, and then the memories grow fuzzy. I know I had a few more, but I've now lost count. I wonder how anyone can drink so much. I know I can't go on like this. I start to worry about my health, beginning the well-trodden road of fear and recrimination: What were you thinking? Don't you care about anything? Anyone? How will it feel if you end up with cancer? It will serve you right. What about the kids? Can't you stop for the kids? Or Brian? They love you. There's no good reason why, but they do. Why are you so weak? So stupid? If I can just make myself see the horror of how far I've fallen, maybe I can regain control. Next come the vows, my promises to myself to do things differently tomorrow. To fix this. Promises I never keep.

I'm awake for about an hour. Sometimes I cry. Other times I'm so disgusted that all I feel is anger. Lately I've been sneaking into the kitchen and drinking more. Just enough to shut down my brain, fall back asleep, and stop hurting.

These early mornings are the only time I'm honest with myself, admitting I drink too much and need to change. It's the worst part of my day, and it's always the same, night after night. The next day it's as if I have amnesia. I turn back into a generally happy person. I can't reconcile my misery, so I simply ignore it. If you ask me about drinking I'll tell you I love it; it relaxes me and makes life fun. In fact, I'll be shocked if you don't drink with me. I will wonder, "Why on earth not?" During the day I feel in control. I am successful and busy. The outward signs of how much I drink are practically nonexistent. I am so busy that I don't leave room for honesty, questioning, and broken promises. The evening comes, the drinking starts, and the cycle continues. I am no longer in control, and the only time I am brave enough to admit it (even to myself) is alone, in the dark, at three in the morning.

The implications of what it could mean are terrifying. What if I have a problem? What if I am an alcoholic? What if I am not normal? Most terrifying, what if I have to give up drinking? I worry that my pride will kill me because I have no intention of labeling myself. I am afraid of the shame and stigma. If my choice is to live a life of misery in diseased abstinence or drink myself to an early grave, I choose the latter. Horrifying but true.

What I know about getting help, I know from my brother who spent time in prison. Prison in the U.S. often involves Alcoholics Anonymous (A.A.) meetings. He says you start every meeting admitting that you are an alcoholic, powerless against alcohol. He says they believe alcoholism is a fatal illness without a cure. And I personally know self-proclaimed alcoholics who, rather than finding peace, fight a daily battle for sobriety. It seems miserable in our culture to be sober. To live a life avoiding temptation. Recovering appears synonymous with accepting life as just OK and adjusting to a new reality of missing out.

The idea of recovering seems to give alcohol more power even, and, maybe especially, when I am abstaining from it. I want freedom. It's now clear that alcohol is taking more from me than it's giving. I want to make it small and irrelevant in my life rather than allowing it more power over me. I want change. I have to find another way. And I have.

I now have freedom. I am back in control and have regained my self-respect. I am not locked in a battle for sobriety. I drink as much as I want, whenever I want. The truth is I no longer want to drink. I see now that alcohol is addictive, and I had become addicted. Obvious, right? Not exactly. In fact, in today's drinking society, it's not obvious at all. Admitting that alcohol is a dangerous and addictive drug like nicotine, cocaine, or heroin has serious implications. So we confuse ourselves with all sorts of convoluted theories.

I've never been happier. I am having more fun than ever. It's as if I have woken up from the *Matrix* and realized that alcohol was only dulling my senses and keeping me trapped rather than adding to my life. I know you may find this hard, if not impossible, to believe. That's OK. But I can give you the same freedom, the same joy, and the same control over alcohol in your life. I can take you on the same journey—a journey of facts, neuroscience, and logic. A journey that empowers you rather than rendering you powerless. A journey that does not involve the pain of deprivation.

I can put you back in control by removing your desire to drink, but be forewarned, getting rid of your desire for alcohol is the easy part. The hard part is going against groupthink, the herd mentality of our alcohol-saturated culture. After all, alcohol is the only drug on earth you have to justify *not* taking.

Experts imply that it takes months, even years, of hardship to stop drinking. A tough riddle can make you crazy, taking forever to solve. But if someone gives you the answer, solving the riddle becomes effortless. I hope this book will be the answer you are looking for.

I offer a perspective of education and enlightenment based on common sense and the most recent insights across psychology and neuroscience. A perspective that will empower and delight you, allowing you to forever change your relationship with alcohol. And remember, sometimes what you are searching for is in the journey rather than the destination.

All my best,
Annie Grace

THIS NAKED MIND

Control Alcohol, Find Freedom,
Discover Happiness & Change Your Life

INTRODUCTION

"We can't be afraid of change. You may feel very secure in the pond that you are in, but if you never venture out of it, you will never know that there is such a thing as an ocean, a sea." —C. JoyBell C.

What if, by reversing years of unconscious conditioning, you could return to the perspective of a non-drinker? Not a recovering (sober) alcoholic but a person with the same desire, need, and craving for alcohol as someone who has never picked up a bottle—a true non-drinker. Well, you can. By the end of this book, you will be free to weigh the pros and cons of drinking and determine alcohol's role in your life without emotional or illogical cravings. You can remain happy about your choice because it will be yours alone, decided from a place of freedom rather than out of obligation or coercion. Your desire to drink will be gone, so no matter what you choose you won't feel like you are missing out. You won't be pining for a drink or avoiding social situations because of temptation. Without desire there exists no temptation. Importantly, you won't have to label yourself as diseased or powerless.

This book will change your perception by showing you why you drink, both psychologically and neurologically. You may believe you already understand why you drink—to relieve stress, engage socially, or liven up a party. These are your rationalizations for drinking, but you actually drink for subtler and less conscious reasons. Understanding these reasons will put you back in control. It will end your confusion and eliminate your misery. But first, we must undo years—decades—of unconscious conditioning about alcohol.

And don't beat yourself up for anything you have struggled with in the past (including unsuccessful attempts to quit). It's counterproductive. There is a powerful misconception that people who can't control their drinking are weak-willed. In my experience it's often the strongest, smartest, and most successful people who drink more than they should. Drinking, or wanting to drink, does not make you weak. You may find it hard to believe, but an inability to control how much you drink is not a sign of weakness. So let's stop any self-loathing right now.

You may find it impossible to believe drinking less won't involve deprivation. The idea of drinking less fills you, as it did me, with dread. You worry that parties and social occasions will become tedious and difficult to attend. If you drink to relieve stress, the thought of losing the added support you believe alcohol provides can be terrifying. But it's true. With this approach you can effortlessly drink less and feel happy about it. What a euphoric, life-changing experience! You'll be excited to go out with friends, even to bars, knowing that not a drop of alcohol will cross your lips.

Does drinking less mean drinking nothing? Do you need to quit forever? That will be up to you. You will make your own decision based on information that empowers you, giving you back control rather than imposing rules on you. We will explore all aspects of the drinking cycle. Don't worry about making a decision about how much or how often you will drink now. What is important in this moment is that you have hope. You need to know this approach can and will work—that you will be released from the clutches of alcohol.

Maybe you think I don't grasp your situation, how dependent you've become on booze. Perhaps you've been drinking heavily for many years, and these claims seem absurd. That's OK. Skepticism won't impact the result.

No matter why you picked up this book, you'll find nothing but great news here. If you read, critically consider, and absorb the information in these pages, you will be inspired to sever or cut back on your relationship with alcohol without feeling deprived. In fact, you'll be happy, possibly euphoric, about your decision. You will feel in control and empowered to make conscious, logical, fact-based choices about the role alcohol will play in your life. I encourage you to read between one and two chapters a day, progressing with momentum, yet allowing sufficient time to absorb the content.

Don't change your day-to-day routine, even if it includes drinking. You heard correctly—feel free to continue to drink while reading the book. This may seem counterintuitive, but you will see that it is important to the process. Of course, if you have already stopped drinking there is no reason to start, and I am absolutely not encouraging you to do so. What's important is that you continue your regular routines so you don't create stress and foster a sense of deprivation while trying to absorb this information. You will need to focus and critically consider what *This Naked Mind* presents to you. However, it is important, if possible, to read sober in order to fully grasp the material. And don't skip ahead. The concepts build on themselves. This book will challenge you, so please be willing to open your mind and question long-held beliefs.

Finally, be hopeful. You are about to accomplish something incredible—regaining control. I know it hasn't happened yet, but you can be excited about it now. So, throughout the book, do your best to maintain a positive state of mind. Change often occurs when the pain of the current situation becomes so great you become willing to change without fully understanding what the future holds. You probably imagine a life without alcohol as painful, even scary.

This perception encourages you to put off change as long as possible. I will show you how altering your drinking habits will not cause pain, but instead allow you to enjoy your life more than you ever thought possible. With this approach, you are not clutching to the proverbial burning platform. You do not have to choose between the lesser of two evils (continuing to drink or living a life of deprivation). Rather, you will make the simple choice between your current state and a bright and exciting future. It's OK, even encouraged, to allow yourself to feel hopeful. This book contains a revolutionary approach. It will change your life for the better.

1.
THIS NAKED MIND:
HOW AND WHY IT WORKS

unconscious: un·con·scious | /ənˈkänSHəs/ *noun.*
The part of the mind that a person is not aware of but that is a powerful force in controlling behavior.

conscious: con·scious | /ˈkänSHəs/ *adjective.*
Aware of something (such as a fact or feeling), knowing that something exists or is happening.

consciousness: con·scious·ness | /ˈkänSHəs-nəss/ *noun.*
The condition of being conscious
: the quality or state of being aware especially of something within oneself
: the upper level of mental life which the person is aware of as contrasted with unconscious processes.

Definitions sourced from Merriam-Webster's.

Conscious or Unconscious Thought?

Did you know your unconscious mind is responsible for your desires? Most of us don't think about the distinction between our conscious and unconscious thoughts, but that distinction forms a vital piece of the alcohol puzzle. Studies confirm we have two separate cognitive (thinking) systems—the conscious and the unconscious.[1] The give-and-take between unconscious choices and our rational, conscious goals can help explain the mystifying realities of alcohol.[2]

We are all fairly familiar with the conscious (or explicit) mind. Conscious learning requires the aware, intellectual grasp of specific knowledge or procedures, which you can memorize and articulate.[3] When we want to change something in our lives, we usually start with a conscious decision. However, drinking is no longer a fully conscious choice in your life. Therefore, when you make a conscious decision to drink less, it's almost impossible to adhere to that decision because your larger, more powerful unconscious mind missed the memo.

Unconscious learning happens automatically and unintentionally through experiences, observations, conditioning, and practice.[4] We've been conditioned to believe we enjoy drinking. We think it enhances our social life and relieves boredom and stress. We believe these things below our conscious awareness. This is why, even after we consciously acknowledge that alcohol takes more than it gives, we retain the desire to drink.

The neurological changes that occur in your brain as a result of alcohol compound this unconscious desire. Thad A. Polk, neuroscientist, professor, and author of *The Addictive Brain* (a 2015 course on the newest science of addiction), says viewing addiction through the eyes of neuroscience allows us to "look beyond the seemingly bizarre behavior of addicts and see what is going on inside their brain."[5] In my early days on this journey, the undermining of my desire to drink less by a strange desire to drink more seemed nothing if not bizarre.

The mind, specifically the unconscious mind, is a powerful force in controlling our behavior. Information suggesting the benefits of alcohol surrounds us, yet we rarely become conscious of it. According to the Neuro-Linguistic Programming (NLP) communication model, we are assaulted with over two million bits of data every second, but we are only consciously aware of seven bits of that information.[6] Television, movies, advertising, and social gatherings all influence our beliefs. From childhood we've observed, with few exceptions, our parents, friends, and acquaintances appearing to enjoy moderate, "responsible" drinking. These images teach our unconscious minds that alcohol is pleasurable, relaxing, and sophisticated.

Your opinions about alcohol and your desire to drink spring from the lifelong mental conditioning of your unconscious mind. This desire has likely been compounded by specific neurological changes in the brain. The goal of *This Naked Mind* is to reverse the conditioning in your unconscious mind by educating your conscious mind. By changing your unconscious mind, we eliminate your desire to drink. Without desire, there is no temptation. Without temptation, there is no addiction.

Like most things that have been ingrained in us since childhood, we believe in alcohol without question, like we believe the sky is blue. Through this book, you will think critically about your deeply-held beliefs about alcohol and strip away those that are false. This will convince the all-powerful unconscious mind and allow harmony and agreement between your conscious and unconscious minds.

When the Brain Causes Pain

I cannot overstate the importance of your unconscious mind. I learned this lesson from Dr. John Sarno, a renowned physician who investigates the connection between physical pain and emotions. A *Forbes* article calls Dr. Sarno "America's Best Doctor,"[7] and his methodology has successfully healed all sorts of people, including controversial radio personality Howard Stern. Sarno coined the term The Mindbody Syndrome, the theory that your mind, below your conscious awareness, rather than any physical injury or ailment, may be responsible for your pain. After the birth of my second son, I experienced crippling back pain. Incapacitated for weeks at a time, I spent thousands of dollars on treatment. I tried chiropractic care, acupuncture, traditional doctors, muscle relaxants, and painkillers. I attended weekly physical therapy, including traction and massage. For three years I was unable to pick up my kids, and no type of treatment helped.

Through Sarno's work I learned the true source of my affliction, and through reading his book I was cured. I know this is hard to believe. Yet here I sit—I've remained pain-free for years. Many thousands of people have been forever cured of chronic pain through Dr. Sarno's work. There is even a website set up by individuals Dr. Sarno has cured. The purpose? To provide a place for people to write thank-you letters to Dr. Sarno to express their gratitude for giving them their lives back. It's truly amazing and can be found at thankyou drsarno.org. Dr. Sarno's approach of targeting and speaking to your unconscious mind is the same approach I employ for regaining control over alcohol.

Dr. Sarno methodically proved to me that the back pain I felt— pain that no medical professional could diagnose—was related to suppressed stress and anger.[8] How do we accumulate all this suppressed stress and anger? Imagine a young father. His wife (who no longer has time for him) hands him their screaming baby. She is exhausted and needs a break. He takes the child and tries everything to comfort him. Forty minutes later the baby is still screaming. The father is frustrated and angry. How can he not be? His needs are not being met, the baby's actions are illogical, and he feels useless. In his mind, it is unacceptable to feel angry at a helpless baby, so these emotions remain buried in his subconscious, or as psychiatrist Carl Jung calls it, "the shadow."[9]

We hide emotions that we feel to be abhorrent in "the shadow." We are unwilling to accept this part of us. So, we assert, "I am a good person; there is no way I want to harm this helpless baby," and we unconsciously repress our negative emotions. In order to deeply bury reprehensible emotions, your brain can cause physical pain to distract you. The pain is real. Laboratory tests demonstrate that the pain is caused when your brain cuts off oxygen to the afflicted area. Epidemiologists call this transfer of symptoms *amplification*.[10] Amplification prevents unacceptable ideas from surfacing.

Your Unconscious Mind at Work

> *"Anything unconscious dissolves when you shine*
> *the light of consciousness on it."*
> —*Eckhart Tolle*

Why am I telling you all this? Drinking and back pain seem like two very different problems. So what do "the shadow" and amplification have to do with drinking? It's hard to believe that reading a book cured my back pain, but perhaps you can see how physical pain could originate in your emotions. Your conscious mind may now be willing to entertain this theory. But if I only needed to consciously accept the fact that the pain stemmed from my emotions rather than a physical injury, the cure would have been instant. Simply hearing the theory and accepting it consciously would have been enough to heal my back. But while my consciousness could grasp the concepts relatively easily, the pain remained. This is because it was my unconscious, rather than conscious, mind that needed to understand, to grasp the reality of the situation. And that process, the process of Dr. Sarno speaking to my unconscious mind, took me reading a 300-page book.

The unconscious mind is not logical; it's all about feelings. It is the source of love, desire, fear, jealousy, sadness, joy, anger, and more. The unconscious mind drives your emotions and desires. When you make a conscious decision to quit or cut back on alcohol, your unconscious desires remain unchanged. You have unknowingly created an internal conflict. You want to cut back or quit, but you still desire a drink and feel deprived when you do not allow yourself one.

Also, the unconscious mind often works without the knowledge or control of the conscious mind.[11] Studies from as far back as 1970 prove our brains actually prepare for action 1/3 of a second before we consciously decide to act. This means that even when we think we are making conscious decisions, our unconscious mind actually makes the decision for us.[12]

You can easily test this and reveal the extent to which your unconscious mind controls your conscious decisions. Remember a day when you were in a bad mood for no reason. You couldn't pinpoint what was wrong; you just felt grumpy. If your conscious mind controlled your emotions, you could simply think, "I am going to be happy," and your mood would change from grumpy to sunny. Have you tried that? Did it work?

When I am in a bad mood, a conscious thought to try to be happier—or, worse, someone telling me to just be happy—does nothing to improve my mood. It does the opposite. Why? Because your conscious mind doesn't control your emotions. Granted, you can train your conscious mind in more positive or negative thought patterns, which ultimately alters how you feel. These repeated conscious thoughts eventually influence your unconscious and therefore your feelings.

So how does your unconscious mind feel about alcohol? Today's society has conditioned your unconscious mind to believe alcohol provides pleasure, enjoyment, and support—that it is vital to social situations and stressful situations alike. This book reverses that conditioning by stripping away your false beliefs about alcohol. We will do this with the help of Liminal Thinking, a method developed by author Dave Gray. Liminal Thinking defines how, through the conscious exploration and acceptance of new ideas and truths, you can influence your unconscious mind. This gives you back your ability to make rational and logical decisions about alcohol, no longer influenced by illogical, emotional, or irrational desires. It will give you control and freedom by changing your understanding of and therefore your relationship with alcohol. While tradition, advertising, and societal norms condition our unconscious to believe that alcohol is beneficial, Liminal Thinking and the material in this book will expose that unconscious conditioning and recondition your unconscious, exposing alcohol and giving you freedom.

Experience and the Unconscious Mind[13]

In order to influence the unconscious mind, we need to first talk about the way in which personal experience ties to the unconscious. Perhaps you've heard the ancient story about the blind men and the elephant. Three blind men are brought into a room with an elephant, and each man touches a different part. One touches the tail, one the trunk, and one the side. When asked what they are touching they begin to argue. The one touching the trunk believes he is touching a snake; the one touching the body, a wall; and the one touching the tail, a rope.

Each blind man is saying what he believes to be true. And their experience proves it. Since we tend to trust our experiences implicitly, we understand how the argument started. Of course, the truth is that none of them are correct. They are all experiencing a piece of reality and forming their own, very different, opinions.

Gray explains that we only see and experience part of reality, and no matter how many experiences we have had, our brains are not

powerful enough to experience and observe everything. Gray makes the point that we are limited by what we pay attention to: "In any given moment, the more you focus on one aspect of your experience, the less you notice everything else."[14] We usually notice only the things specific to our immediate reality: the society we grew up in, the media, the influencers in our lives, and our actual life experiences.

Gray states that upon those relevant experiences and observations we make assumptions, from those assumptions we draw conclusions, and from those conclusions we form beliefs.[15] Gray defines belief as everything we "know" to be true.[16]

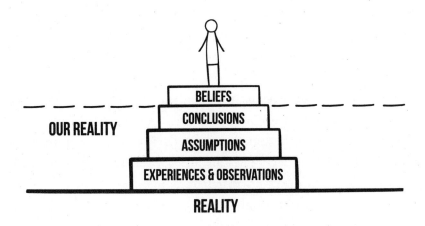

This illustration demonstrates that the things we "know" to be true are not actually formed by reality, but by reality as we have interpreted it from our experiences, observations, assumptions, and conclusions. Consider how this applies to alcohol. Collectively held beliefs are not built directly on the foundation of reality.

These beliefs can include statements like:

· Alcohol provides enjoyment.
· Alcohol provides relief.

- Alcohol is the key to social situations.
- A party can't really be a party without booze.
- Alcohol makes us funnier or more creative.
- Alcohol can relieve our stress or boredom.
- For some it can be hard, if not impossible, to stop drinking.
- The very definition of alcoholic and alcoholism.

These beliefs can be particularly difficult to change for several reasons. One reason is that we unconsciously self-seal them by seeking out things that are congruent with them. This is called confirmation bias, the tendency to search for or interpret information in a way that confirms one's preconceptions. We can find confirmation for our preconceptions about alcohol in many forms, including the media, the people we drink with, and our internal rationalizations. Adages about drinking found hanging in so many households illustrate a confirmation bias. Some of my favorites are:

- It's not drinking alone if the kids are home.
- We have too much wine, said no one ever.
- It's not a hangover; it's wine flu.
- I cook with wine; sometimes I even put it in the food.
- Wine! Because no great story started with someone eating a salad.

The kicker is that these beliefs have become so ingrained in our minds and our society, and so repeatedly self-sealed, that they are programmed into our unconscious. And our unconscious controls our emotions and our desires.[17] By definition the unconscious is not readily accessible or easily changed.[18] We need a specific process to dive into the foundation of our beliefs, examine them, and change our perceived reality.

So what happens when your experiences with alcohol start to contradict your bubble of self-sealing belief? Perhaps your experiences are no longer wholly positive, and you start to question your drinking. Or maybe you hear new information about the dangers of drinking.

Gray says that one of the ways we make sense of these new ideas that don't fit with our current beliefs is to look for external validity. Can we take the new information and test it out to prove its merit? However, especially with alcohol, we often don't make it that far. This is because the new information doesn't have internal coherence—it doesn't fit with what you "know" to be true. And because it is lacking in internal coherence, you will *unconsciously reject it before you have a chance to consciously consider it.* This happens all the time. We both consciously and unconsciously disregard information we don't want to hear. And when we do this, we never have a chance to see if this new information is indeed true; we never move to test it against reality.[19]

Why does this happen? Because we like certainty; it feels safe. Gray explains this unconscious behavior helps us deal with the realities of life, many of which are uncomfortable. It allows us to outsource some of the fear that attacks us when we confront certain truths. Reality is uncertain, and uncertainty causes fear. We try to protect ourselves from this fear by staying inside our bubble of belief until something happens that we cannot ignore. At that point we are forced to confront reality.

For me, it was one hangover too many, leaving me unable to function during the day as a result of my heavy drinking at night. I reached a point where I could no longer ignore the fact that alcohol was affecting my career and my relationships. This forced me to confront new information that said wine was not the joy juice I believed it to be.

But at this stage, attempting to drink less felt practically impossible. Why? I lived with a huge bubble of self-sealing belief around my drinking. I believed alcohol enhanced my creativity, made me funnier and more outgoing, allowed me to enjoy social situations, relieved my stress at the end of a long day, and comforted me when something went wrong. Giving up drinking felt like an incredible sacrifice, like the loss of a close friend. These were beliefs I had never previously questioned that had been built up over a lifetime of experiences, observations, assumptions, and conclusions.

I *knew* these beliefs to be true. I felt I would never be able to relax without a glass of wine. I honestly believed social situations would be boring and even depressing without alcohol. Even when I realized these beliefs were illogical, they still *felt* true because they were embedded in my unconscious and were much stronger than my logical, conscious reasoning. As Gray says, "construction of belief is not something we do consciously, it's something we do unconsciously."[20] In the illustration below you can see how everything shaded in below the line of our beliefs represents the things we are not consciously aware of.

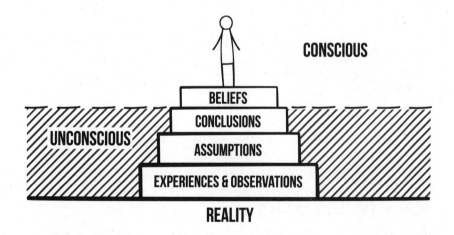

So what can we do? How can we explore reality and change our unconscious belief that alcohol is the "elixir of life" to fit with our conscious desire to drink less? It's relatively simple. We need to bring unconscious experiences, observations, assumptions, and conclusions into conscious thought. This allows your unconscious to change. The concept is scientifically proven—scientists now realize that the brain is able to change and adapt in response to new experiences, in a process called neuroplasticity.[21]

The process of illuminating your unconscious foundation of belief will influence your unconscious mind. To do this, I will logically and critically provide you with information about alcohol and addiction. I will expose your beliefs, assumptions, and conclusions by presenting you with methodical, factual, and rational arguments for you to question and evaluate. You'll be completely in control: I will strip away misinformation and present new concepts you have not yet critically considered. I will give you the tools to discover your own truth, your own reality, to understand that the rope you think you are holding might really be the tail of an elephant. Let's get started.

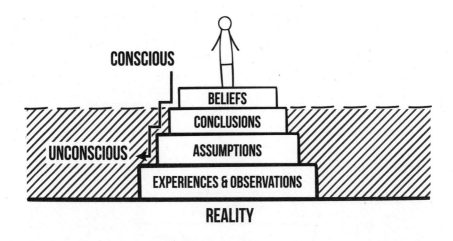

Alcohol: The "Elixir of Life"?

Alcohol is addictive. This fact has been proven over and over again. It is the nature of the substance, and it doesn't matter who you are or how in control you believe yourself to be. Your physical response when you drink alcohol is to want more. Alcohol hooks you through its addictive and dehydrating nature. Again, this is a physiological fact. Before you drank alcohol, you didn't miss it; you didn't think about it. You were happy and free.

If you're having problems with alcohol, you've already realized alcohol is not a miracle elixir. You know it's costing you money, health, friendships, and maybe even your marriage. Your conscious mind knows all of this. The problem is that your unconscious is continuously assaulted with messages about the "joy" it brings and the stress it relieves. These messages come from external sources, friends, family, and of course, advertising. These messages are confirmed by internal sources—your past experiences with alcohol. This book will address both.

Over the next day, notice how many messages you are exposed to about the "pleasures" and "benefits" of alcohol. Look around—from your friends to what you watch on television, almost everything in our society tells you, both *consciously* and *unconsciously*, that alcohol is the "elixir of life," and without it your life would be missing a key ingredient.

The Twelfth Juror

"Truth rests with the minority . . . because the minority is generally formed by those who really have an opinion." —Søren Kierkegaard

Alcoholism appears complex because it is misunderstood, not only by drinkers and their families but also by experts. We must see through these illusions. In short, we need to become detectives and lay bare the information, evaluate it, and discover the truth.

You may wonder, if common knowledge about alcohol and addiction is false, why do we believe it? How do we, as a society, accept untrue propositions as fact? Great questions. To answer them, let's look at a jury deliberating in a trial. It's a large jury with twelve jurors. Eleven of them are convinced of the defendant's guilt and one believes in his innocence. Do we believe the eleven jurors or the one? For the single juror to detain an exhausted jury (the decision must be unanimous), he must be absolutely sure of his position. In fact, you could argue that he is more certain than the eleven. Going against the grain is not easy. He must see something the rest do not. Suppose the eleven are experts? How much firmer in his stance must that single juror be? It appears the one juror is considering a perspective the eleven are not.

One of my favorite authors, Terry Pratchett, famously said, "We must be able, at any time, to accept the fact that we could all be absolutely and utterly wrong." It can be difficult to accept that the majority might be wrong, but it is a possibility we must entertain. It's amazing how drinkers can be incredibly open-minded about many things, yet close-minded when it comes to alcohol. This is because of the compartmentalization that happens within the mind of any substance-addicted person. So keep your mind open.

Visualize Success!

You are now ready to suspend judgment. To explore your unconscious desire to drink, to understand the reasons why you drink. This is great, and if you are willing to be honest with yourself and look deep into your belief system, you will find success.

This Naked Mind will help you explore your unconscious—and therefore influence it—as you work through the book. This type of book encourages your mind to consider the information when you are not actually reading and even when you sleep. That being said, you can take certain steps to ensure success. You may notice repetition throughout the book. You're a busy person and want me to cut to the chase. Rest assured, it is repetitive for a reason. For most of your life you have been repeatedly exposed to media, peer pressure, and many other influences. Repetition is vital to undoing a lifetime of ingrained beliefs. Despite the repetition, I've tried to make the content as interesting as possible.

Emotions and images—not necessarily images you see but images in your mind—comprise the language of your unconscious mind.

When you experience emotions related to the content, you will speak more directly to your unconscious. Importantly, you should feel hopeful when reading this book. The theory is sound, and I've included the most up-to-date scientific, medical, and psychological information. It works. It will work for you. Concentrate on that, and be hopeful.

Visualizing success always helps. A growing body of research suggests our unconscious minds cannot actually tell the difference between a real experience and a vividly imagined fake experience.[22] So visualize success—like being incredibly happy, laughing, and having a great time out with friends while drinking lemonade. You can even spend a few minutes each morning and night imagining the life you want while feeling positive emotions. This inspires success.

Get excited about what the future holds. Cultivate feelings of success even before you are successful. You hold all the tools you need to regain control of your drinking. Begin to think about the power of your mind and the strength of your body. This is exciting! In fact regaining control of my life through *This Naked Mind* is one of the most exciting and life-affirming things that has happened to me. It can be the same for you.

Don't dwell on past experiences. Your past is in the past. You have been caught, and through this book you will see that your alcohol problem is not your fault. Forgive yourself. You are the hero of this story. There is no reason to dwell on the negativity of the past and every reason to forgive yourself. Look forward to an incredible future.

Finally, relax! Let go of expectations, remain positive, and just let it happen. In Shawn Achor's book *The Happiness Advantage,* he states, "positive emotions broaden our scope of cognition and behavior . . . they dial up the learning centers of our brains to higher levels. They help us organize new information, keep that information in the brain longer, and retrieve it faster later on. And they enable us to make and sustain more neural connections, which allows us to think more quickly . . . and see new ways of doing things."

Do what you can to put yourself in a positive frame of mind while reading. There is so much to look forward to! Trust the approach, and more importantly, trust your unconscious to do the right thing for you. You can't control or micromanage your unconscious. Worry and stress are conscious activities—don't bother with them.

2.
THE DRINKER OR THE DRINK?
PART 1: THE DRINKER

"The world we have created is a process of our thinking.
It cannot be changed without changing our thinking."
—Albert Einstein

To find a cure we must understand the problem. What causes the alcohol epidemic in society, the drinker or the drink? We will look carefully at each.

The Blame Game 1.0: Me

Who is to blame? It seems society would have you believe that it is you, the drinker. You probably believe that your inability to control drinking—unlike "regular" drinkers who can "take it or leave it"—is due to a flaw you possess and they don't. What if that's not true?

I bet when you drink more than you should or when you wake up with a hangover, you beat yourself up. I know I did. I would drink a bottle or more of wine each evening and fall asleep quickly. But I awoke at 3 a.m. when the carbohydrates and energy from the alcohol flooded my system. Every night, I lay there and chastised myself for overindulgence, vowing to be better tomorrow.

The next day seemed invariably long and tiring, and by late afternoon I craved my wine. When evening came, I pushed the vows I'd made to the back of my mind. Sound familiar? For you it may be a different drink, a different cycle. Perhaps your drinking is not quite as bad, or maybe it's worse. The bottom line is that when we discover we are unable to control our alcohol, we blame ourselves. It's easy to do. Society blames us; our families blame us; our friends look at us with pity, wondering why we can't get our lives under control. We live in a state of constant self-loathing. What if it's not your fault?

It is difficult to be drinking more than you would like. You start to hate yourself, feeling weak and out of control. If you hadn't hid your problem so well more people would judge you, wondering why you can't simply "get it together," "be responsible," and "take control." After all, they drink but don't seem to have a problem.

If you are like most problem drinkers, you interpret your inability to control your drinking as weak willpower or a personality flaw. If only you had more willpower, you could drink less or abstain. If only you could quit for some unknown length of time, your desire for alcohol would diminish. You would finally be like all the people you know who seem to be in control of their alcohol, who seem to be able to take it or leave it. But wait. Are you weak-willed in other areas of your life or is alcohol a strange exception? I am distinctly not weak-willed, as people who know me can attest. Isn't it strange that I seem to lack willpower in this area?

Does it make any sense that alcoholics—those who need to control their drinking most—are the same people unable to do so? Why can't they simply exercise their free will and stop? Is there something, apparently undiagnosable, that makes certain people less able to control their alcohol consumption than others?

Am I an Alcoholic?

So what is an alcoholic? And how do I know if I am one? The majority of adults drink. According to the National Institute on Alcohol Abuse and Alcoholism, a whopping 87% of adult Americans drink.[23] What differentiates the casual drinker, the moderate drinker, the heavy drinker, the problem drinker, and the full-blown alcoholic?

According to *Paying the Tab* by Philip J. Cook, if you drink a single glass of wine each night you're in the top 30% of all drinkers. If it's two glasses, you're in the top 20%.[24] That means that 80% of adults drink *less* than you. But many people who imbibe a glass or two of wine with dinner do not fit the stereotypical description of an alcoholic. Alcoholism isn't strictly defined by how much or how often you drink. There is an invisible and ill-defined line that categorizes the "true alcoholic." Since the line is arbitrary, and alcoholism does not have a standard definition, how are you supposed to know if you actually have a problem?

A quick Google search reveals dozens of test questions intended to answer the question, "Am I an alcoholic?" They all carry a disclaimer saying they cannot provide a diagnosis for alcoholism. They say that is a decision I have to make.

How is it that the majority of Americans drink, yet for a self-diagnosed select few, a fun, social pastime turns into a dark, destructive secret? And why then do we deny the problem and put off asking for help as long as possible, until the problem becomes truly unmanageable?

It's quite easy for us to self-diagnose as "non-alcoholics" when we start to think we have a problem. Most people believe that alcoholics are somehow different from other people, different from "us." Many assume that alcoholism results from some type of defect. We're not sure if the defect is physical, mental, or emotional, but we're sure that "they" (alcoholics) are not like "us" (regular drinkers).

Jason Vale explains that most doctors belong to the "state the obvious" brigade. They pronounce something like: "You are drinking a lot, and it is starting to affect your health. My recommendation is that you moderate or stop drinking."[25] Then the doctor goes on to say that only you can decide if you are an alcoholic. Really? I might have a fatal illness, but no one can diagnose me? As a drinker, the suspicion that I have a serious problem will likely cause me to drink more. And why not? We believe alcohol relieves stress, and the journey to overcome denial, put away my pride, and determine if I am an alcoholic is terribly stressful.

If there is a specific physical or mental attribute responsible for alcoholism, why can't we test for it and segment the population into alcoholics and regular drinkers? That would enable us to prevent the afflicted individuals from falling victim to drink. If there is something inherently different about alcoholics, surely we could find some indication of it before they harm themselves, their family, and society as a whole.

With good reason, we applaud the strides scientists have made in medicine. Amputees with prosthetic limbs can now control the prosthetics' movements with their thoughts, which are translated to the limb by electrical signals from the brain.[26] Dr. Sergio Canavero, an Italy-based neuroscientist, is preparing to transplant a human head.[27] Recent advances in medicine blow our minds. If there is a specific physical or mental defect responsible for alcoholism, I find it hard to believe that we can't, in this day and age, diagnose and prevent it.

Am I saying every person responds the same way to alcohol, no matter their genetic or physical disposition? Not at all. Like the way one glass of wine affects two people differently, long-term exposure to alcohol has different effects on each of us. I am not debating this. Nor am I saying there is no evidence for a gene that increases a proclivity for alcohol addiction. We have discovered many loose relationships between genes and alcohol use but none definitive enough to declare responsible.

The genetics lab at the University of Utah, a department that studies the role of genes in addiction, says that someone's genetic makeup will never doom them to becoming an addict.[28] Polk confirms that, despite any genetic connections, someone cannot become an alcoholic without repeatedly drinking alcohol.[29]

It seems strange to use the term "alcoholic." We don't have cigarette-o-holics but rather people who have smoked and therefore become addicted to cigarettes. Similarly, you don't hear about people who are cocaine addicts suffering from cocaineism.[30] If you consider yourself a regular drinker, you probably take issue with this sentiment. Why? Because if we agree that no specific, diagnosable physical defect separates alcoholics from the population of "responsible" drinkers, everyone who drinks is susceptible and perhaps on the path to alcohol dependence. I assert that over time, with the right level of exposure, anyone can develop a physical dependence on alcohol. And since we are all built differently, no one can determine at what point an individual will develop dependence. This message isn't popular; it flies in the face of our thriving alcohol industry, our societal dependence on the drug, and the attitudes of "regular" and "responsible" drinkers who pride themselves on maintaining control.

The Blame Game 2.0: A.A. and the Alcohol Allergy Theory

I used to accept the notion that alcoholics were different than regular drinkers. Why not? The alcoholics I knew said they had a disorder or defect, so who was I to argue? Since that time I have done a tremendous amount of research. It took me some time to find out where the belief started and why it was accepted. I discovered at once how genetics play into the diagnosis. Neuroscientist Thad Polk says, "There is no single addiction gene; dozens of genes have been identified that affect addiction susceptibility, and most of them only have a small effect by themselves."[31] We have not yet found a way to diagnose or prevent addiction based on genetics.[32] Understanding why alcoholics themselves believe they are different from the normal population proves more difficult.

We accept this theory for a handful of simple reasons. Regular drinkers like it because it allows them to believe they are in control—safe to continue drinking without any worry that they will cross the arbitrary line into alcoholism. Alcoholics like the theory because once you "come out" as an alcoholic, your friends make an effort to help you abstain, rather than pressuring you to drink. They mix you mocktails and support your journey to fight the disease. It is easier to abstain when no one offers you alcohol. Also, physical difference means you receive less blame. We don't blame people who get cancer; disease allows for forgiveness. Finally, it is easier to maintain sobriety if you believe one slip will bring a fatal disease out of remission.

A.A. is the world's most prolific approach to treating alcoholism, with more than two million members in 175 countries.[33] Let's examine A.A.'s approach to alcoholism to understand what assumptions we, as a society, have made and how these assumptions translate into beliefs about alcoholism. A.A.'s primary documentation is informally called "The Big Book." Its official title is *Alcoholics Anonymous, the Story of How Many Thousands of Men and Women Have Recovered from Alcoholism.* This book describes Dr. William D. Silkworth, who treated but did not cure Bill Wilson, founder of A.A. Dr. Silkworth specialized in treatment of alcoholism, and in 1934 he unsuccessfully treated a patient who he concluded was hopeless. When A.A. later cured this patient, Dr. Silkworth wrote this letter to Bill Wilson:

> *We doctors have realized for a long time that some form of moral psychology was of urgent importance to alcoholics, but its application presented difficulties beyond our conception. What with our ultra-modern standards, our scientific approach to everything, we are perhaps not well equipped to apply the powers of good that lie outside of our synthetic knowledge.[34]*

Here, Dr. Silkworth recognizes that the solutions A.A. forwarded are successful beyond what the medical profession was able to offer. And the "ultra-modern" medicine of 1939 is still in use today.

The letter goes on to speak about how, where medical procedures fell short, the "unselfishness and community spirit of recovered A.A. members, who want to help those afflicted, has been an astounding success."[35]

I will quote the most important part of the letter directly:

> We believe . . . that the action of alcohol on these chronic alcoholics is a manifestation of an allergy; that the phenomenon of craving is limited to this class [of people] and never occurs in the average temperate drinkers. These allergic types can never safely use alcohol in any form at all; and once having formed the habit [they have] found they cannot break it, once having lost their self.[36]

The letter discusses the inadequacy the doctor feels in helping these alcoholics and that he is astounded to see how a psychological change—like inclusion in A.A.—allows alcoholics to heal. You may notice this letter contains a contradiction. How can alcohol be an allergen that is only activated once the habit is formed? It seems to indicate they believe alcohol to be a manifestation of an allergy but that they also must "form the habit" for that allergy to manifest. It makes more sense to believe that alcohol is an addictive substance to which any human can become addicted once enough is consumed.

The idea that alcoholics differ physically from the rest of us was hypothesized without any corroboratory lab findings by a doctor who suspected some people suffered from an allergy to alcohol. Allergens are relatively easy to diagnose, and 76 years later we have not found an allergy to be responsible for the disease of alcoholism. But Dr. Silkworth needed an explanation for A.A.'s success in helping alcoholics for whom medical prowess failed.

How did this belief, that a physical flaw differentiates regular drinkers from alcoholics, become so widely held? A.A.'s response to Dr. Silkworth's theory is telling:

> *In this statement he [Dr. Silkworth] confirms what we who have suffered alcoholic torture must believe—that the body of the alcoholic is quite as abnormal as his mind. It did not satisfy us to be told that we could not control our drinking just because we were maladjusted to life, that we were in full flight from reality, or were outright mental defectives. These things were true to some extent, in fact to a considerable extent with some of us. But we are sure that our bodies were sickened as well. In our belief, any picture of the alcoholic which leaves out this physical factor is incomplete.[37]*

What a relief the pioneers of A.A. must have felt. It is wretched to feel that your mind is not strong enough to resist alcohol. How much better to believe something is wrong with your body, something out of your control. A physical flaw, in a sense, lets us off the hook for our inability to maintain control when drinking. The A.A. literature of today continues to perpetuate the theory that alcohol is an allergen. A booklet that is distributed at today's meetings states,

> *As far as we are concerned, alcoholism is an illness, a progressive illness which can never be 'cured,' but which, like some other illnesses, can be arrested . . . We are perfectly willing to admit that we are allergic to alcohol and that it is simply common sense to stay away from the source of our allergy.[38]*

"Us" and "Them"

While A.A. saves many from alcoholism, I must point out the danger of the physical-flaw theory. Given the widespread drinking in our society, this theory can be dangerous. We continue drinking unchecked, often overlooking the danger of addiction, because we have come to believe alcoholism can only happen to other people. By the time we realize we have a problem, we are faced with self-diagnosing a fatal and incurable illness or admitting to being weak-willed and lacking self-control. We tend to avoid this horrific diagnosis until things have gotten so out of control we can no longer avoid the problem. In some ways this approach has defined alcoholism as a disease of denial. It is standard practice for drinkers to hit rock bottom before they seek help. When I told a friend I had stopped drinking, her immediate response was, "I can't imagine what you must have been through in order to make that decision." The assumption was clear: I must have had a rock-bottom experience.

We see this physical-flaw theory play out in every A.A. meeting. The meeting starts with a round-robin of, "Hello, my name is _____, and I am an alcoholic." By forcing me to name the problem—I am an alcoholic, a person with a physical flaw that gives alcohol unreasonable control over me—they make the affliction easier to deal with. Members of A.A. enjoy the fellowship of like-minded people fighting a similar battle, and through that community and support they find sobriety. But how does this physical-flaw theory affect drinkers who don't (or won't) consider the possibility that they have an incurable illness? Those who don't (or won't) consider themselves alcoholics?

Instead of treating alcohol with caution because we know it to be dangerous and addictive, we reassure ourselves that we are different from those flawed people we know as alcoholics. I speak from experience. And no one treats this as an insult. The alcoholics themselves confirm they are "different" from the normal population. So, millions of "regular" drinkers go through their drinking lives with no fear that they might become alcoholics.

We also believe that addiction to alcohol varies from other addictions because the rate of addiction happens differently for each person. We see many people who seem to "control" their drinking and can "take it or leave it." So it's difficult to understand why some people's first sips launch them into full-blown dependence while others never reach that point. But it is not just alcoholics who systematically increase the amount they drink. Regular drinkers start off with just a few drinks and are soon consuming a nightly glass of wine. In fact, alcoholics start off as "regular" drinkers. In many cases it takes years for them to cross the indistinct line into alcoholism.

The Blame Game 3.0: Alcoholic Genes

The Big Book claims that alcoholism "is limited to this class [of people] and never occurs in the average temperate drinkers."[39] The idea is that alcohol is not a problem for normal people and that many people can drink and suffer no physical, mental, or social ill effects, implying that alcohol is not a problem for normal people. Since 87% of the population drinks,[40] with those drinkers ranging from the person who only drinks during toasts at weddings to the degenerate sleeping in the gutter, it is not hard to see why society struggles to understand this disease.

A.A. members describe themselves as a group of men and women who have discovered they cannot control their drinking.[41] While I don't agree that alcoholics have lost control due to a physical, mental, or emotional defect, I concur that an alcoholic should be defined as someone who no longer has the ability to restrain their drinking.

I realize under this definition many alcoholics don't recognize that they have lost control. Many more drinkers dwell in limbo. Usually, years separate the point where you start to wonder if you have a problem and the moment you accept it. Ten years after a tiny voice in my head began to question my nightly drinking I determined I had to stop denying it and change how much I drank. It saddens me to think of the damage I did to my body, the havoc I wreaked in my relationships, and the pain I caused my husband. I want *This Naked Mind* to be a life raft, a wake-up call well before we reach "rock bottom" and our drinking becomes unmanageable.

If about 87% of people drink, it seems fair to assume that the majority believe themselves to be in control.[42] To be clear, I am not saying that everyone who drinks has developed a physical and neurological dependence on alcohol. It is not that everyone who sips alcohol is addicted but that everyone who drinks alcohol has a chance of becoming addicted. Furthermore, the point of addiction or dependence is unknown to the drinker and is generally not known until the drinker attempts to cut back. The obvious problem is that you can't know when you are in control. Nothing seems different, and in fact as humans we tend to feel in control until something significant shows us that we are not. Even then we will vehemently deny we have lost control.

The End of the Blame Game

Why is it hard for us to admit that alcohol itself is the primary issue? That alcohol, like any other drug, is addictive and dangerous? That life circumstances, personality, and conditioning lead some victims down into the abyss of alcoholism faster than others, but that we are all drinking the same harmful, addictive substance? That alcohol is dangerous no matter who you are? Have you heard the saying, "When you hear hoof-beats, think horses, not unicorns?" Perhaps we need to take another look and realize the simpler answer makes more sense.

If you are not convinced, that's OK. We will talk more about this. What is important now is that you entertain the idea that you might not be fully in control of your drinking. After all, you cannot solve a problem you don't realize you have.

So that begs the question, when exactly did we lose control?

3.
THE DRINKER OR THE DRINK?
PART 2: THE DRINK

"First you take a drink, then the drink takes a drink,
then the drink takes you."
—F. Scott Fitzgerald

A Dangerous Delight: The Nectar of Death

Allen Carr, an author and addiction expert best known for helping smokers overcome nicotine addiction, uses a perfect analogy for how addiction works: the pitcher plant.[43] This analogy is powerful, both in making sense of addiction in your conscious mind and in reconditioning your unconscious mind.

Have you heard of a pitcher plant? It's a deadly, meat-eating plant native to India, Madagascar, and Australia. Imagine you are walking by a Krispy Kreme doughnut shop, and you smell the doughnuts frying. It's hard to resist the smell of doughnuts. A pitcher plant is like Krispy Kreme for insects. You are an unsuspecting bumblebee flying through the woods. Suddenly, you fly through blissfully perfumed air. It makes your little bee tummy start to rumble, and you want to get a taste.

You fly closer to the plant; it looks like a delicious treat of fresh nectar. It smells great. To get a taste you must fly inside the rim. You land in the nectar and start to drink. But you don't notice the gradual slope under your feet. You are caught up in the moment, enjoying the treat. You begin to slide down into the plant without realizing it. You only notice the intoxicating nectar. Then you begin to sense the slight slide; gravity conspiring against you, but you have wings. You are confident you can fly out of the plant at any time. You need just a few more sips. The nectar is good, so why not enjoy it?

You think, as most drinkers do, that you are in control; you can leave the plant at any time. Eventually the slope becomes very steep, and the daylight seems farther away as darkness closes in around you. You stop drinking just enough to see dead, floating bodies of other bees and insects around you. You realize you are not enjoying a drink; you are drinking the juices of other dead and dissolving bees. You are the drink.

But can't we have the best of both worlds? Enjoy the nectar and then fly away? Maybe you can put limits on yourself and monitor your intake. Tons of people can do this and do it well—for a while, until something changes in their lives, some additional stressor or a tragedy. Or perhaps nothing changes and, like me, you gradually find you are drinking more than you ever set out to.

All doctors and alcohol experts agree that alcohol is addictive. How many people do you know who drink consistently less over time? For the moment, let's focus on "responsible," adult drinking patterns. Sure, students are well known for binging while attending university, leaving the party-heavy environment of frat houses for steady jobs and family life can reset the amount they regularly drink. But once they've set their long-term patterns, isn't it true that people tend to drink more, not less, over time?

We used to tease one of my friends because she was tipsy after half a glass of wine. Her low tolerance was the butt of jokes for years; however, when I saw her last week, she drank two large glasses at dinner and felt sober enough to drive home. Alcohol is addictive, and your tolerance increases over time. It's a dangerous road no matter how little you drink or how in control you think you are. In fact, recent neurological studies demonstrate that the brain changes in response to alcohol. These changes increase tolerance, diminish the pleasure derived from drinking, and affect the brain's ability to exercise self-control.[44] We will talk in detail about the effects of alcohol on the brain in a later chapter.

A Neglected Warning: The Homeless Drunk

Why aren't we forewarned by the dead bees at the bottom of the pitcher plant? We have all seen people who've lost everything to addiction, who beg on the street with a bottle of booze in a brown paper bag. Isn't this vagabond like the rotting bodies of the other trapped bees? Does this person help us to see the danger? Perhaps for a few. But most of us hide behind the arbitrary line we have drawn between "alcoholics" and "regular drinkers." We don't blame the addictive drug in our glass. Instead, we believe that there is something wrong with the addict on the street.

Thinking the alcoholic on the street is different allows us to believe ourselves to be immune. What has happened to him cannot possibly happen to us. We are not in danger of becoming one of "those" people. Of course, we don't know his backstory, that he was a smart, successful businessman with a growing family. We don't know how alcohol ensnared him, and he lost everything to the most accepted, deadly, and widely used of all drugs.[45]

Let's look at it a different way. We see the homeless man on the street like a bee views an ant that has crawled into the pitcher plant. The ant doesn't have wings; therefore, he is not like me, the bee. I have wings; I am in control. I can escape whenever I want to. But in reality both the ant and the bee are in mortal danger.

The last time I was on the Las Vegas strip everyone, everywhere was drinking. I mean, hey, it's Vegas. The drinkers came in all varieties, from giggling girls with the "yards" of fruity drinks to the bachelor-party boys with their 40 oz. beers. They were young, vibrant, and full of life. I watched them walk right by a beggar with his bed on the street. He had no food but clutched a bottle of alcohol hidden in a paper bag. It was clear to any passerby that drinking had destroyed his life. All of the "regular" drinkers looked directly at him. Many even gave him spare change.

But did they question the substance in their own cups? Did they realize they were drinking the same life-destroying poison as the homeless man? Did it prevent them from ordering their next drink? Sadly, no.

The Descent: When Did I Lose Control?

Is it so hard to accept that the youngsters, experimenting with alcohol, are like the bee landing on the edge of the plant and tasting the nectar? That the homeless man begging for food is just at a more advanced stage in the descent?

A recent study by the Prevention Research and Methodology Center at Pennsylvania State University measured the college binge drinking habits of students whose parents had allowed them to drink in high school. The findings demonstrate that teens who drink in high school have a significantly higher risk of binging in college. The study also confirms how much influence parental behavior has on teenagers and children. And it's not just boys modeling their dads or girls modeling their moms. If either parent drinks at home, both the son and daughter are influenced.

Starting to drink in high school leads to more drinking in college.[46] Why? Because when the descent begins at an early age, kids enter the college years farther down the slope than those who waited until college to sample the "nectar."

I didn't realize how my drinking increased over time. I shut my mind to the fact that I was drinking more than I ever had anticipated. Are you drinking more or less than you did three, five, or even ten years ago? What about your friends? Are they drinking at the same level, or do they drink more as time goes on? When we realize we are drinking more than we want, we begin the battle to quit or cut back. But, like the bee in the pitcher plant, the more we struggle, the more stuck we become.

When does the bee lose control? When she begins her gradual slide downward? When she tries to fly away and is unable to? That's certainly when panic sets in. But it's clear she lost control well before she realized it, prior to the point she couldn't physically escape. As Allen Carr theorizes, perhaps from the moment she landed on the pitcher plant, the bee was never in control.

When did you lose control? Was it the first time your spouse commented on your drinking? Or someone noticed the smell? When you drank so much you threw up, again, perhaps on your partner? When you got a DUI? Maybe you feel like you are still in control. I'm not asking when you realized you had a problem. That was most likely a definitive moment: another hangover, blackout, or even wrecking your car. Losing control is different from *realizing* you have lost control.

So when was it? Or are we always in control? No one insists we drink; no one holds a gun to our heads. But if we are in control, aren't alcoholics also in control? No one forces them to drink. But that has to be different, right? Is it? Or are there just different levels of the same thing? From the outside no one would have guessed how much I was drinking. I was a "high-functioning alcoholic." I didn't lose my job or miss a single meeting because of alcohol. In fact, I excelled at my job and was frequently promoted. I didn't drink and drive. There were few outward signs of how much I drank. Did that mean I didn't struggle? Or that the alcohol wasn't slowly killing me? On the contrary.

Perhaps it's like the story of the boiling frog. A frog is placed in a pot of cold water, which is moved onto a hot stove. The water heats up, yet the frog does not jump out and save himself. Why not? It happens at such a gradual pace that the moment in which he should jump out passes. When he realizes he is boiling to death, it's too late. Could it be that the 87% of adults who drink are like the frog? Are we all in the same pot of slowly boiling water?

So when did you lose control of your drinking? When you experienced a life-crisis related to alcohol? When you realized it was hurting your health, and you decided to cut back? No, it must have been before that because if you were truly in control, you would not have allowed any of those things to happen. When exactly was it? Can you pinpoint it? Chances are you don't know when normal, habitual drinking became a problem. Can you entertain the possibility that you may never have been in control? That, like the bee, you are not in control of alcohol but alcohol is controlling you? And if you are certain you are still in control and can stop whenever you want to, are you certain you will still be able to next week? Next year? Are you willing to bet your life on it?

Finding Freedom: You Can Do This

You still have many questions. What about the addictive personality? What about the fact that some people have different backgrounds and reasons for drinking? What about our intellect—surely we are smarter than a butterfly? What about all the people who enjoy a single drink with dinner and never seem to slide farther down? What about all the people who actually seem to be able to take it or leave it?

We'll cover these questions in future chapters. But for now, consider the possibility that since we are human, and since alcohol is addictive to humans, once we begin to drink we unconsciously begin the slow slide into addiction. Does this mean everyone descends at the same rate? Or that everyone reaches the bottom? No. Many will drink throughout their lives and never reach a point where they try to stop. Maybe this means they are sliding at a very slow pace, or maybe it means that the alcohol kills them before they realize they have become dependent. Many factors contribute to the speed of a person's slide, and we will explore those factors in detail. Keep asking these questions. Critical thought is the key to understanding.

What is important now is that you can see that alcohol is an addictive substance whose nature does not change depending on who drinks it. This means that you are not weak. It is not your willpower or character that is lacking. You are as much at fault in the situation as the bumblebee that is instinctively enticed by the nectar of the pitcher plant.

Butterflies in the pitcher plant do not have hope. They don't have the intellectual ability to understand, and therefore escape, their tragic fate. We do! We, as humans, have the intelligence and ability to understand what is happening in our minds and bodies. I know the pitcher plant is terrifying, but be hopeful. You can find freedom and it may be one of the most joyful experiences of your life.

When I found freedom from alcohol I felt euphoric. The realization dawned, and I cried tears of joy. You probably still believe alcohol benefits you in some way. So the idea of drinking less or quitting altogether is uncomfortable. I can relate. It is terrifying to think about giving up something you feel brings you pleasure or relief. It's OK. When you understand the concepts in this book you will not feel any apprehension, only joy. Hope is stronger than fear. Try to maintain a hopeful outlook.

And remember, this is not your fault. You have been caught in a deadly trap that was designed to ensnare and slowly kill. It is subtle and insidious, and millions of people are deceived every day. The trap is designed to keep you a prisoner for life by making you believe you drink because you want to. We will expose the truth.

4.
LIMINAL POINT:
IS DRINKING A HABIT?

"The chains of habit are too weak to be felt
until they are too strong to be broken."
—Samuel Johnson

I've organized the book in a unique way in order to use Liminal Thinking to shine the light of conscious thought on ingrained beliefs about alcohol. You will find the narrative chapters of the book interspersed with mini-chapters called "Liminal Points." A Liminal Point will take you on a journey through certain, ingrained beliefs about alcohol. I want to deal with these beliefs throughout the book, instead of all at once, to allow you to test the logic in the midst of your daily life. This will allow you to examine what you believe to be true against external sources. What observations and assumptions have you made? What experiences have you had? What conclusions have you drawn?

To deconstruct why we might believe drinking is a habit, we must look at how this belief was unconsciously created.

We have already discussed how our experiences and observations affect our unconscious mind and our desire to drink. Since it is impossible to notice, experience, or observe everything, we unconsciously put our **experiences** and **observations** through a lens of relevance that is shaped by our personal needs. From these relevant experiences and observations we make **assumptions**, and from those assumptions we draw **conclusions**. From conclusions we form our **beliefs**. Once we've established a detailed framework of why you believe what you believe, I will reveal another perspective, one that may be closer to reality, in narrative form. In this manner we will submerge beneath the surface of your conscious and deconstruct your beliefs about alcohol.

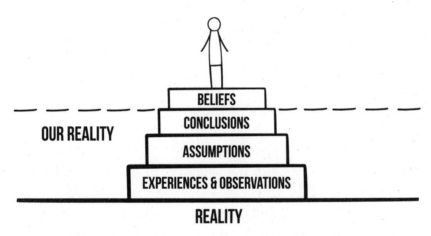

Note: With each Liminal Point we will go through the above steps, so you may want to mark this page and refer back to it from time to time.

Your **experience** is that you regularly drink. You also **observe** regular, habitual drinking around you. You **assume** because of how frequently drinking occurs, not only in your own life, but also in the lives of those around you, that drinking must be habitual. This is an easy assumption. It is more palatable than the assumption that you, and those around you, drink regularly because you have become dependent on alcohol. A habit doesn't feel threatening. You **conclude** that drinking, because it is so regular and you are afraid to look for a more sinister reason, must be a habit.

Let's explore reality:

It's Just a Habit

Many people justify their drinking by saying it is just a habit. And indeed, drinking may have started as a habitual routine. You went to a party and had a drink, or you got home from work and had a drink. The thing about habits is that they, by definition, encourage your brain to think less.[47] Once something has become habitual, like driving or brushing your teeth, you no longer consciously think about it. This is great—it frees up brainpower, allowing us to focus on new and different things.[48] So if your drinking started as a habit, there is a good chance you often drink without thinking too much about it. Over time, drinking became more than a simple habit.

If drinking was truly a habit, when I was pregnant, I would have been perfectly happy drinking non-alcoholic beers. Non-alcoholic beers tasted similar, but I couldn't bring myself to drink more than one. It was the alcohol, not the taste, I wanted. Similarly, if heroin was a habit, perhaps the addict could shoot up a syringe of saline? With some effort, aren't most habits relatively easy to break?

Would you allow your wife to leave you, your kids to hate you, your money to bleed away, and your self-respect to abandon you because of a habit? And if drinking was simply a habit, why does the alcoholic, who has been sober for fifteen years, still take it one day at a time? There is no other habit where this is the case.

When we give up a habit like biting our nails, notoriously difficult to do, we don't feel deprived because we no longer gnaw on our fingertips. We don't worry we will live our lives missing out on an authentic pleasure. We may habitually drink, but drinking is not a habit—it's an addiction. Yet the majority of drinkers believe they drink because they want to, they enjoy it, and they choose to do it.

Say I offered you two hundred thousand dollars to stop drinking. Would you? Do you have to think about it? What about a half million? You can buy a beautiful home, but you can never drink again. If drinking was a habit, there would be no hesitation. For a half million dollars you wouldn't hesitate to break a habit—no matter how much effort it took.[49]

With justifications such as these, we aim to prove we are in control. The fact that we spend so much time defending our alcohol intake proves the opposite. All drugs do this—you try to prove you are not dependent, not controlled. It is the fear that keeps us drinking, and the alcohol itself creates the fear. We fear that we will never be happy or at peace without drinking and that stopping will mean we will feel unhappy—that we are missing out. If you believe these false justifications, even after you stop, when your health has improved and your relationships have been restored, you will continue to envy drinkers. You will believe their reasons for drinking and feel jealous that they are drinking when you are not. But when you recognize that their reasons are unfounded, you're not jealous at all—you rejoice in your newfound freedom.

Is your alcohol habit truly a habit?

5.
YOU: SIMPLY NAKED

"The most fundamental harm we can do ourselves is to remain ignorant by not having the courage and the respect to look at ourselves honestly and gently."
—*Pema Chödrön*

You are the most awesome living organism on the planet. Your mind can do more than any computer. In fact, it creates computers. Your body is self-regulating, self-healing, and self-aware. It alerts you to the tiniest problems and is programmed to protect you, ensuring your survival. It is infinitely more complex than the most intelligent technology. It is priceless.

Since alcohol affects how your body functions, it is vital to understand how your body works when sober. When you are ensnared in the cycle of addiction, it's easy to forget how competent you really are. You are balanced and strong. You are equipped with two phenomenal guidance systems—symptoms and instincts—which help your mind to understand your body's needs.

Your Extraordinary Mind and Body: Complex

We learn more about the human brain every day. We are awed by its abilities, and, despite our technological advances, we cannot come close to replicating it. Your brain is capable of more in a single second than I could describe in hours. It can do more than I could ever explain because much of its power is still unknown. We know of nothing more powerful than the human brain. Astonishingly, the majority of your brain's activity happens without conscious thought. It's designed to keep us alive and highly functional without our direction. When we are asleep, it allows us to breathe, keeps our hearts beating, and regulates our temperature. Our immune system fights a daily battle against millions of toxins, both externally and internally. We take all of this for granted.

Your extraordinary brain is housed in a body that sustains and communicates with it. Your senses alert your brain to new information. Our abilities to smell, feel, taste, hear, and see connect us to our surroundings. They allow us to function and protect us from danger. Survival depends on our senses.

It's astounding how far we've progressed in science and medicine, yet nothing we've accomplished compares to the miracle of a single human cell. And we possess trillions of cells, each unique. Human beings are more sophisticated than anything in our known universe. It can be argued that a human being is the apex of the known universe. It is important to be aware of how awe-inspiring, complex, and powerful your body is. We've been created for the survival of our species and ourselves yet with capacity for emotion, empathy, reflection, and compassion; we are able to accomplish so much more than just survival.

Your Extraordinary Mind and Body: Balanced

One of our miraculous abilities is achieving and maintaining homeostasis. *Merriam-Webster's Medical Dictionary* defines homeostasis as:

homeostasis: ho·meo·sta·sis | /hō-mē-ō-'stā-səs/ *noun*
*: the maintenance of relatively stable internal physiological conditions
(as body temperature or the pH of blood) in higher animals under
fluctuating environmental conditions*
*: the process of maintaining a stable psychological state in the indi-
vidual under varying psychological pressures or stable social conditions
in a group under varying social, environmental, or political factors*

Homeostasis is a vital life force. We must remain in balance to
survive. If we get too much acid (low pH) in our blood, it harms our
organs. Consider how we take care of a houseplant. We need to make
sure the soil is moist but not oversaturated. We need to give it sun-
light but not scorch it. We do all these things to ensure the right
balance of water and nutrients. We as humans instinctually do this
inside our bodies. We sweat when we are hot so that water evaporates. Evaporative water is cooling, so sweating regulates our temperature. When we are trying to rid our body of unwanted intruders
such as bacteria and viruses, we get a fever, but not so high of one as
to kill us. By heating itself up, our body kills the intruders without
harming itself. When we need oxygen to feed our cells, we naturally
breathe at a faster rate. All of these, plus an uncountable number of
other functions, work as your body's optimal survival thermostat,
helping to maintain homeostasis.

Your Extraordinary Mind and Body: Strong

We are constantly exposed to messages from the media about the
fragility of our bodies. Look at how we consume hand sanitizer by
the bucket. America spends more on healthcare than most other
countries, yet has a higher infant mortality rate and relatively lower
life expectancy for the developed world.[50]

We often feel weak and incomplete, yet nothing is further from
the truth. Despite drinking poison in increasing quantities, usually

daily, we still function. By believing we are weak, we foster the misconception that we need something more to thrive.

We are not weak; we are strong. We represent the very pinnacle of existence, stronger and more capable than anything we know of. We populated and explored the entire planet and even the moon before most of our modern medical discoveries.

It's a miracle I survived all my years of heavy drinking and am healthy and thriving. It's a testament to how strong we are. When I decided to stop drinking, I expected to lose weight and improve my health. I was not disappointed—I lost ten pounds in the first month. The real surprise was how my life improved in ways I didn't expect. For one thing, my confidence skyrocketed. Also, when my body healed, I found myself amazed at the difference in how I felt every day. During my years of drinking I didn't feel particularly sick, but I didn't feel physically great either. I completely forgot how it felt to have tons of energy. Now I'm often surprised by how much I can get done, while still feeling motivated and happy. It is staggering to realize what we are capable of when we are mentally and physically strong.

We know more than ever about the dangers of alcohol and drugs, yet addiction is on the rise. As a society we find this confusing. The "Just Say No" campaign, introduced by First Lady Nancy Reagan, remains one of the most famous anti-drug campaigns of all time.[51] Between 1998 and 2004, the U.S. Congress spent almost $1 billion on national anti-drug media campaigns. Why? Because we continue to see addiction on the rise, and we just don't understand why. Youth today drink more than they did in the '80s, and though we are concerned, we can't seem to understand why the rates of drug and alcohol use are increasing. I believe part of the reason is that we inadvertently condition ourselves to believe we are weak. We believe we lack some vital ingredient necessary to the enjoyment of our lives. We conclude that we are deficient; we need substances to enjoy life and deal with stress. We've been unconsciously conditioned to believe alcohol helps us compensate for this deficiency, that it will help us feel strong, uninhibited, creative, and confident. Or maybe we think it will help us deal with the pressures and hassles of daily life.

Your Warning Mechanisms: Symptoms

Now let's look for a couple minutes at the most common way our body warns us when something isn't right: symptoms. When we feel a symptom of illness, we usually hurry to the medicine cabinet or the nearest doctor to make the discomfort go away. The pharmaceutical industry has never been bigger.

Imagine you are on a ship, and you sail into a storm. The captain can no longer see the shore or the stars and is completely dependent on the ship's navigational systems. A bright red light starts flashing. This light lets him know one of his navigational instruments is low on battery. He can't accurately navigate without it. What if, instead of replacing the battery, he removed the red indicator light? Did the captain fix the issue? Nope. He compounded it.

My mother is a health nut. She ate organic food before most people knew what organic food was. She won't even take Advil because she believes our ailments can and should be healed through natural, herbal, and food-based remedies rather than with chemicals. Although I ignored her guidance for many years, especially in college when I rebelled against my healthy upbringing with a diet of Taco Bell and Nerds candy, I have come to realize how poignant and true her advice is: We must exercise caution before doing anything that alters our normal functions. It can be terrifying to realize how little we know about the inner workings of our bodies and minds. When we mess with the functions of our bodies or numb our senses with alcohol and other drugs, we act like the captain, inviting catastrophe.

Tommy Rosen, founder of Recovery 2.0 and an addiction specialist, teaches that we have an "infinite pharmacy within," meaning inside we have every instinct, hormone, and drug we need to help us live long, healthy, and happy lives. If you look at your body's ability to produce adrenaline or endorphins, you see they are supplied in the perfect quantity at the exact time needed. We possess a phenomenal system.

Your immune system is your single most powerful weapon against disease. It is significantly more important to your health than any modern medicine. Ask any doctor and she will tell you the same thing. We've discussed how alcohol severely damages your immune system's ability to function. Drinking is like removing the red indicator light on your immune system.

A rare genetic condition aptly referred to as Congenital Insensitivity to Pain prevents a person from feeling pain. At first this might seem like a good thing. A life with no pain, who'd complain about that? It is actually one of life's scariest disorders. You wouldn't realize the shower was scalding until your skin reddened and blistered. You wouldn't know your bone was broken until it protruded from your arm. People suffering from this disorder have no chance of living a normal life. It would be hard to make it past childhood unless you lived inside a bubble. Pain gets a bad rap, but it is our friend—it keeps us alive.

As kids we longed to be older, to have our own houses, cars, and money to spend. As adults we wish we were young again because we are always tired and life seems to get increasingly stressful. It shouldn't be this way. During childhood and adolescence we undergo more changes than at any other time in our lives. In every other animal, childhood is much more stressful than adulthood.[52]

Think about how tough high school was. Remember the mental strain of the changes you underwent. As a child you don't feel in control of your life and your destiny, which generates fear and stress. When you are mentally at peace and physically strong as an adult, you experience the best of both worlds. You regain the vigor of youth, and your actual age no longer seems to matter. You feel more comfortable in your own skin. You are wiser and better adjusted. These are the best years of your life. You have more energy, joy, vigor, courage, and self-respect than ever before. Alcohol steals this from us. We drink more and more and become sicker and sicker. It is gradual, and we don't realize we no longer feel our best. We become accustomed to it and actually believe it's normal to feel fatigued, stressed, and somewhat unhappy. Now, granted, exhaustion can be caused by many things besides alcohol, but if you are drinking, there is no doubt it exacerbates these stresses, making exhaustion and even regular hangovers an unpleasant way of life. There is not a clear sign that we are doing something to hurt ourselves other than the hangover. Perhaps this chronic exhaustion is the body's way of saying that something's wrong.

These days I have so much energy it's incredible. It took time to regain my energy, but over time I healed from years of drinking poison. When you are physically strong, you feel on top of the world. You are present to fully enjoy the great moments in life. I handle stress better too. Before, my stressors multiplied because, instead of dealing with my problems, I ignored them by drinking. When left unattended, they grew inexplicably large. Without drinking, I can mindfully manage stress. In fact my ability to handle the things I once drank to ignore can be empowering. I don't mean to say I never have hard days—of course I do. But when you are healthy and happy, everything becomes easier.

Your Warning Mechanisms: Instincts

We have a staggering intellect that both helps and harms us. It's helpful when we use that intellect to recognize our bodies' warning lights—symptoms—and search for the root problems. It's harmful when we rely solely on our intelligence and ignore our bodies' instinctual knowledge. Instinct is the work of our bodies' senses alerting us to what will harm us. Sadly, we often ignore this most basic warning system.

When something goes wrong with our body, we visit a doctor. Doctors will tell you that we understand relatively little about how we are made and how to heal ourselves. We continuously learn more, disproving existing medical theories. We used to think that bloodletting—draining blood from a sick person—would cure illness by draining the malady from the body. We now realize this actually harmed the patient, sapping vital strength from an ailing body. Now, of course, our knowledge and technology is growing at an unprecedented rate. We are more informed than at any other point in the history of the world, yet we would be stupid to imagine that our knowledge is complete. You only have to read the news to realize we are constantly discovering new things and disproving existing theories.

Our health is the single most important thing we have, and without it, nothing else matters. Our instincts are specifically designed to guide us. Yet in our stubbornness, we rely heavily on our own intellect, trusting our knowledge more than our senses, even though common knowledge is often later disproven. We ignore our instincts in favor of intelligence, not realizing our instincts are designed to keep us alive and healthy. Alcohol deadens our senses and mutes our instincts. It is important that we do not ignore our natural instincts; they are the most valuable source of information we have regarding our health and longevity.

We need to see that we are strong, whole, and complete. We need to understand that alcohol, instead of acting as a support to help us deal with life, actually deadens our senses and harms our immune system. Consuming chemicals, which affect the functioning of our bodies, is reckless. And in this case, the danger is increased because our chemical of choice is addictive. In truth, you don't need alcohol to enjoy life or to relieve stress. You only think you do. And in reality, it does nothing for us. As you uncover the truth, your perception will begin to change, both consciously and unconsciously, and with this knowledge you will no longer desire alcohol. You will be free.

6.
LIMINAL POINT: ARE WE REALLY DRINKING FOR THE TASTE?

"Recovery is all about using our power to change our beliefs that are based on faulty data."
—Kevin McCormack

Before you ever drank a drop you **observed** everyone around you drinking, seeming to enjoy the taste of alcohol. Yet your early **experience** probably contradicted that belief. Kids generally don't like their first sip of alcohol. Since you continue to observe others around you drinking, you **assume** there must be something good and beneficial about drinking, despite the taste. You **conclude** that you should persevere in drinking; you may even be told you need to "acquire the taste." Over time, you do indeed acquire a taste for alcohol. Now your experience is in line with your observations, and you can more easily conclude that alcohol tastes good, and you do, in fact, drink because you like the taste.

Let's consider reality:

You Just Have to Acquire the Taste

This justification is the great deceit that lures new drinkers in. My colleague, Yani, is French. She told me her parents encouraged her to have sips of wine at dinner from the age of eight, much like my parents encouraged me to at least taste the spinach on my plate. She never liked it and would tell them so, but they would insist on at least one sip telling Yani to just wait and see—she would like it when she is older. Sure enough, Yani now drinks wine every night. When we take our first sips and almost gag, there's always someone there to reassure us that alcohol is an acquired taste.

But let's consider again our awesome bodies, whose purpose is to make sure we remain alive. We know that we need food and water to survive, and if we don't eat and drink, we will die. Other animals are not consciously aware of this, so how does nature make sure they eat and drink? Instinctually, they feel hunger and thirst.

We know that certain things are poison because we are told so or because the label says so. How does a doe know what is poison, which grasses to eat and which will make her sick? It's a brilliant aspect of her design, yet quite simple: Grasses that deer are meant to eat smell and taste nice, while the grasses that will make the deer sick smell and taste bad.

Our sense of smell and taste are vital to our well-being. They help us distinguish between good and rotten food. The products in our refrigerators may carry expiration dates, but our own ability to smell when meat is rotten or taste spoiled milk is more sophisticated than the dates placed on foods. These senses ensure our survival.

I was recently in Brazil and saw ethanol for sale at the gas stations. You may be surprised to know that the ethanol you put in your gas tank is the exact same ethanol in the liquor you drink. Yep, alcohol, without additives, is ethanol. Pure alcohol tastes awful, and a very small amount will kill you. We use extensive processes and additives to make it taste good enough to drink. Unfortunately, none of these processes reduce the harms associated with drinking fuel.

Alcohol destroys our health by attacking our liver and immune system and is related to more than sixty diseases.[53] Yet because we are only peripherally aware of the harms but very familiar with pro-alcohol social messages, we often justify our drinking by saying we drink for the taste. And we believe this is true. We have an uncanny ability to unknowingly deceive ourselves.

Imagine a college kid drinking one of his first beers at a football game. It's cheap and warm, and almost certainly does not taste good. You are fairly sure he would rather be drinking a soda. If you ask him why he isn't drinking a soda, he will probably tell you he likes the taste of beer. In truth, he wants to fit in, and only kids drink soda during football games. He cannot admit this, and might not even realize it, so he tells you he likes the taste. This does not sync with reality as you watch him choke the beer down.

If you ask him a few months later, at the homecoming game, he will again tell you he likes it. Since he has been drinking for a few months, the answer may hold some truth. He has started to acquire the taste. And since the alcohol is addictive, it has created an imperceptible craving for itself, which, when satisfied, gives him the perception of enjoyment.

I don't know anyone who drank so many sodas they puked. Yet, how many people do you know who have drunk enough to throw up? Even the most moderate drinkers I know occasionally take it too far. Throwing up is awful. Awful, but when you think about it, actually incredible. Throwing up saves our lives, protecting us from alcohol poisoning. The implication is clear: Alcohol is not good for us. Yet we are not deterred. We carry on, thinking of our nights "worshiping the porcelain gods" as a badge of honor. It's college after all, and we are determined to acquire a taste for booze.

Finally, you actually like the taste of alcohol, but it is still the same chemical in your gas tank. It is still destroying your liver, your

immune system, and your brain. The taste doesn't actually change—
that's impossible.

Think of the guy who showers in cologne. You can smell him
coming from a mile away, yet he is unaware. It's the same concept. I
went to school in an agricultural town surrounded by ranches and
farms. Aggie towns have a very intense smell. After a few months
there, I couldn't smell it at all. It's remarkable how, given enough
time, senses grow immune to the most unpleasant things.

There's no doubt alcohol tastes bad. Why else would we need to
go to such great lengths to make it palatable with mixers and sweet-
eners? You may be a manly type who now loves to drink whiskey
straight. You acquired a taste for whiskey like I acquired a smell for
animal crap.

Do you really drink just because of the taste?

It Enhances the Taste of Food

The enhancement of food by a particular drink makes sense when
you think about milk and cookies. You actually take a cookie and dip
it into milk, changing the texture and flavor of the cookie. I can
understand how this could enhance the taste. But you don't put wine
in your mouth with your steak, so how can it change the way food
tastes? Not to mention it's been medically proven that alcohol actually deadens your taste buds rather than increasing their sensitivity.[54]

Now, I admit the flavor of wine can be great in sauces, but so can
just about anything depending on what else you mix with it. A popular cooking show forces chefs to cook with all kinds of nasty ingredi-
ents to make them palatable. I find it strange that, with thousands of
beverages in existence, we only use this excuse with alcohol. We don't
hear people claiming they drink Coke because it enhances the flavor
of their hot dog. It strikes me, as a marketer, that this is a genius
marketing tactic. If we can marry the product (alcohol) with the authentic pleasures of eating, we have a much higher chance of selling
a glass of wine, at its incredible markup, every time we sell a steak.

Conversations justifying why we drink happen all the time. We don't sit around justifying other things we like, like why we eat grapefruit. Yet when you turn down an alcoholic drink, it seems everyone around you launches into a diatribe explaining in painful detail all the reasons they are drinking. If you pay attention, you will start to notice how conversations about alcohol are not balanced. When eating a doughnut we will probably mention the calorie count or how much sugar it has. And for good reason—it helps us limit ourselves to just one. Yet when discussing alcohol you never hear someone say, "This booze is delicious. It enhances the taste of my food, but I do worry about liver damage."

Why is this? Why do we group together and chat up the great things about drinking? It's so we can collectively close our eyes to the dangers. Herd mentality makes it easier to believe or do something because everyone else is saying or doing the same thing. This is exactly what happens when people start to talk about the "full-bodied, oaky, lemony, exaggerated, pompous yet fruity" flavor of a Cabernet.

Further, at least when it comes to wine, there is actual proof that almost no one can actually tell the difference between good wines and cheap wines. The American Association of Wine Economists did a study of more than six thousand wine drinkers. In these blind taste tests, wine drinkers were unable to distinguish expensive wines from cheap wines. In fact, the majority claimed to prefer the cheap wines.[55] You might be amused to know that the same association conducted a study two years later and found that people are also unable to differentiate Pâté from dog food.[56]

I Drink to Quench My Thirst

"How can I be so thirsty this morning when I drank so much last night."
—Anonymous

We think a cold beer sounds good on a hot day to quench our thirst. Since beer is about 96% water and 4% alcohol, it's logical to conclude the water content in beer should quench your thirst. Yet alcohol is a diuretic, a substance that eliminates water from your system by making you pee. The beer not only sucks away the 96% of water but further depletes your body's water content. That's why you wake up in the middle of the night with incredible thirst after a bout of drinking. Your mouth is parched, and you feel like you are dying for a glass of water. Dehydration from drinking can actually shrink your brain and its ability to function.[57] This means after one drink you are actually thirstier, and that makes it easier for the next pint to go down. You probably wouldn't drink a six-pack of soda, yet we do that with beer all the time. The more our thirst increases, the better we believe the next beer will taste because of the illusion it is quenching our thirst. Not to mention the alcohol is addictive, and your taste buds are becoming numbed.[58] You want more. What genius product marketing.

I closed my mind to the dangers of drinking. I went to great lengths to justify alcohol and encouraged others to drink with me. Drinking with other people seemed more fun, but I now see it was less stressful. It's not drinking alone, when we are by ourselves, that bothers us. It's drinking by ourselves in the company of people who are not drinking that makes us question our choice. When no one else is drinking you feel quite dumb standing around drinking something that is making you lose control of your faculties. If everyone is doing it, even if it goes against your rational judgment, you don't have to come up with reasons to justify it. If everyone is doing it, there must be good reasons—it must not be that bad. It's amazing how far we will go to delude ourselves. Tell a lie long enough and convincingly enough, and even the liar will believe it.

7.
YOU: POLLUTED

*"Education is the most powerful weapon which
you can use to change the world."*
—*Nelson Mandela*

I didn't intend to write this chapter. In fact, I wrote it after the first
round of edits. Why? I believe a positive outlook is far more produc-
tive than a negative one. I stand by my belief that listing the horrors
of alcohol doesn't help us quit. It gives us the conscious desire to quit,
but if you're reading this book, you probably already have that. It is
your unconscious desire to drink that is causing you so much trouble.
For as long as you can remember, you have been conditioned to believe alcohol provides numerous benefits. These beliefs must be reversed in order to find freedom. A list of the harms does nothing to
undo your perception of the benefits. And chapters like this one can
cause drinkers stress, and we tend to drink more when we are stressed.
In the end, our situation is not improved.

Before you skip on past this chapter, though, as a society, we really
do need an education about what alcohol is and what it does to our

bodies. I had assumed it was common knowledge that alcohol is harmful to your health. I was wrong. More than seven thousand people volunteered to be beta readers—reading early drafts of the book and providing feedback during the editing process. As their comments poured in, I realized that it is not common knowledge that alcohol is harmful. In fact, we have been so indoctrinated that we believe the opposite is true. Common knowledge actually claims that moderate drinking, defined as one to three drinks per day, benefits your health. Given these misconceptions, this chapter became vital, and I will start with the presupposition that you believe some alcohol use is good for your health.

Why All the Misinformation?

I understand where these beliefs come from. Articles come out all the time claiming that wine is good for your heart or that alcohol reduces your cholesterol. A few studies have correlated alcohol consumption and life expectancy. What is bizarre about these studies is that they ignore the cause of death (i.e., did alcohol contribute to death?) and lump all deaths together. Nonetheless, innumerable articles are published highlighting the relatively few studies that claim alcohol is good for you and ignoring the thousands of studies that prove otherwise.

So why do the supposed health benefits get so much publicity that they have become commonly believed? There are a few reasons. First, journalists need to write popular articles that get attention and exposure. This enables them to claim a higher readership, sell more advertisements, and build their business. While there are many more studies about the dangers of drinking, there are far fewer published articles. You can test this with a quick Google search. If you search "alcohol harms" or "alcohol dangers," your results will include numerous studies from organizations like the National Institute on Alcohol Abuse and Alcoholism or medical sites like the Mayo Clinic or

WebMD. My search of both of these terms turned up zero popular publications (*Times, Huffington Post, Washington Post*) on the first page. Try searching "alcohol healthy." Almost no reliable sources will show up, but you'll see dozens of articles with headlines like "Drinking for Health" from popular but unscientific media outlets. These articles invariably point to one of a small handful of actual studies.

We've been duped by media that print what is popular rather than what has been comprehensively demonstrated. But we also dupe ourselves. This is another example of confirmation bias. Articles that claim health benefits from wine or beer get thousands to tens of thousands of shares. They proliferate on social media. With our culture's short attention span and focus on headlines, it is no wonder we have come to believe that some drinking is actually good for you. When you do find an article in a popular media outlet that cautions against alcohol use, you'll notice it has fewer shares, often fewer than ten. This means that only the first line of readership sees these articles, and the information rarely goes viral.

Dr. Jürgen Rehm, PhD, Senior Scientist at the Centre for Addictions and Mental Health in Toronto, cautions that studies claiming beneficial health links to alcohol represent a small fraction of the studies conducted, which generally demonstrate harm. Yet when measured in the press, the studies claiming benefits are more often highlighted. He reiterates, "We have counted how many studies are reported in the press, and there are many more reports on the beneficial link than on the detrimental link between alcohol and health." There is ten times the evidence to support the dangers of alcohol, yet it's the small fraction of the research supporting the benefits of drinking that is published and shared, often with the purported benefits taken out context.

This is again proven with insight into the science of sharing. Why do people share on social media? One of the top reasons for sharing is "social currency." People share things that they think will make them look "good" (smart, cool, hip, informed, etc.) in the eyes of their peers. An article about happy hour doing wonders for your heart carries more social currency than the study that disproves the relationship between wine and heart health.[59]

But it is confusing. There is a lot of misleading information out there. We cannot blame ourselves for being misinformed. This chapter will educate you. The information has been compiled from statistically relevant studies, and I have included data from both sides to allow you to draw your own conclusions. I encourage you to dig deeper into the sources provided and to further your knowledge with your own research. We seem to pay more attention to the side effects of ibuprofen than we do to the beverage society consumes most. It is important that we use our intellect with discernment, keeping up-to-date on the most recent articles and understanding what the study is actually saying. We owe it to ourselves to be informed about what we put into our bodies and to make decisions based on fact.

Let's focus on what alcohol does to our bodies. We will speak more about societal harms and secondhand drinking (effects on those in proximity of the drinker) later in the book.

The Overall Harm Factor

Researchers scored twenty drugs on criteria related to overall harm, considering both the harm to the user and the harm to people who are around the user but not actually using the drug. The majority of the criteria related to the specific harm to an individual. Overall, alcohol scored as the most harmful drug, with an overall harm score of 72. Heroin came in second with a harm score of 55, and crack cocaine scored third with a score of 54.[60]

The World Health Organization (WHO) says that alcohol is a causal factor in sixty types of diseases and injuries. The report goes on to say that alcohol has surpassed AIDS and is now the world's leading risk factor for death among males ages 15–59.[61]

In the United States, excessive alcohol consumption, defined as four drinks in two hours for women (five for men) or eight drinks per week for women (fifteen for men),[62] is a leading cause of premature mortality, with 88,000 alcohol-related deaths in the U.S. every year.[63] This means alcohol causes more than twice the number of deaths as all other drugs combined, both illegal and prescription. All illicit drugs cause 17,000 deaths per year, and prescription drugs are responsible for 22,000 deaths per year.[64]

Benefits of Alcohol?

There are medicinal benefits to alcohol. It is a strong antiseptic and can be used to dull pain. Not surprisingly, doctors have found other methods, such as ibuprofen and morphine, to more effectively relieve pain. But there are numerous claims about more dubious long-term benefits of alcohol. For instance, there is evidence that wine can raise your levels of good cholesterol because of its antioxidants.[65] But is it really about the wine? Many fruit juices contain more antioxidants than wine. Yet I don't know anyone who drinks juice on a nightly basis, while I know plenty of people who habitually drink wine. If you disciplined yourself to drink a glass of antioxidant-rich juice every night, I'd wager you would get the same results. And there would be no harmful side effects or chance of becoming addicted.

We have seen many articles around the supposed heart-health benefits of alcohol, specifically wine. A new study that analyzed the drinking habits and cardiovascular health of over 260,000 people shows that drinking alcohol, even light-to-moderate amounts, provides no heart-health benefit.

The other well-publicized claim is that people who drink live longer than abstainers. One of the most famous studies to this effect is the Holahan study.[66] Charles J. Holahan tracked 1,824 individuals, ranging in age from 55–65 when the study started and 75–85 at the end of the twenty-year period. The majority (65%) were men, and

92% were Caucasian. The study found a correlation (not a causation) between drinking and living longer, meaning a higher percentage of the 345 abstainers died during the twenty-year period than the 1,479 drinkers. Cause of death was not measured or considered. The study gives a caveat to the significance of the correlation by saying that "abstainers were significantly more likely to have had prior drinking problems, to be obese and to smoke cigarettes than were moderate drinkers." The people who abstained seemed to abstain for reasons such as other health issues or prior alcohol abuse, and the reasons the 239 abstainers died between the ages of 55 and 85 is unknown. And I don't want to make decisions about my overall health based on a tiny sample size of 239 individuals. There is a correlation between the stork population and the number of babies born, but surely we aren't tempted to translate this correlation into causation.[67] Why should we treat alcohol differently?

It would not be a good idea to self-medicate with morphine, codeine, or any other prescription drug. In fact, it's probably not a good idea to self-medicate with any addictive substance. Medicating for any condition from heart disease to Parkinson's should be done under supervision with a specific treatment plan and well-documented and understood side effects. While there are correlations between alcohol consumption and health, none make a compelling case that alcohol itself should be medicinally self-administered.[68]

The Dangers of Drinking: To Your Body

As we discussed in the previous chapter, your body is arguably the most complex and capable organism on the planet. Your body's ability to ensure your survival and overcome illness lies beyond our comprehension. If you take care of your precious body, it will take care of you. I would like to outline what alcohol does to your body, so you see why it wreaks such devastation on your health and life. I've compiled this information from several studies with the primary source being the U.S. Department of Health and Human Services.[69]

Your Brain

Your brain's structure is incredibly complex. The brain communicates with neurons, trillions of tiny nerve cells, which translate information into signals that the brain and body can understand. Your brain's network of chemicals (neurotransmitters) carry messages between neurons. These chemicals are powerful, and they change your feelings, moods, and physical responses. Your brain works to balance these chemicals, either speeding up the transfer of information or slowing it down. Alcohol slows the pace of communication between neurotransmitters. It interrupts your brain's communication pathways, literally reducing the speed of communication between parts of your brain by slowing down your brain's neural highways.[70] It slows communications from your senses, decreasing your responsiveness and deadening your senses.

Your cerebellum, limbic system, and cerebral cortex are most vulnerable to alcohol. Your cerebellum is responsible for motor coordination, memory, and emotional response. Your limbic system monitors your memories and emotions. And, your cerebral cortex manages activity, including planning, social interaction, problem solving, and learning. It comes as no surprise that alcohol hinders motor coordination. After all, being tipsy or unable to walk a straight line is a classic indicator of alcohol use. But have you realized that alcohol robs you of your natural ability to manage your emotions? This is why alcohol causes unhappiness and irritability, and why some drinkers describe their binges as either crying jags or fits of rage.

It won't surprise you that severe, chronic depression and heavy drinking are closely linked.[71] What is more terrifying is that over time the artificial stimulation your brain receives from drinking makes you neurologically unable to experience the pleasure you once did from everyday activities, such as seeing a friend, reading a book, or even having sex.[72] Alcohol interferes with your ability to behave, think, and interact socially. Drinking impedes your natural capacity to remember, learn, and solve problems.

Just one bout of heavy drinking, meaning five drinks in two hours for men or four drinks in two hours for women, can cause permanent alterations in your nerve cells and reduce the size of your individual brain cells.[73]

A release of serotonin, a neurotransmitter that regulates emotion, physiologically contributes to the initial tipsy feeling. Sometimes drinking can release endorphins, the neurotransmitter responsible for feelings of euphoria. You might think this is a good thing, but actually it's not. Your brain tries to compensate. It doesn't understand the surge in neurotransmitters and tries to adjust and restore balance.[74] This is one of the reasons you build up a tolerance, become dependent, and experience physical withdrawal symptoms.

Your liver acts as your first line of defense. It breaks down the alcohol so that your body can rid itself of the poison as quickly as possible. When breaking down alcohol, your liver releases toxins and damaged liver cells into the bloodstream. These toxins are more dangerous to the brain than the alcohol itself.[75] The toxins released into your brain are responsible for bad sleep, mood imbalance, personality changes (like violence or weeping), anxiety, depression, and shortened attention span, and they can result in coma and death.

Don't be feeling too discouraged right now. Abstinence can help reverse the negative effects on thinking skills, memory, and attention. And over several months to a year structural brain changes have been shown to self-correct.[76]

Your Heart

Your heart beats over 100,000 times per day, carrying 2,000 gallons of blood through your body. As you probably know, there are two chambers in your heart. The right side pumps blood to your lungs where it exchanges carbon dioxide for oxygen. Your heart then relaxes and allows the oxygenated blood to flow back into your left chamber. When your heart contracts again, it pumps the oxygen-rich blood into your body, nourishing your tissues and organs. On the journey through your body, your blood passes through your kidneys to cleanse it of waste. Blood becomes "dirty" because it is one of our more efficient cleansing systems and constantly removes toxins from your body. Electrical signals ensure your heart beats at the right pace multiple times per second for your entire life.

Alcohol weakens the heart muscle so that it sags and stretches, making it impossible to continue contracting effectively.[77] When your heart can no longer contract efficiently, you are unable to transport enough oxygen to your organs and tissues. Your body is no longer nourished appropriately.

Drinking large amounts in one sitting, even on rare occasions, can affect the electrical system that regulates your heartbeat.[78] This can cause blood clots. During a hard drinking bout, your heart may not beat hard enough, which can cause your blood to pool and clots to form. The opposite can also happen. Your heart can beat too fast, not allowing time for the chambers to fill with blood so insufficient oxygen is pumped out to your body. As a result, binge drinking raises your likelihood of having a stroke by 39%.[79]

Your blood vessels are stretchy, like elastic, so that they can transport blood without putting too much pressure on your heart. Drinking alcohol releases stress hormones that constrict your blood vessels, elevate your blood pressure, and cause hypertension, in which the blood vessels stiffen.[80] Hypertension is dangerous and causes heart disease.[81]

Your Liver

Two million Americans suffer from alcohol-related liver disease,[82] making it a leading cause of illness and death. Your liver stores nutrients and energy and produces enzymes that stave off disease and rid your body of dangerous substances, including alcohol. As we've discussed, the process of breaking down alcohol creates toxins, which are actually more dangerous than the alcohol itself.[83] Alcohol damages liver cells causing inflammation and weakening your body's natural defenses. Liver inflammation disrupts your metabolism, which impacts the function of other organs. Further, inflammation can cause liver scar tissue buildup.[84]

Your liver function suffers because alcohol alters the natural chemicals in the liver. These natural chemicals are needed to break down and remove scar tissue. Drinking also causes steatosis or "fatty liver." Fat buildup on your liver makes it harder for the liver to operate.[85] Eventually fibrosis (some scar tissue) becomes cirrhosis (much more scar tissue). Cirrhosis prevents the liver from performing critical functions, including managing infections, absorbing nutrients, and removing toxins from the blood. This can result in liver cancer and type-2 diabetes.[86] Twenty-five percent of heavy drinkers will develop cirrhosis.[87]

Your Immune System

Germs surround us, making our immune system our most important tool for fighting off disease. Our skin protects our bodies from infection and disease. If germs make it into the body, we have two systems that provide defense: the innate system (which fends off first-time germ exposure) and the adaptive system (which retains information about prior germ invasions and promptly defeats repeat attackers). Alcohol suppresses both.[88]

Our immune system uses cytokines, small proteins, to send out chemical messages about infection in a kind of early alert system. Alcohol disrupts the production of cytokines. When working correctly, cytokines alert our immune system to intruders, and our immune system responds with white blood cells that attack, surrounding and swallowing harmful bacteria. Alcohol impairs both functions, which leaves us more susceptible to pneumonia, tuberculosis, and other diseases.[89] Further studies link alcohol to an increased susceptibility to HIV, not only increasing our chances of contracting HIV, but also impacting how rapidly the disease develops once contracted.[90]

Alcohol and Cancer

> *"Responsible drinking has become a 21ˢᵗ-centry mantra for how most people view alcohol consumption. But when it comes to cancer, no amount of alcohol is safe."*[91]
> —*Laura A. Stokowski*

But wait, light drinking doesn't cause cancer, does it? Yes, apparently it does. In a meta-analysis of 222 studies across 92,000 light drinkers and 60,000 non-drinkers with cancer, light drinking was associated with higher cancer risks for many types of cancers, including breast cancer.[92]

A seven-year study of 1.2 million middle-aged women highlights the direct and terrifying link between drinking and cancer. According to this study, alcohol increased the chance of developing cancers of the breast, mouth, throat, rectum, liver, and esophagus.[93]

The most frightening revelation is that cancer risk increases *no matter how little or what type* of alcohol the women drank. According to cancer.gov, the risk of breast cancer was higher across all levels of alcohol intake.[94] It's not just heavy drinkers or people who drink every day who increase their chances of getting cancer. Compared to women who don't drink at all, women who consume three alcoholic drinks per week increase their breast cancer risk by 15%.[95] According to Cancer Research UK, "There's no 'safe' limit for alcohol when it comes to cancer."[96]

Both binge drinking and daily drinking have the same cancer-causing effect. "Drinking alcohol increases the risk of cancer whether you drink it all in one go or a bit at a time."[97] It also doesn't matter what type of alcohol you drink. It's the alcohol itself that leads to the damage, regardless of whether you imbibe beer, wine, or hard alcohol.[98]

Another study links 11% of all breast cancer cases to alcohol.[99] Since 295,240 new cases of breast cancer were diagnosed in 2014,[100] about 32,476 new cases of breast cancer were connected to alcohol.

Although many of us are not aware of the relationship between alcohol and cancer, it should not come as a surprise. The International Agency for Research on Cancer (IARC) declared alcohol a carcinogen in 1988.[101] Alcohol itself, ethanol, is a known carcinogen, and alcoholic beverages can contain at least fifteen other carcinogenic compounds including arsenic, formaldehyde, and lead.[102] Alcohol causes or contributes to cancer in different ways. When your liver breaks down alcohol, it produces a toxic chemical called acetaldehyde. Acetaldehyde damages your cells, rendering them incapable of repair and making them more vulnerable to cancer. Cirrhosis also leads to cancer. Alcohol increases some hormones, including estrogen, contributing to breast cancer risk. It also causes cancer by damaging DNA and stopping our cells from repairing this damage.[103]

In summary, any level of alcohol consumption increases the risk of developing an alcohol-related cancer.[104] This is a discouraging message. However, I have good news—any reduction in alcohol intake lowers your cancer risk.

Alcohol and Death

You already know that you can die from alcohol poisoning by drinking too much alcohol in one sitting. What you may not know is that alcohol overdose can also occur from a continual infusion of alcohol into the bloodstream over time, resulting in death that does not correlate with a single binge.[105] Early death from alcohol steals more than 2,400,000 hours of human life per year in the United States.

According to the Centers for Disease Control and Prevention (CDC), alcoholism reduces life expectancy by ten–twelve years.[106]

This may lead you to ask what level of alcohol use really is safe. According to the most up-to-date research (2014 and newer), there is no risk-free level of alcohol consumption.[107] Considering how many people still drink every day, this is a sobering fact indeed.

8.
LIMINAL POINT: IS ALCOHOL LIQUID COURAGE?

"The secret to happiness is freedom. The secret to freedom is courage."
—*Carrie Jones*

You have **observed** alcohol used as liquid courage in popular media your whole life. The cowboy who takes a few shots before the high-noon gunfight. James Bond with his martinis "shaken not stirred." Even soldiers sipping from their flasks before battle. You **assumed** alcohol did provide liquid courage. You tried it, and your **experience** taking a shot to rid yourself of your nerves confirmed that your butterflies subsided. You've **concluded** that yes, alcohol helps you take on life with an extra dose of bravery.

Let's consider reality:

Liquid Courage

I get nervous every time I speak in public. Lately I've needed to speak more in front of senior colleagues. I can't recall exactly when, but somewhere along the line I figured that, since alcohol relaxed me, a quick drink before a speech would help me. I would stop at the hotel bar or buy a four-pack of single-serving wine bottles, keeping a few in my purse.

I was convinced drinking gave me confidence. I now realize alcohol actually chipped away my confidence.

In this day and age, most true danger has been eliminated from our daily lives. We live longer than ever before. We are not under attack by neighboring tribes or wild animals. We go to the grocery store rather than hunting for food. As a result we regard fear as weakness when, in reality, fear allows us to exercise caution and make better decisions. We protect ourselves because of fear. Considering that fear is key to our survival, calling someone fearless doesn't seem like much of a compliment. It is good for us to feel fear; it prevents us from taking unnecessary risks. With adrenaline pumping through our bodies we are more alert and responsive and can make faster decisions. Alcohol numbs your senses and prevents you from feeling natural fear. It is not possible for alcohol to give you courage because, by definition, if you've numbed feelings of fear you cannot be courageous. Courage means doing what is right or just, despite your fear. Ignoring, or disregarding, your fear goes against your instincts, which ensure your survival.[108]

So what's wrong with numbing my fear before a presentation? My natural nerves spurred me to prepare. They ensured I wasn't complacent and drove me to rehearse and plan. When I began to rely on alcohol to dampen my fear, I stopped preparing in advance. Instead I stayed up late, drinking the night before and putting off my rehearsals. Preparation made me a good public speaker. But once I started drugging myself with alcohol, knowing I wasn't prepared, my nerves skyrocketed. I actually worsened my fear by drinking, and so I felt I needed a few swigs before I stepped on stage. As you can guess, my speeches got worse. Thankfully it never reached a point where I was visibly drunk on stage, though if I hadn't found *This Naked Mind*, I have no doubt I was heading that direction.

Think about an athlete or a soldier who uses alcohol as liquid courage. The same thing happens—by removing natural apprehension, they rob themselves of important skills. I won't disagree that fear, nervousness, and apprehension are unpleasant feelings, but they are valuable and necessary.

In our society, we have so many ways we protect ourselves that we actually look for activities, like adventure sports, to demonstrate our bravery. I think drinking is one of those things. We know drinking has dangers, yet we brag about our ability to hold our liquor. Like a warrior demonstrating strength through his scars, we demonstrate strength by beating our bodies up and rallying the next morning. After a long night out with colleagues, comparing how much was drunk, who no longer remembers the evening, and who is feeling the best or the worst becomes a favorite topic of conversation. A hangover has become a badge of courage.

We went skiing recently (another, albeit healthier, activity we engage in to inject adrenaline into our safe and protected lives). My husband and I skied the back bowls (all double black diamond runs) while our kids took lessons. My sons, wanting to prove they were brave, courageous, and grown-up, asked to go with us to ski the bowls. When I explained the danger, it only enhanced the allure. If we can't do it, but Mom and Dad can, it must be awesome. We tried to caution them, but nothing we said was as powerful as what we did. They didn't care about the cliffs or that they weren't yet proficient skiers. We are their parents, they admire us, and if we're skiing hard stuff, they want to ski hard stuff.

This also happens during our teenage years—things our parents caution us against become available to try. We learn that some of the stuff our parents warned us about can be fun. We start to wonder if everything they've advised us against will be enjoyable. Danger means excitement, we think.

Do we believe telling our kids that "it's an adult drink" does anything to caution them? Quite the opposite—it enhances the allure.

According to the Substance Abuse and Mental Health Services Administration, more than half of Americans age twelve or older report that they are current drinkers of alcohol.[109] Thirty percent of adolescents report drinking by the eighth grade.[110] Our children do what we do, not what we say. Kids want to be brave, courageous, and grownup. They emulate their parents; it's how they are programmed. When they see us playing with fire, whether it's on the double black diamond ski runs or by drinking poison, they also want to play with fire and prove their bravery. And there is no way we can deny that drinking alcohol is playing with fire. While illegal drugs kill 327 people per week, and prescription drugs kill 442 people per week, alcohol kills 1,692 people per week.[111] We are unintentionally conditioning our children. We are programming them to believe their lives will not be complete without drinks in their hands.

We use our brains to make choices, and choices often come down to fear. We choose what we are less afraid of. Our decisions change once the fear scales tip. For example, a woman in an abusive relationship may not leave the abuser because she fears living without him. If she has a child, however, the fear scales may tip. She may now fear for her child more than she fears being without a partner. In this way, children can be the catalyst for a woman to leave an abusive relationship. The fear scales tipped against cigarettes when new research proved smoking causes lung cancer and takes thirty years off your life. Many people quit because their fear of dying from lung cancer outweighed their fear of a life without cigarettes.

The rational decisions we make change in light of more information. Imagine you are a short, scrawny man. You've managed to piss off some guy who is 6'4" and 250 pounds. He is coming after you and wants blood. You run. You arrive at a wall and find yourself trapped. Without any other option, you turn around to fight. Your odds have not improved—your attacker is still much stronger than you, but your situation has changed. Running is no longer an option. It is not cowardly to run away, nor is it brave to turn around and fight.[112]

Let's say you are the same scrawny guy, but now you've been drinking. Drinking does nothing to improve your position; it makes it worse. You feel a false sense of bravado, and you decide to fight before you are cornered. Further, when you are fighting, your reactions are delayed, and your senses are dulled. You don't feel pain to the same extent, and instead of backing down you are severely injured. Alcohol does not make you brave because there is no such thing as bravery when it comes to the instincts, which keep us alive. Alcohol just makes you less aware of your instincts. In this instance alcohol makes you stupid rather than brave.

If you are hiking alone and see a mountain lion cub, would it be brave to try and get close enough for a photo? The mother lion, despite her natural fear of humans, will kill you to protect her cubs. She is protecting her young, showing courage. Yet, if her family was not threatened would she be showing cowardice by running away from humans? Carr says both bravery and cowardice are human concepts, which don't exist in the animal kingdom.

I believe true bravery does exist. It's shown when you make a decision to override your natural fear in order to do what is morally right, but not when you remove your fear by numbing your senses. Jumping onto the subway tracks to try to save a child is irrational but brave. Your fear of dying is surely greater than your fear of watching someone else die. Yet you can overcome that fear in order to help another person. You cannot be brave without fear. If alcohol removes your fear, it makes it impossible for you to be truly brave. And cowardice? Cowardice is when you do not act according to your moral compass, failing to do what you know to be right, because of your fear. In my experience, drinking, to shut out life and avoid actual issues I knew I needed to deal with, was, without a doubt, the act of a coward.

We fear ridicule as much as bodily harm. Say you are pressured into trying a drug for the first time. The fear of looking weak, cowardly, and stupid in front of your friends outweighs your fear of the drug. You ignore your instincts to avoid scorn. This is cowardice, not bravery. It is much harder to make the right decision, the better decision, and endure the blow to your ego. It is much harder to go against the grain, skipping the drink and showing your children a different way, than it is to be swept along in our drinking culture. That is courage. Drinking because everyone else is doing it or because you are worried about being left out is not. It takes great courage to stand up for what is right, to stand up to the majority even silently by ordering an iced tea rather than a beer. It takes courage to read this book. There is no bravery in using alcohol to rid yourself of fear.

And let us not ignore the fact that alcohol actually makes us more vulnerable. My husband is training to become a pilot. When he flies he depends on instruction and information from the ground crew. They alert him when it is clear to land and where other planes are located to ensure they don't collide. If the communication between my husband and the ground crew is cut off, he will be vulnerable. He will have less information about his surroundings and feel less in control. This is not a pleasant experience, yet we do this to ourselves willingly when we drink. Alcohol deadens the flow of information from our mind and senses. This increases our fear, as we realize we can no longer clearly hear instruction from the ground crew. We realize we are less prepared to deal with whatever situation we find ourselves in; the natural feedback our senses provide us with has been obscured. Drinking during times of danger worsens your fear because you know you are removing your defenses.

But wait, if you believe alcohol provides courage, relaxation, and enjoyment, isn't that almost the same as if it actually provided those things? Are you better off believing you have a helper to get you through life, even if it's a placebo, an illusion? But deep down you know the truth. You know an alcoholic doesn't valiantly face up to the hardships and sufferings of life. I always knew drinking revealed weakness, not bravery. I knew I had allowed myself to become some-one who could not face life on its own terms.

For many, alcohol ensnares them at such a slow pace that it's im-perceptible. The changes are subtle. You come to depend on alcohol, feeling it gives you the courage to face the day, when in reality it steals confidence from you.

9.
OH S#*%! WE'RE STUCK

Trapped Without a Key

In *The Sober Revolution*, Lucy Rocca describes alcohol dependence in this way: "Breaking free from a dependency on alcohol is akin to escaping from a self-built prison . . . in the cycle of addiction you had no idea that you were effectively restricted behind bars."[113] When you're drinking more than you want to be drinking, it's as if you're behind bars. This idea is not unique to Rocca or myself—many other experts are starting to look at alcohol dependence in this way.

Imagine you're in a tight pair of handcuffs, without a key, and everyone blames you for it. You may have put them on yourself, but you don't really remember doing it, and you are very sorry that you did. You feel miserable.

Your wife takes you to see a doctor about the handcuffs. They're chafing your wrists, and your skin is infected. She is upset that you are no longer doing your part around the house. You find it hard to take out the garbage in a pair of handcuffs.

The doctor takes a look at you and tells you how bad it is for you to be in these handcuffs. The infection on your wrists could kill you if you are not careful. You need to get out of them as soon as possible. He goes on to tell you all the reasons you should take them off—they are affecting your family, your health, and your life. He tells you how difficult it is to pick up your kids with handcuffs on and that they will feel unloved. He gives you strict instructions to remove the cuffs. But he doesn't have the key, so nothing he says actually helps you get free.

What a frustrating experience. The doctor thinks you are stupid, and you think the doctor is an idiot. But doctors do this when they tell a drinker, who has become dependent on alcohol, that he needs to stop drinking or he won't live to see his children graduate. You, the drinker, already know this, and you've tried to quit. The doctor also knows his advice hasn't worked with others, and he doubts it will succeed with you either. The same thing happens when a wife threatens to leave her husband unless he stops drinking. More than anything he wants to stop and save his marriage. He would never logically or emotionally choose alcohol over his family, but he can't stop. Yet we believe addicts drink because they want to.

If I drank because I wanted to, why, when drinking began messing up my life, was I unable to stop? Instead, I wanted to stop and didn't stop. If you are making a choice, it should follow that you can reverse the choice. This is not the case with addiction. But we still believe with more willpower we could quit and release ourselves from the handcuffs.

So, we're stuck. But how did it happen? We did not smell enticing nectar like the bumblebee. Actually, alcohol initially tasted bad. So why are we tempted?

Marketing 101: What Are We Really Selling?

Look around or turn on the television. We've been conditioned to drink our entire lives. We're told alcohol calms and relaxes us, gives us courage, gets us through parties and work events, and makes us happy. Younger people even believe alcohol is good for their health.

Yet no one wants to admit that they're influenced. We want to feel in control of our destinies, free to choose our paths, uninfluenced by marketers' ploys. We feel like advertising isn't affecting us because we are not consciously aware of its power. In reality, your staunch belief that advertising does not influence you is one of the reasons it is so effective. Dr. Mark Schaller, a psychologist at the University of British Columbia, says, "Sometimes nonconscious effects can be bigger in sheer magnitude than conscious ones, because we can't moderate stuff we don't have conscious access to."[114] Makes sense, right? How can we consciously counteract a belief that bypassed our conscious understanding entirely?

An article in *Scientific American* says, "The error we often make is to assume that we can control the effects an ad has on our behavior because we are fully (consciously) aware of its content."[115] Consciously rejecting an ad's message doesn't ensure your subconscious doesn't buy the scam. We may think, "What a ridiculous car ad! A handsome guy wearing a fancy suit, zooming around a race course, and picking up a hot date. Who pays for this stuff?" But the next time we look at our worn-out old Ford, our unconscious mind revs up, and we find ourselves daydreaming about updating our ride or bemoaning the lack of cool features that newer car models include. Why? Because our unconscious is responsible for our desires and emotions, and our unconscious bought the underlying message that a new car will improve our overall happiness and success.

Studies in the last eighteen months have brought to light how profoundly our unconscious mind shapes our day-to-day thoughts and decisions.[116] When we make decisions with little to no thought that often actually means little to no conscious thought. This is why advertising influences you in profound ways, especially when you are not consciously aware of it.

In my first job out of college I worked at an advertising agency. A few times a week our founder would get on the intercom and say, "This is your captain speaking. All hands on deck, we have a brainstorming emergency." I'm not kidding; he really thought he was funny. We hailed to the boardroom, where he had plenty of "creative juice." The message was overt and clear—alcohol boosts creativity. To produce great campaign ideas, we needed to get drunk.

Was our best work done in those meetings? Not that I can remember. I actually remember the "aha" creative moments coming from other places. In fact, I don't recall a single big campaign idea from our drunken meetings. Did that stop us? Not at all. I didn't drink a lot at the time, but I was passionate about marketing and advertising. And I soon learned that alcohol was the key to my career.

The agency occasionally produced campaigns for local bars. I remember thinking hard about the methodology of selling alcohol. The marketing formula I often use is "the product's product's product." I realize that sounds confusing, so let me explain. The most successful advertising speaks very little about the product being sold and volumes about what void that product will fill in your life.

Take perfume advertisements. What's the product? A yellowish liquid that looks a bit like urine. Now that doesn't equate to compelling ad copy. What is the product's product? The yellowish liquid smells nice. Yet smelling nice is still not why people buy perfume. Advertisements selling the smell are not very successful. No, it's the product's product's product that you must sell. For perfume? Yes, it's sex.

The Wound of Existence

With this framework in mind, let's talk about another important aspect of marketing. Marketers actually create need by speaking to your vulnerabilities.

How? We play heavily on the human condition. Humans are not satisfied with simply existing. We look for more. No other animal questions their purpose in life or how they fit into the universe. This is one of the remarkable features that makes us uniquely human. But this questioning often creates a void inside us. We have more questions than answers, which causes tension. We desire more. This affliction is often called "the wound of existence."

Marketers play into this. Our natural, internal yearning can be easily and unconsciously directed. We not only sell sex when selling perfume. We also promise fulfillment, completion, satisfaction, and self-actualization. We present a lifestyle that promises to satisfy your restlessness. Through marketing, we tell you that if only you were thinner, smarter, sexier, you would find contentment; your life would be complete. You don't realize that the restlessness you feel is simply part of being human, so you look for ways to eliminate it. But ask yourself, even if you were handed everything you wanted, would it make you truly happy? Dan Harris explains this as hedonic adaptation: "When good things happen, we bake them very quickly into our baseline expectations, and yet the primordial void goes unfilled."[117] Generally, the more we consume the more we desire.

Existentialist psychotherapist Irvin D. Yalom identified what he calls humans' ultimate concerns: death, isolation (loneliness), freedom, and meaning.[118] These concerns reflect our deep fundamental needs. We search to understand the meaning of life, but no question provokes more debate. We feel desperate to experience gratification, so much so that we often rob ourselves of it by overindulging. We grapple with the inevitability of isolation and feel alone even in groups or families. We are painfully aware of the inescapability of death. We pursue pleasure and fulfillment in a never-ending search for satisfaction. Harris says, "It is the lie we tell ourselves our whole lives: as soon as we get to the next meal, party, vacation, sexual encounter, as soon as we get married, get a promotion, get to the airport check-in, get through security and consume a bouquet of Auntie

Anne's Cinnamon Sugar Stix, we'll feel really good . . . and yet the itch remains."[119] Marketing plays directly to these concerns. Alcohol commercials promise friendship, acceptance, gratification, happiness, and youth.

How to Sell Poison

Why do alcohol marketers need appeals that target the most fundamental of human needs? Let's look at this a different way. What if tomorrow we discovered alcohol for the first time, and the discovery included all the known scientific data on alcohol's effects on individuals and society, including that it's now been named the world's number one killer?[120] It's unlikely we would use or promote it recreationally. We might use it as a fuel, an antiseptic, or to dull pain. But we certainly wouldn't promote drinking it.

A good marketer can sell practically anything to anyone. Tobacco is literally dried, decaying vegetable matter that you light on fire and inhale, breathing horrid-tasting, toxic fumes into your lungs.[121] At one point marketers promoted smoking as a status symbol and claimed it had health benefits. Once you give it a try, the addictive nature of the drug kicks in, and the agency's job becomes much easier. If they can get you hooked, the product will sell itself.

Since the product is actually poison, advertisers need to overcome your instinctual aversion. That's a big hill for alcohol advertisements to climb, which is why the absolute best marketing firms on the globe, firms with psychologists and human behavior specialists on staff, are hired to create the ads. These marketers know that the most effective sale is an emotional sale, one that plays on your deepest fears, your ultimate concerns. Alcohol advertisements sell an end to loneliness, claiming that drinking provides friendship and romance. They appeal to your need for freedom by saying drinking will make you unique, brave, bold, or courageous. They promise fulfillment, satisfaction, and happiness. All these messages speak to your conscious and unconscious minds. Look at alcohol advertisements over the next few days. For each ad, try to identify the product's product's product. Try to see which of your most fundamental emotional desires the advertisement is appealing to and notice how unrelated the claim is to the reality of drinking. It's easy to dismiss alcohol advertisements as ridiculous because the claim that your chances of experiencing a threesome go up if you drink a certain kind of beer are absurd (I'm not kidding—this is a real ad). But as ridiculous as these ads seem on the surface, you must remember that consciously dismissing them as absurd is part of how they work in speaking directly to your unconscious desires. You will be amazed at who alcohol ads actually say you need to be to end your isolation, find freedom, maintain your youth (avoid death), and discover meaning in life. You may start to wonder how, as a society, we allow it.

Let's not forget, alcohol gives you no nectar. The reality, when the sexy advertisements have been stripped away, is that the actual product is ethanol.[122] It is a horrible-tasting, addictive poison. So we sweeten it with sugar and flavoring or process it to make it more palatable. The product's product is inebriation, a gradual deadening of your senses until you become completely intoxicated. And the side effects that are never disclosed are many. Think about ads for new medications, like Viagra or blood pressure medication. They are legally required to disclose all the statistically relevant side effects. Alcohol has the same cancer-causing effects as asbestos,[123] and just three drinks per week can increase a woman's chance of developing breast cancer by 15%,[124] yet there are no labeling requirements whatsoever. Yet compared to other drugs (illegal, legal, and prescription), alcohol bears the highest harm rating.[125]

When promoting alcohol, marketers sell a better human experience: relief from the human condition. And in doing so, we promise the opposite of what alcohol really provides. We sell happiness where there is pain. We sell romantic relationships when alcohol destroys healthy, fulfilling relationships. We sell sex when drinking deadens your senses and, as a depressant, actually decreases sexual desire, making it difficult to achieve erections and orgasm.[126] In fact, alcohol is a main cause of sexual dysfunction in men, including premature ejaculation, low sexual desire, and erectile dysfunction. A clinical study done in 2007 revealed that the amount of alcohol consumed was the most significant predictor of developing sexual dysfunction.[127] We sell stress relief when addiction derails your life. We sell increased mental capacity and creativity, yet drinking slows our brain function,[128] resulting in less intelligent and creative thought.

Maybe you still believe you are not affected by advertising. Most people think they're immune, but the data shows otherwise. The evidence is clear—exposure to alcohol advertising impacts subsequent use, encouraging people to start drinking and promoting heavier drinking among existing drinkers.[129] This connection is especially strong in young people.[130] Research demonstrates that your brain not only receives sensory information but also registers information at an unconscious, cellular level.[131] This can occur even when you are asleep![132]

Guess what some of most expensive commercials are for? You guessed it—alcohol. Guinness spent $20 million on the single most expensive commercial of all time. In terms of dollars per second, the priciest ad award goes to a Bud Light commercial. It cost $133,000 per second. The alcohol industry in the U.S. spends more than two billion dollars per year on advertising. Why would Guinness and Bud Light invest that type of money if advertising didn't work? They wouldn't.

Even if you accept that marketing influences you, it's hard to believe that advertisements are solely responsible for your desire to drink. You're right. As powerful as advertising is, it is not powerful enough to create a society where 87% of adults voluntarily drink cancer-causing poison. While the advertising industry contributes to that number, marketers are not solely to blame. We are most influenced by what we observe others doing, especially those we know and respect. Word of mouth is a powerful tool. Advertising is only the beginning. After it's done its job, it passes the task on to a society of walking billboards.

Case Study: The Marketing of Wine

Since marketing is my trade and wine was my drink, I want to take a minute to talk about the absolute genius behind wine marketing. I drank red wine for two reasons: It was touted as the healthiest choice, and it allowed me to feel grown-up at business dinners. I understand that the wine tasting ritual you observe at restaurants began a long time ago when wine occasionally turned sour due to the vinegar content. It was necessary to sample the bottle before it was poured. However, we've taken this ritual to a whole new level. I never thought I would admit it, but the entire thing, with its pomp and ceremony, makes me giggle.

Given my experience in marketing and the lengths I know marketers will go to in order to create a culture around certain products, it seems more likely that this is all a marketing ploy. In fact, I see the pairing of wines with foods and the elaborate tastings as one of the smartest strategies of our time. People will pay hundreds, even thousands, of dollars for a bottle of wine, yet it is consumable, so the pleasure, if there is any, is fleeting.

What we don't realize is that everyone else is likely faking it. It's worth repeating that the American Association of Wine Economists has proven that people cannot actually distinguish between "good" wines and cheap wines.[133] But since there is such a seemingly distinguished culture around wine, you probably felt, like I did, too stupid to admit you cannot tell the difference between certain vintages. So even if we don't see the point, we go along with it. I learned words like "oaky" in order to blend in, yet we had no idea what an oaky flavor actually is. I've still never licked an oak tree to find out. Another clue is that I've been part of hundreds of these rituals, all around the world, and never once was the wine, post swirl and sniff, returned.

Can you imagine if we did this for any other drink? Like milk? And wouldn't it make much more sense with milk? If the milk isn't fresh, you could actually smell the fermentation and send it back. Yet there is no milk ritual.

We start to identify with the type of wine we drink—white or red. This again goes against the idea that certain wines complement certain foods. You will notice that people who have acquired a taste for red wine drink red almost 100% of the time. Since apparently red wine only complements meat and pasta, while white wine complements fish and chicken, how do you explain these red wine drinkers drinking red with their salmon? Generally, if you enjoy the taste of wine, or in fact liquor, it's because of the sugar, not the alcohol. If I mixed enough milk, sugar, and flavorings with Drano, I bet I could make it taste like Bailey's.

Craig Beck, a self-proclaimed ex–wine aficionado describes the fine wine industry in one word: bullshit.[134] Beck says that he, by using the ritual of wine to cover his problem, managed to delude himself that there was nothing wrong. He says, "I couldn't have a problem because I was clearly a cut above the alcoholic in the park who chugged back super-strength tins of beer. I was buying and drinking the stuff of kings, an indication of my social standing and refined palette, and surely not a proclamation of a drug addiction!"[135]

Living Advertisements

Today's data-driven, intelligent marketing targets messages with such precision that the marketing department at Target is said to be able to predict pregnancy before even the mother-to-be realizes she is pregnant.[136] A successful marketing department should be known as a profit center, not a cost center. So we break target markets into audiences and drill down to specific personas. We articulate exactly who we are speaking to and craft our ad campaigns to lever the unconscious desires of the people most likely to be big profit sources. When the sales start pouring in, we increase our marketing budget and target additional segments of the population. This method maximizes bang for our buck, and we then rely on popular opinion and societal conditioning to extend our reach.

How does this societal conditioning play out in real life? As kids we're allowed juice while the adults drink beer. Soon we're teenagers, and we have a powerful urge to prove we're grown-up too. So we sneak our first drinks. And why not? Adults all around us are proclaiming the benefits of alcohol. These influential adults are living advertisements. And we believe them, not only because of their words but because of their actions. Alcohol must be incredible—why else would they drink so much of it?

Our society not only encourages drinking—it takes issue with people who don't drink. Since I stopped drinking I've been shocked by the invasive questions I receive. You wouldn't ask someone who turned down a glass of milk, "Are you pregnant?" "Are you lactose intolerant?" or "Did you struggle with milk?"

Beck explains these reactions in his book, *Alcohol Lied to Me: The Intelligent Way to Stop Drinking*. He says that all humans are motivated by just two component factors: seeking pleasure and avoiding pain. That is a key reason why your friends, no matter how much they care about you, don't want you to stop drinking. When you stop drinking they are forced to confront the fact that deep down they too know alcohol is bad for them. Beck explains, "When you stop drinking you appear to raise your standards above those of the people around you. As you raise your own standards, you automatically highlight their low standards, and this causes psychological pain to everyone around you."[137]

Is it any wonder that more people drink than ever before? And alcoholism now begins earlier in life. In "Alcoholism Isn't What It Used to Be," the National Institute on Alcohol Abuse and Alcoholism (NIAAA) states that twenty-two is now the mean age for the onset of alcohol dependence. The article says, "In most persons affected, alcoholism looks less like Nicolas Cage in *Leaving Las Vegas* and more like your party-hardy college roommate or that hard-driving colleague in the next cubicle."[138]

How do we allow the advertising industry to spend more than two billion dollars to tell us (and our children) that ingesting an addictive substance that drastically shortens our lives, destroys our confidence, causes cancer, and is responsible for death, abuse, violence, suicide, and general unhappiness will make our lives better?

Would we allow cocaine to be advertised in the same way? Can you imagine a $12 million commercial playing during the Super Bowl, with millions of young minds watching, proclaiming how amazing their lives will become if they snort a few lines? Why do we see cocaine and alcohol so differently, especially when, in the United States, alcohol kills 241 people per day[139] and cocaine kills only fifteen people per day?[140] Why do we glamorize the benefits of drinking?

There are complex answers, which lay in alcohol corporations, politics, taxes, lobbyists, and the like. But, in an effort to concentrate on what we can control, let's go back to the initial question. How did this happen?

I know plenty of people who use cocaine. Would I let them pull it out in front of my kids? Never. Between friends, restaurants, and television, my kids don't go a day without seeing someone take a drink. Yet alcohol kills 17.6 times more people than cocaine every year.[141] If we look at drunk driving, the statistics are horrific. Every night and weekend one out of ten drivers on the road are intoxicated, and alcohol-related accidents are the leading cause of death among young people.[142] Half of all fatal highway accidents are alcohol-related.[143] Imagine if a Boeing 747 aircraft carrying five hundred people crashed, killing all its passengers, every eight days. That is how many people die every eight days as a result of drunk driving.[144]

No one intends to be a statistic. We don't intentionally kill another human being by driving drunk. Most drunk drivers don't even realize they are drunk. Their inhibitions have been compromised, and their senses are no longer functioning properly—they literally no longer have the sense to avoid getting behind the wheel.[145]

While we glamorize the benefits of drinking for "responsible drinkers," being a drunk carries a heavy stigma. The stigma is so strong that we've created the belief that becoming a drunk can't happen to normal people, it can only happen to "them." It forces us to lie to others and ourselves about our drinking. Let's be honest—we all drink more than we want to sometimes. You can't tell me that moderate, "in control" drinkers don't puke on occasion or wake up with a killer hangover. No one sets out to throw up or get the spins at the end of the night. Why can't we recognize that, with alcohol, we are not as in control as we think we are?

Why can't we admit it? Why has it become painful to imagine a life without booze? Because marketing, our friends, our families, and our own experiences conspire to create a strong mental desire to drink. Drinking is so ingrained in our culture and upbringing that we've practically been trained, both consciously and unconsciously, to try alcohol. You now have a way to find freedom that will not result in tragedy or deprivation. You will not feel like you are living a boring, deprived life. You will be making a decision based on clear evidence. By the time you are ready to make a decision about how much you will drink, your unconscious mind will retain no desire to drink whatsoever.

10.
LIMINAL POINT: DRINKING HELPS ME LOOSEN UP AND HAVE BETTER SEX

"Alcohol doesn't permit one to do things better but instead causes us to be less ashamed of doing things poorly."
—W. Osler

You have **observed** people who are normally quiet and reserved become loud and obnoxious after a few drinks. You have also observed that people tend to "give it up" easier after drinking. You may have then **assumed** that drinking is vital to loosening up and getting lucky. You've personally **experienced** your inhibitions fade after drinking. Without your typical inhibitions you've become more empowered to go after sex. And maybe this has resulted in you having more sex when under the influence than when sober. The clear **conclusion** is that yes, drinking does help you loosen up and have better sex.

Let's consider reality:

I Drink to Loosen Up

More than half the population considers themselves shy; I know I do. Ironically, if you ask my friends and family, they will tell you I'm outgoing. This shows how different our perceptions are from reality. Yet shyness can be crippling, especially when you are forced to be outgoing with strangers in a social situation. As my friend Heidi calls it, "schmoozing and boozing."

For me it was business trips, networking events, and running booths at conferences. The norm for all us "shy" people was to drink. The conferences reinforced this, and there was never a shortage of free alcohol. Often booths provided free alcohol all day. If you wanted a drink, you could have one. No wonder I started believing alcohol was key to loosening up and being more gregarious while networking.

The important question is, did it work? Drinking didn't make me funnier. How could it? When my brain functioned at a slower pace my wit was dulled. It didn't make me more interesting. It just removed my inhibitions. I thought this was a good thing. I now realize we have inhibitions for a reason. They protect us, not only from physical harm, but from doing or saying things we shouldn't. Without my inhibitions, I talked to strangers like I would speak with close friends. This got me in trouble more than once. Sometimes the trouble was benign, and "drunk Annie" just resulted in a few whispers behind my back. Since I was often the youngest at these functions, people wrote off my silly behavior to immaturity. Other times my loss of inhibitions, combined with my naive nature, put me in awkward and risky situations.

More than once I found myself alone with a man who clearly wanted more from me than a business card. I'm incredibly thankful I was never harmed, but research shows how rare that is. When drinking, men perceive a greater level of sexual interest than women intend to communicate. This perception of feeling "led on" by a woman when combined with alcohol, which can increase aggressive behavior, makes a man more likely to commit assault. Drunk men are more likely than sober men to find the use of force to obtain sex acceptable.[146] Finally, alcohol affects a woman's ability to assess and react to risk. We are more likely to take risks that we would normally avoid, such as being alone with an strange man.[147]

You may argue that having a couple of drinks to loosen up is no big deal. Did you know that sexual assault, especially in universities, is at an all-time high? Authors of a 2015 study from *The Journal of Adolescent Health* say, "Sexual violence on campus has reached epidemic levels."[148] How would you like your son to be loosening up and losing his inhibitions in that environment? The majority of college rapes involving alcohol are not planned. In a major study, a boy who forced sex on a female friend wrote, "Alcohol loosened us up and the situation occurred by accident. If no alcohol was consumed, I would never have crossed that line."[149] In the same study we find that 54% of college women have experienced some form of sexual assault.[150]

Let's put that in perspective. Last October I volunteered at my son's kindergarten and helped carve pumpkins for Halloween. The statistic above means that more than half of these sweet and innocent six-year-old girls will experience some form of sexual assault when they leave their homes for university. Again, when it comes to sexual assault, and especially alcohol-fueled sexual assault, we all seem to have a story. A close friend of mine was asleep in her dorm room when a man, with alcohol on his breath, broke through her window and raped her in her bed. Can you imagine the horror and pain she still feels, decades after the incident? Even if the sex is consensual, alcohol increases other dangers. Sixty percent of STDs are transmitted when alcohol is involved, and young adults who use alcohol are seven times more likely to have unprotected sex.[151]

Shyness and inhibitions are not negative, yet we've been conditioned to think they are. These emotions protect us, helping us to navigate life with grace. It's not a lot of fun to be shy, but it's normal. Everyone feels it. In Susan Cain's book *Quiet, The Power of Introverts in a World That Can't Stop Talking,* she discusses what a gift it is to listen, a gift to the people we are listening to and to ourselves. You won't learn anything new by talking. When our talkative nature stems from drinking, it's neither thoughtful nor eloquent. Our brains function at a slower pace, and we have fewer filters between our thoughts and our mouths. What we talk about is less filtered and less interesting—not a great combination.

Despite introversion's positive qualities, as a society, we have been conditioned to believe shyness is a curse. We have a societal bias toward extroverts[152] because we are ashamed of our natural inhibitions. It's no wonder we try to escape our true nature by drinking. We hope that our personalities will change after a few drinks, and we will become the outgoing, engaging person we aspire to be. A more effective approach is to accept ourselves, realizing everyone is in the same boat, and allow conversations to unfold naturally. When we take the time to get to know someone, asking questions instead of speaking to fill the silence, the result is amazing. It's a gift to learn from other people. Asking questions, listening, and learning, these things make *you* a more interesting person. You become the type of person others want to be around.

Losing inhibitions is dangerous in sexual interactions. It's worth repeating that a loss of inhibitions is deadly when it comes to driving. When you are sober you don't imagine you would ever get behind the wheel of the car when drunk. But when you are drunk, what seemed like a terrible idea suddenly makes sense. With your heightened sense of bravado, you feel more in control than you actually are. Before you know it, it's the next day, and you think, "Wow, I probably shouldn't have driven last night." Half of all traffic accidents are linked to alcohol.[153] The majority of drunk drivers don't mean to drive drunk, but when drinking they can no longer judge how drunk they are. The roads have become more dangerous than ever. Inhibitions are protective, both to us and the people around us.

If we agree that alcohol has some control over you once you start drinking, enough that drinkers regularly drink more than they set out to, surely alcohol can make you do something you never imagined yourself capable of. I am appalled by how many awful things I did under the influence. Addiction is humbling, and I have been humbled enough to know that I am capable of anything, no matter how abhorrent, if the circumstances are right. Anyone is. Believing yourself immune to mistakes increases your chance of committing a repugnant act. All humans are painfully capable of failure. We are only human. It only takes one slip-up, one lapse in judgment. Don't be fooled—everyone makes mistakes. No one intends to kill another person while driving drunk. Yet it happens all the time. In the U.S., someone is killed by a drunk driver every 51 minutes.[154]

Have you ever gotten so drunk you threw up? Did you set out to do that? If your judgment is perfect, would you have allowed that to happen? Even if you consistently make great decisions and keep yourself and others out of harm's way, do you want to be the person at the party who cannot shut up? The person whose breath reeks of wine but can't tell because their senses have been numbed to the smell? We all know the person who goes on and on, and unfortunately, unlike on Facebook, we can't skip to the next interesting story. I know from experience, no one wants to spend time with "drunk Annie," who can't stop talking or laughing loudly at her own jokes.

You may feel that a little alcohol is good for your conversation skills or your golf game. The problem with alcohol is that once you start drinking you can't judge the point where a little is good and a lot becomes a disaster. When you are making a fool of yourself, or when your conversation skills wane, you remain unaware. Even if you could gauge the exact amount to drink, booze doesn't make you cleverer, funnier, more creative, or more interesting. There is nothing inherent in alcohol that can do this. More often when a shy person gets drunk, they end up emotional, weepy, and repetitive. We don't realize how bad we look when drinking because we are drunk and so is everyone else. It's the old question: If everyone jumped off a cliff, would you? With alcohol, as a culture, our answer is disturbing—yes.

I Drink to Have Better Sex

We have already discussed the fact that alcohol is a main cause of sexual dysfunction in men, that it makes it harder to become and remain sexually aroused.[155] What about women? I spoke with women who no longer drink, and the overwhelming sentiment is that sex is much better sober. One said, "My libido has taken a full-on, diva-style return to center stage." Another called it a "sober mojo revolution." I agree, sex is much better when you aren't deadening your ability to feel. Not only is it easier to have orgasms, but they seem to last significantly longer.

I experienced another positive in the sexual arena when I stopped drinking. Becoming alcohol-free made me happier than I'd been in years, and while this may not apply to everyone, it allowed me to get off an anti-depressant that I had been taking for a long time. The result? Libido! Sex has been more fun and more frequent these days.

The one downside everyone mentioned was that it's not all that fun to have sex sober with someone who is drunk. One woman said, "I agree that sex is so much better without booze, but I have to try and get my naughties in the mornings now because I hate wine breath on my husband." Another said, "I've discovered sex when you're both drunk is OK, and sex when you're both sober is amazing, but sex when one is sober and the other is drunk is the worst. Timing is everything, if you know what I mean, and when he is drunk things end much too soon." No matter how you look at it, alcohol does not lead to better sex. And the good news is that you don't have to take my word for it. This is something I hope you will enjoy finding out for yourself!

11.
A QUEST FOR SOBRIETY

*"Be patient with yourself. Self-growth is tender; it's holy ground.
There's no greater investment."*
—Stephen Covey

Let's imagine you've decided to try and stop drinking.

The first thing you do is research the evils of alcohol online. What you learn reinforces the reasons you want to quit, so your motivation is higher than ever. But you haven't addressed the actual reasons you drink. As Charles Duhigg demonstrates in his book *The Power of Habit*, willpower is a muscle that fatigues and eventually runs out.[156] Eventually, after a hard day, you get frustrated, your willpower muscle weakens, and you decide to have just one. One turns into many. Since you weren't successful stopping, you start to believe you are truly addicted. Quitting suddenly seems as difficult as you've heard.

When quitting is hard, it reinforces our belief that alcohol holds a great deal of power over us. It must be incredibly addictive, and we must be incredibly addicted. The more you dwell on reasons not to drink, the more upset you feel when you abstain and the worse you feel when you give in to temptation.

Yet this seems illogical. We've determined that alcohol causes us problems, and our efforts to cut back have taken the joy out of drinking. We no longer enjoy it, and drinking bouts are filled with self-loathing and regret. We are miserable when we give in but cannot understand why we can't quit. What do we need to know to find freedom? We must begin by understanding how our descent began.

My Descent

Your circumstances will differ from mine, but the principles remain. Here is where it started for me.

When I was a kid, I was full of enthusiasm and energy, without a drop of alcohol. I didn't need it to enjoy slumber parties, playgrounds, school dances, or anything else.

It all began in high school. At first I didn't like the taste. The only person I know who actually liked the taste of their first drink is my friend Jenny. She was on the beach in France drinking Malibu and Coke. Of course it tasted good—it was 95% sugar. Her surroundings were exotic, and she will tell you she liked her first drink. Let's be honest and realize she did not like the alcohol; she enjoyed the sugar and the environment. If her first drink was hard liquor in a dark basement, she would have spit it out. Even rats won't touch the stuff. In *Introduction to Learning and Behavior*, Powell and Symbaluk write that most laboratory rats will not voluntarily drink alcohol when it is presented to them.[157] In fact, rats only voluntarily drink alcohol after they have been force-fed it and developed a physical addiction.

In any case, my first drinks weren't all that good. I remember a lot of peer pressure. I was dating an older guy who hoped to lower my inhibitions. He bought me sugary wine coolers, but they didn't taste great. I longed for acceptance, so I worked to acquire a taste, although I would have preferred to drink something else. I was young, happy, and healthy. I didn't need the alcohol.

Disliking the taste of our first drinks helps us become stuck. If the first drink tasted amazing, we would be more cautious. Since those early drinks aren't very good, we throw caution to the wind. After all, how could we become addicted to something we don't like? I remember my first taste of vodka-infused orange juice. I was twelve years old, and my cousins and I had backpacked ten miles into the wilderness to a natural hot springs. A water bottle with what I now know to be filled with a screwdriver was passed around. When I had a sip I almost spit it out, asking, "Who ruined the orange juice?"

This is a great example of ignoring our instincts in favor of our intellect. If an animal drank something that tasted bad, instinct would kick in. They would not drink more because they would instinctively know the foul taste meant it was harmful. That would be the end of it.

Instead, we use our intellect, our reasoning abilities. We see everyone drinking. We have our first drinks and are surprised they don't taste all that great. We reason there must be something truly incredible about drinking. It must be a special treat if parents drink wine every night when it doesn't even taste good. We reason that there must be amazing benefits to drinking. Why else would everyone be doing it? This happens consciously, and, more dangerously, it happens unconsciously. So we work hard to develop a taste.

Suddenly, without realizing it, drinking has become part of our lives. We never make a conscious decision to drink as much as we now do. It just happens. Now we can't imagine dinner without wine or football without beer. Our tastes become accustomed to it. Over time we develop a tolerance. We experiment with stronger drinks and drink more often. Consuming this much was never a conscious decision.

My career contributed to my becoming dependent on alcohol. Early in my career I was promoted to senior roles, and at twenty-six I became the youngest VP in the company. I found myself traveling the country on business trips. Dinners out were characterized by heavy drinking, and of course, everyone could drink more than me.

I was called "kiddo" more often than I care to admit, and I had a chip on my shoulder to prove I deserved the promotions despite my age. I dedicated myself to building a tolerance in order to keep up with my colleagues. I had a routine: a glass of wine, a glass of water. This way I could drink more wine without feeling as tipsy, and it minimized the morning-after effects. It's pathetic to admit, but often I would sneak back to my hotel room, stick my finger down my throat to get the last glass or so out of my system. This allowed me to go on drinking. Or at the end of the night I would puke to get the last few glasses out before bed. I was on a mission to fit in, to prove myself, and sure enough I built a formidable tolerance.

Before I quit drinking, I, at 5'8", 140 pounds, could easily drink two bottles of wine in an evening. I often bragged about my ability to keep up with anyone in my company. Considering the company is headquartered in London, I felt this quite the accomplishment. I worked hard for my tolerance, for my unique ability to poison myself, and I was proud of it.

Not surprisingly, wine became part of every day, whether I was at work or not. I drank as much at home as I did at work and more when out with my friends. I can honestly say that in my last years of drinking I consumed more calories in alcohol than in food. It wasn't that there was always a reason to drink. It was just that there was never a reason not to.

When I was questioned about the amount I was drinking, I remember justifying it, saying that alcohol doesn't really affect me, that it wasn't hurting me. What else do we justify because it isn't hurting us? We don't rationally justify things this way. It's especially stupid when it's abundantly clear that alcohol was destroying my body.

I can't pinpoint exactly when things changed. If you haven't slid as far down as I had, take this as a warning—things do change. It sneaks up on you no matter how smart, successful, and in control you believe yourself to be.

I was often on international, overnight flights in business class. In business class the flight attendants seem on a mission to get the passengers drunk so they fall sound asleep for the journey. I would astound the flight attendant by how many times he had to fill up my glass. I would land in another country in the early morning hours, still tipsy. I inevitably had meetings first thing. So I would shower and change in the airport lounge before taking a taxi to the office. Soon I began to see things differently. I thought, "Hmmm, Annie, time isn't relevant anymore. You may be landing at 8 a.m., but it's 10 p.m. at home. Why not make yourself feel better and have one more when you land?" And it was easy to do. Alcohol flows freely at airport lounges twenty-four hours a day.

Hangovers caught up with me, either because I was drinking more or because I was so focused on the wine that I forgot the water. I'd heard that alcohol is the best cure for a hangover, so a beer or two at lunch (or earlier) began to sound like a good idea.

If you believe you are in control of your drinking, you are now thinking this could never happen to you. You may be right. You may have what I call "guardrails" in your brain where you have such a stigma against drinking in the morning that you would never let yourself fall that far. I hope you are right. In fact, I believed it would never happen to me. But my rationalizations became so powerful that I blinded myself to reality. I didn't see it as a problem, rather a temporary fix, all in the name of being more successful in my high-pressure, international role.

When you reach this point on the alcohol continuum, people around you start to see your problem before you do. You receive comments from family, friends, colleagues, or even your boss. You decide to prove you are indeed in control and determine to drink less. You've always said, "I can take it or leave it," and you have no doubt this is true.

You try to abstain completely on certain days or drink less per day. This is a critical change. Before this point you haven't questioned each and every drink. You drank what you wanted, when you wanted and didn't give it much thought. I definitely didn't think about how much I was drinking. I just drank.

Since alcohol has now caused an issue—enough of one for someone in your life to call you out on your drinking—it would seem you should want to drink less. Consciously you do. Unfortunately, your unconscious has not gotten the message, and it still desires alcohol, believing it is your key to enjoying social situations and relaxing.

You abstain and feel bored, annoyed, or grumpy. Everyone else is enjoying a drink after work, and part of you desperately wants one. You may give in, saying you will have only one or two. And you realize it's not fun to worry about how much you are drinking. After a few, it doesn't seem to matter anyway. You decide you will drink less tomorrow. Tomorrow comes, and you beat yourself up over your lack of willpower, wondering why you can't simply drink less. The fact that you are having a hard time keeping your commitments to cut back compounds the problem. You worry that alcohol must have power over you. Why else would it be so hard to drink less?

Before you decided to cut back, your drinking wasn't a problem; at least you didn't realize it was. You, like me, probably didn't give it much thought. Now every time alcohol is in the picture, you face a stressful dilemma. If you normally drink every day, this stress becomes a daily occurrence. I relied heavily on wine to help me relax and relieve stress. As soon as something stressful happened, I would reach for a bottle opener. When my beloved wine became the source of my stress, I found myself in a vicious cycle. This is a painful position to be in. You are simultaneously drinking too much and not drinking enough. I've heard it said, "One drink is too many and a thousand is not enough." This is truly a pickle—the part of your brain that sees alcohol as a problem is at odds with the part of your brain that wants a drink whenever you feel like it.

The struggle at this stage is palpable. You are incredibly stressed and end up drinking more than before. Eventually you realize, much to your horror, that you are not in control and probably need to stop drinking altogether.

This news, for many, is tragic. Mary, a former blackout drinker who found her freedom with *This Naked Mind*, described it like this: "I remember thinking, I think I just need to stop drinking. My entire body deflated as the words crossed my lips, overcome with sadness at the thought of giving it up forever and at the same time not believing I was capable. It felt so unfair. Why couldn't I just learn to drink like other people? Why did it have to come to this?"

The first few weeks and months of sobriety are described by some as the hardest thing they have ever done. My friend Beth, who quit drinking with A.A., said it was like losing her best friend. She mourned for alcohol and went through an intense grieving process. Quitting is a horrible experience for someone who believes that life will never be as sweet without alcohol.

No one plans to become an alcoholic, just like no one thinks they are capable of cheating on their spouse. We mentally segregate ourselves from "them," believing we would never allow these things to happen in our lives. The truth is they do happen. They happen all the time to people just like you and me. I was taught that a marriage is safest when you accept that you could cheat—that anyone could—and take precautions to protect your marriage. Alcoholism is no different. Alcohol is physically addictive, and a physical dependence on alcohol can occur in anyone.

Since I was high-functioning, it was easy for me to see alcoholics as separate from me; I couldn't possibly become one. It was easy to close my mind to the amount I was drinking because I was so successful in my family life and career. I even gave alcohol some of the credit for my success. I mean, how would I have had all those great ideas or done all that networking without booze? Now I know I'm much better at my job when I'm not drinking. One of the great things about the life you are about to lead is how much fun it is to disprove your false notions about alcohol. Realizing my ideas come from my brain, not from the bottle, is empowering. It feels great to know I don't need alcohol at all, for anything. I am strong, happy, and whole just as I am.

The Quest Begins

And so, once you realize alcohol controls your life, the quest to regain control begins. Sadly, many people avoid this journey, even though they dearly want freedom from alcohol's control, because they're afraid it will be impossible or result in lifelong pain. Remember the alcoholic living on the street in Las Vegas. Obviously he is no longer happy; alcohol is not giving him any real relief or enjoyment. In fact it's clear that alcohol is to blame for his tragic situation—sleeping on the sidewalk, hungry, filthy, begging for money, and being harassed by the police. Yet we observe his brown paper bag and wonder why, beyond all logic and reason, he continues to drink.

We might interpret his situation to mean that quitting must be an almost impossible feat. Why else would people allow their entire lives to be ruined? We are bombarded with statistics about how few people successfully stay sober. The task before us appears monumental. We start off with a feeling of apprehension and terror.

We hold on to the illogical hope that someday, if we can abstain for long enough, we will be miraculously released from our desire to drink. Why would that happen? All around you booze is still held up as the "elixir of life." Your friends are drinking and seeming to enjoy it. Nothing has changed, so why would you somehow, someday, be spontaneously freed?

When you stop drinking through sheer willpower, you start to see the benefits. You become healthier, and your situation in life improves. The reasons you quit begin to fade into the background. Inevitably you start to feel healthy and strong. You feel empowered because of the strength you have shown by quitting. You forget the reasons you quit to begin with. Humans have selective memory. We tend to remember the good things rather than the whole picture. You forget the fights with your spouse, the hangovers, or the stupid things you did and said. You forget your misery, and the reasons you quit no longer seem as important as they did before. You heal, and in healing the reasons to avoid drinking lose their immediacy.

You find an excuse for just one, and suddenly you are back in the mental misery of alcohol addiction. It makes no difference if you go straight to the blackout stage or if it's a gradual descent that takes years. You have not changed. Alcohol has not changed. Society has not changed. What would make this time any different than the last?

How will you know when you have succeeded? If you live waiting to see if you ever drink again, you won't know you are successful until you are dead. Living a life in recovery, yet never recovered, implies you have no greater expectation than for life to be OK. But when you completely change your mental (conscious and unconscious) perspective on alcohol, you begin to see the truth about drinking. When this happens, no willpower is required, and it becomes a joy not to drink. This is the mystery of spontaneous sobriety, which we will talk about after our next Liminal Point.

12.
LIMINAL POINT: I DRINK TO RELIEVE STRESS AND ANXIETY

"You cannot find peace by avoiding life."
—*Virginia Woolf*

You have **observed** people saying they need a drink after a long day. You have also poured yourself a drink to take the edge off, and your **experience** showed it did take the edge off your stress and anxiety. It was easy to **assume** alcohol was a stress reliever and quieted your anxiety. Eventually you came to the **conclusion** that alcohol was necessary to relieve stress and anxiety.

Let's consider reality:

Alcohol Relieves My Stress and Anxiety

I started as a social drinker, but during the last five years I used it to relax. Ironically, drinking made my life much more stressful. My health was affected. I compounded the natural stress of my job with the anxiety of wondering what stupid comment I'd made to whom during nights of drinking. Glass by glass I poured stress into my life, all the while deluding myself into believing alcohol helped me relax.

What is actual relaxation? You could say that being completely relaxed means having nothing to worry, irk, or annoy you either physically or mentally. How can alcohol do this for you? It does not fix the annoyances and stressors but temporarily dulls the symptoms. And guess what? As you build a tolerance, the actual effect of alcohol decreases, and your need for it increases. Soon the things that are making you upset are barely muted by alcohol, and you are addicted. Of course, addiction is a much bigger stressor than the stressors you drank to remove. You've created a mental craving for alcohol that did not exist before, one that you now have to either feed (with more alcohol) or deprive. Wanting something you shouldn't have does nothing to relax you; it creates a mental divide inside your mind, which is the very definition of frustration and agitation. It's the opposite of relaxation. Drinking to treat your problems ensures you will not address the true source of your discontent. It ensures you will remain stuck, treating the symptoms of stress rather than their causes. Things go from bad to worse when you add alcohol dependence to the mix.

A few years ago in Windsor, England, I stepped off the stage after speaking to about seventy people. I usually know I've nailed it, and this time I wasn't so sure. Something felt wrong. I knew I was not responding to the audience well, and they were not responding to me. Sure enough, a friend took me aside to ask what was wrong. He was, as good friends are, honest with me, saying I had lost my spark. I was not the animated, funny, and relatable communicator I used to be. I knew he was right and burst into tears. I didn't understand what was wrong, why I was so on edge. What I did know was I wanted a drink to calm my nerves. Alcohol caused the sharp decline in my speaking abilities. Yet in the moment I thought alcohol was the only solace I had.

I had that drink to "calm my nerves," but I was so stressed it didn't help. Heavy drinking and lack of sleep were why I had lost my spark.

When I reflect now on why I was such a mess, there was no real reason. While my career can be stressful, I thrive on a fast pace and constant change. I am in my element when I am responsible for large budgets and international teams. I was never in a life-or-death situation. All my stress came from my drive to improve and excel. Drinking to dull my stress made it worse. Now that I no longer administer myself a powerful poison on a regular basis, I can handle all sorts of situations, even the most daunting. Are they all easy? No. Do I feel stress? Of course. But the stress is never multiplied because I don't have the energy, self-confidence, or courage to deal with the issue at hand. Alcohol seemed to give me an easy way out. Have a drink, deaden my senses, and let stress seep from my mind. But it worsened every situation because I drank instead of facing the problems head-on.

I am writing this on a plane ride home, returning from a six-day, four-country business trip. I'll want to relax when I get home. At the end of a trip like this I inevitably feel wound up. I used to believe this was stress, and I needed alcohol to unwind. I admit, some of it is stress, but most of it is the responsibility of my role. I now see that I thrive when I am pushed. I crave speed with my job, my family, and the other projects I am involved in. I have been told, when I was especially on edge, to slow down, but slowing down does not make me happy. It's not the pace that is the problem; the problem is poisoning my body and mind so that I am physically unable to keep up with the life I want to live.

Imagine the intensity of sinking into a hot tub after a rigorous workout on a blistering summer day. A chilly and refreshing shower would feel better. However today, after twenty-nine hours of traveling, the hot tub sounds great. It will relax my muscles and help me sleep. Lying in bed with a good book is a treat for me. My son, at three, would find that very stressful. He is full of energy and can't yet read, so he would be frustrated by having to sit still. In order to relax, we need to figure out why we are not relaxed and address the problem.

If we are tired, we sleep. If we are cold, we start a fire or put on a sweater. If we itch, we scratch. You get the picture.

If I am stressed because I forgot to return an important phone call, I can either make the call or write myself a note to ensure I do it when I am able. This will relieve my stress. If I am experiencing stress because of a deadline, I can schedule time to work on the project or just get to work. The most thorough road to relaxation is removing the specific irritation that is causing you stress.

I have an executive mentor and coach. A few years ago we were discussing the fact that I was distracted by work over the weekends, and I couldn't unwind enough to relax and enjoy family time. This was when I was drinking, which further proves to me that a drink is not the magic relief button I once thought it to be. My coach gave me some great advice. He said there are really only three types of things that cause stress to creep into our minds outside of work. The first is something you forgot to do. In this instance, write it down and re-solve to do it first thing Monday morning. The second is something you realized you'd messed up. In this case, decide if it's fixable. If yes, write it down, making a note to fix it as soon as possible. If not, you might need to make amends, but then you need to let it go. The third is a new idea, and if a new idea pops into your head, you should write it down and act on it once you are back in the office. This advice relieved my work-related stress more than any drink ever has.

You achieve relaxation by removing the source of discontent. Al-cohol, by definition, cannot relax you. Now you may wonder about the numbing effects of alcohol. Surely alcohol would help numb pain. Yes, alcohol will numb your brain and your senses. It will numb you in such a fashion that, if you drink enough, it will render you unconscious. And unconsciousness will relieve your pain. But saying this is a good idea is like saying it's a good idea to go under the guil-lotine because you have a migraine. There are better solutions.

A 2012 study shows that alcohol makes you less capable of dealing with stress and anxiety. Researchers gave mice doses of alcohol for a month, then ran tests to compare the mice that had been drinking with normal mice. The mice were put in stressful situations to measure their reactions. Alcohol literally rewired the mice's brains to make them unable to deal with anxiety and stress.[158] Many find this shocking, but if you drink regularly you probably already know this is true.

Why do we believe alcohol helps stress and anxiety? Because it can make you oblivious to your stressors even when it's worsening them. You already know that when you sober up, unless you've done something to actually improve the situation, your stress remains.

On the beach with an excellent book, enjoying the sun and the breeze off the ocean, without a care in the world, I am fully relaxed. Alcohol can't improve that feeling. I was recently on the beach in Hawaii enjoying this very sensation, and I considered having a drink. I had always had a Mai Tai (or eight) while on the beach. When I thought about it, I realized a drink would make me tired and cranky. And since one would make me thirsty and awake my alcohol craving, I doubted I would stop at just one. Then instead of spending the next day sunning myself on the beach, I would spend it in bed, hung over. When I thought about it, I realized I didn't want a drink. Mental peace is having no distress. It is a feeling you can never achieve with a drug.

If you are truly happy and relaxed, you have no need or desire to change your state of mind. Looking back, I see that my constant need to drink to relax myself was really proof that alcohol was not relaxing me. If alcohol helped me achieve relaxation, wouldn't it follow that I wouldn't need as much of it? If alcohol cured my stress, wouldn't I need less, not more, of it over time? No, alcohol does not relax you. It does not fix the stress in your life. Rather, it inebriates you, which covers the pain for a short amount of time. As soon as it wears off, your stress returns and, over time, multiplies.

Being happy and stress free, dealing with the root cause of stress rather than numbing the symptoms is the only sure way to find relief.

Then you no longer need to cover the symptom with poison. I am heartbroken to know more than one person who has taken their own life. It's tragic that we deal with our unhappiness in this way, by rendering ourselves forever unconscious, believing the only cure to our depression or unhappiness is to erase ourselves altogether. Alcohol erases a bit of you every time you drink it. It can even erase entire nights when you are on a binge. Alcohol does not relieve stress; it erases your senses and your ability to think. Alcohol ultimately erases your self.

The Opposite of Relief: What Happens in Your Brain

So if alcohol doesn't relax you, what does it do? Quite simply, alcohol slows down your brain function. It does this by affecting two neurotransmitters (chemicals that transmit signals between brain cells): glutamate and GABA.[159] Glutamate is an excitatory neurotransmitter that increases brain activity levels and energy. Alcohol suppresses the release of glutamate, resulting in a slowdown along your brain's neural highways.[160] You literally think more slowly. GABA is an inhibitory neurotransmitter. Inhibitory neurotransmitters reduce energy and slow down activity. Alcohol increases GABA production in the brain, resulting in sedation, diminished thinking, reduced ability to reason, slowed speech, diminished reaction time, and slower movement.[161]

When drinking, science shows that you also alter brain chemicals that increase depression.[162] Your brain counteracts alcohol's artificial stimulation of your brain's pleasure centers, diminishing enjoyment until the illusion of pleasure no longer exists. At this stage the dopamine levels are high, which increases the craving for alcohol but without the illusory pleasure.[163] Neuroscience demonstrates that desire for alcohol can transition into a pathological craving that is associated with dependence.[164] Drinking creates a compulsive need for alcohol, but you don't actually receive any enjoyment from it. How long this takes is person-specific. In some people it can happen almost immediately, and in others it can take several weeks, months, or years of drinking.[165]

Alcohol affects your cerebral cortex, especially your prefrontal cortex. It depresses the behavioral inhibitory centers, making you less inhibited. This also inhibits the processing of information from your eyes and mouth[166] and further inhibits your thought processes, making it more difficult to think clearly.

In addition to slowing brain function, episodic drinking (defined as four drinks in two hours for women and five drinks in two hours for men)[167] can injure the brain by causing the death of neurons.[168] Finally, alcohol depresses nerve centers in the hypothalamus, which control sexual performance and arousal. Sexual urges may increase, but sexual performance and sensory pleasure decrease.[169]

To summarize many of the things we've been discussing about what alcohol actually does to you, I will use an excerpt from Jason Vale's book *Kick the Drink . . . Easily*:

"Alcohol has been proven to:

- Depress your entire nervous system.
- Undermine your courage, confidence, and self-respect.
- Destroy your brain cells.
- Break down the immune system, making you less resistant to all kinds of disease.
- Interfere with the body's ability to absorb calcium, resulting in bones that are weaker, softer, and more brittle.
- Distort eyesight, making it difficult to adjust to different light.
- Diminish your ability to distinguish between sounds and perceive their direction.
- Slur your speech.
- Dull your sense of taste and smell.
- Damage the lining of your throat.

- Weaken your muscles.
- Inhibit the production of white and red blood cells.
- Destroy the stomach lining.
- Cause obesity."[170]

Vale goes on to say, "When you stop putting a poison like alcohol in your body, it literally breathes a sigh of relief."[171]

13.
THE MYSTERY OF
SPONTANEOUS SOBRIETY

"No one saves us but ourselves. No one can and no one may.
We ourselves must walk the path."
—Buddha

Have you ever heard of spontaneous sobriety? It's a strange-sounding phrase, but it really just means recovering from alcohol dependency without any formal treatment. And the secret to spontaneous sobriety has everything to do with reconciling the internal conflict caused by your desire to quit drinking and your fear of missing out.

Sobriety Without Rehab

You may be surprised to know that in the U.S. people who spontaneously recover from alcohol dependence are between four and seven times more successful than participants in our main alcoholism treatment approach: A.A. According to a recent study by the NIAAA, more than one-third of individuals with alcohol dependence fully recovered without any treatment. They went from alcohol dependence, defined as demonstrating tolerance, withdrawal symptoms, and unsuccessful attempts to reduce or stop their consumption, to not drinking at all or drinking at levels that were no longer harmful and no longer characterized as dependence.[172] In comparison, Dr. Lance Dodes, a recently retired professor of psychiatry at Harvard Medical School, says, "Peer reviewed studies peg the success rate of A.A. somewhere between 5 and 10 percent, about one of every 15 people who enter these programs is able to become and stay sober."[173]

Not only are people who simply quit, without programs or outside help, more successful in maintaining a healthy relationship with alcohol, they appear to be more at peace with and happier about their decision. A significant portion of their time and energy is not dedicated to maintaining success. Instead of sobriety becoming a daily focus with meetings, readings, and devotionals, it fades into the background, allowing them to be truly free. Further research shows 75% of people who recover from alcohol dependence do so without seeking any kind of help, including specialty alcohol rehab programs and A.A.[174]

How can this be? It does not seem to make sense that simply quitting, without any assistance whatsoever, could be more effective than formal support programs. I found this incredible not only because of the success rates but also because the phenomenon of spontaneous sobriety is not publicized. If there is a way to quit or cut back without a lot of effort and without heartache, sign me up. I needed to understand what this phenomenon was and how it was done. I wanted to understand if there was something that happened inside these spontaneously sober people that I could replicate and teach.

Spontaneous Sobriety: Case Study

Fortunately, one of these spontaneously sober people is my dad. He smoked cigarettes for twenty years and drank heavily. One day he up and quit both, never looking back. My dad leads a unique life. After graduating college, he gave up a promising Manhattan-based future in film production to move into a tiny (twelve foot by twenty-four foot), one-room log cabin in the middle of the Rocky Mountains. There, my parents raised my brothers and me without running water or electricity. At that altitude, the roads are closed from November to May. We had to ski or snowmobile to get to the nearest town.

This is where I grew up—and where he still lives, forty-four years later. It is nestled in a basin at 10,500 feet above sea level, almost at the timberline, and the closest neighbor is miles away. In fact, I remember developing a fear of neighbors because I heard the term in school, and since we didn't have any neighbors I didn't realize what they were. In fact neighbors sounded quite terrifying, and I went home and asked my mom, "Do neighbors bite?"

I never knew my dad to drink, so I assumed he never had. In reality, he was known for his heavy drinking and drank as much or more than any other fraternity boy in the '60s. So why was his "recovery" nonexistent? When I asked him, he replied, "I realized it wasn't doing me any favors, so I decided to stop. I never looked back."

How is this possible when so many spend their lives in recovery, consumed by the fact that they no longer drink? How did my dad simply decide he didn't want to drink alcohol and never look back? My dad wasn't aware of the psychology or science behind why, when he made a firm decision to quit, he was able to stop without pain or longing. The answer is not immediately obvious, but it's actually very simple. I will explain with a story.

Cognitive Dissonance: Disagreeing with Yourself

My friend Chelsey is now happily married to an amazing man. Before meeting her husband, she traveled a long, bumpy road of suitors. One in particular rubbed me the wrong way. Many of the guys weren't good enough for her, but Jesse hit well below the mark. And she liked him, a lot.

My opinion created tension between us. We are close and have a hard time hiding anything from each other. I couldn't sugarcoat it. I didn't have a great reason why I so disliked him. I underestimated how much she liked him, and suddenly we were at odds about something that we couldn't easily reconcile. Usually, if we disagreed on something, we could chat for long enough and eventually see each other's point of view. With Jesse, I couldn't see why she liked him, and she couldn't understand why I didn't. While she dated him, it hung over us and affected how much she shared with me about her relationship.

The reverse happened a few years later when I was still deeply addicted. She did not approve, and though she wanted me to be honest with her about what I was going through, I couldn't. I couldn't explain what I was doing and how I didn't like myself because of it. So I didn't share with her as much as I should have. In both instances we had differences we couldn't reconcile, and we grew more distant than either of us wanted.

This is exactly what happens inside your brain when you realize you are drinking more than you should. In psychology this phenomenon has a fancy name—cognitive dissonance, defined as the mental stress or discomfort that is experienced by someone who holds two contradictory values, ideas, or beliefs at the same time.

Let me give you another example. It's Halloween, and the receptionist at your office brought in a bowl of candy. It sits on her desk, which you walk by every day. You want to eat some, but you've promised yourself that you're going to stay away from sugar.

You have an internal struggle, which creates mental stress. You now have two contradictory trains of thought. You don't want to eat the candy because you don't want the sugar. Yet you crave the candy, believing it will provide pleasure and satisfaction. You give in and eat some. This is when problems with cognitive dissonance begin. You've done something you are not happy about, which creates discomfort.

This internal struggle has been studied in-depth. It is very difficult to be happy or at peace when we do something part of our brain doesn't agree with. We will go to incredible lengths to overcome the dissonance and restore internal peace. We do this both consciously and unconsciously. And because not all our attempts to remove the struggle are conscious, we can, unknowingly, lie to ourselves.

There are a few ways to overcome this division and restore our inner harmony:

1. We can change our behavior: "I won't eat any more candy."
2. Or we can justify our behavior by changing the conflicting idea or information: "I can cheat every once in a while. I deserve it."
3. We can justify our behavior by adding new behaviors: "It's OK. I will go to the gym later today."
4. Or we can delude ourselves by ignoring or denying the conflicting information: "Candy isn't that bad for me."

With addictive substances, we find more complications. You have a strong unconscious belief that alcohol relieves your stress and enhances your life. You have both a conscious and unconscious belief that cutting back or quitting is a legitimate sacrifice. You worry that quitting will be stressful. You don't have a substitute to take its place. In fact, life seems cheerless without it. And to make it all worse, everyone around you drinks!

You now have a strong, conscious belief that the amount you are drinking is harmful to your health, hurting your relationships, and negatively affecting other areas of your life. Since alcohol is an addictive substance, the conflict becomes physical as well as mental. You develop a tiny, almost imperceptible, physical craving for the addictive substance, which makes it more difficult to quit. With time, this craving grows powerful. This is a neurological fact—brain circuitry changes as a result of repeated exposure to an addictive substance, and over time cravings grow in strength through increased dopamine levels, which are the result of a learned chemical response in your brain.[175] Even when you're not drinking alcohol, the internal conflict rages because the craving is in constant disagreement with your desire not to drink. Add deteriorating health and relationships to the equation, and the internal conflict becomes increasingly more painful.

This phenomenon is the basis of addiction. All addicts lie to themselves and others. They do this to protect themselves and minimize the internal trauma caused by their conflict of wills. We become so good at making excuses, at blinding ourselves to the truth, that we believe our own lies. Being unable to trust yourself is terrifying and causes an incredible amount of pain. This is the pain of addiction. Contrary to popular belief, it's not the physical consumption that destroys our lives but the internal conflict and our determination to fix it while retaining an unconscious belief that the drug is somehow vital to our lifestyle.

With alcohol, we can rarely solve the conflict by simply changing our behavior. Since the unconscious mind has been conditioned to believe alcohol is our friend, that it helps us handle stress and improve our lives, we still desire to drink after we decide to quit or cut back. We need willpower to abstain. But, as scientists now know, willpower dries up.[176] And the few drinks we allow ourselves to have become coveted. We give in, drink, and then feel guilty. We are in the midst of cognitive dissonance, a divided mind, experiencing internal conflict.

When we realize we cannot stop drinking via willpower, the conflict in our brains increases. We have tried to change our behavior and found that difficult. We have tried to change our cognition, or thoughts, by reviewing lists of the horrible effects of drinking, and that too has failed. We try to justify our behavior by making excuses for drinking. We may not believe these rationalizations at first, but it's so much easier to tell myself that it's OK to have a drink at 8 a.m. because it's 10 p.m. at home than to experience internal conflict. Part of our brain realizes the excuses don't hold up, so we numb ourselves by drinking more. We try anything to overcome the conflict. We ignore and deny information that conflicts with our desire to drink. We are running out of options, and we don't understand why we can't overcome this. Then we start to blame ourselves.

You can see why scare tactics are rarely successful in overcoming an alcohol problem. We have known all our lives that alcohol is addictive and that it ruins people's lives, but we choose to ignore or deny such information, which compounds the conflict in our brains. Drinking becomes an illogical activity.

The belief that alcoholism only happens to other people, people with a physical or mental defect, gives us an easy way to address the conflict in our brains. It gives us a reason to believe we are in control even when we know we are not. It helps us deny our problem. You can observe how drinkers deal with cognitive dissonance by paying attention to the reasons people give for drinking. If you are honest with yourself about why you drink, I bet it will be difficult to find a reason that truly stands up to logical, critical examination.

Stopping the Internal War

So how did my dad overcome his cognitive dissonance? How did he achieve spontaneous sobriety? He chose the first way, to stop drinking once and forever. But when he made this decision, he had long since determined that alcohol was not doing anything positive in his life. He realized this with 100% of his mind, leaving no lingering doubt, no room to question his decision. He chose to stop drinking with all of his brain, and by doing this he ended the conflict, achieving peace. The personality characteristic that allowed him to do this, his decisive and definitive nature, is also a quality that contributed to his drinking. When he was a drinker, he drank with his entire mind. He didn't doubt or question every drink. If drinking a little was good, drinking a lot was better. This commitment is both what pushed him to become dependent on alcohol and what ultimately helped him find freedom.

I won't tell you what my dad did is easy to do. It's not. It takes a mind that is pliable enough and strong enough to change all of itself—both the conscious and the unconscious. *This Naked Mind* does that work for you. By reading this book, you are changing your unconscious mind, so you can easily and peacefully end the conflict inside your brain. You may have been living with division in your brain for years, even decades. Only you know how much pain and suffering this has caused.

Why is this division so painful? Conflict causes pain, which explains why we are, by nature, averse to conflict. It hurts to disagree with a close friend. We suffer pain when we don't see eye-to-eye with strangers or even when we witness conflict. How much more painful to fight with ourselves? If you've suffered from addiction, doing something you hate, you know the intense pain. I have not, in my life, experienced anything worse. There is nothing scarier. The conflict was so painful that I would "obliviate," rendering myself completely intoxicated in order to ignore the mess my life had become. In doing this, I lost my trust in myself. I did stuff I didn't want to do, and I didn't understand why I continued to do it. The misery was powerful and all-consuming. I no longer saw a familiar face in the mirror. I didn't know who I was; I lost myself. To find yourself again, and to restore your happiness, it is vital that you remove the disagreement inside your mind. And the first step is to examine the asserted benefits of alcohol, and prove, logically and rationally, with our Liminal Points that there are few benefits to drinking.

14.
LIMINAL POINT: I ENJOY DRINKING; IT MAKES ME HAPPY

"Addiction begins with the hope that something 'out there' can instantly fill up the emptiness inside."
—*Jean Kilbourne*

You have **observed** people "enjoying" alcohol in every conceivable manner for as long as you can remember. Advertisements promise alcohol will make us happy as we develop relationships, have sex, ignite the party, and enjoy our everyday activities. It's practically impossible in western society not to form the **assumption** that alcohol makes people happy. You determined to try alcohol, and over time your **experiences** confirmed this. Not necessarily because alcohol actually made you happy, but because once you built even the smallest tolerance you became slightly, almost imperceptibly, unhappy when you couldn't drink. In fact the **assumption** that alcohol makes you happy includes an unspoken **assumption** that not drinking will make you unhappy. And in this way your **experience** confirmed your assumptions, so you've **concluded** that yes, alcohol does in fact offer enjoyment and make you happy.

Let's consider reality:

Alcohol Makes Me Happy

Studies show that alcohol causes a lot of unhappiness in our society. It makes the drinkers unhappy, but it also makes the people around drinkers unhappy. It causes homelessness, joblessness, poverty, abuse, depression, pain, rape, misery, and death. There are support groups for victims of emotional, physical, and sexual abuse resulting from alcohol. Alcohol has devastated families, with 70% of alcohol-related violent incidents occurring in the home. Of these incidents twenty percent involve a weapon other than hands, fists, or feet.[177] Orphanages exist for children whose parents have died or can no longer take care of them because of alcohol. Alcohol causes arguments, fights, stabbings, murder, and unwanted pregnancies. In violent crimes, an offender is far more likely to have been drinking than under the influence of other drugs.[178] And people who drink regularly have a higher rate of death from injury or violence.[179]

Alcohol and the damage it causes in society is so rampant that I have yet to meet anyone who doesn't have a story of heartache, tragedy, pain, or regret. My beautiful cousin died the day after Christmas when she was twenty-three. She was crossing a street when she was hit by a drunk driver. Her face was barely recognizable. She made it to the hospital, where she died. We all have horror stories.

The effect of alcohol on children is the most heartbreaking. It is incredibly painful for children to see their parents—around whom their entire worlds revolve—stumbling, sick, arguing, or being mean to each other. My friend Julie's parents divorced when she was quite young, and her mother remarried a heavy drinker. I spent the night a few times, and her room lay directly beneath her parents'. I remember lying in bed, listening to alcohol-fueled fights and feeling so helpless. My friend pretended she was asleep. She must have been embarrassed. Her mom never drank, and the arguments seemed one-sided. We could only hear a male voice yelling while her mom cried. Yet in some ways Julie was lucky. Many children lie in bed or hide in closets while their mom is physically harmed. Often it's the children who are victims of abuse. It's terrifying to know more than half of all confirmed child abuse reports and 75% of child deaths from abuse involve alcohol.[180] Mothers convicted of child abuse are *three times* more likely to be alcoholics, and abusive fathers are *ten times* more likely to be alcoholics.[181] And the cycle continues because children of alcoholics are up to four times more likely to develop alcohol addiction later in life.[182]

Even without abuse, a drunken parent terrifies a child. They are either doting on you, constantly telling you they love you (which you realize is false, empty, and fueled by the drink), or they seem to disappear, and you no longer recognize your parent. They are no longer the person you know and trust. Although they may be physically present, you feel abandoned and afraid. You wish they would just go away. Being around them, even if they aren't violent, is painful. When a child can't communicate with their parents, it spawns hurt and neglect. Kids are also subject to morning-after abuse, when the hangover causes parents to snap at their kids, leaving them wondering why. Children hate to see their parents drunk; there are few things more upsetting.

You may argue these are extreme cases, and surely alcohol in moderate quantities helps you enjoy life. While you can see that on the whole it causes more misery than happiness, you are the exception. These horrible things happen to other people, but you find true joy in drinking. By some miracle, the substance that causes fathers to hurt their children, drivers to kill entire families, and drinkers to take their own lives makes you happy.

Perhaps I am not being fair. How can I dispute the euphoric tipsy feeling? I can't. You get a bit of a rush when alcohol first enters your system. That is a fact; it happens. Alcohol, unlike food, can be absorbed directly through the stomach lining. This means alcohol reaches your brain cells quickly. But have you noticed how quickly the feeling dissipates? Pay attention the next time you are drinking. It comes on quickly, but it's gone within twenty minutes. Some experts theorize that the "rush" is simply a boost in blood sugar as alcohol is made up of sugars and carbohydrates. To combat the rush of glucose and balance out your blood sugar, your body stimulates the production of insulin. The insulin causes your blood sugar to fall, resulting in lower blood sugar than when you began drinking. With low blood sugar you feel empty and tense. And perhaps another drink will relax you—for another few minutes—because it will give you the next rush of glucose.[183]

That feeling hooks you. Observe how you feel when drinking. After that initial tipsy feeling passes, it won't come back in quite the same way, no matter how much you drink. You drink more to chase the initial rush. After a few drinks, your senses are dulled, and your perceptions change. Life no longer feels quite real. You believe you are in control but can no longer gauge how drunk you are. You have lost your ability to moderate. This is why, despite warnings, danger, and the threat of a DUI, smart people get behind the wheel when they shouldn't.

Vale asks, "Each time you have had a drink, can you honestly say that you have been happy? Have you been uptight or argumentative when drinking? Have you ever been stressed out, felt depressed or cried during a drinking session? Have you become obnoxious or unreasonable when drinking?"[184]

He goes on to make the point that in theory, if alcohol made you happy, every time you drank you should be full of happiness. Let me ask you, from a purely physiological perspective, how could alcohol possibly make you happy? The effect of alcohol is to deaden all of your senses, to numb you, to inebriate you. If you are numb, how can you feel anything, happiness included? Surely you are not happy every time you drink.

None of us are proud of everything we have said or done while drinking. Yet in the moment we believe we are on top of the world, saying and doing anything we please, deluding ourselves into thinking it's making us happy. Are you happy when the room starts to spin, or your dinner comes back up? Is the drunk on the street in Vegas who has lost his home and his family to booze truly happy?

You might take issue with this and tell me that of course none of those things are enjoyable, but moderate drinking makes *you* happy. How is that logical? How does a substance that makes people act in ways they are ashamed of suddenly turn into joy juice when we drink a little of it? Wouldn't it make more sense that if a little alcohol made us a little happy, a lot of alcohol would make us a lot happy?

You may argue that you see drinkers all the time who are happy. They're drinking, joking, giggling, and enjoying themselves. I am willing to bet they are enjoying the situation, conversation, and time with their friends rather than the booze. You may argue that if the booze wasn't present, the situation would become somber. I agree—if the drinkers believed, as most drinkers do, that they couldn't enjoy themselves without alcohol. It's not that alcohol makes drinkers happy; it's that they are very unhappy without it.

It's hard to measure this because we have nothing to compare against. I don't remember attending a wedding, or for that matter a funeral, where alcohol wasn't provided. I certainly never went to a business dinner where drinking wasn't involved. I can't remember a single barbecue without booze. Looking back on my adult years, I don't remember any social occasions where alcohol wasn't available. We live near one of the world's best concert venues, and they serve alcohol but charge a lot for it. I was at my friend Laura's house, and we were in the kitchen. I noticed a loaf of bread with a piece broken off. I went closer and saw that a bottle was baked into the loaf of bread. Laura's husband is a whiskey fan, and they were planning to attend a concert. He didn't want to buy drinks and preferred his own brand, so Laura emptied the bottle and baked a loaf of bread around it. It was cooling, and then she was going to fill it back up. They planned to pack the bread as part of their picnic lunch in order to sneak the whiskey into the concert. You can bring as much food as you want, you just can't bring in booze, and they actively search your bags. As you can imagine, Laura was pleased with herself, and her husband was ecstatic.

My point is that when we are enjoying social occasions, which by their nature create true enjoyment, there is almost always alcohol present. Can you think of many social occasions where drinking was not an option? I don't mean that you were refraining or trying to drink less but that drinking simply wasn't part of the party? Even that statement sounds like an oxymoron. If you are part of a subculture that doesn't serve alcohol at every wedding or party, you have a better point of comparison than most of us. Think back to some of the most fun parties you've attended, with and without alcohol. You've been able to relax and enjoy yourself at both types of parties, haven't you? You've had a great time in social gatherings without booze. Doesn't this lead you to believe that maybe you had fun because you were talking and laughing with friends, rather than because you were drinking?

Now, instead of comparing myself to other drinkers at social gatherings, I can compare my non-drinking self against my former, drinking self. It's almost a joke how much more I enjoy my life. I actually know when I am having a good time, or a not-so-good time for that matter, but my emotions are one hundred percent mine. There are a million reasons why I am happier now, but above all I know myself. I feel comfortable and confident in my own skin. I love being alive, love being me. This is true happiness. After *This Naked Mind*, Mary describes it like this: "I don't drink anymore because all of these feelings are more euphoric and fulfilling than any experience alcohol has provided me."

It's hard to accept this when all your hipster friends are "enjoying" wine with dinner. It's the thing to do. Yet, deep down, we all sense that alcohol may be harmful. It's why we feel the need to justify how much, or how often, we drink. It's the black shadow hanging over the times you drink and the times you don't. We've convinced ourselves that we cannot enjoy life without booze, so we close our minds to the shadow. How is it possible that, at one time, we enjoyed life and found happiness before we ever drank? Happiness is feeling physically and mentally healthy, feeling great to be alive. How can anyone who is dependent on a drink that destroys their health and ensnares them be truly happy? Your mind is extremely powerful and what you believe will be true. If you believe you can't party or hang out with friends without a drink, you won't be able to.

If you are looking to turn off your brain, you can do this with alcohol. When you come out of your alcohol-induced stupor, your pain will still be there and quite often compounded. Will you magically be happy when you wake up from your night of drunken oblivion? Will your situation have somehow improved? Or will it be worse? You now feel both mentally and physically awful. Drinking has frayed your nerves, and you are less prepared to deal with the reason you started to drink to begin with.

A real sorrow or distress cannot be fixed by alcohol. You can't drown out things that are truly tragic. By drinking enough you can close your mind to them temporarily, but they will remain. The more you drink, the harder it is to deal with your problems when you finally sober up. When you wake, tragedy will still be there. Your loss will remain, seeming worse than before.

It's eye-opening to realize who is happy and who may not be. It's hard to be happy when we are obsessed with where our next drink comes from or how much alcohol we can put away in an evening. I often notice people who aren't drinking or are drinking so little you can tell it's for show. They are enjoying the atmosphere, laughing, and talking with friends. They are not controlled by alcohol—they seem at peace and truly happy. Make your own observations. Look around next time you are out to dinner or at a club. See who seems happy and relaxed. Then pay attention to whether they are heavily drinking. The results might surprise you.

If you feel you need alcohol to make you happy, relax you, or help you enjoy your evening, you are already in trouble. Just because your body is not yet falling apart and you have the means to feed your craving doesn't mean you aren't addicted. Maybe you have not reached the chronic stage where you are completely physically and mentally dependent on alcohol. But if you think you need alcohol to enjoy social occasions or to relieve the stress of the daily grind, you have already become emotionally dependent. The cumulative effect of alcohol, on any drinker, is unhappiness, not happiness.

Don't worry if you feel I am being unfair and painting too harsh a picture. The great news is that you don't have to take my word for it. Once you are free, you will prove these things to yourself over and over again. You will live your life to the fullest, attending dozens of social functions, happier than alcohol could ever make you.

15.
DEFINING ADDICTION: PART I

*"Progress is impossible without change, and those who
cannot change their minds cannot change anything."*
—George Bernard Shaw

Characteristics of Addiction: Abuse, Dependency, Craving

The term addiction is tossed around all the time. We can be addicted to chocolate, shopping, television, or really anything. The word has so many different meanings that psychiatrists prefer the term "Substance Use Disorder." Substance use disorders are classified based on certain characteristic features that fall into three categories: abuse, dependence, and craving.[185]

Abuse is characterized by significant negative consequences to the addicted. These can be health consequences, relational consequences, and consequences from no longer doing what you should be doing—like going to work in the morning.

Dependence happens when the addict depends on the drug psychologically and sometimes physically. Dependence is characterized by tolerance, when you need to consume more of the drug to get the same effect, and withdrawal, when you have unpleasant psychological or physical symptoms when you stop taking the drug.[186] Both occur when your body and brain have changed to compensate for the chronic presence of the drug.[187]

Craving is an extremely strong, illogical desire to use the drug. Cravings can contradict your feelings, meaning you may consciously desire to take the day off from drinking, but an intense craving for alcohol still exists. When an addict attempts to abstain, cravings can be so strong that the addict finds it hard to think about anything else.

For simplicity, let's define addiction this way: doing something on a regular basis that you do not want to be doing. Or doing something more often than you would like to be doing it, yet being unable to easily stop or cut back. Basically, it's having two competing priorities, wanting to do more and less of something at the same time. The addictive substance creates a psychological need for itself in your thoughts and a biological need in your gray matter. This need grows, and a cycle begins where the body tries to compensate for the presence of the substance, but it goes too far, creating a need for the drug.

Eventually the need—the craving and the desire for the addictive substance—is so all-consuming that choice is no longer involved. In studies of addiction, the subject will continue to self-administer the addictive substance ad infinitum at the exclusion of everything else in their lives, including taking care of their young or even feeding themselves. Rats in these experiments will starve themselves.[188]

When we reach that compulsive stage we must sever the cycle completely. We must starve the substance's need for itself.

We all have many addictions. In a way, we are an addictive species—we use the same skills to learn and adapt as we do to become addicted. Learning happens in the same part of the brain as addiction. Polk cites studies that confirm addiction is intrinsically tied to our brain's ability to learn. We will cover this in detail in the next chapter.

The Cycle of Addiction

This is one of the most important parts of this book. We must understand why we drink.

When crack addicts run out of crack, they freak out. They become anxious, irritated, and severely paranoid. They go to great lengths to get their next fix. Some people do things they could never have imagined before the addiction, even prostituting themselves for another hit. Their entire world revolves around the drug. They are miserable. When they find and smoke crack, they relax. It seems logical to conclude that crack is just the thing to alleviate misery, paranoia, and panic. Look at the evidence. One minute they are a wreck, and the next they seem happy and at peace. We know this is not true. In reality, the crack addict smokes crack not for the benefits of the drug, but to relieve the withdrawal the previous dose created.

It would seem that we only undergo withdrawals when we quit. In reality, every time we take the drug we experience withdrawal as it leaves our system. This is the reason we feel the need to take the drug again. We endure withdrawals constantly when we are repeatedly taking a drug or drinking alcohol. If the crack addict had never smoked crack, they would never suffer from the panic, the cold sweats, and the misery of a crack withdrawal. Isn't it clear that the drug creates rather than relieves these symptoms? We can see this from the outside, yet it's not clear to the person who is addicted.

Addictions vary from substance to substance, but the patterns are the same. The addict is conditioned to believe the substance will provide enjoyment or relief, that it will help them enjoy life more or ease their stress. The addict generally believes they are somehow incomplete and need something more than what their body can naturally provide. They may believe there is something missing inside of them, an empty space that can be filled with their substance of choice. These beliefs are not generally conscious.

Addicts usually take time to acclimate to the experience of using the drug. The first time I smoked marijuana, it wasn't pleasant; I felt paranoid, and I didn't like it. My friends told me that was normal, and the next time would be better, so I tried it again. Since the initial experience is less than ideal, whether it's the foul taste of your first beer or the paranoia of your first bowl, your fear of becoming addicted fades. How can we possibly become addicted to something that isn't all that great? According to Vale: "The irony is that the awful taste is part of what springs the alcohol trap."[189]

When we take a physically addictive substance, from caffeine to crack, we suffer withdrawal as it leaves our system. With some harder drugs it's intense, but with most addictive substances, like nicotine, sugar, caffeine, or alcohol, it can be a small, almost unnoticeable, feeling of discomfort. A vulnerable, anxious, empty feeling. The uneasy notion that something is not quite right, or missing, and that life is incomplete. Since alcohol can take days to leave the system, drinkers might experience this feeling almost constantly.

Since we don't suffer this feeling when we are taking the drug, we don't connect the feeling with the drug. The feeling of something being amiss is similar to stress or hunger, so we can't pinpoint it. When we drink another drink, we feel better. We have a drink and feel more relaxed, confident, and in control than we did just moments before. Since the relief is real, we start to believe the drink provides enjoyment. We are happier when we take a drink, not because drinking makes us happy, but because the drink relieves the withdrawal that drinking caused. This illusion confirms what we've been unconsciously conditioned to believe, that alcohol provides relief or pleasure.

We continue drinking to get rid of the empty, uneasy feeling that alcohol created. When we enjoy the "pleasure" of a drink, we restore the wholeness and peace of mind we knew our entire lives before we ever drank a drop. Since alcohol is harmful, we begin to build an immunity to it. We need more to achieve the same effect, more to relieve the empty, insecure feeling. Since addictive substances create the vulnerability to begin with, they cannot help us relax. They are the reason we feel tense, weak, and insecure. Vale says, "The beautiful truth is that you won't need to find different ways to relax as you will be far more relaxed as a non-drinker anyway. It is alcohol that causes you to feel un-relaxed in the first place."[190]

The immunity grows, and eventually you are unhappy, even when drinking. The drug destroys us mentally and physically. Our health falters, our nerves suffer, and the feeling of dependence becomes greater. We take more. The cycle continues. And suddenly we see how, without ever realizing it is happening, we have become dependent. We see how the drunken partier in Vegas becomes the homeless man clutching his paper bag.

As the cycle continues, the feeling of dependence becomes greater, and we begin to believe alcohol is the most important thing in our lives. Just as bad food would taste amazing if we were starving, our perception of booze is altered. Alcohol seems more valuable. Our loved ones see us slipping. By the time they say something, we have become so afraid of losing what now feels like our only solace that we unknowingly and unconsciously close our minds to what they are saying.

Eventually our tolerance is high and we are drinking so much that much of our mental and physical health has been stolen. The illusion of gratification is practically nonexistent. We start to listen to family and friends or pay attention to the small, cautionary voice inside our heads. We wonder if we should cut back or quit. Yet we've been unconsciously conditioned to believe cutting back or quitting is difficult, so we sadly begin to prepare for an uphill battle.

We try to abstain, but our unconscious mind still believes we are getting something positive from alcohol. Because of this we are tormented when we try to quit. We believe we are sacrificing something that has become important. Since everyone around us is "happily" drinking, we feel like we are missing out. Ultimately our actual experiences confirm our belief that it is hard, if not impossible, to stop drinking.

The longer we deprive ourselves, the greater the satisfaction when we finally give in. Why? Through abstinence, the feeling of misery has grown—and so has the relief. We translate this relief as pleasure when we finally give in and drink. In this cycle of addiction, both the misery of abstinence and the "pleasure" of surrender are real and intense.

Aftereffects of the Alcohol Cycle

I like how Allen Carr describes causation between alcohol consumption and the misery we suffer between drinks. These five points are his, but I've fleshed them out a bit for clarity's sake.[191]

First, we experience the immediate aftereffects from our previous bout of drinking. You are familiar with the general low mood, tiredness, hangover, headaches, and sluggishness.

Second, we have the mounting physical harms caused by ongoing drinking. These occur so slowly we don't notice they are happening.[192] Feeling sluggish, stressed, and chronically tired becomes the new normal. Ongoing drinking affects your mental well-being, with alcohol being a major cause of depression.[193] Drinking begins to affect our finances and relationships.

Third, we face the real stress in our lives. In *The Sober Revolution*, Lucy Rocca explains that since alcohol depresses the central nervous system, exacerbating depression and anxiety, a drinker often finds it difficult to cope with everyday stressors. Small, daily problems that shouldn't be much of an issue become an "ever-increasing mountain of the unachievable."[194] While the initial issues are not necessarily related to drinking, we would have dealt with them, improving upon or solving them rather than feeling overwhelmed, reaching for a drink, and putting them off until tomorrow. Without alcohol, we would be able to handle them as they arose rather than putting them off and making them worse.[195]

Fourth, we feel the empty, anxious, insecure feeling we only know as, "I want a drink." It's the imperceptible twinge that something's missing. These four factors combine to create the real reason we drink, an incredibly strong psychological craving.

It's obvious that the immediate aftereffects of drinking are caused by alcohol. The cumulative effects are harder to pinpoint, but they make up the fifth factor. We don't realize that our chronic exhaustion is related to continuously poisoning our bodies. We blame these feelings on life in general or on aging. We don't think about the actual stressors in life, things we've procrastinated on or blocked from our minds when drinking.[196] We don't consider the subtle, "A drink sounds nice" feeling because it is generally small, almost unnoticeable. All of these factors work together to create the fifth and final factor. This factor—the mental craving for alcohol—is much stronger than all the others put together. Alcohol, along with all addictive drugs, actually re-wires our brains, changing their function.[197] The craving becomes more than a mental illusion; it's a neural reality—a reality of dependence and withdrawal.[198]

The Itch to Drink

When you are between drinks, you crave a drink. This can happen either consciously or unconsciously. You want a drink, and you don't see a reason not to have one. If you can't have one in the moment (say you are driving), you look forward to drinking later.

When you decide not to satisfy your craving because you want to drink less, you become miserable. The little feeling of wanting a drink grows intolerable. Why? Any provocation can be small until you can't fix it. It's like getting a blister while hiking. The feeling is faint at first, almost unnoticeable. You could fix it by removing your shoe, but if you keep hiking, it will continue to rub, and the irritation will grow until you can't stand it.

A craving, when unsatisfied, becomes so strong you cannot concentrate on anything else. It's like the neighbor kid is playing the drums. The sound is in background, and you don't notice it. But eventually it seems like the drums are being played in your living room. Drum practice becomes overpowering, and you can't think, much less relax. Drumming dominates your mind until practice is over or you have a nervous breakdown and shove his drumsticks down the garbage disposal.

You drink to end the distress. The drink itself does not provide enjoyment, but you sincerely enjoy ending the nuisance of wanting a drink. The relief is so strong you feel happy, even giddy. You drink to get the feeling of peace that someone who is not dependent on alcohol always feels.

That's why the mental desire for alcohol is far stronger than all the aftereffects. When a drinker decides she needs a drink to satisfy her craving, she is unhappy until she consumes one. The longer the drumming continues, the more refreshing the silence. Similarly, the longer you crave alcohol, the greater the illusion of enjoyment or relief when you satisfy your desire.

You know the feeling—the misery of wanting a drink and not allowing yourself to have one. You know how real these feelings are, so real that you end up justifying the next drink in ways you never imagined. You also know how intense the relief is when your craving is satisfied.

The deception is the belief that alcohol itself provides the enjoyment and the relief. It does not. The misery you feel when you abstain is actually caused by drinking. It doesn't matter if you have just started drinking or are at the chronic stage, this is true. It's the reality of addiction, the reality of alcohol.

Claiming alcohol gives you pleasure is like saying it's enjoyable to create blisters for the relief of taking off your shoes. Alcohol doesn't satisfy your desire for alcohol; it is what created your desire for alcohol. Alcohol is the only reason you continue to crave alcohol and the only reason your cravings get worse over time.

When it was my turn to be the designated driver, I couldn't help feeling grumpy. I didn't think I would have as much fun without drinking. Since I believed it, it was true, and when I didn't have fun, my unconscious mind concluded that drinking was key to enjoying a party. I was duped into believing drinking made the difference. The deception is clear. It's not that alcohol is inherently enjoyable, but that because I was addicted, an evening without alcohol was miserable. The truth is that you don't need alcohol to enjoy yourself; you only think you do.[199]

The great news is that you are not stuck. Your life can be complete and whole again without alcohol. You don't have to continue to suffer.

The Ultimate Test

At the end of a long day, my mood used to change as soon as I ordered a glass of wine. I became upbeat and excited, and the cares of the day seemed to fade away. I couldn't have felt any of the physical effects of the drink just by ordering it or within seconds of my first sip. Yet my mood drastically improved. My mental craving was relieved. I would continue drinking, and the next three or four glasses wouldn't actually provide pleasure. My senses were numbed, and I became less sharp, less witty, and less interesting.

You can actually test this. I did. I wanted to see if alcohol provided me with honest enjoyment. Despite the fact that I drank every day, I couldn't accurately explain to you what it was about drinking that I enjoyed. I hoped to understand how alcohol made me feel. Was there, apart from the circumstances or the relief of ending my craving, any true enjoyment?

I did this at home, alone. It wouldn't be a fair test around friends who actually make me happy. And I couldn't be out at some sort of event that would have made me happy. I made a video of the experience so I could objectively view myself later. I opened a bottle of wine and drank it.

At first I had a tipsy, light-headed feeling, like blood rushing to my head. I was a little off balance. It didn't feel all that great but was the most pleasant part of the experience. This feeling came and went in less than twenty minutes. Eventually I got drunk and sat down to tell the camera exactly how I felt—out of it, like my vision was narrowing and the walls were closing in on me. I felt much less capable of doing the things I had planned for the evening, like reading or writing. Before the experiment I thought as soon as I got a buzz, I would want to do something fun, like go in the hot tub or play video games. I thought I would want to capitalize on and enjoy the feeling. I had no desire to do anything. I had zero energy, and nothing sounded like fun. It wasn't bad, but I couldn't say it was fun. It was more like everything got a bit soft around the edges, a bit less sharp, less real. I had a hard time putting my thoughts together and communicating.

I was horrified when I watched the video. I had slowly transformed from my generally energetic, confident, and happy self to a complete idiot. Alcohol stole my smarts. I sounded so dumb. I was shocked and embarrassed. I didn't expect it to be so bad. I knew talking to someone who has been drinking can be painful, but I had been so certain I was funnier, wittier, and more fun to be around when I was drunk. My perception was completely out of sync with reality. I thought I was making great jokes on camera. I wasn't.

And think about your own experiences. When you are talking to someone who has been drinking, you aren't envious of how they are feeling. Usually the last thing you want is to feel like they do. I don't remember ever talking to someone who was noticeably drunk and wishing I could have as much fun as they were having. Why? Because it was clear they were not having fun. They were no longer themselves. The real person had left the building. Only when you aren't drinking does this become crystal clear.

Drinking felt like tunnel vision. I was no longer aware of all my surroundings but only what was right in front of me, and even that took more effort and concentration than I had energy for. After an hour, the only thing that sounded good to me was sleep. Instead of staying up late to enjoy my night of drinking, I went to bed. My big party ended before 10 p.m. It was strange and disorienting. I certainly didn't feel happier.

As a marketer, I often ponder how I could sell something, a product or an experience. The experience of that night was something I would struggle to sell. I couldn't put the "amazing feeling" of alcohol into positive words. What is that feeling anyway? How is it possible, when we know all alcohol does is deaden our senses, to claim it gives us a truly amazing feeling that we enjoy? I consider myself an excellent marketer, yet from that night of experimental drinking, I could not find any benefit worth putting into an advertisement. I would have had to, as all alcohol advertising does, make it up.

Before the test I stopped drinking with *This Naked Mind* so I had no craving for alcohol. Without a craving, I experienced no relief. Alcohol creates an appetite for alcohol. It gets upset when you don't feed it, and you feel relieved when you do. The feeling of relief is a huge contributor to the illusion of happiness. As Jason Vale says, "The only reason a little alcohol appears to create happiness is because it removes natural fears and satisfies your psychological dependency on the drug."[200]

If you do try this test, it's important to minimize any external factors that make you authentically happy. Pick a day when you are not overly happy or overly sad. Don't watch TV, movies, or listen to music. It's important that you experience just the alcohol to see if you enjoy it. Be honest with yourself, and make it a true test. Ask yourself if you are happier than before. Ask yourself if you want to spend the rest of your life dumber, with your senses deadened, experiencing tunnel vision, and unable to concentrate on more than one thing at a time.

I made a big deal out of eliminating outside factors—friends, fun locations, even TV or music—because enjoying a situation that includes alcohol doesn't mean you're enjoying alcohol. Look at your life. You have enjoyed tons of occasions, but can you separate the drinking from the activity and realize you had fun because of the company or the event, rather than the "joy" of poisoning yourself and numbing your senses? Think back to before you drank, when you were perfectly capable of enjoying all sorts of things without drinking. That enjoyment is what's still present in social situations, only now it's clouded by alcohol.

What about when you didn't think much about drinking, so it was just something you did? Did you get excited about your night out because of how incredible the alcohol was going to be? Or can you entertain the idea that you don't actually enjoy drinking but feel deprived and unhappy without it? Can you see how ending a low, created by alcohol, is not the same as experiencing a true high? Do you realize that a fun evening with friends is fun for every reason except alcohol? In fact, during most of your drinking life, when you took alcohol for granted, the illusion of enjoyment was barely noticeable.

And what about the other times? Was the boozy moms' group really fun when you realized you're back home but have no memory of how you got there? That's called a blackout, and though they are rarely discussed, they happen more frequently than we realize. In fact, a 2002 study published in the *Journal of American College Health* found that more than 50% of drinkers at Duke University had experienced blackouts.[201] If you can't remember it, how can it be fun? And don't forget all the times you said something stupid, went home with someone you didn't want to, or puked for hours on end. Don't forget when your speech became slurred, or when you got in trouble with your spouse because she found the bottles you'd been hiding in the closet. Or perhaps your trouble was with the law when they pulled you over for swerving and served you with a DUI.

The irony is that the times you're drinking are no better than the times of misery between drinks. It provides no enjoyment. It provides no relief.

One of the first times I got drunk, I remember feeling out of control, like the room was spinning. It was horrible. This feeling ended in terrible sickness, which I now know was my body's ingenious survival mechanisms at work. My body saved my life by purging the alcohol that could have killed me. My first time was long ago, but the feeling hasn't changed. At the end of my drinking days it just took me a lot more booze to get to that stage. In fact, I had built such a tolerance that I didn't feel that way after two bottles of wine. I didn't actually feel much of anything. When I was drinking, though I never consciously thought about it, I believed I was drinking because I liked it and because I chose to. Now I see I was drinking so much because I was addicted. If drinking made me giggly, it was never the same as true, fulfilling happiness. Laughing gas also makes me giggly, but it certainly does not make me happy.

16.
LIMINAL POINT: IS ALCOHOL VITAL TO SOCIAL LIFE?

"Dear alcohol, we had a deal where you would make me funnier, smarter, and a better dancer . . . I saw the video . . . we need to talk."
—Anonymous

Before you ever drank a drop you did not need alcohol to enjoy yourself socially, yet as you grew older, you **observed** everyone around you drinking in social situations. In fact, you almost never **observed** social situations without alcohol. You **assumed** alcohol was a key ingredient for a good party. You began to drink socially, and initially you probably still didn't find alcohol vital to socializing. Since alcohol is part of practically every social situation, soon you only **experience** social situations with alcohol. Eventually you developed a small dependence, and you missed alcohol if it wasn't available. Your **experience** confirmed your observations. You didn't have quite as much fun if you didn't drink. You **concluded**, yes, alcohol is vital to social life.

Let's consider reality:

I Drink for Social Reasons

Clearly drinking is a social pastime. At many occasions, alcohol turns a great event into a mess. At our wedding we only offered beer and wine to guests. We knew providing certain guests with liquor would mean trouble. We all have stories of the uncle or friend who gets drunk and ruins the wedding. And that doesn't only happen at weddings. There are plenty of nights out at the club or the bar where social drinking quickly turns antisocial.

I knew a girl whose boyfriend would get drunk and pass out so hard he repeatedly wet the bed. He was thirty years old. His problem was well-hidden, as most are. At the party he was the happy-go-lucky drinker, yet bed-wetting was a nightly occurrence. You cannot tell me this is a social activity.

My brother, a non-drinker, is a second-degree black belt, something he would not have had the discipline to achieve in his drinking days. We relish competition, experiencing new things, and meeting new people. We enjoy these things because our senses are engaged. It's part of our nature as human beings to pursue the company of other humans. According to research by Johann Hari, social activities can help prevent addiction. If rats are put in cages alone with both drug-laced and clean water, the rats quickly become addicted to the drug. But if rats are in cages with lots of friends and social activities—Hari says to imagine a rat park—they ignore the drugs and prefer plain water. And before you think rats might not be a good representation of human nature, you should know their genetic, biological, and behavioral characteristics closely resemble those of humans, making them excellent test subjects.[202] Hari believes the antidote to addiction is actually companionship.[203]

With my personal experience, I can't help but agree. Addiction turned me into a loner. I had secrets and couldn't connect with others as well as before. My cravings drove me to a point where I valued the drug more than people. This is hard to admit, but it's true. When drinking we become insular, we lose ourselves, and we miss out on true opportunities for companionship. It's not the drinking that makes these activities fun; we enjoy them because we are with friends and doing something we like. When was the last time you came home from a football game and raved about the quality of the beer instead of talking about the amazing touchdown pass?

We have become accustomed to drinking on these occasions. We didn't need alcohol to enjoy them before, but now we have developed a habit of drinking. We have intertwined, within our minds, the alcohol and the joy we feel from the occasion. This is for a few reasons:

- The idea that drinking enhances experiences has been ingrained in our conscious and unconscious minds through advertisements.

- We reconfirm this when we develop an almost unnoticeable physical dependence on alcohol. Alcohol can take ten days to fully leave your system, and your body physically craves a drink. You probably don't even notice this, or you just notice the feeling as, "A drink sounds good." The relief of feeding this craving makes alcohol seem as if it is contributing to your enjoyment of the occasion.

- The mental belief that drinking enhances the occasion creates a placebo effect. This makes two things happen.

  1. Since you believe alcohol is helping you have fun, it does. Your mind is incredibly powerful.
  2. If you skip a drink, you feel deprived. You believe you are not enjoying yourself as much as you would with a drink in your hand. You come to believe that you won't have fun without a drink.

- This cycle continues, and as drinking is addictive, you eventually create a physical addiction. At this stage, once you are addicted, you will feel tormented when you do not allow yourself to drink.

How can you know this is true? You don't have to look further than people who don't drink at all to realize it's not the alcohol that makes social occasions amazing. Think about a school dance. There was no alcohol, yet it was fun and exciting. You scoped out girls or guys, enjoyed looking at everyone's outfits, and spent social time with friends with no parents allowed.

As Rocca says, "Alcohol stifles your creative mind, dulls your senses and turns you into something of a slave to its every whim, the real world shrinks drastically until it is nothing more than a cycle of hangovers, booze and falseness."[204] Alcohol homogenizes life, meaning you experience the same deadened sense of drunken reality at a hockey game as you feel at a fancy dinner. And you won't remember much of either. Instead of enjoying the wide variety of social activities available to us, drinking makes them all blend together. Rocca describes it as life becoming small, a boozy Groundhog Day in which you become ensnared. You don't realize you are caught fast in your small life until you crawl out of it and re-enter the land of the living.[205] Drinking ensures social events become unmemorable and monotonous. After all, drunkenness feels the same no matter what you are doing.

You dumb down every experience. Instead of making sharp, crisp, lifelong memories, you recall social occasions through a haze or not at all. You know the saying—"It must have been fun; I don't remember it."

I now have more fun than when I was drinking. I no longer worry about what I will drink next, where it will come from, or how much I will have. I can't wait for you to experience this. At a restaurant or sporting event, you will be amazed at how much you're enjoying yourself and truly happy you no longer drink. When you stop believing you need to drink to have fun, you won't need to. You'll realize that alcohol can actually hinder your fun.

What about Hindu weddings? Talk about a party! The joy is palpable, and the dancing goes on until dawn. Everyone is laughing, eating, talking, and celebrating. These parties go on for days. No joke, literally days on end of amusement and joy. And guess what? Generally, Hindus don't drink. It's definitely not the alcohol that make these occasions fun. If everyone was drinking, the party couldn't go on for days on end. The second day would be full of hangovers and headaches.

You may worry that you'll only want to spend time with others who don't drink. You don't want to give up your friends or avoid situations where alcohol is present. I don't blame you. I don't want to limit my social activities either. But don't worry. When your unconscious desire to drink is gone, you won't be pining for a drink. You won't feel that you are giving something up. The bar will be a reminder of the freedom you have gained, not of what you feel you've lost. No, once your mental, unconscious, desire goes, your cravings are purely physical, and they last only as long as you are healing from the drug. In fact, you'll feel completely different. When you see alcohol as your mortal enemy instead of your best friend, you will love going out and not drinking. It will give you pleasure. Instead of hiding in the shadows, you will dance on your enemy's grave.

I remember pressuring my friends to drink. I would tell them they weren't being any fun as a ploy to get them to drink with me. Now when I order a non-alcoholic drink people call me boring. Why do we do that? Probably because we don't want to question our own drinking. Why do you think drug addicts and heavy drinkers hang out together? Could it be because no one makes them feel guilty about how much they are consuming? I found it easier to drink as much as I wanted in the company of other heavy drinkers. It seems OK to poison ourselves if everyone else is doing it—our dependence is masked. It eases our guilt and our misery.

High school hallways are filled with laughter, shouts, and jokes, and there is no alcohol. The locker room after a winning game has a buoyant, joyful atmosphere, again with no drinking. Is it so hard to accept that what you enjoy about social activities are your friends and the experiences? Do you remember how great the beer tasted? Of course not. You remember how much your friend made you laugh or the good-looking girl who kept smiling at you.

You may think alcohol helps people get over their initial shyness, encouraging a party atmosphere. Alcohol—by deadening your natural senses, including apprehension—removes the filters between your brain and your mouth. This gives us the illusion that the party is starting to kick off. Everyone is getting chatty, and conversation is starting in earnest. In truth, people take a bit of time to warm up. Even as kids, everyone is unsure of how they fit in. Give it a few minutes, and they are off and running, having a great time. It's a good thing to be cautious at first. It helps you understand your surroundings and take the time to get to know the people you are with. Our initial shyness not only protects us but also ensures we don't do or say something we will regret. You might even like being the person breaking the ice, introducing yourself and asking questions. Everyone else feels just as nervous, and all it takes is one person to start the conversation. Taking a little time and asking a few questions is much better than breaking out the booze and then sending everyone home in their cars. Already one in ten drivers during the night and weekend hours are drunk.[206] Let's take the time to get to know each other, break the ice naturally, and make our streets safer.

Isn't it strange that, in studies, the most popular reason we give for drinking is that it's a social thing to do? Especially when we know drinking is harmful and addictive. Aren't we actually saying we don't know why we do it? We don't have a truly good reason? We might even be saying that we don't actually enjoy it. And if we don't enjoy it, why do we drink? We drink because we are addicted to a drug.

17.
DEFINING ADDICTION: PART II

"There is no greater misery than false joys."
—Bernard of Clairvaux

The Lowdown on Alcohol-Induced Lows

You may feel there is something wrong with you, that you have no choice but to desire alcohol. The truth is we only want something we think provides a benefit. Addicts crave drugs because they are deceived into thinking drugs will enhance their lives. Once you see the drug for what it is, the cause of your misery and cravings that gives you nothing in return, the desire for the drug dies.

It's easier to see this with cigarettes. As a society, our entire perspective has changed regarding smoking. It is no longer socially acceptable. Social cues strongly influence your unconscious mind. Through numerous messages, both overt and subliminal, we are now conditioned to believe that there are few benefits to smoking. In Australia the government mandates all cigarettes to be sold in packages that visually depict the harms of smoking. When someone pulls out their pack of smokes, they see gruesome images: holes in tongues from mouth cancer, feet with toes missing from vascular disease, gray and black teeth. The images are disgusting and hard to look at. You can Google them if you want to see for yourself.

Further, nicotine acts quickly. In an hour it has left your body, so the craving for a cigarette happens almost immediately. This leads to chain smoking and panic when a smoker doesn't have cigarettes. Alcohol, however, takes between 72 and 240 hours to leave your body.[207] It can take up to ten days to recover from the lows of drinking. A heavy drinker starts to regard these lows as normal. The lows are created when your brain releases a chemical called dynorphin, which counteracts the "pleasure" from alcohol in an attempt to maintain homeostasis. Again, you know this phenomenon as tolerance. Dynorphin not only dampens the effect of alcohol, it also turns down the natural pleasure you get from everyday activities.

According to Polk, the drinker's body becomes used to the presence of alcohol in such a way that eventually the chronic drinker will need alcohol just to feel normal. And at some point no matter how much you drink you will be unable to feel anything but misery. Yet because of your brain's conditioned response to the drug, you will crave alcohol constantly.[208] The descent can be long or short, depending on your individual chemistry and the amount and frequency of your drinking. The following graph is a visual demonstration of the peaks and troughs that alcohol causes, and how it can impact your ability to enjoy everyday pleasures.

The time it takes for a drinker to move through the stages of alcoholism, from imbibing their first drink to needing vodka before breakfast, varies. But because alcohol is addictive, consuming it changes the way your brain works, meaning that no matter how slow you descend, everyone is moving the same direction—down. The descent happens faster when you drink to combat stress. Social drinking is limited to certain circumstances, which slows your

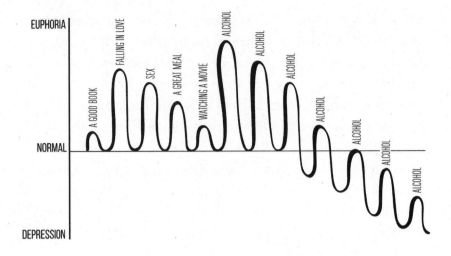

inevitable descent. If you are drinking to hide from life, to block stress, you can always find a reason to drink. The more you drink, the more stressful your life becomes. Soon there are good reasons to drink at lunch or to have a screwdriver with breakfast. You drink to dull your problems, but drinking never solves your problems. It compounds them. At some level you know this, and it bothers you. The easy solution is to take another drink, pushing this from your mind.

After a hard day I would kick off my shoes, pour myself a glass of wine, and sit down to relax. I would feel happy and calm after the first sip, well before the alcohol took effect. It was not the alcohol helping me unwind. If alcohol truly helped us relax, we would encourage drinking before a job interview or college exams. If someone was aggressive and violent, we would give them a drink to calm them down.

What is important now is to realize that alcohol does pick you up, but only from how far it kicked you down, never up to where you were before you started drinking. Since alcohol takes up to ten days to leave your body, the lows can be ever-present for regular drinkers. It is not that the alcohol makes you happy. It's that as a drinker, you are unhappy when you are unable to drink. Scratching an itch is pleasurable, but you would never purposely sit in poison ivy just to scratch your ass. This is a key to all drug addiction—the drug creates the low and then deceives its victims into believing that, by ending the low, it is providing a high.

That's how drugs work, and the further they take you down, the greater your perceived need becomes. With alcohol it can be so gradual you barely notice you are falling. As you drink, your tolerance grows, and soon you need to drink more to get the same effect. It can happen quickly, but often it happens slowly, over a lifetime.

At some point you realize you are drinking more than before, more than you ever wanted to, but life is so stressful. The stress mounts, and there's never a good time to cut back. You decide to put it off until your life becomes manageable again. You see the difficulty—as long as your intake increases, your life becomes less manageable. You started drinking to hide from stress, but you've only worsened it.

The Science of Addiction

The neurological and physiological evidence to back this up is overwhelming. I will do my best to explain. Let's start with dopamine. Dopamine is a neurotransmitter, which means it is a chemical produced in the brain that transmits signals from one neuron (brain cell) to another. Dopamine plays a central role in addiction and is commonly known as the addiction molecule. This is in part because alcohol and other addictive drugs chemically release dopamine in the brain.[209] Until recently, scientists believed dopamine was linked to pleasure. We now see that while higher levels of dopamine give us increased motivation to seek reward, the dopamine itself does not provide an actual reward or any pleasure. Scientists now believe dopamine is responsible for cravings. If you have experienced intense cravings, you know that the craving itself is not pleasurable, and craving something is very different from liking it.

In one study, scientists genetically modified rats by breeding brothers and sisters for twenty generations so that their genes were similar. They bred rats that were dopamine-rich, meaning they had more dopamine at all times, and dopamine-poor, meaning they had less. The dopamine-rich rats were more motivated to seek out any type of reward—food, companionship, or sex—but did not demonstrate any greater level of pleasure when enjoying the reward. The dopamine-poor rats were unmotivated to seek rewards. In fact, they were so unmotivated they would starve rather than make the effort to walk to the food dish. Yet when they were nursed, they demonstrated the same levels of pleasure in eating as any other rat.[210]

It's important to understand the difference between wanting and liking. When I was in the deepest levels of my addiction, the cravings were overwhelming to the point where I felt I was no longer in control. Yet the pleasure I got from drinking was practically nonexistent. I remember drinking all night long, coming back to the hotel room, and thinking about how much I'd consumed and how I didn't feel it at all. My tolerance was so high that it was hard to drink enough to get drunk. My craving was increasing, yet my enjoyment was decreasing. I thought this strange; however, studies of the brain make sense of it.

While dopamine does not trigger pleasure, it does motivate us. Dopamine is key to learning and is vital to our survival. Say you live in the caveman era and are exploring a new area in search of food. You find a thicket of raspberry bushes. This discovery causes a rush of pleasure. The pleasure occurs in another part of your brain, the nucleus accumbens, or pleasure center of the brain. Dopamine is also released, which signals that something important has happened. The beauty of dopamine is that it helps your brain process environmental cues, including cues from before you discovered the raspberries. You subconsciously learn how to best find raspberries. You will not be consciously aware, but your mind is remembering the vegetation around the bush, the amount of shade nearby, and the texture of the soil. Soon you are finding raspberry bushes more frequently without realizing how or why. We are amazing creatures with an incredible capacity for learning. Unfortunately, when addictive drugs chemically release dopamine in the brain, you are learning addiction.[211]

The ventral tegmental area of the brain, or the VTA, stimulates dopamine release.[212] The VTA is one of three parts of the brain involved in processing reward. We briefly mentioned the nucleus accumbens, and the third area in the reward circuit is the prefrontal cortex. Liking and enjoyment happen in the nucleus accumbens. James Oldes and Peter Millner of McGill University inserted electrodes directly into this region of the brain in rats. When the subjects were allowed to self-stimulate the region by pushing a lever, they continued to push it thousands of times to the exclusion of anything else. They neglected their young and forwent sex and food, even to the point of starvation, to continue stimulating this part of the brain. They even endured severe pain in order to push the lever. Pain they would not endure in order to get food, even when they were starving.[213] This has been demonstrated in humans as well. Robert Heath performed controversial experiments on humans where he observed the same repeated and seemingly uncontrollable self-stimulation.[214]

You won't be surprised to learn that addictive substances stimulate this area much more effectively than everyday rewards. While watching a movie or eating a good meal will stimulate it, drugs stimulate it more directly, producing activity levels well beyond the normal range. This sounds great on the surface—a way to stimulate the part of the brain that causes us the most pleasure. But really, it's terrifying because, in an effort to maintain homeostasis and protect itself, your brain will decrease the stimulation it is receiving. When alcohol overstimulates your nucleus accumbens, your brain produces CREB, which allows for the production of dynorphin, a natural painkiller.

The dynorphin inhibits the stimulation of the nucleus accumbens in an attempt to maintain internal equilibrium. You, in turn, feel less pleasure from drinking. You know this feeling as your tolerance increasing. You will need more alcohol to get the same effect, and eventually you will become physically dependent. Your brain will have compensated so much for the chronic ethanol exposure that you will need to drink to feel normal. Worse, you become less sensitive to all types of natural stimulation. Pleasures such as eating a delicious meal or spending time with friends no longer activate your pleasure center in the same way. The nucleus accumbens becomes numbed.[215]

The final change in your brain occurs within your prefrontal cortex. This is the part of your brain responsible for decision-making. It allows you to make well-thought-out decisions, exhibit self-control, and prevent the more reptilian parts of your brain from running the show. Alcohol damages your prefrontal cortex, resulting in a decreased capacity to make good decisions.

To summarize, three changes happen in your brain as a result of drinking:

- First, alcohol increases cravings (but not pleasure) by releasing dopamine.
- Second, alcohol artificially activates the pleasure center of your brain, the nucleus accumbens. Your brain tries to compensate for this overstimulation, leading to tolerance and the eventual numbing of your pleasure center.
- Finally, alcohol damages your prefrontal cortex, decreasing your ability to exercise self-control and making it more difficult to abstain.

You are caught in the horrible cycle of addiction—more cravings, little to no pleasure, and an impaired ability to break out of it.

As we've learned, it's difficult to control how much you drink because, over time, drinking will actually alter your brain. You have no way of knowing when that change will happen or to what degree. And just as dieting makes food more attractive psychologically, trying to control your intake increases temptation. The good news is that by overcoming the mental desire to drink, you can more easily resist the physical craving. When you stop drinking, your brain will stop compensating and repair itself. You can again find pleasure in simply living—as you could before you ever started drinking.

18.
LIMINAL POINT: IT'S CULTURAL.
I NEED TO DRINK TO FIT IN.

"Whenever you find yourself on the side of the majority,
it's time to pause and reflect."
—*Mark Twain*

You **observe** everyone drinking all the time. In fact, at almost every occasion, from grade school fundraisers to "wine and women" church groups, and even the finish lines of marathons. You **experience** all manner of conversations about alcohol—at work, after work, at home, on the weekends, and in the media. You **assume** our culture is so intertwined with alcohol that living a life without it will be next to impossible. You **conclude** that our culture dictates, even mandates, drinking, and you will find it too difficult and lonely to live without drinking.

Let's consider reality:

We Live in an Alcohol-Centric Culture

This is our last Liminal Point, and it is the most difficult to combat because it's closer to reality than any of the others we've explored. Our culture is alcohol-centric. In the last few decades we have collectively thrown caution to the wind, even deluding ourselves into believing that drinking is a healthy and vital part of life. But although this is true today, it doesn't have to be true tomorrow. We can educate ourselves and our children and work toward labeling and promoting alcohol the way cigarettes are now labeled and advertised. Although we can work for a better tomorrow, tomorrow is not yet here, so we need to explore some things about today.

Those Who Defend Alcohol the Loudest Are Often the Most Worried About How Much They Drink

More than seven thousand people volunteered to read this book, providing feedback before it was published, and many readers believed they were unique in their struggle, believing that everyone around them was perfectly happy with and in control of their drinking habits. I have discovered this is just not true! If you regret last night's bender, so do the people you were out with. If you sometimes worry about drinking every day, chances are so does your partner. If you wish you could stop after just a few, odds are so does your best friend. Alcohol addiction is so insidious because of how well we hide it, even from ourselves. We are ashamed to question our drinking. We worry that by asking a question we may be forced to quit drinking and live marginalized from society. We keep our fears to ourselves. Our questions hidden. Because no one is talking about the problem that so many have, we allow it to grow.

Since I stopped drinking, dozens of people have confided in me that they too want to cut back. Remember how my career contributed to my descent? Many of my colleagues read the book, and it turns out we were all trying to keep up with each other! While everyone worried about how much they drank, no one wanted to say it. One of my former bosses read the book and told me, "Annie, it's like your book has lifted a burden. I felt drinking was practically mandatory. There was so much social pressure that I didn't feel like saying no was an option. I now realize I can simply say no. That is empowering, thank you."

We Think the "Cool" People Drink (a.k.a. People Who Don't Drink Are Lame)

I am guilty of this one! I remember looking down my nose at people who weren't drinking as much as I was. I felt proud of my drinking lifestyle and how much "fun" I was having. I imagined that people who didn't drink must be downright boring! It is common to hear people say, "I don't trust someone who doesn't drink." The truth is that the cool people are cool if they drink or not. The funny people are funny if they drink or not, and the lame people are lame if they drink or not. Now I will add a caveat that if you feel you are making a sacrifice by not drinking when you are out with friends, of course you aren't going to be (or have) any fun. The beauty of *This Naked Mind* is that you will not feel that way. So your coolness is not going anywhere. I love being the life of the party and making people laugh. This is still true! In fact, since my wits aren't dulled, my jokes are much funnier than they were in my drinking days, and we all laugh harder.

I can't tell you how much it surprises people when I am the life of the party without a drink in my hand. I have a friend who can't get over it. He just stares at me; I think he is trying to figure out if I'm putting on an act. Why is it so surprising? Because we truly believe that alcohol is the fuel to our fire, and we are gobsmacked when that is not true. I offer one warning: You will be ready to have fun before your friends. I show up to the party ready to crack jokes, but everyone else thinks they need a few drinks in them before it's OK to "let loose." This is not because the alcohol is the key to their enjoyment but because they believe it is. Thinking something is true often makes it so.

How Will My Partner React?

One of my readers has had a boozy relationship with her partner of more than two decades. He has no interest in changing, and she is fearful their relationship will weaken. Another reader drank wine with his wife every night. When he decided to stop drinking, she thought it was a phase that wouldn't last. As the weeks went by and he kept declining wine at dinner, it began to bother her. She would say things like, "So you are still on this kick, huh? I thought it would have blown over by now." She even began to pressure him to drink with her.

These are not pleasant outcomes. When readers shared them with me, I worried about the unintended consequences of change. The truth is that any change, no matter how positive, disrupts the synergy of a relationship. Even if your partner is happy about your decision, it will change the dynamic of your relationship. Be conscious of the fact that a change for you will mean a change for them. Be aware and treat them, whether they continue to drink or not, with respect. Don't force a change on them or feed them advice. Do share as much as possible about your journey, how you are feeling, and what you are thinking. Honest and compassionate communication is key.

How Can I Keep My Friends or Make New Ones?

Making friends, especially if you believed people who don't drink are boring, might be a real concern. What will people think about you? How will you navigate ordering a tonic without making them feel awkward for ordering a gin? First, let's explore your perception of people who don't drink. Do you truly know any? If the answer is yes, and you still feel they were boring, was it because they didn't drink or were they not that interesting of a person anyway? But it doesn't really matter because perception is reality, so if you thought they were boring it was true to you. How do you overcome this perception when so many people feel exactly the same way?

The best way is through experience. First you need to know without a doubt that you are the same person (even better!) without a drink in your hand. This will take time. You will need to experience many different events without alcohol for your anxiety to fully go away. You will probably be anxious before every experience without alcohol. The exciting news is that each experience will show you how much fun you can have without drinking. It's a process. This is a change that will affect every aspect of your life. You will need to be patient as you adjust, but I believe that each experience will bring you closer to knowing, without a doubt, that you are the same person (even better!) than you were when you were drinking.

It's true that some people will write you off before getting to know you. You can deal with this however you see fit. In the days when my confidence was low, and I was adjusting to not drinking, I dealt with it in all sorts of ways. You can pretend to be drinking: Order a gin and tonic, then get up to use the restroom, find the waitress, and ask her to hold the gin, or order a beer in a dark bottle, pour it out, and fill it back up with water. Readers have also contributed some things they say to avoid drinking without having to declare themselves the dreaded non-drinker:

- I can't tonight; I'm driving.
- I overdid it last night, so I'm taking the night off.
- I'm on a detox that doesn't allow alcohol.
- I'm watching my weight.
- I'm trying to cut back.
- I'm doing an alcohol-free challenge.
- I don't feel like it tonight.

- I have an important meeting tomorrow, so I want to keep a clear head.

Dating is another concern. How will you meet people without drinking? How will they react when you tell them? You must realize if a hundred people are drinking heavily, eighty of them wish they were able to enjoy themselves while drinking less. You might be surprised to know that, when looking for a partner, people find minimal alcohol consumption attractive. It's partially subconscious but true. We respect the non-drinker, admiring their character and self-discipline. We even feel they will ultimately make a better partner and parent. The bottom line: Not drinking is sexy!

Telling Your Friends Without Losing Your Friends

I made these mistakes so you don't have to. I am an excitable person, and when I was discovering *This Naked Mind*, I was vocal with my friends. I would say things like, "You'll never believe it! Just one drink causes cancer; there is no way I'm putting that shit in my body," or "You don't need alcohol to have a good time! It's crazy, but we've all been deluded by media and society."

As you can imagine, I was annoying. A friend even told my husband, "Yikes, I can't imagine what it's like living with the anti-alcohol evangelist." It wasn't pretty. Drinkers are fearful of having to quit. Without the reverse conditioning that *This Naked Mind* provides, they still believe that alcohol is vital, and not drinking (or feeling like they are being judged for drinking) creates stress. If they have developed a psychological, physical, or emotional dependence on alcohol (practically everyone I know), reminders of the harms of alcohol create stress. This needs to be a positive experience. When they see you enjoying yourself, it will give them hope rather than fear.

Often when someone stops drinking, they wish they were able to drink "normally" and are jealous of people who are still drinking.

Drinkers know this and have pity on the non-drinker. They separate themselves, believing that the non-drinker has a problem to which they are not susceptible. With this dynamic, there is little to no tension between the parties. The drinkers are, in fact, very accommodating, even ordering mocktails for the non-drinker to support them in overcoming their "problem."

A different dynamic occurs when you stop drinking with *This Naked Mind*. Rather than admitting to a problem, you have been educated and enlightened. You will no longer want to drink. Drinkers may have a hard time with this. How can you not want to drink? It won't seem possible. You may even feel smug that you no longer need alcohol when everyone around you does. Since drinkers are unable to pity you, it's possible that they will begin to feel sorry for themselves. They may feel judged when you decline a drink. You are now holding yourself to a higher standard. You are demonstrating you care more about what you put in your body and how it affects you. This is great, but not everyone will see it that way.

So how do you deal with this? How can you gracefully tell people about your decision without alienating your friends? I think the answer is relatively simple. It's not about pleasing everyone all the time. You did this for you, and by making this decision, even though you may cause tension at first, you will soon become a beacon of hope that they too can change.

In terms of specific phrasing, you will need to figure out what works for you. Try a few things. Make sure you are truly without judgment; speak truthfully about you, your decisions, and your story without imposing your beliefs on others. And try not to condemn their drinking habits, as your friends undoubtedly see alcohol as you once did—a companion, comfort, and friend. These are some phrases that have worked for me: "I realized I'm happier when I don't drink," "I'm on a health kick and giving up booze is part of it," "I decided drinking was no longer doing me any favors, so I quit," and "I feel better when I don't drink."

19.
THE DESCENT: WHY SOME
DESCEND FASTER THAN OTHERS

"Genius is more often found in a cracked pot than in a whole one."
—*E.B. White*

My husband blamed my compulsive nature on an "addictive personality." This always rubbed me the wrong way. So I asked him to define what exactly he meant by "addictive personality." He named people he thinks have an addictive personality and others who don't. The common trait among the addictive set was that we were, or had been, addicted to something. His definition never satisfied me. You can imagine my vindication when I discovered that scientists and doctors now agree that there is no such thing as an addictive personality. Despite trying for years to define what personality traits make someone prone to addiction, the scientific community has been unable to do so with any degree of certainty.[216] In fact, attempts to identify an addictive personality by linking a specific configuration of personality traits to addictive behaviors has been largely abandoned.[217]

But wait. Isn't it common knowledge that some people are more prone to addiction than others? As you've probably realized by now, common knowledge about alcohol and addiction is more likely myth than fact. So let's look at why some people fall into the addiction cycle faster than others, and why some people never seem to become dependent.

To review, addiction is doing something on a regular basis that you don't want to be doing, or that you want to be doing but find yourself unable to easily stop or cut back on. In the previous chapter, we explored how the cycle of alcohol-induced lows pushes us into a state of addiction where our desires (to drink and not to drink) are at war with each other.

We've also established that addicts go to great lengths to protect their drug of choice. They are loath to blame the substance for any ills they experience when using it. If they blame the substance, the next logical step is to eliminate it from their lives—which seems terrifying. Since the majority of Americans drink, it's not a stretch to assume that we have an addicted society: a society that protects alcohol by portraying alcoholism as a personality defect.

We take the existence of an addictive personality for granted. It's an inescapable prop of mainstream conversations about alcohol. We protect alcohol by blaming addiction on a person's personality rather than on the addictive nature of alcohol.

Am I saying that personality doesn't affect how quickly we become addicted? Not at all. Many factors impact the speed at which we slide into addiction—environmental and social factors, genetic factors, and, yes, personality factors. Just as personality affects every other aspect of your life, it must factor into how quickly you become dependent on alcohol.

So if I believe personality can play a role in addiction, why am I taking issue with the term "addictive personality?" I think it's negative and misleading. The same personality traits that caused me to drink more, like commitment, decisiveness, and a strong will, are primarily positive attributes. In fact, these "addictive" attributes played a vital role in finding my freedom.

The nebulous idea of an addictive personality allows us to protect our precious alcohol. We focus on the addictive personality, which makes alcohol dangerous for them but not for us. We protect the alcohol and blame the individual. This takes hope away from the alcoholic, encouraging them to believe they are powerless against their personality. The concept of addictive personality lets us close our minds to the fact that alcohol is addictive, period. If there is an addictive personality, and we don't feel we have one, we no longer need to exercise caution with alcohol.

"Addictive" Personality Traits

While I want to point out the fallacies in the broad brush and ill-defined concept of an addictive personality, it is worth noting that personality traits are potentially linked to problematic alcohol involvement. Interestingly, while some of these traits can be viewed as negative (including being more independent and less agreeable) most are neutral—or even positive—including extraversion and openness to experience.[218]

The negative concept of an "addictive personality" leads us to feel there is something wrong with us and implies that traits having some link to addiction are wholly negative and harmful. Not so. Some traits can, in fact, be desirable and positively influence a person's character and experiences. Other linked traits include experience seeking, decisiveness, impulsiveness, and nonconformity. As you can see, every personality trait that may contribute to a person's slide into addiction has both negative and positive sides. A collection of traits, which can have positive or negative implications for someone's life, should not be stigmatized and labeled as "addictive."

Let's look at my father again. He is a person who makes up his mind and sticks with it. Once he decided to stop drinking, he had no internal struggle and no pain because his decision was definite and permanent. He uses this decisive quality in other aspects of his life. He realized at the age of thirty-seven that he needed daily exercise to enjoy a full life. He found mountain biking and skiing most agreeable, so for the last thirty years he has biked sixty to a hundred miles every week and skis forty to eighty times per winter. He determines something is good, and he goes for it. He's also a nonconformist, not generally influenced by what other people think or say.

I believe his decisiveness, consistency, and nonconformity may be the same personality traits that led him to drink heavily. He determined he was receiving some pleasure from a little alcohol and concluded he would receive more pleasure from a lot. So he drank whenever he wanted with no qualms. Since all drug addiction escalates, he drank more and more. When he realized that alcohol was not providing any true pleasure, it was his decisive, consistent, and independent personality that made it easy for him to quit.

Here is another scenario. At a restaurant, a friend of mine, who is conscious of what others think of her, was the first to order and ordered a beer. After everyone else ordered, she realized that no one else in the group ordered alcohol, so she changed her mind and asked for water instead. She obviously wanted the beer, but in her mind, the stigma of drinking alone outweighed her desire for a beer. My bet is that her descent, so long as she continues to spend time with people who rarely drink, will be slow. Alternatively, if she spends time with heavy drinkers, this same personality trait may push her into drinking more than she wants.

Millions of factors contribute to the pace at which you become alcohol dependent. Perhaps you're someone who paces yourself, never jumping into anything. It stands to reason that you wouldn't jump head-first into drinking. On the other hand, if you are like me and get passionate about everything, including drinking, it makes sense that you would drink more, crave more, and fall faster.

Our finances can affect how fast we descend. I have a friend who tells me she loves to drink and would be an alcoholic if alcohol wasn't so expensive. Another friend truly enjoys dessert, and since she is on a tight budget, she weighs an alcoholic drink against dessert. Though she would like both, the dessert wins every time. In both cases, my friends desire to drink more, but either finances or a sweet tooth prevent them. This slows their descent.

Our surroundings also play into how quickly we descend. For me, moderate drinking evolved into heavy drinking when we moved from Colorado to New York City. When we lived in Colorado, we hiked, skied, camped, and enjoyed the diverse activities available there. In the big city, drinking was the main social pastime. Social life in Manhattan, London, and most of the other large cities I visit revolves around drinking.

And don't forget the effect of family opinion. A friend of mine was raised in a household where drinking was "of the devil." Though she does drink, the stigma she grew up with ensures that she limits her intake to limit her guilt.

No One Is Immune to Addiction

Countless motives, personality traits, and circumstances contribute to the speed at which someone falls into alcohol addiction. It is true that most drinkers will drink until they die, never suspecting drinking is taking years off their life, never feeling out of control, never suspecting they have a problem. But not realizing they have a problem does not mean they don't have one.

No one is immune from addiction to alcohol. The more you drink, the more you will want to drink. When a stressful life event occurs, the most moderate drinker can slide into either physical or emotional alcohol dependence. Even when the fall is nearly imperceptible, it is still happening. Barring a hindering circumstance, do the people you know drink more than they did a few years ago? Do you? Everyone who drinks now drinks more than they used to; I know this is true because at one time they didn't drink at all. You and the drinkers you know will be drinking more in five years than you are today—that is how alcohol works.

It's terrifying how fast you start to sink when you begin to suspect a problem. You have become dependent on an addictive substance. It is a vital part of your life, and you cannot imagine dealing with stress or enjoying social situations without it. Drinking more than you want creates panic and stress. You are accustomed to drinking when stressed, so you drink more of what is causing your stress. The cycle spirals out of control. Whether you feel life would be incomplete without your weekly beer or your daily bottle of vodka, the problem is the same.

We spend a lot of time trying to categorize drinkers: moderate, heavy, problematic, regular, alcoholic. We spend even more time trying to figure out what category we are in. This makes the entire topic of addiction more confusing, and if we are honest, it's a silly conversation. Perhaps we are all in the same dire predicament: all caught. As Lucy Rocca says, you have "positioned yourself at the top of a very slippery slope and with each drink you consume you're sliding ever quicker toward the bottom."[219]

Why is it so hard to believe that when you are in high school and start to experiment with alcohol, you are the bee drawn to the pitcher plant? Can you see the bee struggling on the sticky slope as the drinker trying to cut back or quit? Is it still hard to believe that your favorite beverage is a highly addictive drug? Why else would our society continue to consume it despite the epidemic alcoholism has become?

Why is it so hard to see the obvious truth? If alcoholism was due to a physical or mental flaw or a defect in my personality, I would have been incurable. How do you explain the fact that I have been cured, completely and painlessly, of this incurable disease?

There is no inexplicable defect in our personalities, no elusive flaw in our bodies. Alcohol is simply a highly addictive drug.

There is a logic principle called Occam's Razor. It states that, all else being equal, the simplest explanation is most likely correct. The explanation that alcohol is an addictive substance is far simpler than the convoluted theories (none of which we can prove or satisfactorily explain) around personality and physical and mental defects leading to alcoholism.

We find it hard to accept that we are all drinking the same addictive poison. Doing so means we must accept that the difference between the alcoholic and the moderate drinker is only how addicted they have become and how quickly. How far they have progressed on the alcohol addiction continuum. We must accept that alcohol cannot change in nature if it's consumed by an alcoholic or a moderate drinker. It is the same substance, with the same poisonous qualities.

Over time, drinking provides no honest enjoyment. When you reach the point of dependence, this truth is inescapable because, at the chronic stage, even the illusions of pleasure disappear. Alcohol is a physical depressant that poisons your body and ensnares your brain. It destroys you physically and mentally. It deadens your senses, thereby deadening all your survival instincts. It takes the happiness of this beautiful life with it.

Yet what message does our drinking generation send to our children? When I was drinking, my kids often asked if they could have a sip. I didn't realize it, but they saw alcohol as a coveted, adult treat that they couldn't wait to try. This now fills me with dread; I never want them to experience addiction. I have never felt more worthless than when I was addicted. Alcohol addiction is so scary that contemplation of suicide is 120 times more likely among adult alcoholics,[220] with alcohol involved in a third of all suicides in the U.S.[221]

Debating alcohol's inherent addictive nature with moderate drinkers is not generally useful for you or them. I've made that mistake. The new information you provide creates internal conflict, which is painful. They will do everything they can to convince you and themselves that they are enjoying their drink, remain fully in control, and can stop whenever they want to. You can't undo decades of unconscious conditioning with a quick conversation. As John A. Bargh, a professor of psychology at Yale, put it, "Unconscious systems are continually furnishing suggestions about what to do next and the brain is acting on those, all before conscious awareness. Sometimes those goals are in line with our conscious intentions and purposes and sometimes they're not."[222] They may consciously see your point of view, but their unconscious attachment to alcohol is strong and controlling.

If you do want to convince a friend or loved one, let them see how free and happy you have become, and let them ask you how you did it. Then go slowly and carefully. It is rewarding to help others, but trying before they want help will be frustrating for both of you. And give yourself a high-five. Consider how far ahead you are of the "take it or leave it" group. Why? Because you cannot fix an issue you don't know exists.

Time for a Self-Check

So am I saying that anyone who drinks any alcohol at all is addicted? No, that is clearly not true. I think anyone who illogically or unconsciously desires alcohol is addicted whether or not they are consciously aware. Anyone who feels fear at the thought of never drinking again is already emotionally dependent. If someone told me I could never eat another apple because they will eventually kill me, I would stop eating apples. It would be a logical decision, and it wouldn't fill me with dread. While I may be a bit bummed, I would also feel relieved that I was no longer going to die early and thankful that the truth about apples and my health had come out. I would certainly quit eating apples as soon as I was presented with the evidence. If you only drink on occasion and can "take it or leave it," why not leave it?

Take a moment and make a list of everything you get from drinking. This is important because you need to clearly understand that alcohol does you no favors. If you feel afraid, just realize that your fear is proof of what I am telling you. If I was lecturing on the harms of red meat, you might feel disappointed, since you like a good steak, but you wouldn't feel dread in the pit of your stomach. That feeling of dread is the manifestation of addiction—fear that is created by drinking.

Is ignorance bliss? If I thought I was getting pleasure from drinking, isn't that basically the same as getting actual pleasure? Wouldn't I rather go through my life with the perceived pleasure than nothing at all?

It's a valid concern, but ignorance is only bliss if nothing can be done to make things better. In this case, through knowledge and education you achieve freedom. You are about to be free. You will experience so much more pleasure being whole, healthy, and happy than you ever did from drinking. You will no longer see quitting as "I never get to drink" but "I never have to drink." So let's move on toward finding your freedom.

20.
LIVING A NAKED LIFE IN OUR SOCIETY

"Yesterday I was clever, so I wanted to change the world.
Today I am wise, so I am changing myself."
—*Rumi*

Freedom at Last

Once you've finished this book and freed yourself, you have some important lifestyle choices to consider. Deciding not to drink will be a pleasure, so you will not suffer by being out at a bar or around your friends who are still drinking, and you won't need to avoid situations that you enjoy. You don't have to change anything about your lifestyle. But we should talk about a few exceptions. Be honest with yourself. Are there activities in your life that are only reasons to drink, and which will no longer give you any pleasure?

You may find once-desirable activities to be nothing more than a waste of time. Some people may have only been fun because alcohol slowed down your brain enough to make them so. I'm not talking about spending time out at the bar with your real friends or doing anything you actually enjoy where others are drinking. But you may discover that you were choosing activities that aren't actually fun and are with people you don't truly care for, just to have somewhere to drink. These activities now feel like a waste of your time.

After I stopped drinking, I went to Las Vegas. The trip had been planned before I quit. Before *This Naked Mind*, the idea of a trip to Vegas without drinking would have been unbearable. I would have canceled the trip. Once I quit, the idea of going to Vegas without drinking was not a concern. I was looking forward to the trip with the absolute certainty that drinking is not needed to have a good time. That's exactly what happened. I have never had more fun in Las Vegas. I was with my closest friends, enjoying engaging and hilarious conversations. I laughed until I cried. I didn't suffer a single hangover, and there was no black shadow hanging over me. I reveled in my freedom. I had no worries or cares and woke up each day with tons of energy. Every meal seemed to taste better than the last. Interestingly, alcohol deadens your ability to taste,[223] so food really did taste better.[224] Without drinking I was better able to experience one of life's greatest pleasures: eating.

During this trip drinking occupied zero percent of my brain space. I was more present and engaged than I could ever have been while drinking. And I secretly reveled at breakfast when all my friends had headaches, wearing their sunglasses and ordering mimosas to try to rid themselves of massive hangovers. I felt great, headache-free with no nausea, full of energy to meet the day, and I couldn't help smiling to myself about how far I'd come.

I ended up leaving Vegas a day early to go abroad for a work trip. As you know, my career, with its heavy drinking dinners, was a big factor in my descent. This trip was no different and included plenty of nights out for drinks. I was out four nights in a row with different colleagues, vendors, and clients. I enjoyed the dinners and conversations. It was my first business trip without drinking, and I was determined to do everything I used to do, including going out for more drinks after dinner. That's when things got weird. I didn't understand why I wasn't having fun. I had done this so many times before and always seemed to enjoy myself (though I admit I don't remember a lot of specifics). I must have enjoyed myself, since I did it every night, often staying out well into the next morning.

When I got back to the U.S., I was a bit panicked. I worried that I was no longer having fun without alcohol and couldn't think of a good reason why. I discussed this with my husband, who immediately knew the answer. It was simple, and I have been on many business trips since without any problem. Late-night drinks after dinner with colleagues or vendors with whom I don't have any real relationship are not actually fun. We weren't close friends enjoying each other's company and conversation; in fact, if we left the company, we'd probably never see each other again. We were only getting together to drink. The conversations were repetitive and centered around office gossip, which is never very nice. The reality is that the situation, without my senses thoroughly deadened, is not that pleasant. I now go out and enjoy great dinners in exotic places and then retire to my hotel room. There, I read, write, or, most fun (if the time zones allow), Skype with my kids. In the mornings I no longer drag myself out of bed fifteen minutes before my first meeting. Now I often wake up early and explore the city before I go into the office.

Last night I was at a London train station, Charing Cross. I was with my UK-based marketing team, having coffee and a chat. Next to us, lone commuters also enjoyed a quick drink before their commute home. Everything about the situation looked sexy. The beer was in a proper pint glass, very British. The British accents lent sophistication to the scene. The act of enjoying a pint, in a busy train station, while transitioning from the grind of work to the relaxation of home, was glamorous.

Before my experience with *This Naked Mind* it would have been almost impossible for me to resist ordering a beer. I would have bought into the societal cues, the ambiance, and the experience.

Yesterday I had no desire to drink a beer. I saw the situation for what it was. I was saddened to see a smart, healthy group of people unwittingly sinking into a deadly pit. The pitcher plant is a beautiful but lethal flower. The experience was freeing because I was not tempted. I could see the truth.

As a reaction to the damage alcohol is doing to British society, public health organizations have introduced Dry January and Stoptober (Stop October). In Australia they have Dry July. These are months when people are encouraged to experience life without drinking. This year I was in London during Dry January. You could tell who some of the participants were because they walked around with a holier-than-thou attitude. They seemed to feel superior to those who had not manned up enough to give up booze. At first I didn't understand the bravado, but soon I realized it was a defense mechanism. In order to maintain sobriety, they needed to minimize their desire for a drink. So they looked down on drinkers. Nothing says addicted more than trying to prove we're not.

You are about to have a completely different perspective. Instead of feeling a desire to drink and needing to avoid places where people are drinking, you will feel freedom. Actually, being around drinkers is one of the best reminders of your freedom. You'll see the irrational reasons people give for drinking. If I'd asked the guy at the train station why he was drinking, he probably would have told me he likes the taste. He ordered and drank the beer in less than two minutes so he could make his train. He didn't have time to savor the taste. I was drinking fresh-squeezed orange juice and taking it very slowly. England has amazing juice, and I wanted to enjoy every sip.

You can easily investigate these collective reasons for drinking. Look around and observe why others are drinking. You will see they are not making rational decisions. In fact, the reasons they give for drinking are simply excuses. They don't understand why they are drinking. These "regular" drinkers, rather than tempting you, become a powerful reminder of how lucky you are to be free.

Not only will you watch regular drinkers without resentment, but you will start to recognize drinkers on the slow (or fast) descent into the abyss of addiction. Most drinkers are unwittingly drinking more over time, perhaps more than they ever wanted.

It can become confusing because drinking is so prevalent in our society. We build bars like shrines to booze, and some are beautiful, even striking. Your unconscious mind is vulnerable, and although you are freeing your emotional desires from alcohol through the education in this book, you will need to ensure you don't allow the garbage back in. If day after day you see people happily drinking alcohol, you may trick yourself into believing there is something special about drinking after all. The most important tool is to use your brain. Drinkers don't yet know what you know, and as a society we collectively close our minds to the risks of drinking. When I tell people that alcohol is a known carcinogen, a fact that was scientifically proven in 1988, they are surprised. Not so long ago I was shocked to discover that my dear wine was not the life-affirming drink I believed it to be. The key is to think. Be mindful and aware of the constant barrage of messages you are subject to every day. When you start to question, remind yourself of the truth about alcohol and consciously undo these influences as soon as possible. Your unconscious mind is susceptible to the influences that tell you alcohol is key to life. You must be on your guard, not allowing your mind to be a guesthouse or storage area for junk. Take out the trash as soon as you realize it is coming in.

Take control of your mind and fight to see the truth. You will probably find this fun and empowering. I was eating at a restaurant with a beautiful bar in another London train station, King's Cross. It has huge brick walls with ceilings at least four stories high. This bar was truly a sexy and incredible shrine to alcohol, with shiny glass bottles full of rich, amber liquid stretching up all four stories. In reality, the architecture and design were beautiful. Marketers have done specific studies on how much more alcohol they sell—up to 40%

more—when the liquor bottles are properly displayed and lit. It's amazing how much influence beautiful presentation has on our minds. I took a minute to admire the architecture, but instead of wishing I was part of something with so much apparent beauty, I made a conscious decision to see the amber liquid for what it was: a substance that would destroy my brain and body. A drink that would render me tired, insensible, and hung over.

I know a consultant for bars and restaurants. His main job is to help bars become more profitable, which means selling more alcohol. He told me that pubs should always be set up with clear pathways to the bar. The bar should, if possible, have multiple access points. Bottles should be displayed up high so that customers can see them over the heads of other customers, and these bottles should always be lit from below. He says that if a bar provides water with every drink, the customers will not get drunk as quickly, and the bar will sell more booze. There's even a correlation between bathroom accessibility and noise levels to encourage the most alcohol consumption. That day at the spectacular alcohol shrine at King's Cross, I smiled to myself and smugly ordered my tonic and lime, knowing without a doubt that the beauty of the alcohol display only ran skin deep.

Don't believe you're immune to the constant assault of pro-alcohol messages. No one is. We must recognize the lies and put them in their place. Realize how powerful the bombardment must be to convince the majority of adults to regularly drink poison. If the majority boarded a ship that hit an iceberg and was sinking, would you envy them? You, hopefully, would feel compelled to reach out and lend a hand to help others escape from the sinking ship.

Is Moderation an Option?

While I've presented you with analogies, facts, and scenarios that favor leaving alcohol completely behind, I have not given you definitive direction to stop drinking altogether. I have a hard time with rules. If there is a rule I must follow, my every instinct is to break it.

A definitive statement to answer this question is difficult. I don't want to write a rule and have the rebels, like myself, feel that they are bound. I would much rather present you with all the facts, allowing you to come to the decision that is best for you.

Moderation with any addictive substance is difficult, and for some it becomes impossible. Brain changes from drinking can be permanent. Theoretically, when someone develops a strong physical dependence, their brain and body may have altered to such an extent that they can't function without alcohol. Let me explain.

We spoke about the changes that happen in your brain as a result of drinking. We've discussed how alcohol increases cravings but not pleasure by releasing dopamine. I want to expand on the dopamine relationship to explain why some people are unable to stop at just one drink.

To review, addictive drugs, from nicotine to heroin, release artificially high levels of dopamine in the brain. While scientists used to believe dopamine was linked to feeling good, they now believe that dopamine is linked to learning, and learning includes wanting, expecting, and craving.[225] Rather than giving us pleasure, dopamine teaches us how to get pleasure. It helps us learn the most effective ways to stimulate the brain's pleasure center.

We know that alcohol artificially stimulates the brain's pleasure centers. We also know that to maintain homeostasis and protect itself, the brain turns down the pleasure received from alcohol over time.[226] This is tolerance. This is why at the end of my drinking career I was desperate to drink, yet I received little to no actual pleasure even after two or more bottles of wine. The explanation is clear: My brain was repeatedly, artificially overstimulated by alcohol, so it built a tolerance and produced a counter-chemical, dynorphin, which turned down the stimulation. Over time it took more and more alcohol to feel any stimulation. And everyday pleasures wouldn't even register because of the high levels of dynorphin my brain was producing. This is why neuroscientist and professor Polk says:

"Consider what happens in a drug addict when they repeatedly over-stimulate the brain with their drug of choice. The brain will continue to turn down the overstimulation, and over time the addict will feel less pleasure from the drug. The high won't be as rewarding, and the addict will require more and more stimulation to get the same level of reward. And of course that is exactly what drug addicts report, they need more and more of the drug to feel the same high: And eventually they need to take the drug just to feel normal."[227]

Let's dive deeper into the role of dopamine in addiction to understand why some people become unable to stop at just one. Basically, dopamine's role in learning is to ensure pleasure can be found again. Wolfram Schultz says, "An adaptive organism must be able to predict future events such as the presence of mates, food and danger . . . predictions give an animal time to prepare behavioral reactions and can be used to improve the choices an animal makes in the future."[228] Dopamine plays a central role in how adaptive species, including humans, are able to anticipate and be motivated to pursue a reward.

Terry Robinson and Kent Berridge formulated a theory for the neural basis of drug craving called the incentive-sensitization theory of addiction.[229] The theory states that repeated use of addictive drugs makes the brain's dopamine center hypersensitive to that specific drug. This will happen differently in different people. Some people have higher natural levels of dopamine and some naturally lower levels. However, as I understand it, it is possible for this hypersensitivity to a specific drug (in this case alcohol) to happen in anyone over time with repeated use.

According to Robinson and Berridge: "The repeated uses of addictive drugs produces incremental neuroadaptations in this neural system, rendering it increasingly and perhaps permanently hypersensitive to the drug." This hypersensitive dopamine system creates a craving for the drug that can occur separately from liking the drug. And this can produce "addictive behavior (compulsive drug seeking and drug taking) even if the expectations of the drug's pleasure is diminished . . . and even in the face of strong disincentives, including the loss of reputation, job, home and family."[230]

Did you catch that? This means if you drink enough alcohol, over time you can change the response of your brain to alcohol. And once the change has occurred, it may never return to normal. This explains why someone can be sober for thirty years, drink a single beer and be thrown back to drinking past the point of throwing up, until they are unconscious. This means that one drink, even after prolonged abstinence, can stimulate craving for alcohol so that you will continue to drink no matter the consequences and worse, that *you won't even enjoy it.*

This is how we explain the alcoholic whose spouse threatens to leave if they don't stop, yet remains powerless against the pull of alcohol. This is how we explain the illogical and irrational behavior of alcohol and other drug usage. After enough dopamine is repeatedly released, your brain responds to alcohol in a completely different way.[231]

I would like to note here that if you have altered your brain to this extent, there is hope. Once you have broken the cycle, your cravings will go away. You will never be back in the misery of addiction if you never drink that one drink. Even though the dopamine hypersensitivity to alcohol will exist, it will remain dormant as long as you introduce no alcohol into your body.

For me, craving something I no longer enjoyed felt like someone had moved into my brain and was calling the shots. It was like being held captive by an adversary who was constantly growing stronger as I grew weaker. An enemy that would kill me if I didn't kill him first. Lucy Rocca describes it this way: "The monster wants to be fed . . . alcohol keeps people pushed down . . . alcohol makes people powerless and turns them into slaves of drinking."[232]

It is interesting to note that more dopamine is released by alcohol in men's brains than in women's,[233] which may be a reason why, on the whole, more men drink alcohol and develop alcohol addictions than women. In fact, men made up 70% of all alcohol-related deaths in the U.S. (88,000) in 2014.[234]

I would also like to say that if you have already reached the point where you cannot resist a drink, if you are unable to stay sober long enough to read this book, you need to go somewhere for help: a place that will prevent you from drinking and make alcohol unavailable to you as you detox. The good news is that once the alcohol is out of your system, and your mentality has changed, meaning you see that you no longer need alcohol, you can regain control.

"Trying to have 'just one drink of alcohol' is like trying to knock just one domino down in a huge line of them." —Craig Beck

The Stress of Decision-Making

Did you know that making decisions causes stress and expends our brain's resources? Studies show that little decisions appear to take as much neural energy as big ones.[235] And brain energy, like any other type of energy, gets depleted. When you use your brain's energy on tons of little decisions (should I drink today? how many will I allow myself to have tonight?), you deplete your decision-making abilities. Not to mention that the alcohol itself, once it enters your brain, negatively affects your ability to make sound decisions. Don't forget that over time alcohol chemically damages your prefrontal cortex.[236] This is the part of your brain that is vital to making sound, long-term decisions. The prefrontal cortex balances out the pleasure-seeking, animal regions of your brain, and when it is damaged by alcohol abuse, its effectiveness is decreased. You make worse decisions, and temptation is harder to resist because the animal regions of the brain, the parts that seek pleasure without considering consequences, become stronger than the more measured areas of the brain.[237]

For me it was a cycle of insanity. I would make myself promises about moderation, which I would keep at first. Success gave me a profound sense of satisfaction, of control. I felt proud, invincible. I could enjoy the nectar and then fly away. Then I would stumble upon more reasons, seemingly legitimate reasons, to drink more or to give in to temptation. Eventually it became clear that moderation was not working, that I had crossed the line, but at that point I could not stop. In the cycle of addiction, the funhouse, nothing is as it appears. I felt let down, ashamed of myself. I didn't understand why I continued to do what I had come to hate, and it terrified me. I felt alone and began to isolate myself from those close to me, who I knew would be disappointed. I became a miserable shell of myself. Sometimes I was so deceived that I was not aware of how far I had fallen. How dependent I had again become. My tolerance would build, and within days, weeks, or months, I'd return to the chronic stage.

Before addiction, I had a typical capacity for reward. When I was addicted, I no longer enjoyed normally rewarding experiences. In a situation like this, you start to fear you can only find joy with the assistance of the drug. This fear keeps you in the clutches of addiction. Experience confirms that you only get pleasure from drinking. What you don't realize is that drinking "pleasure" is not true pleasure, and everyday pleasure will return as soon as you stop drinking and allow your brain and body to heal.

You will recognize the deception and realize you don't need alcohol to relax or to enjoy yourself—you were duped into believing you did. In order to reach that place you must defeat your mortal enemy.

At the beginning of the book we broke down our problem into two areas: the drinker and the drink. On the surface it seems that you, the drinker, should be able to control yourself. But the reality of addiction, once it's taken hold and changed your brain, is that you can't. Addiction takes control away from the drinker. The good news is that you can control the drink. You can—now that the unconscious conditioning has been reversed—make a conscious, logical, and rational decision about drinking. You can control alcohol so it does not control you. While being fully in control will mean different things for different people, for me it means staying away from booze. The great news is that I no longer have any desire to drink an addictive poison that does nothing for me. Miraculously, as a result of this process, I am thrilled that I no longer drink. Few things have made me happier than gaining my total and complete freedom from the clutches of alcohol.

It is important that you not make the mistake of clinging to any former illusions about alcohol. If you retain the desire to drink, you will spend the rest of your life wondering when it will be a good time to have that next drink.

Don't underestimate the power of your mind. I was contemplating the power of the human mind on a recent flight. There I was, 35,000 feet in the air, and if something happened to the pilot, the plane would have been able to fly and practically land itself. Humans built this technology. We built global positioning systems that broadcast the plane's exact location. We have the intelligence to understand gravity and space; we launch satellites into orbit so GPS can work. We are powerful.

My first conscious experience of my mind's power was when my back was healed through mental education and understanding. Through Dr. Sarno's work, I realized my mind was more powerful and influential in my physical body and emotions than I could have possibly imagined. I now know, without a doubt, that if I choose to believe I will be miserable without alcohol in my life, I will be; if I choose to believe I can't relax without a drink, I won't be able to. I also know that if I choose to see alcohol as it really is, a toxic and addictive drug that should be treated with caution and doesn't deserve a role in my life, I will have no desire for it. The choice is mine.

Now that you know the naked truth about alcohol and what it has been doing to you, your body, and your mind, you'll be able to act. Your unconscious mind is changing, and drinking is again becoming a fully conscious decision. You can use your powerful mind to find freedom from alcohol.

When you see the truth, you realize you are able to let go of your desire to have an occasional drink. You realize one drink can create the physical addiction, which in turn creates the mental addiction. The cycle will continue. If you retain your desire to drink, it will be difficult, if not impossible, to find freedom.

Alcohol is addictive, and if you have been presented with all the facts and continue to desire alcohol, it's difficult for me to believe you are fully in control. Just because people seem to be in control of their drinking doesn't mean they are. There are a few things you can observe to see if someone is really as in control as they think they are:

- Do they willingly offer a fair conversation about alcohol? Can they comfortably discuss both the pros and cons of drinking?
- Do they make a big show of explaining why they drink in a way that they would not do with other things they choose to do (for example, drinking soda)?
- Is drinking daily and habitual, done without any real or conscious thought as part of their everyday life?
- Do they feel uncomfortable around you if you are not drinking? This is a definite sign that they're not making choices they are fully comfortable with.
- Do they feel the need to justify their drinking to you? Especially when you haven't asked?
- Do they seem unable to have a good time if they are unable to drink?

Again, be gentle. Even if someone is controlled by alcohol, they may be unaware, and we humans hate it when our self-control is questioned. You may need to smile and nod, realizing that everything you have read is true and that you are no longer caught up in the alcohol cycle—a cycle that only leads one way: downward.

Recently on a ski vacation, everyone was sitting around drinking while I enjoyed my soda, cranberry, and lime (which is an excellent drink!). My friends were discussing plastic bottles and how the plastic can leach into your drinking water and poison you. Everyone at the table was intelligent and seemed very in control of their drinking, yet there they were, drinking a known poison in massive quantities and speculating about the possibility of plastic leaching into their drinking water. It was a startling demonstration that even when we know the research and understand everyday pollutants, alcohol gets a free pass.

Moderation is a dangerous game. It's like saying you want to jump a little way out of a plane or lose your virginity but just a little bit. Alcohol tricks us because drinkers hide how much drinking affects their lives. Many don't outwardly hit rock bottom. Millions worry they may be in danger, but asking for help means enduring the stigma. Instead, they spend years worrying, wondering if they actually have a problem.

Let's End It Now

My goal with *This Naked Mind* is to help people before they reach a stage where alcohol has such a hold on them that their lives are unmanageable. I hope to give people freedom before they slide so far down into alcohol addiction that their brains are forever altered by the drug. To make them aware of the dangers of alcohol before they become slaves to it. Surely we should focus on arresting alcohol abuse well before the disease has progressed to full-blown alcoholism and begins ruining lives.

Alcoholics, because of the stigma, usually sink low, often harming themselves and others, before they ask for help. It's not OK. We place this stigma on people who have done nothing more than become addicted to an addictive substance, like the bee in the pitcher plant. The stigma and the diagnosis of an incurable disease conspire to ensure we don't ask for help at the early stages when we can still avoid deeply hurting ourselves.

Let's change it. Let's lose the stigma and admit that when it comes to alcohol and drugs, none of us are in control. In fact, let's stop calling it "alcohol and drugs" and acknowledge that alcohol is a drug— the most dangerous drug on the planet.[238] Addiction blocks your mind from the drug's harms and deceives you into believing you are in control, despite the irrationality of your decisions. All alcoholics started with one drink. The only difference between drinkers who feel they are in control and those who admit they are not is what stage the disease has progressed to. How much their bodies, their situations, and their wallets can cope with how much they drink. They are not in control. You were not in control, and if you decide to drink again, you will give up control.

Don't envy people who seem to control their drink. Just because alcohol seems to enhance a pleasurable occasion does not mean it actually does. I, as the non-drinker, feel amazing at occasions I would once have drank at. I am free. I have all my wits around me, and as a result, I laugh a lot more. I am funnier and smarter without drinking than I ever was while deadening my senses. I still have bad days, of course, but even then I realize that self-medicating with alcohol is a horrible idea. My friend Mary puts it this way: "The bottom line is, if I am unable to find joy in a situation, it's most definitely not the lack of alcohol to blame." If you struggle with depression or anxiety, it's time to get help. Continuing to self-medicate with booze will only make things worse. I say this from experience.

Placebo Effect

"Man is what he believes." —*Anton Chekhov*

The placebo effect demonstrates the incredible power of our brains. Basically, the placebo effect occurs when someone is given a substance they believe will cure them. Even though the substance lacks the active ingredient, the person still experiences the anticipated cure or result. A study by Slavenka Kam-Hansen in the journal *Science Translational Medicine* showed that, for some drugs, more than half the impact of the drug is due to the placebo effect. People improve while taking them not because of anything in the substance but because of the staggering power of human belief.

I was eating alone in Paris, and the table next to me filled. They sat down, clearly in a funk from a long day of work. There wasn't a ton of conversation. The wine came, and they became instantly happy. They started laughing and talking excitedly about the wine. Someone said it was not his favorite kind, but "it does the job," which is apparently a French saying. It struck me that they began to have a great time as soon as the wine came. Without any drinking, the mood transitioned from slightly weary, just off work, to buoyancy and giggling. The fact that the mood changed before they drank a drop proved to me that the wine itself did not create happiness. No, this was clearly the placebo effect. It was the promise of wine that changed the mood. If someone took the bottle away, surely the long-day-at-the-office misery would have returned.

Can you see how addiction, until you drink enough to change your brain, is mostly mental? Relief was coming, and that was enough to change the mood even before anyone drank a drop. I had an early morning, so I didn't stay to watch the dinner play out. However, I have been the lone sober person at many of these occasions. Here's what happens. The wine comes, and the mood changes, so the conversation is intelligent, quick-witted, and full of life. Fast-forward two or three glasses, and conversation grows a bit dull, even among some of the most intelligent people. The wine does exactly what it is supposed to; it slows your brain function and dulls your senses.

Drinking does not make dull people fun. Alcohol makes smart and engaging people dumb and boring. Its very nature slows your brain function and dulls your wit and senses. People rendering themselves senseless are not entertained. What could be more boring than the monotony of experiencing life with only part of your senses? It is no fun to be controlled by a poison.

Remember the relief that the group of diners demonstrated when the wine arrived? The relief that a craving would soon be assuaged? The beauty of being a non-drinker is that I live in the place of relief, or rather freedom, from craving. I never again have to endure that painful, anxious craving. I don't experience withdrawal symptoms. I am ready for a good laugh and to enjoy whatever's next. I love the fact I don't need to stop at the liquor store to enjoy my evening. And while everyone has bad days, mine have become fewer and easier to deal with. I no longer make one bad day into two by getting drunk and spending the day after with a hangover. It's time for you to find that same freedom.

21.
THIS NAKED MIND

"Knowledge itself is power."
—*Francis Bacon*

You are close. With every word you have read, every idea you have contemplated, you have been undoing the lifelong conditioning of your unconscious mind. You have used Liminal Thinking to dive deep into the foundation of the obvious, examining your observations, experiences, and assumptions. You have slowly but surely been regaining the perspective of someone who has never had a drink, who has never been addicted to alcohol.

And now you have the advantage. You've experienced alcohol addiction, and you know how vile and insidious it is. I have perspective that the non-drinker doesn't have—I've seen the evils firsthand. Survival deserves a medal, not a stigma. I am stronger than before. I now have a shield of experiential armor against the horrors of alcohol. I feel strong enough to stand up and fight. My mission, the mission of *This Naked Mind*, is to change how our society views alcohol, to expose the truth and to provide tools to change our direction.

In writing this, my research has brought me to tears on numerous occasions. Why? I hurt for all of us. The most destructive part of this, the most rampant of all drug addictions, is how it steals our ability to respect and care for ourselves. Without self-respect, everything else falls apart. We are blinded, naively destroying our loved ones and ourselves. We unknowingly contribute to our children's future struggles. A recent study shows that kids who are allowed sips of alcohol are more prone to abuse alcohol as adults, and kids with alcoholic parents are four times more likely to have problems with drinking in adulthood.[239] At school, kids receive a message of caution against alcohol, but at home, our kids receive another, much stronger, message from the ever-present bottle of wine.

Alcohol is society's most dangerous addiction, causing four times as many deaths as prescription and illegal drug overdoses combined.[240] And it's growing. Death by alcohol consumption is increasing every year, and it has now surpassed AIDS as the world's number one killer of men aged 15–59.[241] More people are addicted to alcohol than any other drug on the planet.

Yet we've stigmatized not drinking. I experience this all the time. Refusing a drink invites criticism and judgment. The assumption when someone doesn't drink is that they must be recovering from a serious problem. Not only is it insulting, but it encourages this rampant and most destructive of all addictions to thrive unchecked.

If we don't change, we are on a terrible trajectory. In every category, misery from alcohol increases. We spend more money advertising alcohol than ever before, and more teenagers are trying alcohol, more college students binge drink, and the suicide rate among students is higher than ever. We're seeing more deaths from alcohol than ever before. Yet we continue to embrace alcohol as the "elixir of life." Our generation perpetuates this; I know I did. We are consuming so much wine that the latest trends are wine clubs and boxed wines. Our children see alcohol as vital to life's enjoyment. It is up to us. It is our responsibility to change this and expose alcohol. Once your eyes have been opened, it is clear. You see our entire society trapped in the pitcher plant, sliding downward, and it is terrifying.

Alcohol causes poverty, homelessness, domestic violence, child abuse, homicide, rape, death, and destruction. Alcohol doesn't just affect the drinker but everyone around them. We have an obligation to ourselves and the generations to come to expose this hideous disease for what it is. And we have a choice. We are doing this to ourselves. We can be the change. We can stop the cycle. We've put tobacco in its place. Why can't we do the same for alcohol?

At the beginning of this book, I assumed the thought of never drinking again filled you with apprehension, possibly panic. I dreaded the idea of spending my life without alcohol. By now alcohol's grip on you should be starting to loosen. The idea of not having to drink is exciting and welcome.

If the idea of giving alcohol up forever still makes you apprehensive, that's OK. For many, the proof that life can and will be enjoyable comes in living free from the insidious clutches of alcohol. Only then do you experience the joy of knowing you never have to drink again.

No matter where you are mentally, it's important to consider all the facts as you make a decision about alcohol in your life. Again, it truly doesn't matter if you are still attached to alcohol and feel afraid of life without it.

It's important to make a decision, a commitment, even if it's just a commitment to try an alcohol-free life for a period. This is for two reasons. First, the effort it takes to make one decision is the same amount of effort it takes to make each of a thousand decisions. Allow yourself to feel the freedom that comes with a single commitment, a single definitive choice—it is intoxicating. Second, without a decision you won't know when you are free. Our society is filled with conditioning; it's all around us. We got together with some other couples and their kids for St. Patrick's Day, and everyone was drinking. It's hard when you see people you know, love, and respect drinking alcohol as if it were the elixir of life. It's hard not because you want to pour poison down your throat, but because you know that truth. You have a perspective they don't, and you are grateful to know you are free.

But it is hard for the same reason cognitive dissonance is hard. You know something is true, yet the evidence in front of your eyes, in the form of your close friends casually drinking, telling you they can "take it or leave it," creates disagreement. Not because you think they are correct, but because you can't understand why they cannot see what you can. Remember their unconscious minds that control their desires and emotions still believe that alcohol is necessary to having fun at social occasions. Their nonchalant manner toward drinking is contrary to all of the truths you now know. These experiences don't make you question your commitment or point of view, but they create difficulty because it is hard to have different opinions than the people you care about.

Humans like to belong. You won't feel tempted to drink for the sake of drinking; in fact, at home, drinking won't even cross your mind. But in a social situation, you may be tempted because of a desire to fit in or to relieve the division you now feel between you and your friends. It's not easy to be different. Remember in grade school, when everyone got into certain brands and you begged your parents to buy you the same clothing your classmates had? It's human nature to want to be part of a group, to fit in.

While it's not easy to be different, it is good. And you are strong. It is a testament to the addictive nature of alcohol that your quitting evokes such emotional reactions from those around you. When I stopped eating eggs, no one got emotional or offended or questioned if our friendship would be as close as it was before. As much as your friends care about you, no matter how graceful you are about your decision, a divide will likely spring up between you and them. If they worry that they may have a problem, your not drinking will increase their anxiety, yet they will still feel all the emotional and mental attachment to alcohol as you did before you began reading this book. This is another important reason to make a commitment to yourself: When you are committed, it will be easier to prepare for these situations.

It's OK if it's not always easy. Nothing worth doing is completely easy. By being different you are making a strong statement. I laughed a lot at the St. Patrick's Day celebration. Your friends see you laughing and enjoying the evening sans booze, and it has an impact. And at some point, if you go gently and don't adopt a "holier-than-thou" attitude, they may ask you for your secret. They may open the door for a conversation about their struggles with alcohol.

Let's look again at Beth, a recovering alcoholic who is in A.A. and has been sober for five years. She knows I am writing this book and asked me if I could teach her to drink in moderation. I asked her if she wanted me to teach her how to drink motor oil in moderation. She looked at me as if I were crazy—why in the world would she want to do that? That's exactly the point. If you see alcohol as it truly is, nothing but an awful tasting poison that is destroying our society, our families, our relationships, and our bodies, why would you want to drink it? Even on occasion?

As part of my research into moderation, I read some forums about an approach called moderation management. The participants check in on online platforms and report on how many drinks they consume in a week. They count each drink, trying to obtain a target number of drinks per week. They are consumed every day by when they will drink, how much they will drink, and if they will keep their drinking goals. Instead of finding freedom from alcohol, they've become consumed by it. It is like our friend the bumblebee. She enters the plant trying hard to avoid slipping in while still drinking the nectar—nectar made from decay and rot. If she makes one misstep, she gets stuck, slides down, and becomes the nectar.

If you have no desire to drink, why would you try a single drink and give your enemy power again? As Carr says, once you see the truth about drinking, the fear of never being able to drink again is replaced by the excitement of never *having* to drink again. The experience is euphoric. You see your entire life, long and healthy, stretch out before you. You are proud. You have done something amazing. You are excited to enjoy this remarkable life and all of the many, wonderful human experiences it holds.

I drank for so long I forgot how beautiful life could be. I forgot how it feels to wake up energized about what the day can bring. Drinking drags you down. When you drink, you're inviting your mortal enemy to move back in. It's the alcohol monster who only feeds on more alcohol and destroys you in the process of feeding himself. His thirst is always growing and never satisfied. Of course, one drink will partially relieve the craving. It may quiet the monster for a little while. Yet it's this temporary solace that deceives us. Soon, you can see the bottom of your empty glass. I clearly remember thinking about my next drink before I had finished the drink in my hand. It's the same with all addictive substances—they all create an insatiable thirst for themselves.

Imagine that you arrive at an open house. The realtor has opened the home for prospective buyers, and you are one of many on the tour. You walk in and start to explore. The realtor has baked cookies so that the house smells wonderful. You are offered these fresh-baked cookies. You eat. You explore for a while, but then you realize there is something wrong about the home. It is certainly not the home you thought it was from the outside, and it's not for you. You decide to leave, and upon trying to walk out the front door, you find you have become lost. You wander through long, dark hallways, past eerie doorways, up and down stairs until you no longer recognize where you are or how you came to be there. The house has turned into a frightening maze. You realize the cookies are making you ill, but they're the only food available so you are compelled to eat them. It's a chilling experience. You see other prospective buyers, still walking around and enjoying the cookies. They haven't realized the cookies are poison or that the house is a deadly maze. Just because they don't find the house alarming yet doesn't mean they are any less stuck or that the cookies are less poisonous. The reality is terrifying whether they understand it or not.

A comparative risk assessment of drugs including alcohol and tobacco was done using the margin of exposure (MOE) approach. MOE is the ratio between intake and toxicology. A MOE of less than 10 is categorized as "high-risk," an MOE between 10 and 100 falls into a "risk" category. Cocaine, alcohol, nicotine, and heroin were the only drugs to fall into the high-risk (less than 10) category. When the population was taken into account, only alcohol fell into the high-risk category. All other drugs (with the exception of cannabis, which had an MOE of more than 10,000) fell into the "risk" category.[242] These are facts; they are not up for debate. Our society insists that alcohol is somehow separate from drugs; we even say "drugs and alcohol" rather than accepting that alcohol is the most dangerous drug of all.[243]

You will need to be on your guard because it's easy to believe drinkers who say they have no problem with alcohol and can take it or leave it. We have no reason not to believe them. We trust our friends. And they are not deceiving you on purpose; they believe what they say. They still seem to be enjoying the tour of the house. Often the main reason they believe they can take it or leave it is that they have never tried to leave it.

Imagine if I told you I could sometimes go a day without chewing gum. Wouldn't you immediately think I was obsessed with gum? Or consider smokers. It would seem that someone who smokes three packs a day enjoys smoking more than someone who smokes a single pack per day. If you ask the person who smokes three packs, they will tell you that they wish they could only smoke one. They envy the person who smokes less.[244] Why don't they just cut back? If they aren't enjoying all the cigarettes they are smoking, why smoke at all? Like drinking it is because they are tortured when they try to moderate or quit. A chain smoker no longer believes they are getting honest pleasure from smoking; in fact, they hate smoking but don't feel they can deal with life without cigarettes. This is not control; this is addiction.

Perhaps you feel you can, equipped with this new knowledge, drink only at a moderate stage again and stay there. Maybe you can; if alcohol hasn't yet changed your brain, moderation might be possible for a while. I have no desire to spend effort trying to moderate because alcohol no longer holds any allure. If I decided to moderate, it would be to fit in rather than because I desire to drink. I am aware that is a stupid reason to poison myself. I wouldn't take Advil if I didn't need to in order to be part of the crowd, and drinking is so much more dangerous.

I didn't mean to slip from "enjoying" a glass of wine with dinner to "enjoying" a bottle. Alcohol builds a tolerance, an immunity, which is simply our body trying to protect us from the poison we are consuming. We are compelled to drink more and more. When did I decide to drink more? I didn't. Slowly the wine wolf moved in and developed an insatiable thirst. I fed that thirst and it grew. Once I was poisoning myself every day, life became truly stressful. The subtle, "I need a drink" feeling was constant. Since life was stressful, I drank to deal with the stress. I cannot express how grateful I am to be out of that horrible nightmare. Alcohol is just not worth the risk of re-entering addiction's cycle of misery.

Look back at your drinking career. How many times did you have a few too many and throw up? What about a hangover? Or a headache? How many nights are fuzzy or completely erased? What about saying and doing things you regretted later? Maybe you said unnecessarily mean things to your friends or family. Are you starting to see how lucky you are? Can you start to see the delight of never, ever having to experience any of those things again?

A Brief Review

Perhaps you already feel the wonder of never having to make yourself stupid, hung over, or miserable again. The wonder of never *having* to drink again. If you haven't had that experience yet, don't worry. You may not experience it for weeks or months after you stop drinking. Your body will need to heal. You may need to actually experience life without alcohol to realize the truth of what I am telling you. That's OK. Since your unconscious mind is changing, it will be easier to abstain, to allow yourself to heal and to experience an alcohol-free life. You will now recognize the lies society feeds you. If you're still feeling specific doubts, go back and re-read the chapter that addressed those questions.

You started reading this book because you felt like alcohol was a problem in your life, and you wanted to regain control. However when you tried to cut back, you discovered that controlling alcohol intake was practically impossible, and the thought of not drinking again was terrifying. This reaction was different than what happened when you tried to control other food intakes in your life. Consider this example.

I became allergic to eggs after my second son was born. I liked eggs, and at first I would absentmindedly eat eggs, forgetting about my allergy. I would get a brutal allergic reaction. After a few of these painful reminders, I completely removed egg from my diet. It was not all that difficult, and it certainly wasn't emotional. I don't spend my life thinking about the fact that I no longer eat eggs. I barely give it any thought unless someone offers me an egg, and then I easily decline. Although eggs are delicious and nutritious, I do not mourn them. I feel no pain because I no longer eat eggs. When my doctor ran tests and initially diagnosed me with this allergy, I knew it would be a lifestyle adjustment, but I did not feel any dread; there was no emotional dependence. Instead, I was thankful that I finally understood the source of my painful allergic reactions.

By comparing these two experiences, you can recognize that we deceive ourselves when we believe we can control alcohol just like any other food. Alcohol's not just another food; it's an addictive drug. But we deny our dependence on it and say we can take it or leave it. This is because of the divide between your conscious mind and your unconscious mind. Once you see that drinking is creating problems for you, you consciously want to drink less. However, evidence clearly demonstrates that routine and customary decision-making processes (like regular drinking) do not occur fully within your conscious mind. According to Dr. Chris Firth, a professor of neuropsychology at the University College of London, there is a "bottoms-up" decision-making process, in which the unconscious parts of your brain weigh the rewards, make a decision, and interact with your conscious regions later, if at all.[245] Your unconscious mind controls your desires and your emotions. The unconscious runs on known programs, which exist from years of environmental conditioning.[246] It is in your unconscious mind that your beliefs, habits, and behaviors are formed and reinforced over time.[247]

The divide between what you consciously decide (to drink less) and what you unconsciously feel (you want a drink) creates heartache. Internal division, or cognitive dissonance, results in anguish and sorrow. You choose to obey your conscious mind and feel deprived when not drinking. Or you choose to give in to your deep cravings and drink. When you drink but don't consciously want to, you cannot understand why you've lost control. You feel weak and unable to stick to decisions or commitments.

You drank, your body became immune to drinking, and you drank more. You were in the habit of listening to that small voice saying, "A drink sounds good," so you drank anytime you wanted to. This is your baseline. Your baseline increases over time because your tolerance increases.

At the end I was drinking two bottles of wine a night. Moderating my drinking meant spending a lot of time and energy denying my cravings. This caused stress because my brain was split, my inner self divided. Soon life was dominated by when I would allow myself my next glass and how many glasses I would have. I may have been drinking in moderation, but I was far from free. I was more controlled by alcohol than I had ever been.

We only decide to cut back when our drinking starts to cause issues in our lives. Although we are duped into believing drinking provides pleasure or stress relief, alcohol wasn't that important when we did it all the time. We didn't think about it before it became a problem. We can't remember it that well. It certainly seems we took it for granted. It was simply part of our lifestyle.

Spending your life wanting something you can't have is not freedom. When you spend your day waiting for five o'clock, you don't enjoy the day. Five o'clock comes, the waiting is over, and you are duped into believing that the drink was the magic bullet—in reality it was relieving a craving. Ending the wanting.

Initially, when your resolve was strong, it seemed you could drink less. As a result you felt more in control and better about yourself. You suddenly had more money, and your health improved. These improvements actually conspired against you, making you forget why you quit. Like how food becomes more precious when you diet, alcohol becomes more precious when you abstain. Moderation is like an alcohol diet that will continue for the rest of your life. The longer you crave a drink, the greater the illusion of enjoyment when you give in.

And willpower is a finite and exhaustible resource, much like a muscle, that can be fatigued. Mark Muraven, a PhD candidate at Case Western Reserve University, wanted to understand why, if willpower was a skill (like riding a bicycle), he seemed to have it sometimes but was missing it at other times. He conducted an experiment to prove that willpower was more effective when conserved and that, when taxed, it could run out. Subjects, under the guise that they were participating in a taste-based experiment, were placed in a room with two bowls on the table: a bowl of fresh-baked cookies and a bowl of radishes. Half of the subjects were told to eat the cookies and ignore the radishes and half were told to eat the radishes and ignore the cookies. After five minutes they were given a puzzle that appeared easy but did not actually have a solution. Because the puzzle was impossible, continuing to work on it required willpower. The subjects who had previously exercised willpower by ignoring the cookies worked on the puzzle for 60% less time than the subjects who had not used any of their willpower reserves. Furthermore, the contrast in attitude between the subjects forced to eat radishes and those allowed to eat the cookies was drastic. The radish-eaters were surly, frustrated, and some even snapped at the researchers.[248]

It's easy to see how exercising and fatiguing our willpower to avoid alcohol, day after day, can make us bitter and unhappy. Willpower runs out, and you drink. This drink provides illusory relief, the forbidden fruit syndrome. The "pleasure" of relief is intensified because you've abstained. You regret the drink almost as soon as you consume it, and you deal with this regret by pouring another. The more dependent you are on alcohol, the more you convince yourself that you cannot enjoy life or cope with stress without it, and the quicker it eats at you. Your life becomes less fulfilling. You develop or reinforce a physical dependence, which ensures you stop receiving pleasure or stimulation in your nucleus accumbens from the activities you used to enjoy. This experience is like opening the front door of your mind and inviting depression in to live. You need to remember this: Alcohol physically alters your brain to remove your ability to enjoy normal things.[249]

Clearly, willpower is not the answer. The answer is simple. We must become aware that alcohol is creating our problems. Once the lifelong unconscious conditioning has been reversed, the unconscious mind, which is responsible for desires and emotions, will no longer desire a drink. Now drinking, or not, becomes a fully conscious decision. You only struggled to make rational decisions about alcohol because your unconscious mind had been conditioned to believe lies about alcohol and because alcohol's addictive nature physically affected you. The key is to make a conscious decision to see alcohol in its true form. To allow yourself to see what it really is and smugly decide that it is the last thing you would ever want to put in your amazing body. You will need to make a conscious and continuous effort to see alcohol as it really is from now on. What is so clear now may not be obvious in the future. Why? Because nothing has changed in our society. The media, your friends, and even family will continue to bombard your unconscious mind with the benefits of alcohol. Your unconscious mind will continue to be susceptible to all types of conditioning. The key is to realize this so you can make a deliberate and conscious effort to combat it. You fight the unwanted conditioning by being aware that it is happening. When a desire for a drink creeps back in you must immediately realize that you are being conditioned. You then can consciously question where that desire is really coming from. Examine it and understand if it is a solid, rational reason for drinking or if you have unknowingly allowed false truths to creep back in. As long as you are aware of what is happening, the conditioning will be easy to undo, and over time you will build solid armor against it. You can resist societal conditioning by being aware of it and taking immediate action to reverse it by recalling the truths you now know.

The new perspective you have gained cannot easily be unlearned. It is like an optical illusion—you see one thing until you gain a new perspective and see another. Once you see the new, it is difficult to go back to what you originally saw. I once believed the lie that drinking a liquid that systematically poisoned me and stole my confidence and my health was a good thing. How much easier it is to believe the truth that alcohol is an addictive poison. That all I have to do to be free forever is to stop drinking.

Once I was educated about the science of addiction and what alcohol was doing to my body and my brain it was easy to stop. Every day that goes by I am more, not less, sure of my decision. My eyes have been opened to the plight of others, and as a result my life is filled with gratitude for my freedom.

Again, it isn't easy to be different from the majority, especially my friends, but I am happy to be standing for something I know is right. As a result, self-loathing and a lack of self-respect have been replaced with confidence. I like who I am when I go to bed at night and when I wake up in the morning. My mind has more time and space, now that addiction doesn't dominate my thoughts. Time to spend with my family, to take care of myself, to progress my career, to write this book, to think about how to help others. Time to think about how to start a revolution in our society to wake people up to the danger we face.

It was strange at first. When I was drinking, my nights faded into oblivion. Now I am fully aware and alert from the moment I wake up until the moment I go to bed. What a gift. I make a conscious decision about when to sleep, based on feeling tired, not on how much I've drunk. My memories are not fuzzy, and I have no regrets. It's incredible to live a life where you don't need to hide anything, where you can be honest with yourself.

It takes a lot of courage to be different, to go against the majority. Courage I wouldn't have if I were still drinking and hating myself for it. I am no longer controlled by something I hate. There is true pleasure in leaving shame and misery behind. I find joy in the challenges before me—breaking the sober stigma and helping to eliminate the shame for all who choose to live free from the groupthink of alcohol by choosing a different path.

22.
THE SECRET TO HAPPILY AND
EASILY DRINKING LESS

"The first step toward change is awareness. The second step is acceptance."
—*Nathaniel Branden*

Special note: Reading this chapter before the rest of the book won't work. I know it's tempting, and I'm glad you share my eagerness, but the answers you seek are in the journey, not the destination. If you haven't read or understood the rest of the book, your unconscious, which is slow to change, will not have caught up with your conscious mind. You will still unconsciously believe that alcohol is your friend. Applying the approach, while this division of both wanting to drink and not wanting to drink exists inside you, may make things worse.

We've covered a lot of ground together, and you are now ready to embrace your new understanding and change. Congratulations! You've realized by now that I believe you are happiest when you are not drinking at all. When I talk about drinking less, I mean much less—in fact, I mean nothing. This idea may provoke some anxiety, and if you are still apprehensive, that's OK. You may need to experience the joy of life without alcohol to realize the truth of what you have read. That's no problem. This is new territory, and you don't know what to expect. You don't want to make a commitment you're not sure you can keep.

What is important is that you are wary, for all the reasons we've discussed, of moderation. There is no halfway once you are addicted. Your brain physically and chemically changes, which makes moderation next to impossible. If your brain hasn't suffered chemical changes, they can happen at any time. It is the accumulation of alcohol in your body, no matter how little you drink each time, that creates pathways of addiction in your brain. The problem with alcohol is that the brain doesn't simply forget it. Dopamine is the learning molecule, and your brain has learned to crave alcohol. You can abstain, and these cravings will disappear, but if you drink again your brain immediately remembers. A conditioned response usually stays.[250]

This is why a single drink can land you back into the painful cycle of addiction. You go directly from the enjoyment of one drink to the lowest point of your descent. The key through every cycle is to remember you are strong. In order to be strong enough to choose freedom, you must forgive yourself for each failure. Forgiveness and gentleness with yourself, no matter how long your personal journey takes, are vital and central to finding your freedom.

The beauty of making a decision is that once that decision is made, you will see alcohol as a villainous traitor instead of an alluring seductress. One overarching choice frees you from all the little daily choices that alcoholics suffer for a lifetime. Instead of deciding to forgo every beer presented to you for the rest of your life, you decide once and forevermore to see the truth about alcohol. This single choice means freedom and is much easier on your psyche than daily decisions. A single choice can be made in conscious knowledge, whereas daily decisions rely on constant willpower.

The true difference is that this single choice decides not whether to drink the one drink in front of you, but the amount of space you will give alcohol in your life. A single choice is like a breakup, or better yet, like a marriage to a new, healthier life. Once you are married you no longer have to decide every day that you won't flirt with the handsome man on the airplane. That decision is already made. You are married. At first, when someone flirts with you, it takes practice to consciously think of your husband and how lucky you are to have him. Likewise, it takes practice to remind yourself of the amber death that is in the bottles in the beautiful bar. You will need to make a conscious effort to protect your unconscious mind.

Once a firm commitment is made, you face no decision. When the handsome man smiles at you, there is no willpower required to remain faithful. You simply remember that you are married, for better or worse. At the bar, again there is no wondering if now is the time to have that one drink—after all, this beautiful display of alcohol is so tempting. You simply remember your decision and remind yourself of the truths you now know. A single, strong choice made with all of your brain liberates you from willpower. It frees you from the hundreds of decisions you would have to make if you decided to take it one drink at a time.

And don't forget. If you do give in and have that one drink, your enemy, addiction, can immediately move back in. He plants himself in your brain and starts exactly where he left off. The pathways of addiction are still there. You will not notice him when he is starved and weak, but once he is fed, he grows strong. Why? Because your brain remembers. This enemy is physical dependence. Irrational cravings. Inexplicable behaviors. If you let him in by feeding him, his thirst for booze can be stronger than anything in your arsenal. You are easily overcome by your cravings. Remember that wanting is not enjoying.

The addiction adversary does not just attack a certain defective segment of our population called alcoholics. Sure, he might move in at a different pace depending on how your brain is wired. And sure, there are different physical reactions in each of us that make the artificial high alcohol provides more or less powerful inside our minds. The point is that you cannot become addicted to alcohol if you don't drink.[251] And no matter who you are, if you drink enough, you will become addicted. No one is safe; everyone needs to approach alcohol with caution.

Even if you drink moderately, it is vital to be aware that your drinking is most likely increasing, not decreasing, over time. There are some exceptions. Let's take my friend Todd. He approaches alcohol with extreme caution, and for this reason he allows himself a single beer on Friday and a single beer on Saturday. He never drinks more than one, and he doesn't drink on other occasions. He is strict with these rules, and it is his way of ensuring addiction does not take over. He will probably, as long as he maintains this same level of staunch self-control, go his entire life without developing a physical dependence. That being said, Todd's body is building a tolerance to even those single beers, and the actual effect he believes them to have is probably nonexistent.

While it's great to have that level of self-control, the majority of us are not like Todd. His commitment to this moderate drinking is a result of his religion and his commitment to his faith. Yet even in this situation, I wonder, why drink at all? Over time the beers cease to have any effect whatsoever, so why even drink them? In my mind, this behavior is like smoking two cigarettes a week. Perhaps there is some placebo effect of self-indulgence, but personally I just don't see the point. And further, if Todd really desires the beer, surely he wants more than just one. Surely every Friday and Saturday night he feels some sort of sadness when this single beer has been drunk. "Oh well, that's it then. I'll enjoy another one next week."

It is important to realize that even in Todd's extreme case we can't assume that he will be able to keep his two-beers-a-week limit forever. The very fact he drinks those two beers means he enjoys drinking beer. If something was to change in his life, who's to say he wouldn't use this coveted beverage to self-medicate? And even if he limits himself forever to these two beers, who's to say it won't become an obsession where he spends his week looking forward to his weekend beer? No one can predict when we will slide from drinking without physical dependence to drinking with physical dependence. With some alcoholics it happens within the first few drinks. With others it may never happen during their lifetime. There are a million reasons for this. It is impossible to predict.

It is important to realize when it happened to you, or to accept the fact that if you have not yet reached a point of physical dependence on alcohol, you have no way of knowing what drink will push you across that line. With every glass, you are one drink closer to a physical alcohol addiction.

> *"When you can stop you don't want to,*
> *and when you want to stop, you can't . . ."*
> —*Luke Davies*

Your enemy becomes strong when fed, and he will push you around. You may have kicked him out of your house, but he is waiting outside, plotting. Imagine moderating a cocaine or heroin habit. If you want your mind to be free, and you want complete control back, remember that moderation is not control or freedom. Unless you want to be consumed by an addictive poison that will do nothing for you except eventually kill you, you need to make a commitment to fly away from the pitcher plant, starve your mortal enemy, and revel in your freedom.

So what's the secret? It's simple, and it has two parts: awareness and acceptance.

First, be aware that you have become emotionally and/or physically dependent on alcohol. You cannot fix an issue that you don't realize is there. You are in the grasp of your adversary: alcohol.

You may still think that stopping will be hard, that you won't be able to resist social pressures, and you will feel deprived. The truth is that if you decide in your heart and mind that you never again want to be a slave to alcohol, you have removed any indecision. You have ended your cognitive dissonance. You have ended the internal conflict.

I won't lie to you, depending on how much alcohol you have consumed and for how long, you may have some physical withdrawal symptoms. But when your mind is in the right place, the physical symptoms are greatly diminished because you know why they exist, and you know they will end. They may not be comfortable, but with each physical discomfort, remember alcohol is creating the discomfort. If you are fearful of withdrawal symptoms because of your level of dependence, please seek medical attention to assist you in the process. Think of it this way: You are in a battle, and withdrawal symptoms mean you are winning. You are killing off your mortal enemy. There may be some trauma in the fight, but once he is dead, you are free. You can start to live a happier, healthier life than you ever imagined possible.

You are strong, and by making your commitment you have already won. The fight may not be fun, but it won't last forever—hopefully no more than a few weeks, with the worst part over by the end of the first week. You can do this, and each day will get easier. You are fighting for your life, and victory is yours. I know you can, and deep inside you, you know you can too.

It may be easier than you think. It was for me. Why? Because it is the mental craving that makes it hard to stop. In the Vietnam War, many American soldiers began using heroin with alarming regularity. The government was sure they were going to have an entire generation of heroin addicts on their hands when the war was over, and they tracked these soldiers carefully once they returned to the states. Yet once the soldiers were home and reunited with their families, they quit heroin, easily, with almost no withdrawal symptoms or relapses. This demonstrates how much addiction is in your mind and how freedom comes with a clear decision. The soldiers were not willing to use heroin at home, so they decided not to.[252] There is a good chance you won't experience any withdrawals, and if you do they will be minimal. Who wouldn't be ill for a few weeks to cure themselves from an incurable disease? Don't forget, every symptom you feel was caused by alcohol. You will never, ever have to feel it again.

What to expect? It depends on how long and how heavily you have been drinking. I suffered anxiety and a lack of concentration. I had night sweats; I think that was my body ridding itself of the toxins I had consumed. Some describe the experience like a mild flu. I didn't mind my symptoms because they spelled victory. I knew a drink would make things worse, not better. I was overcome with happiness and the euphoria of knowing my life had forever changed, which made the physical discomfort minimal. It felt like my desire to drink had been surgically removed from my brain, and the result was giddiness. This far outweighed any physical discomfort.

"You are in the midst of transition and . . . sickness is the means by which an organism frees itself from what is alien; so one must simply help it to be sick, to have its whole sickness and to break out with it, since that is the way it gets better."
—*Rainer Maria Rilke*

Something else happens after you stop. You start to look back at your drinking career in a different light, through the lens of self-acceptance and honesty. It's not easy to face all of the things you did and said, perhaps all of the people you hurt. It can be very hard to forgive yourself. You need to let it go, apologize to people if you feel compelled to, but most importantly forgive yourself. Realize that you were captive, a prisoner of your adversary, in the prison of addiction. There is no reason to waste your bright and exciting future dwelling on past mistakes, though now and again you may revisit your past and remember the horrors of addiction. Addiction takes a considerate, honest person and tears them down until they're doing the most horrible things. Also, remember it was not your fault. Alcohol physically changed how your brain works. You were deceived. You are healing, and you don't have to be sick again.

When a former alcoholic continues to crave alcohol months or years after reaching sobriety, it's not because of the addictive nature of the drug—that craving is physical and relatively easy to deal with once the alcohol is purged from the body. The physical addiction will go away when the alcohol is completely out of your system. If you are a chronic drinker and drink to the point that you are ill yet keep drinking, you may have altered your brain to such a degree that you need to be isolated from alcohol while it leaves your system. You may need professional help in the form of a rehabilitation center, and I encourage you to get that type of help. For most others, you will easily be able to overcome the physical cravings because you know the cure. You know you are on your way to being happy and whole. The mental craving, which is generally stronger, only comes when you feel you are making a sacrifice, giving up something desirable. Once you see there is nothing worth desiring, your mental cravings will be gone. You will crave alcohol as much as you crave drinking motor oil.

The beauty of *This Naked Mind* is that once you understand the scientific basis for your inexplicable behaviors and the truth about what alcohol does to your body and mind you are not likely to fall victim to addiction again. Even if it takes you a few cycles of relapse to fully grasp the truth, you will be aware, educated, and knowledgeable. That is vital to your permanent freedom. You will no longer suffer the mental division caused by one side of your brain wanting a drink and the other side feeling like you should cut back. Both sides of that struggle are driven by fear. Fear that you will be unhappy without drinking, and fear that you are harming yourself by drinking. You are about to end that struggle. You didn't suffer from it before your first drink, nor will you after your last.

> *"The more you depend on alcohol, the more convinced you are that you cannot cope or enjoy yourself without it and the quicker you die inside. Then your life is less fulfilling and when this happens, the more you rely on alcohol to fill that gap. This is why I was so afraid of stopping."*
> —Jason Vale

Second, you must accept the truth about alcohol. Decide to let go of your attachment to alcohol by accepting that it does nothing for you. When you stop drinking, you are killing your mortal enemy. He has stolen or will steal more from you than you can imagine. He steals more than 2.4 million hours of life (just in the U.S.) every year.[253]

You now know that you are gaining everything rather than giving anything up. You are killing your enemy, not losing your friend. You can be free the easy way, by accepting the truth about alcohol or you can make it difficult for yourself by retaining some of the unconscious conditioning and seeing alcohol as desirable. If you retain a desire to drink you will have to deprive yourself every time you decide not to drink, for the rest of your life. Why not make it easy for yourself? Why not allow yourself the freedom you deserve? All the pain you have been in, all the pain you have caused, was because of alcohol. You may feel excited, or apprehensive, or not quite prepared. That's OK. It's natural to feel a bit afraid. You're venturing into the unknown, which can cause apprehension. Don't worry. Sometimes you need to go ahead and jump, and let the joy of living without alcohol demonstrate how much better your life has become. Start the journey with joy—you are about to accomplish something truly awesome.

Start Now!

The first secret to happily and easily stopping drinking is deciding you want to be free. Have a good talk with yourself, with those close to you, those who will hold you accountable as you make this decision. There has never been a better time than now.

If you have lingering doubts or still believe that alcohol provides enjoyment or relief, re-read the Liminal Points or join thisnakedmind .com/next for community and support. Believing that you will get enjoyment from a drink is different than having a few cravings. Cravings are normal and relatively easy to deal with. You are changing your entire life, and it may take some getting used to. You might crave a drink in the next few days, months, or even years, but the craving will be small and entirely conscious. The understanding you've gained from this book will allow you to approach the craving rationally, making a fact-based decision. Remind yourself of the principles in this book, and the cravings will die. Since you will not suffer from an unconscious and unexplainable desire to drink, you can easily put any cravings in their place by remembering the truth about alcohol and by seeing that there is nothing to crave.

You may find that your brain has been conditioned to believe it wants a beer at a sports game; you will need to change that. You've been drinking for a long time, and this is a big change. It will take some getting used to. If you let yourself continue to crave a drink or wonder if drinking is pleasant, you will start reconditioning your unconscious to believe all the same old lies. Don't do that; there is no need. Look honestly at the feeling, identify where it is coming from (most likely it will be because everyone around you is doing it and you feel out of place), and realize how stupid it is to drink bad-tasting poison just to fit in. Take a stand for yourself, realizing you want nothing to do with the groupthink of alcohol. Be brave and be different.

Make a choice to let go of your desire for alcohol. Choose to see alcohol in her true form. Society paints alcohol as beautiful, but look beyond all the enticing social cues that conceal the danger. Our conditioning draws us to her like moths to a flame, like a bee into the pitcher plant. But the beauty is an illusion. You now see beyond the surface, and there is nothing but death.

> *"Every time you wake up after drinking, you are physically, mentally, emotionally, socially and financially worse off than if you had not taken the drug in the first place."*
> —*Jason Vale*

Once you realize you want to be free there is only one thing left to do. Deliver the fatal blow to your adversary. Cut off his food supply:

Stop Drinking

Allow yourself to see alcohol in its true form, eliminate your desire to drink, and free yourself completely from the misery of addiction.

Sometimes it is a good idea to have a final drink. This marks the occasion, letting you know you are truly free. Don't make it your favorite drink—use some kind of hard alcohol. You can make it a ritual, a commitment to your new life. Concentrate on how bad it really tastes and wonder how you ever let this toxic liquid control you and why you ever paid for the privilege (heavy drinkers can spend about $400,000 on alcohol during their lives, which makes your last drink akin to winning the lottery!).[254]

Whether you decide to have a final drink or not doesn't matter. What's important is to know, *without a doubt*, that you are free. Free to enjoy this beautiful life. The reminders below will help you navigate this new, abundant life.

Reminders for the Journey

"If you really want to remove a cloud from your life, you do not make a big production of it, you just relax and remove it from your thinking."
—*Richard Bach*

This Naked Mind speaks to both your conscious and unconscious mind by reversing the conditioning you have received from the media, friends, family, and society. You must not forget you are still surrounded by these messages, and you will still be bombarded with them every day. It is difficult not to be influenced. Each one is targeted to deceive you into believing that you are missing out by not drinking. For me, revisiting the principles of the program quickly reverses any unintended conditioning. You can do this by joining us in community at thisnakedmind.com/next. Journaling, blogging, and community have been shown useful in this process. Our community site allows you to have your own blog where you can give and receive encouragement and support. If you want, you can join under a pseudonym, making it anonymous. It can be useful just to hear about other people's journeys or to bounce around ideas.

You can re-read part or all of this book. One of my early readers read the book four times in her first sixteen days of becoming alcohol-free. She is still happily free but the conditioning in her life was such that she needed to ensure the information stuck. That's OK. Do what you need to do to make sure you fully understand the truth both now and in the future.

Here are a few tips that have helped me:

Don't put off the day you decide to stop drinking. Why not make it today? There will always be an excuse. Isn't there a wedding coming up? Or a football game? Perhaps there is stress in your life that you need to deal with. Don't fall for that. That is what you've been doing your entire life, and it hasn't worked. Drinking just pours more stress into your life. There is no need to wait and no need to be frightened. The instant you decide to be free, you will be free. You won't need to avoid your friends or social situations. In fact, you will enjoy them much more.

Today can be the first day of the rest of your life. Make it a celebration—you have done something incredible. Celebrate however you choose, but do something special and commemorative. Declare your freedom. Your entire life is about to start. Relish the moment. Going back to a naked mind is no small thing. You are already free. Own it. Make a commitment to yourself, and if you want, declare your freedom to your family and friends. The moment I knew I was free, I sent an overly-excited group email. Cheesy, I know, but it made me feel great. You deserve to feel great. Well done and congratulations!

You may have already experienced the incredible realization that your whole life has changed, and you are free. I remember it vividly; I was in awe. It is one of the happiest moments of my life. If this hasn't happened for you, it's OK. For some it happens by the end of the book, and for others it happens a few weeks or months after stopping, when you realize that it's all true—that life is amazing without alcohol. Importantly, don't try to force it. It will come. It might be after an occasion you never imagined you could enjoy without drinking, like a tailgate party, a BBQ, or a nightclub. You suddenly realize you had a great time and drinking alcohol didn't cross your mind. Just let the moment come. Go and be surprised when it suddenly dawns on you that you are free.

For the first few days to a week, your body will be going through detox. It takes ten or more days for alcohol to fully leave your system. Since you have altered your dopamine levels, you may experience cravings. This is a reality, and you have to starve those cravings, allow them to die. They will die. When the psychological desire to drink is eliminated, the physical aspects are manageable. Since your mind is free, killing these cravings can be an enjoyable experience. You are starving your mortal enemy. Your cravings may take some time to go away. That's normal. Think of it as your dopamine monster, a monster you want to make smaller and smaller until it shuts up and leaves. And it will. You are now in control, not your cravings. Don't forget that. And take care of yourself. Do things that make you feel good; you deserve it.

Feel free to think about the fact that you no longer drink, but think in terms of "I don't have to drink" rather than "I don't get to drink." It's true. You are free. You never have to experience another hangover, embarrassment, or headache related to drinking. Best of all, you won't experience the mental stress of wondering how much is too much or the black shadow that comes when you know you are drinking more than you should. You never have to drink again. No one will force you. You are again in control of your destiny. This is great news.

Remember, this new life will be an adjustment. You have reached for a drink for every conceivable reason for years, maybe decades. It's understandable that habits can linger. But if you pinpoint why you actually want the drink, you'll soon find that your craving will disappear again. You will realize the reason is just an excuse, and you don't actually want a drink. It's just your mind playing tricks on you. If your craving continues, re-read sections of the book or visit this nakedmind.com/next where you will find additional tools to support this amazing adjustment you are making.

Having just one drink causes the vicious cycle to begin, but you might be stubborn and need to find that out for yourself. If at some point you do, don't beat yourself up. Learn. And love yourself. Remember you are only human. But be on your guard. Society will continue to tell you how amazing alcohol is, and a voice may creep in suggesting that you are missing out. It's all lies. The further I get from my drinking past, the better my life becomes.

The "just one" game will cloud your judgment and cause you pain. Nothing has changed, alcohol is still addictive, and the danger is still present. You've realized there is no true pleasure in drinking. You understand you don't need to drink; you only thought you needed to. When you start to play the "just a few" game, you allow yourself to be duped again. You allow yourself to be deceived into believing there is pleasure in drinking. You have been fighting this mental battle long enough. Remind yourself of alcohol's true nature, that all it actually does is deaden your senses to the point of oblivion . . . oh, and fuel your car. Remind yourself that life with alcohol is homogenous and that with each drink you are not only losing years of your life, but also precious memories of the only life you have.

Sometimes when society all around me is lauding booze as the "elixir of life," it's hard to see the harm in just one drink. But when I start to entertain the idea of "just one," I become very uncomfortable. It's clear why. Indecision creates mental division, which causes pain. As soon as I realize what is happening, I remind myself that alcohol was never my friend but an enemy in disguise. I remember the pain of addiction and how thankful I am to be free. I also realize that I don't get any real joy from drinking; it just makes me tired and grumpy. The pain evaporates. Just remember, you are stronger than any craving. You are in control. And try not to worry about it. It's OK. It will pass. Your brain can crave anything, and if it starts to shout at you that you need a drink, just remember who is boss—you are.

Your change won't be easy for the drinkers you spend time with. They may mourn it. It's easy to understand why. If you are in a room full of people all taking the same drug, it is easier to not think about it. They are unknowingly deceiving themselves, telling lies and believing them.

If you forget you no longer drink, that's OK. I was drinking tonic and lime, and the waitress asked if I wanted another one. I said, "Yes, gin and tonic please," then caught and corrected myself. It was embarrassing. I'm sure she thought I was jonesing for some gin. The truth was that I wasn't thinking about not drinking, and habitual words just slipped out. If you've ever tried to stop cussing (a serious vice of mine), you know how words can just come out. This is actually great news; it means you are not thinking about alcohol. When you are consciously trying not to drink and exercising willpower, you don't make that type of mistake. Alcohol was so far from my mind that I didn't remember I didn't drink. Talk about being free.

This is life, real life. You will have good days, great days, bad days, and horrible days. That's OK. Remember, if drinking made you happy, you would never have been unhappy as a drinker. Alcohol doesn't make you happy, but we know it can make you very unhappy. It's OK to live this life as it is, in all its raw, naked beauty. It's OK to cry, to scream, to be frustrated, and to feel. This is your life, and it's the only one you get. Accept it and accept yourself. You are an incredible human being, and you have so much to give. If you have a great day—live it up. If you have a shit day—remember it will pass. And if for some reason it doesn't pass, if ceasing to self-medicate through alcohol reveals that you are indeed struggling with depression or anxiety, please get help. Remember, alcohol was never helping. It was hiding a real issue that needs to be fixed. It is important to find the right treatment. Depression is not a weakness; it is a disease. You can find help that will actually improve your life rather than steal it like alcohol does. Please do so.

There are a few things that, contrary to popular belief, you should do. First, with the *Naked Mind* approach, it's OK to think about the fact that you no longer drink. There is no reason not to. You got here by questioning everything, examining everything, and allowing yourself to see stuff differently. Don't stop thinking critically now. Finding your truth, in all areas of life, is a beautiful thing.

Many people report dreaming about drinking after they have stopped. That's OK; it's natural. It's happened to me plenty of times.

I would realize I was halfway through a pint (in my dream) and panic (in my dream), worried that I was again caught in the tangled web of alcohol addiction. Waking up reminds me how grateful I am to be free. If you dream-drink and enjoy it, that's OK too. You've been drinking for years. It's understandable that your dream self will need a bit of time to catch up. It doesn't mean you are sliding back or that you have a sincere desire to drink. There is no need to worry about it. Most likely you will be like me, waking up with relief that you are free and that drinking is in your rearview mirror.

Second, there is no need to avoid your drinking friends or places you used to go to drink. You are free to do whatever you want. But be kind to yourself, and only go if you truly enjoy the activity and the company. There is no point in wasting this beautiful life doing things or spending time with people that don't bring you authentic pleasure. You are free. Enjoy it. The more you remind yourself of the fact that you are free from alcohol, the happier you will be.

I was not prepared for how strong the reactions would be when I stopped drinking. Drinkers are very curious when someone suddenly stops drinking. It's assumed that you lost control and are an alcoholic. Ironically, you are the one who no longer drinks, but you're supposed to be the one with the problem. They are still drinking while asking if I have a drinking problem.

People can be aggressive in demanding my reasons. Then after I explain, everyone starts to tell me all the reasons they drink. Unprompted, they all start to tell me why they don't have a problem with booze. Funny, right? When I told people I was no longer eating eggs, no one started to tell me all their justifications for eating eggs or insisting that they didn't have an egg-eating problem.

Be prepared for mixed reactions. It's OK. You didn't do this for anyone else; you did it for you. They may now be jealous of you. They are wondering how you're still enjoying yourself, how you're still happy and relaxed. They will wonder how in the world you did it; they will be baffled by your strength.

Remember, ignorance isn't bliss. Even if someone is completely unaware of being stuck, they are not experiencing bliss. Alcohol doesn't change; it is still harming their health, stealing their money, robbing them of energy, and fraying their nerves. They are building a tolerance to it, and there is no doubt that they will be drinking more a year from now or five years from now than they are today. With alcohol, ignorance is not bliss.

You have so much to look forward to. It was such delight for me to realize it was the company of the people I enjoyed, not the alcohol, that I loved. Enjoy doing all sorts of things for the first time. Start today. And with every experience marvel at the fact that it's life, not alcohol, that makes things worthwhile. Before *This Naked Mind*, you thought quitting drinking would be miserable, that life would be such a bore. The opposite is true, and it's glorious. You can have an amazing time without inebriating and poisoning yourself. This is great news.

Now that you are free, make sure to guard your freedom by guarding your mind. All decisions are yours, but when making them please remember that alcohol does not change; it will trick and deceive you. It will create a need for itself, and when you become physically addicted (which may happen after a night of drinking or just a few drinks), your mind will no longer be entirely yours. You will start to believe the tricks your mind will play on you. These tricks get you to feed the physical aspect of alcohol addiction, to feed alcohol's need for itself. You will feel divided again, and you will do things to end that division. You might justify your behavior or close your mind to the truths you know now. It is a slippery slope and alcohol itself will not change. Alcohol is addictive, and when you attempt moderation, you end up spending excessive time and effort, not on living but on moderating, determining when to and when not to drink. There is an easy way out, but you need to decide to take it. Today your unconscious mind, your entire mind, no longer craves alcohol like it once did. Take this opportunity to free yourself.

Some drinkers think quitting is like losing a best friend. You know the truth: This friend is actually a backstabbing fiend who wants to slowly kill you by destroying your body and your mind. This friend is your mortal enemy—who, if given the chance, will keep you engaged in a horrible, confusing battle until your death. Don't let him. Kill him now and forever. Enjoy his death, dance on his grave, and remember there is absolutely nothing to mourn.

Revisit the truths in this book and find additional community and support at thisnakedmind.com/next. It is difficult to live in this world where we are constantly assaulted with hundreds of pro-drinking messages every day. You will need to be on your guard, or you will again fall victim to your mortal enemy, and he will slowly, cunningly steal your life.

Finally, be happy. You can now see that quitting does not have to be tragic. When you see the truth you can't help but feel joy at your newfound freedom. There is nothing to mourn, you have killed your enemy, not lost a friend. You have just added precious hours to your life and put a significant amount of money back in your pocket. Spend your time and money doing things that bring you true happiness. It can be fun to make a list of what types of things you enjoy and are looking forward to. Then do them. And enjoy your wonderful *Naked Life*!

23.
THE JOURNEY: "RELAPSE"

"It's better not to give in to it. It takes ten times longer to put yourself back together than it does to fall apart."
—*The Hunger Games: Mockingjay*

This Naked Mind is about being aware, stripping away that which is false and finding truth. Your life will be so much better when alcohol is a small and irrelevant part of it. I believe your best chance at peace in your relationship with alcohol is by starving the alcohol monster and letting him rot.

I don't like the word relapse. It seems to impose unspoken rules and judgments, reeking of stigma. But we cannot ignore it. Your alcohol monster may reawaken, maybe more than once, during your journey to his final death. You must know that even with the best intentions and the strongest commitments, you may, someday, allow alcohol back into your life. We must face this reality. We cannot hide from it. Our intelligence allows us to protect ourselves, avoiding traps by understanding how they work. Awareness of risk diminishes it.

Drinking again may not be a big deal. But more likely it will become incredibly painful. The alcohol monster will awaken stronger than before. You may find yourself deeper in the pit than ever. Your loved ones have seen you healing. Even if you never verbalized commitments, they have been made through your actions. Drinking will mean breaking those commitments, not only to those you love but, even harder, to yourself. You may lose trust in your own judgment, resolve, and strength. This is not a reason to avoid commitments. Your strong decisions are a vital part of destroying your thirst for alcohol. But if you do fall prey, you may find yourself deep in a pit of self-loathing, addiction, and despair. So deep that freedom appears impossible.

Addiction is a war with the highest stakes imaginable. For me, the most terrifying thing about relapse is how easy it is to believe that, by relapsing, we have lost the war. Society tells us that if we are unable to stick to our decisions, we are weak. If we break promises, we cannot be trusted. It's easy to believe that making mistakes makes us useless. We figure that if we "fall off the wagon" we might as well "go all the way" because "it's too late now." We feel beyond repair, no longer worth fixing. We pile up internal guilt, convinced we deserve the hatred of those we love. So we punish ourselves, often by drinking more—even to the point where we are sick. We drink to oblivion, binging to numb ourselves to the horror of our failure. Hating ourselves more each time. Falling further and feeling lower than ever before.

It is a mistake to believe that by losing a battle we have lost the war. The truth is that each battle makes us stronger as long as we remain committed to a better tomorrow. We must fight this battle with compassion and forgiveness. We must allow that lost battle to be a reminder of all the reasons we quit rather than an unforgivable mistake. We must remember: Losing a battle does not mean we have lost the war.

Drinking will remind you why you stopped. You will remember how much effort it took to moderate. How painful hangovers are. You will remember the internal struggle, the recrimination, and deception. It may come after that first drink or down the road after a time of successful moderation when your willpower runs out. Let your mistakes become powerful reminders of your freedom. Let them tell the story of how far you've come. Let them be a stepping stone on your journey.

Examine why you drank. Perhaps, as you heal, your reasons for not drinking alcohol seem less important. The pain fades, and you wonder: Is alcohol really as bad as I imagined? Am I missing out? Can I now, with enough distance, moderate?

Maybe you feel socially isolated and desire connection. You wonder if you would fit in better and have more friends if you had an occasional drink. If you struggle from loneliness, you must find connections. But alcohol will never heal your loneliness or provide friendship.

If you are struggling with depression or anxiety, you may begin to wonder if a drink would take the edge off and provide relief. Remember, drinking is like turning off your check engine light. It may temporarily numb your symptoms, but it can never heal you.

You may drink to fill a void in your life. Societal conditioning convinces you that alcohol is key to filling the holes inside you. This will never happen; alcohol can only tear you further apart.

And again, if you have a strong physical addiction, freedom may not be easy or even possible without others to fight alongside you. You may need a rehabilitation center or an ongoing support group. You may need to call for backup. Call for backup now. Discuss this possibility with those close to you; ensure they are prepared to fight with you when the battle comes. Get whatever help you need. Asking for help does not make you weak; it makes you strong.

You will overcome this. Let each temptation, each battle bring you closer to winning the war. Learn from each fight, discovering your truth about alcohol and its role in your life. Alcohol does not define you. It does not give you worth. It is not who you are. It will not fix your problems, solve your loneliness, or provide any of the answers you seek.

This is a journey, not a destination. It is a road that no one can walk but you. These are choices that no one can make but you. But know that by committing to a different future, no matter how many battles you have ahead of you, the war has already been won.

24.
PAY IT FORWARD

"Don't spend your precious time asking 'Why isn't the
world a better place?' The question to ask is 'How can I
make it better?' To that there is an answer."
—*Leo F. Buscaglia*

Life is an incredible journey. It can be hard to understand why we are
here and what it all means. I am convinced that our responsibility, as
humans, is to take care of and respect each other and this planet, our
home. But in order to do that we must first take care of and respect
ourselves. You are one of the brave. You will pioneer this change,
helping save our children, our society, and our future.

We must love ourselves first, take care of ourselves, change our
habits and behaviors, and then we can change the world. How do we
have a chance of overcoming war or hunger or saving our beautiful
Mother Earth if we don't first love ourselves? How can we become
enlightened, open-minded enough to accept other humans with love
and respect, when we don't respect our own decisions?

I can't begin to tell you how much you will accomplish when you
are mentally and physically healthy. When you combine your health

with a true sense of self-acceptance, self-respect, and self-love there is nothing you can't do. This is the way to change our world; it's cliché, but it truly starts within. By solving our own problems with alcohol, we will have the mental capacity, the internal love, and the drive to solve the world's problems. They say peace begins at home, and your truest home is inside yourself.

Take your time; adjust to your new life. Enjoy breaking all of the associations. It's a game for me, doing something I couldn't have imagined without a drink and enjoying it more than before. It reinforces my resolve and fills me with gratitude.

> *"Life is a series of natural and spontaneous changes. Don't resist them; that only creates sorrow. Let reality be reality. Let things flow naturally forward in whatever way they like."*
> —*Lao Tzu*

Your body and mind will soon heal from the trauma of drinking and hating yourself for it. Your body is incredible; it will quickly purge itself of the poison. Your mind may take a bit longer. You may have doubts, lingering cravings, or times of disbelief. That's all OK; don't worry. And don't try not to think about it. A 1987 study from Harvard confirmed that when you try to repress certain thoughts, you think about them more.[255] It's OK to think about what comes naturally into your head; just think—that's the important part.

Take care of yourself; you deserve it. One day, in the very near future, when you feel at peace and whole, perhaps your gratitude will overflow. There is incredible power in giving to someone else the gift you have been given, in helping someone become free. It is an amazing and life-affirming thing to help another person. Either individually or by joining me in this movement, let's ensure we and our children exercise the right level of caution with alcohol. There is so much to be done, from simply helping one person to getting in touch and spreading the word.

Helping other people is one of life's great secrets of happiness. Compassion is actually quite selfish. The Dalai Lama said in a TV interview on ABC News, "The practice of compassion is ultimately to benefit you. So I usually say: We are selfish, but be wise selfish (helping others) rather than foolish selfish (only helping yourself)."[256] In fact, exercising compassion and helping other people is incredibly satisfying. Brain scans show that acts of kindness register in our brain's pleasure centers much like eating chocolate. The same pleasure centers in the brain light up when we get a gift as when we donate to charity.[257] Helping others ultimately helps you. It is an amazing and completely natural high. Over and over it has been shown that service to others is a vital part of our happiness as humans.

Do it. Pay it forward. Go gently and remember never to judge. Change starts here, change starts now, and you are the most important part of this change. The world needs you to be your best. The world needs you to help save it, one person at a time. At the end of the day, *This Naked Mind* is about a mind that comes to care for and respect itself, just as it is, just as it came into this world—simply naked. Remove the pollutants you struggle with. When we do that, we save ourselves and prepare this amazing planet and all its incredible inhabitants for the next generation, for our children.

Pay it forward; it's your turn.

Dear Reader,

If you feel inspired to pay it forward, there is one simple and powerful action you can take immediately. Share your story. You might worry that your story isn't relevant, or that no one can relate. Alcohol addiction does not discriminate; it touches people from every walk of life. No matter your story, someone will be touched and inspired by what you have to say. Your story will provide hope; it may change someone's life.

Perhaps you are thinking, "Wait, I'm not ready to commit to give up drinking." That is not important. *This Naked Mind* is not about rules. It's about knowledge and awareness. It's about ending internal struggle and finding peace with yourself—no matter what that means for you.

What will inspire people is how your perspective has changed. If you have taken small actions, like choosing not to drink on a single occasion and realizing you enjoyed yourself, that is powerful! That is worth sharing. Together we can break down the societal conditioning that constantly tells us alcohol is a vital part of life.

Your voice is important. It can be just as significant to give someone hope that they could enjoy a dinner out without wine than to tell them you've sworn off booze forever. Tell *your* story, as raw and real and true as it is. If there is hope, write about it. Peace? Write about it. Fear? Write about it! Struggle? Write about it! Just tell it honestly and from the heart.

Alcohol addiction remains a hidden and stigmatic problem marked by denial and fear. There are millions suffering alone, afraid to ask the question, "Am I drinking too much?" We worry others will think we have a problem or that we will have to admit to having an incurable illness. So we tell ourselves, and everyone around us, that we are fine, saving our concerns for midnight Google searches with our private browsers turned on. This is where your story, anonymous or not, will greet others just like you. This is where your story will make a difference, sparking hope for someone. We must be brave and vulnerable, letting those who still suffer know they are not alone in their struggle. We must force these questions and answers out into the open. We must let people know that there is hope and that life truly is much better when alcohol is a small and irrelevant part of it.

If you are considering it but are stuck on what to write, I recommend starting at the beginning. When did you start to drink, and how did you feel about it? Talk about your drinking life and how it progressed. Share some of the more poignant moments in your journey. Describe when you realized you needed to change and why. What has that journey looked like? Conclude with how you feel today, in this moment. Do you feel a glimmer of hope for the first time in a long time? Share that. Are you planning to give up drinking? Share that. Again, the only requirement is that you are heartfelt and honest. And you might be surprised—writing your story may prove a powerful step in your own journey. You may find writing to be freeing and healing.

There are many ways to share your story. I would be honored to feature your story on my blog or on my podcast. Your words will be invaluable for people who are looking for support and inspiration.

Thank you for considering sharing your story, and no matter what you decide I wish you the best in your journey.

You are amazing—never forget it.

"You are very powerful, provided you know how powerful you are."
—*Yogi Bhajan*

Love,
Annie Grace

P.S. If you are looking for more support in your journey visit this nakedmind.com for additional resources and next steps or sign up for my weekly newsletter at thisnakedmind.com/reader.

Maybe you need a practical way to get started. Why not simply commit to thirty-days alcohol free? Join me for a thirty-day "Alcohol Experiment" at alcoholexperiment.com.

ENDNOTES

1 Bergland, Christopher, "New Clues on the Inner Workings of the Unconscious Mind," *Psychology Today*, March 20, 2014, psychologytoday.com/blog/the-athletes-way/201403 /new-clues-the-inner-workings-the-unconscious-mind.

2 Carey, Benedict, "Who's Minding the Mind?," *The New York Times*, July 31, 2007, nytimes .com/2007/07/31/health/psychology/31subl.html?pagewanted=all&_r=0.

3 Bergland.

4 Ibid.

5 Polk, Thad A., *The Addictive Brain*, The Great Courses, 2015.

6 "The Conscious, Subconscious, and Unconscious Mind–How Does It All Work?," The Mind Unleashed, March 13, 2014, themindunleashed.org/2014/03/conscious-subconscious -unconscious-mind-work.html.

7 Siedle, Edward, "America's Best Doctor and His Miracle Cures: Dr. John E. Sarno," *Forbes*, September 26, 2012, forbes.com/sites/edwardsiedle/2012/09/26/americans-best-doctor -and-his-miracle-cures-dr-john-e-sarno/.

8 Sarno, John, "The Manifestations of TMS," in *Healing Back Pain: The Mind-Body Connection*, New York: Warner Books (1991), 16.

9 Hoyt, Terence, "Carl Jung on the Shadow," Practical Philosophy, practicalphilosophy .net/?page_id=952.

10 Ozanich, Steven Ray, "The Mind's Eyewitnesses," in *The Great Pain Deception; Faulty Medical Advice Is Making Us Worse*, Warren, OH: Silver Cord Records (2011): 145–151.

11 Anando, "It's now a proven fact—Your unconscious mind is running your life!," *Lifetrainings*, lifetrainings.com/Your-unconscious-mind-is-running-you-life.html.

12 Ibid.

13 Gray, Dave, "Liminal thinking The pyramid of belief," YouTube, youtube.com/watch?v= 2G_h4mnAMJg.

14 Gray, Dave, *Liminal Thinking: Create the Change You Want by Changing the Way You Think*, Two Waves Books, 2016.

15 Gray "Liminal thinking."

16 Ibid.

17 "The Conscious, Subconscious, and Unconscious Mind."

18 Weller, Lawrence, "How to Easily Harness the Power of Your Subconscious Mind," Binaural Beats Freak, binauralbeatsfreak.com/spirituality/how-to-easily-harness-the-power-of-your -subconscious-mind.

19 Gray, "Liminal thinking."

20 Ibid.

21 Harris, Dan, *10% Happier: How I Tamed the Voice in My Head, Reduced Stress Without Losing My Edge, and Found Self-Help That Actually Works: A True Story*, It Books, 2014.

22 Weller.

23 "Alcohol Facts and Statistics," niaaa.nih.gov/alcohol-health/overview-alcohol-consumption /alcohol-facts-and-statistics.

24 Cook, Philip J. *Paying the Tab: The Costs and Benefits of Alcohol Control*, Princeton University Press, 2007.

25 Vale, Jason, *Kick the Drink . . . Easily!*, Bancyfelin: Crown House, 1999 (77).

26 "Prosthetic Limbs, Controlled by Thought," *The New York Times*, May 20, 2015.

27 Fox, Maggie, "Surgeon Promising Head Transplant Now Asks America for Help," *NBC News*, June 12, 2015.

28 Genetic Science Learning Center, "Genes and Addiction," *Learn. Genetics*, June 22, 2014, learn.genetics.utah.edu/content/addiction/genes.

29 Polk.

30 Vale.

31 Polk.

32 Genetic Science Learning Center.

33 A.A. General Service Office, "Estimates of A.A. Groups and Members as of January 1, 2015," aa.org/assets/en_US/smf-53_en.pdf

34 Alcoholics Anonymous World Services, Inc., *Alcoholics Anonymous: The Big Book—4th ed.*, New York: Alcoholics Anonymous World Services, 2001.

35 Ibid.

36 Ibid.

37 Ibid.

38 Ibid.

39 Ibid.

40 National Institute on Alcohol Abuse and Alcoholism, "Alcohol Facts and Statistics," March 1, 2015, niaaa.nih.gov/alcohol-health/overview-alcohol-consumption/alcohol-facts-and-statistics.

41 Anonymous, "Alcoholism: An Illness," in *This is A.A.: An Introduction to the A.A. Recovery Program*, New York: A.A. Publications, 1984.

42 Carr, Allen, *The Easy Way to Stop Drinking*, Sterling Publishing Co. Inc, 2003 (167).

43 Carr.

44 Polk.

45 Kraft, Sy, "WHO Study: Alcohol Is International Number One Killer, AIDS Second," *Medical News Today*, February 11, 2011, medicalnewstoday.com articles/216328.php.

46 Task Force on the National Advisory Council on Alcohol Abuse and Alcoholism, "High-Risk Drinking in College: What We Know and What We Need to Learn," September 23, 2005, files.eric.ed.gov/fulltext/ED469651.pdf.

47 Castillo, Stephanie, "How Habits Are Formed, and Why They're So Hard to Change," *Medical Daily*, August 17, 2014, medicaldaily.com/how-habits-are-formed-and-why-theyre -so-hard-change-298372

48 Ibid.

49 Vale.

50 National Foreign Assessment Center and Central Intelligence Agency, *The World Factbook*, n.d.

51 Berger, Jonah, *Contagious: Why Things Catch On*, New York: Simon & Schuster (2013), 150, 151.

52 Carr.

53 Kraft.

54 Vale.

55 Goldstein, Robin, et al., "Do More Expensive Wines Taste Better? Evidence From a Large Sample of Blind Tastings," *Journal of Wine Economics*, 3(1), Spring 2008: 1–9, wine-economics .org/aawe/wp-content/uploads/2012/10/Vol.3-No.1-2008-Evidence-from-a-Large-Sample -of-Blind-Tastings.pdf.

56 Bohannon, John, et al., "Can People Distinguish Pâté From Dog Food?," *Chance*, June 2010, wine-economics.org/workingpapers/AAWE_ WP36.pdf.

57 Kempton, Matthew, et al., "Dehydration Affects Brain Structure and Function in Healthy Adolescents," *Human Brain Mapping* 32(1), January 2011: 71–79, ncbi.nlm.nih.gov/pubmed /20336685.

58 Carr.

59 Berger.

60 Nutt, David J., et al., "Drug Harms in the UK: A Multicriteria Decision Analysis," *The Lancet* 376(9752), November 2010: 1558–1565.

61 Kraft.

62 Centers for Disease Control and Prevention, "One in 10 Deaths Among Working-Age Adults Due to Excessive Drinking," cdc.gov/media/releases/2014/p0626-excessive -drinking.html.

63 Stahre, Mandy, et al., "Contribution of Excessive Alcohol Consumption to Deaths and Years of Potential Life Lost in the United States," *Preventing Chronic Disease*, June 26, 2014.

64 Centers for Disease Control, "2013 Mortality Multiple Cause Micro-data Files," December 2014.

65 De Oliveira, E. Silva, E.R., et al., "Alcohol Consumption Raises HDL Cholesterol Levels by Increasing the Transport Rate of Apolipoproteins A-I and A- II," *Clinical Investigation and Reports* 102, 2347–2352, doi:10.1161/01.CIR.102.19.2347.

66 Holahan, Charles J., et al., "Late-Life Alcohol Consumption and 20-Year Mortality," *Alcoholism: Clinical and Experimental Research* 34(11), November 2010: 1961–1971.

67 Höfer, Thomas, et al., "New Evidence for the Theory of the Stork," *Paediatric and Perinatal Epidemiology* 18, 2004: 88–92.

68 Carr, 144.

69 "Beyond Hangovers: Understanding Alcohol's Impact on Your Health," 2010, Bethesda, MD: U.S. Dept. of Health and Human Services, National Institutes of Health, National Institute on Alcohol Abuse and Alcoholism.

70 "Neuroscience: Pathways to Alcohol Dependence." *Alcohol Alert* 77, 2009.

71 "Beyond Hangovers."

72 Polk.

73 DiSalvo, David, "What Alcohol Really Does to Your Brain," *Forbes*, October 16, 2012, forbes .com/sites/daviddisalvo/2012/10/16/what-alcohol-really-does-to-your-brain/.

74 "Beyond Hangovers."

75 Ibid.

76 Ibid.

77 Ibid.

78 Ibid.

79 Ibid.

80 Ibid.

81 "Hypertensive Heart Disease, Medline Plus, May 13, 2014, nlm.nih.gov/medlineplus/ency /article/000163.htm

82 "Health Consequences of Excess Drinking," AlcoholScreening.org, alcoholscreening.org /learn-more.aspx?topicID=8&articleID=26.

83 "Beyond Hangovers."

84 Ibid.

85 Ibid.

86 Ibid.

87 Ibid.

88 Ibid.

89 Ibid.

90 Ibid.

91 Rehm, Jürgen, et al., "Alcohol Consumption," in *World Cancer Report 2014* (Stewart & Wild, eds), Lyon, France: International Agency for Research on Cancer, 2014: 96–104.

92 Bagnardi, Vincenzo, et al., "Light Alcohol Drinking and Cancer: A Meta-Analysis," *Annals of Oncology* 24, 2013: 301–308.

93 Allen, N.E., et al., "Moderate Alcohol Intake and Cancer Incidence in Women," *Journal of the National Cancer Institute* 101(5), 2009: 296–305.

94 "How Alcohol Causes Cancer," Cancer Research UK, cancerresearchuk.org/about-cancer /causes-of-cancer/alcohol-and-cancer/how-alcohol-causes-cancer.

95 "Drinking Alcohol," BreastCancer.org, breastcancer.org/risk/factors/alcohol.

96 "How Alcohol Causes Cancer."

97 Ibid.

98 Ibid.

99 "Alcohol and Breast Cancer Risk," Susan G. Komen, ww5.komen.org/breastcancer/table3 alcoholconsumptionandbreastcancerrisk.html

100 "U.S. Breast Cancer Statistics," BreastCancer.org, breastcancer.org/symptoms/understand _bc/statistics.

101 "Alcohol drinking," *IARC Monographs on the Evaluation of Carcinogenic Risks to Humans* 44, 1988: 1–378.

102 Lachenmeier, Dirk W., et al., "Comparative Risk Assessment of Carcinogens in Alcoholic Beverages Using the Margin of Exposure Approach," *International Journal of Cancer* 131, 2012: E995–E1003.

103 "How Alcohol Causes Cancer."

104 Stokowski, Laura, "No Amount of Alcohol Is Safe," Medscape, April 30, 2014, medscape .com/viewarticle/824237.

105 "Alcohol Use Disorder," *The New York Times*, nytimes.com/health/guides/disease/alcoholism /possible-complications.html.

106 Ibid.

107 Stokowski.

108 Carr.

109 Lynsen, A., "Alcohol."

110 "Parenting to Prevent Childhood Alcohol Use," National Institute on Alcohol Abuse and Alcoholism, pubs.niaaa.nih.gov/publications/adolescentflyer/adolflyer.htm.

111 "One in 10 Deaths Among Working-Age Adults Due to Excessive Drinking."

112 Carr.

113 Turner, Sarah and Rocca, Lucy, *The Sober Revolution: Women Calling Time on Wine o'Clock*, Accent Press Ltd., 2013.

114 Carey, "Who's Minding the Mind?"

115 Koch, Christof, "Probing the Unconscious Mind," *Scientific American*, November 1, 2011, scientificamerican.com/article/probing-the-unconscious-mind/.

116 Ibid.

117 Harris.

118 "Yalom's Ultimate Concerns," Changingminds.org, changingminds.org/explanations/needs /ultimate_concerns.htm

119 Harris.

120 Kraft.

121 Carr.

122 "Ethyl Alcohol," *Encyclopedia Britannica*, britannica.com/science/ethyl-alcohol.

123 Janet Hall, "Cancer figures prompt calls for health warnings on alcohol products," *Northumberland Gazette*, July 16, 2015, northumberlandgazette.co.uk/news/local-news /cancer-figures-prompt-calls-for-health-warnings-on-alcohol-products-1-7361758.

124 Weiss, Marisa, "Alcohol and Cancer: You Can't Drink to Your Health," BreastCancer.org, November 9, 2011, community.breastcancer.org/livegreen/alcohol-and-cancer-you -cant-drink-to-your-health/.

125 Dubner, Stephen J., "What's More Dangerous: Marijuana or Alcohol? A New Freakonomics Radio Podcast," Freakonomics, freakonomics.com/podcast/whats-more-dangerous -marijuana-or-alcohol-a-new-freakonomics-radio-podcast/.

126 Iliades, Chris, "Why Boozing Can Be Bad for Your Sex Life," Everyday Health, everyday health.com/erectile-dysfunction/why-boozing-can-be-bad-for-your-sex-life.aspx.

127 Arackal, Bijil Simon and Benegal, Vivek, "Prevalence of Sexual Dysfunction in Male Subjects with Alcohol Dependence," *Indian Journal of Psychiatry* 49(2), April–June 2007: 109-112.

128 Fillmore, Mark, "Acute Alcohol-Induced Impairment of Cognitive Functions: Past and Present Findings,:" *International Journal on Disability and Human Development* 6(2), April 2007.

129 Anderson, P., "Is It Time to Ban Alcohol Advertising?," *Clinical Medicine* 9(2), April 2009: 121–124.

130 Smith, Lesley A. and David R. Foxcroft, "The Effect of Alcohol Advertising, Marketing, and Portrayal on Drinking Behaviour in Young People: Systematic Review of Prospective Cohort Studies," BioMed Central, February 6, 2009, biomedcentral.com/1471-2458/9/51.

131 Bergland.

132 Ibid.

133 Goldstein.

134 Beck.

135 Ibid.

136 Hill, Kashmir, "How Target Figured Out a Teen Girl Was Pregnant Before Her Father Did," *Forbes*, February 16, 2012, forbes.com/sites/kashmirhill/2012/02/16/how-target-figured -out-a-teen-girl-was-pregnant-before-her-father-did/.

137 Beck.

138 "Alcoholism Isn't What It Used To Be," NIAAA Spectrum, spectrum.niaaa.nih.gov/archives /v1i1Sept2009/features/Alcoholism.html.

139 "Alcohol Deaths," Centers for Disease Control and Prevention, June 30, 2014 cdc.gov /features/alcohol-deaths/.

140 "Overdose Death Rates," National Institute on Drug Abuse, drugabuse.gov/related-topics /trends-statistics/overdose-death-rates.

141 Ibid.

142 "The Impact of Alcohol Abuse on American Society," Alcoholics Victorious, alcoholics victorious.org/faq/impact.

143 Ibid.

144 Ibid.

145 Polk.

146 Mohr, Morgan, "The Role of Alcohol Use in Sexual Assault," Kinsey Confidential, April 28, 2015, kinseyconfidential.org/role-alcohol-sexual-assault/.

147 Ibid.

148 Carey, Kate B., et al., "Incapacitated and Forcible Rape of College Women: Prevalence Across the First Year," *Journal of Adolescent Health* 56(6), June 2015: 678–680.

149 Abbey, A., "Alcohol-Related Sexual Assault: A Common Problem Among College Students," *Journal of Studies on Alcohol Supplement* 14, March 2002: 118–128.

150 Ibid.

151 Iliades.

152 Cain, Susan, *Quiet: The Power of Introverts in a World That Can't Stop Talking*, New York: Crown, 2012.

153 "The Impact of Alcohol Abuse on American Society."

154 "Impaired Driving: Get the Facts," Centers for Disease Control and Prevention, cdc.gov /motorvehiclesafety/impaired_driving/impaired-drv_factsheet.html.

155 Arackal and Benegal.

156 Duhigg.

157 Powell, Russell, et al., *Introduction to Learning and Behavior*, Wadsworth Publishing, 2012: 441.

158 Holmes, Andrew, et al., "Chronic Alcohol Remodels Prefrontal Neurons and Disrupts NMDAR-Mediated Fear Extinction Encoding," *Nature Neuroscience* 15, September 2, 2012: 1359–1361.

159 Polk.

160 Danbolt, Niels, "Glutamate as a Neurotransmitter—An Overview," *Progressive Neurobiology* 65, 2001: 1–105.

161 DiSalvo.

162 Ibid.

163 Ibid.

164 "Neuroscience: Pathways to Alcohol Dependence."

165 DiSalvo.

166 Watson, Stephanie, "How Alcoholism Works," How Stuff Works, June 8, 2005, science. howstuffworks.com/life/inside-the-mind/human-brain/alcoholism4.htm.

167 One in 10 Deaths Among Working-Age Adults Due to Excessive Drinking."

168 "Neuroscience: Pathways to Alcohol Dependence."

169 DiSalvo.

170 Vale.

171 Ibid.

172 Hitti, Miranda, "1/3 Fully Recover from Alcoholism," WebMD, January 19, 2005, webmd .com/mental-health/addiction/news/20050119/13-fully-recover-from-alcoholism.

173 Flanagin, Jake, "The Surprising Failures of 12 Steps," *The Atlantic*, March 25, 2014, theatlantic.com/health/archive/2014/03/the-surprising-failures-of-12-steps/284616/.

174 "Alcoholism Isn't What It Used To Be."

175 Polk.

176 Duhigg.

177 "Alcohol, Drugs, and Crime," National Council on Alcoholism and Drug Dependence, ncadd.org/learn-about-alcohol/alcohol-and-crime.

178 Ibid.

179 "Alcohol Use Disorder."

180 "The Impact of Alcohol Abuse on American Society."

181 Ibid.

182 "Alcohol Awareness," National Clearinghouse for Alcohol and Drug Information, 1993.

183 Vale.

184 Ibid.

185 Polk.

186 Ibid.

187 Ibid.

188 Ibid.

189 Vale.

190 Ibid.

191 Carr, 154.

192 Ibid, 60.

193 Brière, Frédéric, et al., "Comorbidity Between Major Depression and Alcohol Use Disorder from Adolescence to Adulthood," *Comprehensive Psychiatry* 55(3), April 2004: 526-533.

194 Turner and Rocca.

195 Ibid.

196 Carr, 144.

197 Polk.

198 Ibid.

199 Vale.

200 Ibid.

201 Hepola, Sarah, *Blackout: Remembering the Things I Drank to Forget*, New York: Grand Central Press (2015), 17.

202 Melina, Remy, "Why Do Medical Researchers Use Mice?," Live Science, November 16, 2010, livescience.com/32860-why-do-medical-researchers-use-mice.html.

203 Hari, Johann, "The Likely Cause of Addiction Has Been Discovered, and It Is Not What You Think," *Huffington Post*, January 20, 2015, huffingtonpost.com/johann-hari/the-real-cause-of-addicti_b_6506936.html.

204 Turner and Rocca.

205 Ibid.

206 "The Impact of Alcohol Abuse on American Society."

207 "What Happens During an Alcohol Detox and How Long Does It Last?," Hologik.biz, December 19, 2016, holologik.biz/how_long_to_detox_from_alcohol/1886-1/.

208 Polk.

209 Ibid.

210 Ibid.

211 Ibid.

212 Ibid.

213 Ibid.

214 Ibid.

215 Ibid.

216 Littlefield, Andrew, and Sher, Kenneth, "The Multiple, Distinct Ways That Personality Contributes to Alcohol Use Disorders," *Social and Personality Psychology Compass* 4(9), September 2010: 767–782.

217 Ibid.

218 Ibid.

219 Turner and Rocca.

220 Pompili, Maurizio, et al., "Suicidal Behavior and Alcohol Abuse," *International Journal of Environmental Research and Public Health* 7(4), April 2010: 1392–1431, ncbi.nlm.nih.gov/pmc/articles/PMC2872355/.

221 Pedersen, Traci, "One-Third of Suicides Involve Heavy Alcohol Consumption," Psych Central, June 21, 2014, psychcentral.com/news/2014/06/21/one-third-of-suicides-involve-heavy-alcohol-consumption/71515.html.

222 Carey, "Who's Minding the Mind?"

223 Horsley, Victor and Sturge, Mary, *Alcohol and the Human Body: An Introduction to the Study of the Subject*, London: Macmillan and Co, 1909.

224 Carr, 262.

225 Polk.

226 Ibid.

227 Ibid.

228 Schultz, Wolfram, et al., "A Neural Substrate of Prediction and Reward," *Science* 275(5306), March 14, 1997: 1593–1599.

229 Robinson, Terry, and Berridge, Kent C., "The Neural Basis of Drug Craving: An Incentive-Sensitization Theory of Addiction," *Brain Research Reviews* 18(3), September–December 1993: 247–291.

230 Ibid.

231 Ibid.

232 Turner and Rocca.

233 Gupta, Sanjay, and Cohen, Elizabeth, "Brain Chemical May Explain Alcoholism Gender Differences," CNN, October 19, 2010, thechart.blogs.cnn.com/2010/10/19/brain-chemical-may-explain-alcoholism-gender-differences/.

234 "One in 10 Deaths Among Working-Age Adults Due to Excessive Drinking."

235 Levitin, Daniel J., "Why the modern world is bad for your brain," *The Guardian*, January 18, 2015, theguardian.com/science/2015/jan/18/modern-world-bad-for-brain-daniel-j-levitin-organized-mind-information-overload.

236 Polk.

237 Ibid.

238 Lachenmeier, Dirk, and Rehm, Jürgen, "Comparative Risk Assessment of Alcohol, Tobacco, Cannabis and Other Illicit Drugs Using the Margin of Exposure Approach," *Scientific Reports* 5, 2015: 8126.

239 Jackson, Christine, et al., "Letting Children Sip: Understanding Why Parents Allow Alcohol Use by Elementary School–Aged Children," *Archives of Pediatrics & Adolescent Medicine* 166 (11), November 2012: 1053–1057.

240 "Overdose Death Rates."

241 Kraft.

242 Lachenmeier and Rehm.

243 Ibid.

244 Carr.

245 Carey, "Who's Minding the Mind?"

246 "The Conscious, Subconscious, and Unconscious Mind."

247 Ibid.

248 Duhigg.

249 Polk.

250 "Is There a Cure for Alcoholism?," DrugAbuse.com, drugabuse.com/is-there-a-cure-for -alcoholism/.

251 Polk.

252 Hari, Johann, *Chasing the Scream: The First and Last Days of the War on Drugs*, New York: Bloomsbury, 2015.

253 Stahre, et al.

254 Carr, 262.

255 Najmi, Sadia, and Wegner, Daniel M., "Hidden Complications of Thought Suppression," *International Journal of Cognitive Therapy*, 2009 (210–223).

256 Harris.

257 Ibid.

Also by
Annie Grace

INCLUDES A DAY-BY-DAY JOURNAL

THE ALCOHOL EXPERIMENT

EXPANDED EDITION

A 30-DAY,
ALCOHOL-FREE CHALLENGE
TO INTERRUPT YOUR
HABITS AND HELP YOU
TAKE CONTROL

ANNIE GRACE

author of ⟡ THIS NAKED MIND

THIS NAKED MIND

NICOTINE

The Science-Based Method
to Reclaim Your Health and
Take Control Easily

Annie Grace and William Porter

AVERY

ABOUT THE AUTHOR

Annie Grace has had a unique life from the very beginning. She grew up in a one-room cabin without running water or electricity in the mountains of Colorado and then, at age twenty-six, became the youngest vice president in a multinational corporation. Success, however, led to excessive drinking and the possibility that she might lose everything. Annie recognized her problem but chose to approach it in an entirely new way. Annie's program has been featured in *Forbes*, the New York *Daily News*, and the *Chicago Tribune*. Annie is successful, happy, and alcohol-free and lives with her husband and three children in the Colorado mountains.

PRAISE FOR

The Alcohol Experiment

"45 days alcohol-free. I didn't think I could make it through the first week, and now I can't imagine ever drinking again. The Alcohol Experiment saved my life. It's so worth the journey!" —R.D., New York, New York

"Day 60 alcohol free [AF]. Just did karaoke sober. I didn't know that was possible. I had even given myself permission to have one cocktail (to loosen the vocal cords, you understand?). But after looking through the menu, I just didn't fancy anything! Stuck with water all night. Now on the train heading home, looking forward to waking up tomorrow with a clear head, money in my pocket, my dignity (if you ignore the singing), and possibly a sore throat. The Alcohol Experiment is incredible. Thank you."

—M.K., London, England

"Annie Grace, I just wanted you to know you've touched the lives of many people. This is such a huge movement that you started. You are talked about, I just want to thank you from the bottom of my heart (tears are coming down right now). You saved me after almost 27 years of drinking daily, since I was 13 years old when I started. I never thought I would be able to do what I am doing now. Thank you." —S.J., Sydney, Australia

"I loved The Alcohol Experiment for so many reasons. Most important, I put down the bottle of wine (every day) and haven't touched it since. I am amazed that I am over 30 days in and feeling strong. I don't even think about it too much anymore, and I have been drinking since I was a teen. (I will be 59 on Thursday!) Thank you so much, Annie, for your courage. This was perfect for me." —H.N.R., Pittsburgh, Pennsylvania

"I completed the 30-day Alcohol Experiment today—and have been AF for all 30 days, which makes me very happy, as it's been a long time since I've gone 30 days without a drink. The readings and writing exercises of this 30-day program have enhanced my understanding—of alcohol and of myself—considerably. This has been a powerful experience, for which I am thankful. I may try moderation . . . but perhaps I never will try it. Certainly not worth it now. I like who I am, AF. I could go on, but for now I simply wanted to let you know that I am grateful. I am not the same person I was 30 days ago. Thank you!" —J.L., Maryland, US

"31 days ago, I started your alcohol-free experiment. I haven't touched any alcohol in the past month and cannot thank you enough for giving me the kick in the ass to get started! I wanted to share a story with you about how much you have convinced me to stay sober. I'm a night nurse and was just returning home this morning at 8:30 when I got a call from my youngest daughter's school confirming that she was not indeed present today. Because I don't make it home in time to put her on the bus, my husband routinely does this, and I know he would have let me know by text if she were sick and couldn't go in. He had not. I completely panicked. In the remaining two minutes it took me to get home, every single scenario raced through my head, and I ran into the house calling for her. Of course she wasn't there. The phone was ringing as I came through the door, though, saying that the homeroom teacher had marked her absent incorrectly. It was actually the student below her on the roster, and my daughter was definitely at school. I was so upset and angry, I had to go for a walk to calm down. It took a while. And then the thought came to me that a month ago I would've been pouring myself a glass of wine, or more likely two—yes, at 8:30 a.m., to relax—but it hadn't even occurred to me. I knew it wouldn't help and in fact would probably have made things worse—I might have called the school back and berated them. It's in large part due to you, Annie. Thank you for your daily teachings. Thank you, thank you, thank you."

—C.R., Costa Mesa, California

"Your 30-day experiment was so helpful. I learned so much! I'm well on my way to being AF completely—from drinking daily to drinking five times in 110 days. And I don't plan on drinking anytime soon. It was so in-depth and educational. Thank you."   —G.P., Austin, Texas

"Thank YOU for this amazing gift you have given so many with first your book and now The Alcohol Experiment! It has truly been life changing for me, and at three months alcohol-free tomorrow, I am more hopeful than I have been in a very long time."   —L.K., Windsor, England

"You are changing the lives of so many people. Thank you. I feel like someone woke me up from a very, very long nightmare. Really, Groundhog Day. There are no words to express my gratitude. Thank you, Annie Grace, for saving my life."   —B.K.R., Portland, Maine

"Day 67, Saturday-morning trip to the farmer's market—weekend mornings are the best. This has been an incredible journey so far. I jumped in to 'get healthy' over the summer, and I had no idea how much freshness and joy I was inviting back into my life. I'm never going back. Not that it's been easy, and my body and brain are still healing, but today I feel sparkly and grateful. Annie Grace, 'thank you' doesn't begin to cover it."

—M.K., Yarmouth, Massachusetts

"I've been wanting to message you for a while to say thank you. I've been trying to moderate my drinking for years and find it's a daily fight. Having a dad and brother who are alcoholics, I was resigned to the fact it runs in the family! My sister introduced me to The Alcohol Experiment after I had just completed Dry January—wow! It absolutely changed my perspective on alcohol, and I haven't touched a drop since, nor do I intend to! Thank you so much for setting me free."

—I.G., Brisbane, Australia

"Yesterday was the end of my 30-day experiment. As I reflect on my life 30 days ago, I cannot believe how much has changed. I have survived a family function, pool party, and work trip (there is always a lot of booze involved) without alcohol. I don't feel deprived or like I am missing out. I am much happier and way less stressed. My relationship with my son is better. I now spend the evenings doing activities with him instead of drinking. My romantic relationship is amazing. I spent years trying to quit or moderate unsuccessfully. This time everything feels different. I have absolutely no desire to drink. I couldn't have done it without you. I have no intention of going back to that life. I am excited to see the changes that will happen in a year. Thank you."

—G.D., Las Vegas, Nevada

"Just wanted to say a huge thank you, Annie Grace. You are a remarkable person who has changed my life. I'm on Day 18 of The Alcohol Experiment and still reading the daily lessons. At first I was looking for support to go 30 days alcohol-free in preparation for training for the Race for Life for cancer research on July 1. I downloaded your book *This Naked Mind* on my Kindle, and only a few pages in, my mind-set was changing. All the things you have taught me have made me see I don't want to drink ever again. It's my 40th birthday next month, and honestly I'm looking forward to facing the rest of my life alcohol-free. I know there will be challenges ahead, but your lessons will help me stay strong. Thanks so much.

"I'm writing this on the eve of my 30 days without alcohol . . . I did actually slip on Day 3, but I'm just ignoring that. From that day on, I can honestly say it's been a breeze. Not because I'm superstrong or anything, but because your alcohol experiment was exactly what I needed to break my 25-year drinking habit.

"The information you've given me about what alcohol is and what it was doing to me has left me never wanting to put it in my body again. Now I know why I've been depressed and tired for 25 years. Five years ago my darling daughter Jenny was diagnosed with cancer, and sadly, a year ago, at the age of 19, she lost her fight. She died in my arms and I thought I'd never feel joy again. A month ago I made a choice between life and death. Did I want to live, flourish, speak her name to anyone who will listen, make her count, enjoy this precious life for both of us? Or did I want to retreat beneath my duvet and drink myself to death?

"Your Alcohol Experiment came along at that point. I guess it was my last stab at giving life a chance. You would not believe the change in me. Yes, I still cry. Yes, the missing is still agony. But alongside that grief I'm now full of energy, I'm happier than I've been in as long as I can remember. Happy with myself. Jenny would be so very proud and pleased if she could see me. Part of me feels sure she can . . . did she lead you to me? I won't know on this side, but one day I'll find out. In the meantime I feel ready to live again. I know this might all sound a bit cheesy, but I just had to say thank you, you darling girl, for all your bravery and hard work and your caring heart. You've given me life when I thought all was lost. I can't really find the words to tell you how grateful I am."   —G.S., Los Angeles, California

"Thank you so, so much, Annie. You are such an amazing force for good in this world! The Alcohol Experiment changed my life."
                                                                —H.R.T., Palm Beach, Florida

"I am now 37 days AF and have never felt so relaxed and happy. I just want to thank you for being brave enough and for caring enough to create The Alcohol Experiment. Without your support I wouldn't be where I am. I wouldn't be going to a weekend of camping and family fun looking forward to not drinking. It's made such a difference to my life. You make me feel humble and so, so grateful. Thank you."   —F.C., Brooklyn, New York

"Day 60! What!? Always dreamed of being AF. Didn't think it was possible. Thank you for my life, Annie Grace!"   —O.F., Dublin, Ireland

The Alcohol Experiment

EXPANDED EDITION

A 30-Day, Alcohol-Free Challenge to Interrupt
Your Habits and Help You Take Control

ANNIE GRACE

AVERY
an imprint of Penguin Random House
New York

AVERY

an imprint of Penguin Random House LLC
penguinrandomhouse.com

Most Avery books are available at special quantity discounts for bulk purchase for sales promotions, premiums, fund-raising, and educational needs. Special books or book excerpts also can be created to fit specific needs. For details, write SpecialMarkets@penguinrandomhouse.com.

ISBN 9780593330241
eBook ISBN 9780593330821

Printed in the United States of America
7th Printing

Book design by Laura K. Corless

Turner, Trace, and Daelyn.
You are why I dream of a better tomorrow.

Brian. My favorite person.
Thank you for creating this life with me.
Thank you for trusting me enough to double down
on this dream and follow the road wherever it leads.

Jesus. Your Grace. Your Love. Your Mercy.
Your Breath in my lungs.

Contents

Introduction

It's YOUR body . . .
  It's YOUR mind . . .
  It's YOUR choice . . .
  During The Alcohol Experiment, you'll make a choice to go 30 days without alcohol. Just to see how you feel. You'll become a detached reporter, researching the facts, writing down your observations, and possibly drawing new conclusions. This is an exciting experiment, not a punishment. You're not weak-willed for questioning your drinking. There's no judgment or labeling here. You have a unique opportunity to remember how to enjoy life without alcohol. And with this book's unconventional approach, I'm willing to bet you'll enjoy the process!

▍ WHO IS THIS FOR?

This experiment is for you if you're curious about your relationship with alcohol, and you're thinking about drinking less often or not at all.
  It is also for you if

- You are of two minds about alcohol—you want to drink less, but you also feel deprived or upset when you abstain.
- You drink out of habit or boredom—only to regret it later.

- You are starting to wonder if alcohol is taking more than it is giving.
- You are curious about a life without booze but do not feel you are an alcoholic.
- You want to drink less, but life is just too stressful.
- You have a love-hate relationship with alcohol—and find yourself setting limits and then breaking them when happy hour rolls around.
- You have tried to cut back or stop drinking (possibly many times) using willpower alone and found it ineffective.
- You fell into drinking more than you ever wanted—without making a conscious decision to do so.
- You can stop drinking for a few days but find yourself feeling deprived.
- You are ready to regain control—of your drinking, your life, your health, and your happiness.
- You are looking forward to feeling great on Saturday night *and* Sunday morning.
- You are ready to be your best self, get in shape, regain your self-esteem, and change your life.

It's NOT for you if you have a strong physical addiction to alcohol—if you are physically dependent and suffer from serious withdrawal symptoms, such as delirium tremens or hallucinations, when you attempt to stop or cut back. This book may help with your emotional and psychological addiction by changing your perspective and erasing your desire to drink. However, I am not a doctor, and alcohol withdrawal can be extremely dangerous. You should seek professional medical assistance so your detoxification is medically supervised.

Is life better without alcohol? That's up to you to decide. My own experience with this experiment proved that, for me, life was absolutely better when I chose not to drink. However, your experience might be different. It's your body. It's your mind. It's your choice. I'm simply inviting you to open your mind to the possibility of making a different choice and then encouraging you to see how it changes things in your daily life.

It's 30 days, not forever . . . Many people ask me if they will have to give up drinking forever if they try the experiment. My answer is it's up to them. My only goal is to offer you a shift in your perspective and to show you some of the neuroscience behind why you might be drinking more than you'd like to.

You might go back to your regular drinking habits after the 30 days, you might drink a bit more mindfully (and less often), or you might decide to give it another 30 days just for the heck of it. You might also decide you feel so good you never want to go back.

Whatever you decide, I'd love to hear your experience with the experiment. If you'd like to share your story, email me at hello@alcoholexperiment.com.

WHY WE DRINK MORE THAN WE WANT TO

Since you're reading this right now, you're probably questioning how much you drink. Maybe you know you drink too much and want to quit. Or maybe you're just curious about what life is like with a bit less alcohol. Maybe you're questioning whether you might be overdoing it a bit. No matter where you are on the spectrum, you're not alone. I've been there. And tens of thousands of people inside The Alcohol Experiment community have been there, too. You're probably wondering why in the world you keep drinking even though you've made a conscious decision to cut back or stop altogether. Why do we do things we no longer want to do?

I wondered the same thing. When I first started drinking, it seemed to be a natural, normal thing to do. I saw nothing wrong with it. I didn't know all the negative ways alcohol could affect my health. I was a drinker, and I was proud of it. I tried hard to develop a tolerance so I could keep up with my colleagues. It was fun. It was relaxing. I had better sex when I was drunk.

. . . Or so I thought.

Eventually, I came to a point in my life when I started to question my drinking. I didn't like waking up with a hangover. I didn't like having to piece together conversations and wondering if I said or did anything embarrassing. I wasn't even enjoying myself anymore. I could drink two bottles of wine and not even feel it because I had such a high tolerance. So I made a conscious decision to stop drinking. And I thought that would be it. I just wouldn't drink. Easy-peasy.

Sound familiar?

If you've tried to give up or moderate your alcohol consumption in the past and failed, I want you to know it's not your fault. There's something going on you're probably not aware of. And once you understand it, your eyes will be opened and you'll be able to undergo this experiment in a meaningful way. It won't be just another failure of willpower.

To understand what's going on, we need to explore a concept called cognitive dissonance. *Cognitive* means "the way you think." And *dissonance* means "disagreement." So, cognitive dissonance is when there's a disagreement in your thinking. Well, how can that be? You've got one brain, right? Actually, your brain has many parts, and they can come into conflict with one another. But what we're really talking about here is your conscious mind and your subconscious mind. Your conscious mind is everything you're aware of. You're tired of waking up with a headache. You don't like spending your money on alcohol. Maybe your relationship is suffering, or your kids don't even know you anymore. Because you're aware of those things, you make a conscious decision to stop drinking.

Ahh, but there's another powerful part of your mind: your subconscious. That's where you've stored a lifetime of subconscious conditioning and beliefs that, by definition, you're unaware of. Our subconscious mind controls our emotions and desires. And society's attitudes about alcohol are programmed and fixed in our subconscious minds by the media, our parents, our friends, and our role models. We don't consciously adopt these beliefs. They are imprinted on us. Take, for example, the belief that drinking helps you relax. That's a belief you formed a long time ago after careful observation and experience. You weren't born with this knowledge. But you watched your parents drink after a long day. You've seen movies and TV shows where characters drink to relax. And you've experienced it yourself and found it to be true. So you formed a strong belief that alcohol helps you relax.

Here's the thing about subconscious beliefs—they're not always true. We form our belief systems when we're very young, and sometimes we'll carry those beliefs our whole lives without ever questioning them. Most of the time, this is fine. The sky is blue. Ice is cold. If I fall down, it's going to hurt. Cognitive dissonance happens when one of our subconscious beliefs disagrees with a conscious desire or decision. If I believe alcohol helps me relax, but I've decided not to drink after work anymore, that's a problem! Part of me desperately wants a drink to unwind after a long day, and another part of me doesn't want to overdo it and wake up with a hangover. There are two conflicting desires. Cognitive dissonance. To drink or not to drink, that is the question.

This is one of the reasons we continue to drink more than we want to even after we've decided to cut back. This is why willpower doesn't work in the long term. *Merriam-Webster*'s dictionary defines *willpower* as "energetic determination." That means it takes energy, conscious thought, and effort. This is especially true when you are trying to stop doing something that you believe provides a benefit. We don't have to exert conscious effort and energy not to drink something we believe is bad for us if we see no benefit in it. For example, there is no effort involved in turning down a glass of motor oil.

If you believe, even subconsciously, that alcohol provides a benefit, you will be exercising willpower to cut back or avoid drinking. The problem with willpower is that since it is energy, willpower runs out. And if you use your willpower on one thing—like being patient with your kids or paying attention during a boring work event—you will have less willpower to use when you try to turn down that next drink.

That is why I say we need to get out of the willpower game altogether. Until we resolve the inner conflict, we cannot hope to succeed.

Let's pretend we're trying to avoid sweets because we're trying to lose weight. Yet someone at the office brings in a big plate of freshly baked cookies and we mindlessly grab one and eat it. (Okay, who are we kidding . . . we eat like three cookies.) Bam! Dissonance. Your brain doesn't want to eat cookies, because you're on a diet. But you did. There's an internal conflict. Our brains immediately try to restore internal harmony in a few ways:

1. We can change our behavior. Make a vow not to eat another cookie no matter how good they look.

2. We can justify our behavior and say, "Oh, it's okay to cheat every once in a while. We all need a little sugar now and then. I deserve it."

3. We can add another behavior to counteract the first one. "Well, I ate the cookies, but that's okay. I'll go for a long run after work to burn off the extra calories."

4. We can delude ourselves by denying or ignoring the conflicting information. "Those cookies are probably not all that bad for my diet. They seemed pretty small anyway."

We delude ourselves all the time when it comes to alcohol or any addictive substance. We ignore the fact that alcohol isn't doing us any favors and it's actually harming us. We do it as a defense mechanism because we're trying to solve this internal disagreement. Conflict hurts. Humans are hardwired to avoid it whenever possible. When you're divided—when you're not whole—it's incredibly painful. And what do we drinkers do to numb pain? We drink! And then we drink more. And sometimes we drink until we black out to avoid something painful, even temporarily.

The more we drink, the worse we feel (mentally and physically) and the more we don't want to drink.

The more we don't want to drink, the more internal conflict we create.

The more conflict, the more pain.

The more pain, the more we drink.

It's a cycle that spirals out of control. It's not intentional. We may not even know we're doing it until something terrible happens. At some point, we wake up to the reality and try to change. But unless we address the dissonance, change continually eludes us. I tried to drink less, to set limits on my drinking. I could do it for a little while, but eventually my willpower would give out, and I'd be right back to waking up wondering how many glasses I'd had the night before. I felt helpless. I felt weak. And I felt alone. I'm smart and capable. Why did this have such a hold on me? I would intend to drink a single glass of wine, or maybe two, but would wake up the next morning being unable to count how many I'd had. And that would make me want to drink more because then I wouldn't have to think about the fact that I'd broken a commitment to myself—again. Drinking erased the conflict, even for a little while.

What I didn't know was that there was something much bigger at work. The subconscious mind is where our desires originate. So part of me was so much stronger than my conscious desire to get my act together. The deck was stacked against me, and I didn't even realize it.

The good news is that I discovered a way to truly resolve my cognitive dissonance around drinking. And it works for anything, by the way. If you're eating sugar when you don't want to, or you're gambling when you don't want to, or you're watching too much television— whatever. This method works to resolve the conflict and get your conscious and subconscious minds on the same page. When that happens, you get what you want with no effort. You can go to a party with all your friends and have a great time without even thinking about alcohol. You can ring in the New Year with ginger ale. You can save your relationships. You can change your life.

Want to know the secret?

It's all about awareness. If you're struggling because you're unaware of your subconscious beliefs, then the solution is to become aware of them. Shine a light deep into the nooks and crannies of your mind and figure out what beliefs are holding you back. What beliefs are in conflict with your desire to drink less or stop drinking?

I've developed a proven, scientifically based process to do exactly that. The process is based on a technique called Liminal Thinking, created by the bestselling author Dave Gray, and The Work, by author Byron Katie. The liminal space is the area between your conscious and your subconscious, or subliminal, mind. The technique I've developed is called ACT: Awareness, Clarity, and Turnaround. You're going to become aware of your belief by naming and putting language to it. Next, you clarify the belief, where it came from and how it feels inside you. Finally, you will turn around the belief coming up with a few reasons why the opposite of your long-held belief may be truer or as true as the original belief. As with many of the most profound tools for change, it is a simple process of deconstructing your beliefs by asking yourself questions like these:

What do I believe?

Is it true?

How does it make me feel?

Is it helpful?

Remember when I said sometimes our beliefs just aren't true? Well, that's how you untangle this mess—by discovering the truth. Does alcohol truly relax you? Or do you just think it does? Do you really enjoy sex more when you're drunk? Or does it become a sloppy, embarrassing mess you can barely remember?

I'm not going to suggest the answer is one or the other. I can't make you believe something you don't want to believe. Your subconscious beliefs remain deeply entrenched until *you* become aware of them and decide to change them by questioning their validity. Every few days during this 30-day experiment, you'll see bonus ACT chapters. You can read them as they come up, or you can read them first if you like. These special chapters present you with some facts regarding certain common beliefs about alcohol. All I ask is for you to keep an open mind and carefully consider what you're reading. It might take a few days or weeks of mulling it over before you decide one way or another. You might need to test out some theories. That's okay. Take as much time as you need. This is your experiment. Here's a preview of how the ACT technique works:

▎ THE ACT TECHNIQUE

1. **AWARENESS.** Name your belief. In the context of alcohol, this is your conscious reason for drinking. Simply put it into words:

   Alcohol relaxes me.

2. **CLARITY.** Discover *why* you believe it and *where* it originated. You do this by asking questions—both of yourself and of the external evidence—and uncovering truths about your belief.

   What have I observed that supports this belief?

   Happy hour. And the idea that everyone unwinds with a cocktail after a stressful day at work.

   Every time I talk to my friends about my struggles, either with my kids or husband, they always say something like, "Oh, no! Don't worry, I know just the thing—you need some wine immediately!"

   What are my experiences with alcohol and relaxation?

I've felt the relaxing effects of alcohol myself. After a stressful day at work, a drink seems to calm my nerves and allows me to transition from the hard workday to a relaxing evening.

Then it's time to do some detective work and compare this belief with both your internal and external realities. Internally, you will ask yourself questions like these:

What do I mean by "relax"?

How do I feel when I'm not relaxed?

How do I feel when I am relaxed?

Does anything else make me feel the same way?

How do I feel while I'm drinking? Is that the same feeling as "relaxed"?

How do I feel the next day? Is that relaxed?

Externally, you will examine the evidence.

Is it true, scientifically? Does alcohol relax human beings?

Does research support this belief? What do external sources say about this belief? Do they support or contradict it? And don't worry, you won't have to do a bunch of research—throughout the 30 days of the experiment I'll be supplying the studies and data.

And finally, in the Clarity step, you want to reflect on two questions:

• How does this belief make me feel?

• How does it make me behave?

This check-in with you about what the belief is doing in your life can often provide the most clarity and motivation for change.

3. TURNAROUND. This is where you allow your subconscious to let go of the belief, deciding if after exploration it is indeed true for you. There are two steps here.

First, you turn the initial belief around and find as many ways as you can that the opposite of your initial belief is true. For example, if your belief is *"alcohol relaxes me"* the opposite becomes *"alcohol does not relax me"* or *"alcohol stresses me out."*

Now that you've stated the opposite, come up with as many reasons as you can that the opposite is as true as or truer than the original belief. Examples might include

- Alcohol stresses my body out; a hangover is evidence of that.

- Alcohol prevents me from taking the action necessary to truly relieve my stress, so in that case it does not relax me.

- When I drink, I am more likely to get in an argument with my spouse, and fighting is stressful.

- When I drink, I beat myself up about it the next day, and that is stressful.

Once you've done that, the final step is simply to decide if this belief still holds true for you and if it is serving you or if you would be better off letting it go.

ACT: Awareness. Clarity. Turnaround. It's an effective, scientific way to shine a light into your subconscious and figure out what's actually causing your behavior. And you can find a guided worksheet in the back of this book to apply this process to any belief that comes up about alcohol, or about anything else in your life.

The important thing to remember is that there is no wrong answer! You are not messing up if you go through this process and still feel the belief is true for you. I know it sounds counterintuitive, but trust me on this—this process is about presenting your subconscious mind with information, facts, and logic. It's about shifting your mind-set. And while that can often happen quickly by simply reading through the ACT chapters, it can also happen more slowly over time. Again, there are no wrong answers.

Now you know there's something deeper at work here, and there's something you can do about it, I hope you're excited about this experiment! My ACT technique works. You can use it to enact change in so many areas of your life. It's so empowering. You can use it to lose weight, start exercising, stop procrastinating, and be a better parent. For now, though, let's focus on your drinking.

| STICKING WITH IT

Often we don't think about how much we drink or why we drink—like we're doing in this experiment—until drinking is no longer an option. We don't know if we drink because there's chaos in our lives, or if there's chaos because we drink. Suddenly, when the option to escape through drinking isn't there, we're forced to take a look at what's going on in our lives and what might be triggering us. What are we trying to distract ourselves from? Sometimes the answer is obvious. Work is stressful. The boss yelled again. But other times there doesn't seem to be an obvious trigger. Sometimes we drink to avoid anything unpleasant or stressful. This experiment offers us the option to switch from seeing stress as a reason to drink to seeing it as an opportunity to be creative and find other ways to deal with our problems. Maybe addressing the source of the stress is a good idea. Maybe blowing off steam on the driving range or at a boxing gym would be equally satisfying, and you could get a healthy workout in as a bonus.

As adults, we develop all sorts of coping mechanisms to handle stress. Maybe you like to read a book, meditate, knit, watch TV, or exercise. When I was in New York, I used to go for a long run at the end of the day. Then when I was encouraged to attend all sorts of boozy work events, from happy hours to networking meetings, that healthy habit got replaced by alcohol. Over time, all my healthy coping mechanisms were replaced with alcohol, and my life was thrown completely out of balance. What I've learned is that when we're tired, stressed out, cranky, or upset, we don't need alcohol. What we need is to change our emotional state. We need to do something to go from tired to energized, from cranky to happy. And we turn to alcohol.

You are going to experience stress over the next 30 days, I can pretty much guarantee it. But rather than saying, "Screw it!" and giving up, stop and think through it. If you have a drink now, how will that make you feel later? It might make you feel better temporarily, but you'll probably feel even worse the next morning when you realize you broke your promise to yourself. But here is the thing—every day that you read a chapter, you are learning, and so I strongly encourage you to pick up right where you left off and keep going. If you make it 30 days with just a few drinks, that is a huge improvement, and you will have learned so much. This experiment is about getting through all the information and staying curious about your behavior, whatever it is. I recommend keeping a journal (you can even jot down your thoughts in the notes app on your phone) or a video diary to record your thoughts each day. Notice how your body feels physically and emotionally. You might be surprised by the changes you see from day to day.

I'm not here to tell you to stop drinking. Or to keep drinking. I'm simply here to provide you with a framework to discover your truth through logical reasoning based on scientific information. At the end of the day, you are the only one who can make the choice. My only goal is to challenge some of the beliefs that might be holding you back. It's a terrible feeling to want something new or different and feeling like you're stuck, unable to move toward it in any meaningful way. One way or another, you'll be able to make a move by the end of this experiment. Your job is simple. Observe and become aware for 30 alcohol-free days. Be a reporter. Just the facts, ma'am.

If you're used to beating yourself up over your drinking, give yourself a break during the experiment. And if you slip up, give yourself a break then, too. The goal is not to be perfect. The goal is simply to test out a new way of thinking and behaving to see how it feels. To see if it moves you closer to those desires you have for a new life. In fact, imperfection can be a wonderful tool to help you see yourself even more clearly.

What I ask of you now, for the next 30 days, is to keep an open mind. Consider the possibilities presented in each day's reading. Is it possible that you could have the facts all wrong? For example, could anxiety be a heavy influence on your drinking? Is it possible that there is more going on with marketing and the profit engine of the alcohol industry than you currently realize? Is there something going on within the brain that makes alcohol seem more attractive than it truly is? Again, all I ask is that you keep an open mind. At the end, you might decide to keep drinking, and maybe you'll naturally cut down on the amount you drink. Or you might decide to stop altogether because you feel so good. It's your body, your mind, and your choice.

| A FEW TIPS BEFORE YOU START

One of the most interesting things I've found in my years of research is just how many people want to change their drinking. I thought I was alone. I thought I was the only one who was questioning my drinking habits. Nothing could be further from the truth! It's not that we are alone. In our society, questioning our relationship with alcohol is a taboo, even among our closest friends. An honest conversation around drinking seems to invite judgment. Yet the statistics are staggering. Eighty percent of Americans drink alcohol, and a huge majority drink it regularly. And think about this: Out of the people you know who drink alcohol regularly, how many of them have said something like "I overdid it last night" or "After last night I am never drinking again" at one time or another? Most of them, right? Almost everyone I know, and certainly everyone I drank with, has told me that they wanted to change their drinking at some point, to some degree.

So you are not alone in wondering about this topic. You are in the vast majority.

Another thing I've realized after reaching hundreds of thousands of people with this message is that drinking more than you want is not a weakness. If you've tried to stop drinking in the past and failed, I want you to know it's not your fault. Some of the smartest and most successful people in the world drink more than they want to, including lawyers, doctors, corporate executives, psychiatrists, professors, you name it. And when they try to cut back, they don't find it easy. And when it is not easy, we blame ourselves, believing there is something wrong with us. As you will discover, there is nothing wrong with you; it's simply that you are a human being who is drinking a substance that is addictive to human beings.

Why is this happening to even the smartest and best of us? Because we're going about it all wrong. The entire conversation around alcohol is flawed. And by the time you finish this book, and the 30-day experiment, you'll see that it's not black-and-white. You're not either "a normal drinker" or "an alcoholic." Most of us fall somewhere in the middle. So relax and let go of your anxieties. There are no judgments here. And even though I've decided to stop drinking indefinitely, you might make a different decision after doing this experiment. My only goal is to give you as much truthful information as I can so that you can make the right decision for you. An *informed* decision.

| WHAT TO EXPECT OVER THE NEXT 30 DAYS

Magic happens in 30 days. It's a period of time when the brain can actually change—by making new neural connections—to build great new habits or to eliminate habits that have held you back. But to experience that magic, you may have to deal with a few side effects. After all, alcohol is a toxin and your body needs to cleanse itself. You might experience some cravings and irritability at first. This is completely normal and will pass as the alcohol leaves your system. It takes about a week for the body to detoxify itself, so be gentle with yourself during this period. Once your system is clean, you're going to feel amazing! You'll have more energy. Your brain will feel like a fog has lifted. And it's possible you'll feel happier than you have in a long time. Here are a few things you can do to help the process along.

- **Make a firm decision to commit to this experiment 100 percent.** One firm decision takes all the stress out of the thousands of smaller decisions you have to make every day. You want to burn the boats here like there's no going back. It's only 30 days. And at the end, you get to make the final decision about whether you continue on alcohol-free.

- **Tell someone you trust about what you're doing and why.** It's okay if you don't want to announce it to the world quite yet. But there's incredible power in having someone you can confide in. Do this and you're much more likely to follow through with the whole 30 days.

- **Drink plenty of water to flush out all the toxins in your system.** The more you drink clean, pure water, the faster your body can cleanse itself.

- **Get lots of sleep.** Your body repairs itself when you're asleep, so give it all the time it needs. If you're worried you won't be able to sleep without drinking, we'll cover that later in the book.

- **Get some exercise.** You'll feel better when you get your blood moving. And I've found vigorous exercise to be a great way to overcome both cravings and irritability.

- **Eat healthy foods, especially protein.** Your body needs protein to make amino acids, which help elevate your mood.

- **Start a journal.** You're going to want to "talk" through what you learn in this book, and a journal is a great place to record your thoughts.

- **Take a photo and weigh yourself.** You might be surprised at the differences you see in your physical appearance after 30 days without alcohol.

- **Stay social.** Now is not the time to isolate yourself or lock yourself away from your friends and family. You need your social life. You need your friends. You might be nervous about going out to places where you regularly drink. But this is an experiment. You have to get out there and try it. You are experimenting with how your real life will be without alcohol. As you go along, you will be amazed to realize you don't need alcohol to socialize or have a good time. You only thought you did. Think back to when you were a child or in high school—did you need alcohol then? Weren't you having the most fun? And what's the worst that can happen? You go out to happy hour, you order a refreshing glass of iced tea, and you have a miserable time. So what? It's just one evening, and it's all part of the experiment. That is great data. You can examine exactly why you had a miserable time and whether the lack of alcohol is truly the reason. I bet you will surprise yourself by having an amazing time.

- **Be positive!** Many people tell me their biggest fear is they don't think they can do it. They aren't sure they're strong enough to make it 30 days. Don't kick off this experiment by feeling sorry for yourself. You have so much to look forward to. Sure, the cleansing process takes a little while and it's not entirely pleasant, but you are strong and you can handle it. The same people who thought they couldn't do it write to me after a week or two to say they can't believe the difference in themselves. They now know they are stronger than they thought.

- **Join this book's online social challenge at alcoholexperiment.com.** There you can do this experiment with thousands of like-minded people from all over the globe. You will get amazing community support, plus daily video resources and a private online journal to document your progress. Consider posting your selfie and get encouragement from others. Use it as a reminder and as a way to track your progress. One of the most amazing changes is how much clearer, more peaceful, and alert your eyes will look after 30 days alcohol-free. And when you join the free online experiment, there are even Alcohol Experiment mentors who've already gone through this process and are committed to helping you make it to the end. There are even Alcohol Experiment mentors there who've already gone through this process and who are committed to helping you make it all the way to the end. (For a reader's discount, please visit alcoholexperiment.com /reader) Throughout this book, you'll find stories and observations from actual community members. The comments are real, though the names have been changed.

- **Consider hosting The Alcohol Experiment in your community!** Change is more fun with friends! I've put together some ideas for how to make this super fun in a group and you can find all the details in the back of this book on page 329.

This is a 30-day experiment, right? So I just want you to read the short lesson for each day. Try to read it in the morning, if you can, and put the recommendations into practice during the day. Don't be surprised if you find yourself having epiphanies in the shower or shouting, "Holy cow!" while you're driving. Once your mind starts mulling over some of these ideas, there's no telling where your thoughts can go.

As with almost everything in life, your perspective can determine your outcome. So instead of thinking about giving something up, think about what you're going to gain: self-respect, more money in your wallet, a better relationship with your spouse and your kids, better health, better working relationships, a leaner body, and more.

This is exciting! You are embarking on an amazing journey. And don't worry—it's only 30 days. You can do anything for 30 days.

Are you ready?

Let's go!

JOURNAL QUESTIONS:
YOUR DAILY WISDOM: DIRECT FROM *YOU*

I am so excited to include journal questions for you at the end of each day. Here's why: Besides the fact that my own personal experience of journaling has been one of the most helpful and profound tools in my life, journaling has also been scientifically proven to reduce stress, boost immunity, sharpen memory, improve mood, and increase emotional awareness and function.

All of these benefits will be so helpful as you navigate this journey, and I especially love the last one—increased emotional awareness and function—for our purpose here. As you begin to experience life without alcohol, there will be so much rebalancing on a cellular, hormonal level in your brain and body and on an emotional level. Becoming more aware of your emotional landscape and increasing your natural ability to regulate emotions with the help of journaling throughout this process will be so beneficial in both the short and long term.

Yet, science aside, I believe the most important and profound benefit of honest journaling is that you access the deep wells of wisdom that already exist inside of *you*. Have you ever had an "a-ha!" moment when something falls into place and the insight feels familiar? Like it was something you have known all along but just needed to remember? I believe that journaling gives us that. And I've created these daily questions not only for the scientific and neurological benefits but to allow you to learn from your most important teacher throughout these 30 days—YOU.

You may feel some resistance in regards to journaling. I know I did. For a long time I didn't write just for myself but as if someone was going to find it later, even if that someone was me! (Yes, I filtered my own writing for myself! And I am not the only one!) We often miss out on some core benefits of journaling because we won't let down the barriers or self-judgment as words come out on the page.

In order to cross the threshold of resistance that you may feel in regards to journaling, here are some tips that have helped me a ton:

- **Become aware of your filters, and remove them.** Most people write (and live!) with filters. Some of these filters may include: writing what we think we should write, writing with a specific purpose in mind, trying to write beautifully, trying to write "correctly," trying to sound smart, etc. This is one of the biggest hindrances to journaling, and right here, right now, I'm inviting you to toss those filters out the window.

- **WRITE LIKE NO ONE IS READING.** Seriously though. Not even yourself at a later date. When I got that I wasn't writing for anyone else to read, not even myself, it shifted everything for me.

- **Plan to burn everything you write.** You don't actually have to, but write like you plan to. When I did this, my ability to write what I was actually feeling, in all of its human ugliness and imperfection, increased greatly, and thus the positive effects of journaling increased as well. I started to be able to truly just empty my brain of everything rather than holding back.

- Don't underestimate this profound tool (the tool of writing) because of its simplicity.

- **Be gentle on yourself with the discipline of it.** Don't beat yourself up for missing a day or a week. Jump back in whenever you can, whenever you want to or need to, especially when you're having a hard time.

- And finally, allow yourself to marvel at and celebrate the incredible insights and wisdom that only you can bring to this 30-day experience. Remembering that none of my words will be half as important in your life as the words you write to yourself.

❚ DAY 1 ❚

What's Your Why?

The best day of your life is the one on which you decide your life
is your own. No apologies or excuses. No one to blame. The gift
is yours–it is an amazing journey–and you alone are responsible
for the quality of it. This is the day your life really begins.
–BOB MOAWAD

We've talked about how you've been unconsciously conditioned to
believe alcohol is a vital part of life for relaxing, socializing, and everything in between. And you know there are competing desires inside
your mind. Your conscious mind wants to drink less, or even stop
drinking completely. And your subconscious mind believes you need
to keep drinking for some very good reasons. Before we dive into
those beliefs and stories and deciding if they're true, we need to know
what those beliefs actually are. After reading literally thousands of
stories from people who've gone through this process, I'm pretty sure
I know what your beliefs are. But that's not important. What's important is that YOU know what they are. So let's start this experiment
by writing a list.

| WHY DO YOU DRINK?

Write down a list of every reason you drink. There's no judgment here. We simply want a list.

To get you going, here's a look at part of my list. You might have some of the same reasons.

- Work is stressful and drinking helps me relax after a long day.
- Drinking helps me be more creative on the job.
- Drinking helps me be more outgoing at networking events.
- Drinking is important to my social relationships.
- I love the taste of wine.

Don't stop with a few reasons; keep going until you can't think of any more. You might come up with 50 or 100 reasons, and that's fine.

You've brought your subconscious beliefs up to the surface of your mind. Now we can shine a light on them, examine them, and you can decide for yourself whether those beliefs are true. And you can make that decision based on the facts, not social conditioning from the media and your peers. Don't do anything with this list right now. Don't try to change your mind. At the moment, these are your beliefs, and they're currently true in your life. As I present you different ideas over the next 30 days, you may think about this list differently.

| WHY THE ALCOHOL EXPERIMENT?

Okay, next I want you to pull out another piece of paper and make a second list. Write down all the reasons you want to take part in this experiment. WHY do you think you might want to drink less? Here's a peek at my list:

- I'm tired of waking up slightly hungover.

- I no longer want to worry that I said something stupid the night before.
- I am sick of the internal dialogue about my drinking—I am tired of thinking about drinking.
- I saw a photo of myself out with friends and my teeth looked purplish from wine—it was disgusting.
- I look back on certain days and my memories are so fuzzy. I am afraid I am missing my life because I can't clearly remember it all.

TODAY, read over both your lists and notice how they are in conflict with each other. This is the whole source of your cognitive dissonance. It's the battle going in your mind all the time, written in your own words. Over the coming weeks, it might help you to picture these lists on either side of a seesaw or a balance. Right now, the first list might be longer than the second one. In a few weeks, check back in to see if the balance has shifted at all.

▌ DAY 1 JOURNAL QUESTIONS

Remember, all the wisdom you seek is actually inside you; the most important words in this Experiment are the ones you tell yourself. Take some time and answer these questions in here or a separate journal (most effective), a voice memo to yourself, or simply by speaking the answers out loud for only you to hear.

1. *Why You Drink—Your Big List*

Reflect and read over each reason you wrote down. How do they make you feel? What reasons do you wish weren't there? If you could take an eraser to your brain and change some of these reasons and thoughts, would you?

_____

_____

_____

_____

_____

_____

_____

_____

_____

_____

_____

_____

_____

_____

_____

_____

_____

_____

_____

_____

_____

_____

_____

_____

_____

2. *What's Your Why?*

Why do you want to take part in The Alcohol Experiment? Why do you want to take a break? To drink a bit less in the future? Have a look at my list and make your own. Dig deep on why you are doing this in the first place.

_____

_____

_____

_____

_____

_____

_____

_____

_____

_____

_____

_____

_____

_____

_____

_____

_____

_____

_____

_____

_____

_____

_____

_____

_____

3. *Let's Get Excited*

Allow yourself to dream. If this experiment delivered everything it promises, what would that look like in your life? How would you feel at the end of 30 days? A year from now? What would have changed in your life? Don't focus on the pain of what you don't yet have, but allow yourself to feel hope and focus on the joy of what is yet to come.

_____

_____

_____

_____

_____

_____

_____

_____

_____

_____

_____

_____

_____

_____

_____

_____

_____

_____

_____

_____

_____

_____

_____

_____

_____

Day 1 Reflections from alcoholexperiment.com

"I am sick of alcohol damaging my life in so many ways, including making an idiot of myself, hangovers, feeling violently ill, wasted time and opportunity, horrendous fights with my husband, putting a strain on my marriage, weight gain, no exercise, loosened stomach, way too big an appetite, anxiety, smoking, money, no time." —JULIANNA

"Today is the first day of the rest of my life." —BRIAN

"Hey guys. Day 1 here. Interested to see if my list of reasons why I drink was smaller than my list of reasons why I am here. I am taking that as a sign that I have more reason to stop than to continue drinking. I have more to gain from being AF [Alcohol Free]. I feel quite motivated by that." —ROMERO

"I decided that my life is my own and I am ready to live it the way I want to, and that doesn't include alcohol." —LIZA

||| ACT #1 |||

The Taste of Alcohol

NOTE: The idea of the ACT technique—Awareness, Clarity, Turnaround—is to give you an alternate perspective. It is an exercise to help you resolve your external or internal disagreement around alcohol. First, we'll become aware by naming a belief you have about drinking. Then we'll gain clarity around that belief, looking at where it came from and how you may have picked it up without even knowing it. We'll also look at the internal and external evidence that supports that belief (or doesn't). Finally, we'll decide if the belief holds true through a turnaround. We will look at the opposite of the belief, and decide if the opposite is as true as or truer than the original belief. When this process is complete, you get to decide if you still believe this and, more important, if that belief is serving you or if your life would be better by simply letting it go. No matter what you decide, you will gain a new perspective. The whole idea is to play detective and look at the evidence and form an objective opinion.

What's your all-time-favorite drink? The one you can't wait to get your hands on at the end of a long day or on Friday night? I bet if you think about it hard enough, you can even taste it right now. Taste is an innocent reason for drinking. After all, no one thinks twice about eating ice cream or nachos. They taste good! And our favorite alcoholic beverages are the same way. But for the sake of this experiment, let's dig a little deeper.

| AWARENESS

Many people tell me they really like the taste of their favorite drink. I get it. I was a red wine girl all the way. Maybe you're a margarita lover. Or maybe you enjoy the taste of a good scotch on the rocks. Let's name this belief:

"I drink for the taste."

I know a woman who drinks a shot of Baileys in her coffee every morning before she drives her child to school. She doesn't think it's a big deal. It's just a shot, and nothing else makes her coffee taste as good. Her concerned husband tried to get her to try Baileys-flavored coffee creamer, but she insists it doesn't taste the same. But if you think about it, she's not actually tasting a lot of alcohol—it's mostly the flavorings, cream and sugar. So what do you think? Is she truly enjoying Baileys for only the taste? Or is there something else going on?

| CLARITY

In order to gain clarity around your beliefs, you need to look back at the past and figure out why you have this belief in the first place. Where did it come from? There are no right or wrong answers here, and everyone is different. So ask yourself, what observations and experiences have you had in your past that might have made you believe alcohol tastes good? Maybe it's something as simple as watching your parents pour themselves a drink at the end of the day. Or observing how they drank glass after glass in the evening. Why in the world would they drink it all the time if it tasted so bad? They're smart, right? They're grown-ups. So it must taste good, or they wouldn't keep drinking it.

I have a friend from France whose parents made sure she drank a little wine with dinner from the time she was eight years old. She hated how it tasted, and told her parents so frequently. But they continued to press on, saying she would appreciate the taste when she got older. The implication was that when she became more mature and grown-up, she would enjoy the taste of wine. We all want to appear more grown up when we're kids, don't we? Sure enough, over time my friend became a great wine lover and now drinks it every night.

Think back to your first drink and remember the experience. What were you drinking? Maybe it was wine at dinner when you were young. Maybe it was champagne on New Year's Eve when you were allowed to stay up until midnight for the first time. Maybe you snuck into your parents' liquor cabinet with a friend on a dare. Or maybe it wasn't until much later—maybe your first beer was in college. Regardless of when it was, think back to your first sip. Did you actually like it? Or did you choke and sputter, maybe even spit it out?

Who was with you at the time? Was it a friend you wanted to impress? Was it a parent you wanted to make proud? Were you trying to find a place to fit in with a new group of people? If you're like the vast majority of people I talk to, your first experience tasting alcohol was not pleasant. You didn't like it. But someone was there to say, "Don't worry, it's an acquired taste. You'll get used to it."

So take a few minutes to write down where your taste for alcohol came from. What was it like the first time you tried a new beer or hard liquor? Was it always an amazing taste you immediately loved? Did you acquire the taste over time? Or did you fake liking it because you wanted to impress someone?

Now that you have an idea where your beliefs came from, let's play detective and look at the internal and external evidence. This evidence will help you decide whether your belief that you like the taste of alcohol is true or whether you have been fooling yourself.

People have some pretty intense reactions when they taste alcohol for the first time. They talk about it burning on the way down. They wrinkle up their nose because it doesn't even smell good. Their eyes start watering. They might even spit it out. Why? One of the major reasons we don't like the taste of something is because it's harmful to us. We don't like the taste of rotten food because it can make us sick. Well, what's going on when you have a hangover? You're sick! Our taste buds react negatively to alcohol to protect us from a harmful substance.

Let's think about the idea of acquiring a taste for something. Whatever your drink of choice is, you probably didn't like it immediately. But your body allowed you to get used to it. Why? Because your brain assumes you have no choice in the matter. If you did, it would make no sense for you to keep drinking. So your body does the logical thing—it makes it easier for you to deal with the taste. You acquire it. Which, if you think about it, is the same thing as becoming immune to alcohol.

Let's look at it another way: My brother has a goat farm, and whenever I walk into the barn, there's an intense, unpleasant odor. As my sister-in-law says, it smells "very goaty." But guess what? My brother and his family don't even notice the smell anymore. Because they've gotten used to it. They have to go into the barn to feed the goats, so their brains no longer register the odor. That doesn't mean they like it. But they have, over time, gotten used to it.

If you did happen to love the taste of your first drink, it was probably something fruity or creamy that was more sugar than anything else. Am I right? Some drinks go down more easily than others. Straight alcohol is ethanol. The same stuff you put in your gas tank! A few sips will make you vomit and a few ounces of pure ethanol will kill you. I think it's safe to say you would never go suck on the end of a gas pump nozzle because it tastes good! No matter what your favorite drink is, the alcohol makes up only a small percentage of the liquid. The rest is flavorings, sugar, carbohydrates, and other additives.

Now of course there are things we appreciate as adults that we did not appreciate as children. We clearly grow a more refined palate as we age, but let's not kid ourselves: If we were purely drinking for the taste, we could certainly find other substitutes that are similar and wouldn't cause any of the side effects alcohol causes. I am intolerant to gluten and I've managed to find plenty of substitutes that aren't exactly the same but are now a natural part of my life and don't create the stomach pain gluten does. The fact is ethanol doesn't taste good. Consider this: When scientists want rats or mice to drink alcohol for a study, they have to force-feed them because they will not naturally opt to drink it.

So are you honestly drinking it for the taste?

If not, then why *are* you drinking it?

You've almost certainly observed characters in the movies and on TV enjoying the taste of alcohol, or giving a satisfying burp and a smile after chugging a beer. Even if the actors are actually drinking whiskey-colored tea, the message still gets across—it tastes good. We all tend to choose our alcohol to match our identities. If we're refined and classy, maybe we drink red wine. Or if we like old cowboy movies, maybe we lean toward whiskey. Of course, if you're an international spy, you've got to order a martini—shaken, not stirred. We identify with the characters and tend to like the same drinks they like. I used to love chugging Guinness and was so proud of my chugging ability. It made me feel tough and like "one of the boys" in that masculine work environment.

Maybe you see yourself as a discerning wine lover, and your cellar has become a status symbol. If that's the case, you probably pride yourself on your ability to discern the toasty-smoky-oaky flavors with their fruity or floral overtones. Or whatever. Here's a fun fact—the American Association of Wine Economists conducted a study of more than 6,000 wine drinkers. In this blind taste test, they discovered that people cannot tell the difference between cheap wine and expensive wine. In fact, most people preferred the taste of the cheaper varieties. And you know what else? The same blind research later found that people can't tell the difference between pâté and dog food!

So what about the argument, "alcohol enhances the taste of my food"? Do we say that about any other beverage-and-food combination? People say milk enhances the taste of cookies, but could that be because we physically dip cookies into milk? No one dips their steak into their wineglass. The truth is, alcohol is actually an anesthetic. It numbs our ability to taste, making it more difficult to savor our food.

Imagine we could remove all the physical and emotional effects of alcohol. If it couldn't actually make you drunk, would people still drink it? There's a body of pretty convincing research suggesting they wouldn't. It tastes bad. It's poisonous. Drinking for the taste is a convenient, innocent excuse. At the end of the day, is it a possibility that there's something more going on with your drinking than just the taste? Humans are incredibly adept at lying to themselves and believing their own stories. It's possible that you actually do love the taste of a cool, frosty margarita. But is it really the alcohol you like? You may not have tried a delicious virgin margarita, but the truth is, they taste as good, maybe even better! And you'll be surprised and empowered by how much you enjoy yourself without the tequila—or the hangover.

▌ TURNAROUND

This may be the most important part of the ACT technique. Here you want to dig into the turnaround, or the opposite of the belief. You'll want to take the time to come up with as many ways as you can (at least three) that the turnaround is as true or truer than the original belief. In this case, the opposite of "*I drink for the taste*" is "*I don't drink for the taste*" or maybe even "*I don't like the taste.*" Now it's your turn to come up with as many ways as you can that the turnaround is true in your life.

| DAY 2 |

It's Not What You Give Up, But What You GAIN

One reason people resist change is because they focus on
what they have to give up, instead of what they have to gain.
—RICK GODWIN

As a participant in this experiment, you're obviously giving something up. You're giving up alcohol for 30 days. But there are two ways to look at it. You could focus on how hard it's going to be and all the things you're going to have to give up and go without. Or you could think about all the amazing insights and experiences you're going to gain as a result of the experiment.

We all undoubtedly control our destinies through our expectations. In other words, we get what we expect. If we expect this experiment to be miserable, then that is what we're going to get. And so to make this a more pleasant experience, we have to change our thinking. We have to *expect* to go into this and experience 30 days of amazing epiphanies, better health, higher energy levels, and systematic shifts in our thinking. How do we do it? We decide to focus on the positive. It's that simple. You might feel weird at first focusing on all the good things that are going to happen, especially if you're skeptical that they will happen. But when you shift your thinking to what you will gain, the good things will come. They truly will.

| BENEFITS

For me, I lost 13 pounds in the first 30 days. My marriage has never been better, and I've finally started doing all the things I'd wanted to do for years and years. Things alcohol kept me from doing, such as starting a business, writing a book, creating a mindfulness practice, and building a strong family life. I've become much happier socially because I'm never worried about what I said the night before. I've become much more successful. I think I look significantly better—my eyes are clearer, my hair is thicker. But these are my stories. What about other people who've gone through the 30-day experiment? What have they gained? Here's a short list from other Alcohol Experiment participants:

- Clearheaded mornings
- Better health
- Less anxiety
- True relaxation
- Better relationships
- Self-love
- Happier family life
- Freedom to fully participate in life

| PAY ATTENTION TO YOUR LANGUAGE

So how, exactly, do you focus on the positive? The easiest way to do it is to pay attention to your language, the words coming out of your mouth. Saying something like "I can't drink" is pretty negative. It sends all the wrong messages to your subconscious because it leaves you feeling deprived and thinking about something you can't do. On the other hand, saying "I'm going to enjoy drinking an iced tea tonight" or "I really love this lemonade" is saying the same thing in a different way. You're telling yourself you're not going to drink alcohol, but you're doing it in a positive way. And you're giving your subconscious the message that you're going to *enjoy* what you're going to do instead of that you're deprived or you can't.

Saying "I'm giving up alcohol for the month" also sends a negative message to your subconscious. But saying "I'm experimenting to see how much better I feel" is totally different. Positive phrasing sends all the right messages and will help you be more successful. So start to be mindful and conscious of how you talk to yourself.

You don't *have to* do this experiment. You *get to* do it. You have the opportunity to do this. You are excited to do this. You are *choosing* to participate. Recognize your old, disempowering words around alcohol and replace them with new, empowering words. This is important. The brain loves anything that gets you out of pain and into pleasure. It loves that shift both consciously and subconsciously, so choose the words you want to use. When you start consciously choosing your words, you'll even start to get a little buzz, especially if you reinforce your statements afterward. If you say, "I'm going to enjoy some iced tea tonight," reinforce it by actually feeling it. "Wow, I did enjoy that iced tea tonight!" The brain will latch on to the experience and repeat it more easily the next time.

Labeling

Another type of language you'll want to pay attention to is how you're labeling yourself and others. There's a ton of research showing how labels can limit your experience. When we put a label on something, we create a corresponding emotion based on our beliefs and experiences. That's especially true when we label ourselves and say we're depressed or we're alcoholics. It's true that we might be suffering, but by labeling ourselves that we *are* those things, we ingrain the negative feelings and end up believing them subconsciously.

It might take a little while to start catching yourself focusing on the negative or unnecessarily labeling yourself, so keep at it. If you catch yourself once a day, it's a great start. Over time you'll get better and better at it, and you'll develop ways to reprogram your language and be more positive naturally. Don't be surprised if people start noticing and telling you how much happier and upbeat you seem. That's because you *are* happier and upbeat when you expect to be and use language to reinforce the idea.

The Power of Positive

Staying positive is one amazing tool you can use to stay alcohol-free for the next few weeks, and beyond if you choose. Positive thinking and believing in yourself are helpful, but I'm also talking about how you use words in sentences. Psychologists have studied how our brains process negative statements and found that the way a sentence is constructed affects brain activity. Negative constructions can cause higher levels of activity, which means we have to think harder.

Let's keep this easy, okay? If we don't have to think hard about drinking, the experiment will be less stressful.

So, say someone asks you, "Would you like a drink?"

You could answer in the negative: "No, thanks. I'm not drinking tonight."

Or you could answer in the positive: "Yes! I'd love a club soda with lime."

By speaking with positive statements, your subconscious mind isn't triggered into activity. It's happy. It believes you enjoy drinking, and so you're enjoying a drink. It just happens to be a nonalcoholic drink this time.

How We Talk Changes Our Experiences

Furthermore, according to Albert Ellis, one of the fathers of modern psychology, how we talk about what is happening to us and around us actually changes our emotions around our experiences! One of the most powerful things I want you to learn in this experiment is that you are much more in control of your life than you may realize. Sure, it takes practice and awareness to begin to shape our emotions and experiences through our language—specifically the language we use when speaking to ourselves—but, wow, is it worth it!

I honestly can't believe the changes that have happened inside me once I learned the importance of how I talk to myself—the words I use and even the tone. Do yourself a favor: Over the next few days, start to pay attention to how you speak to yourself. Ask yourself if you would speak to a stranger like that? What about someone you consider a friend? What about your child?

Listening to Your Inner Voice

You may find it hard to "hear" your inner voice. If that's the case, do this—notice your emotions. When you start to feel anxious, upset, or stressed (or any other negative emotion), use that as a signal to pause and reflect on what you were just saying to yourself.

How we speak to ourselves has a huge impact on our emotions. This is true not only around drinking but in all areas of our lives. Studies show that the majority of most people's thinking is negative and self-destructive. However, since our inner dialogue is constant, we are not often aware of it. The next time you start to feel badly about yourself, I want you to stop and notice the words you just said inside your head. Write them down. And then ask yourself, Was it nice? Was it helpful? Was it something you would say to someone you love? Was it even something you would say to a complete stranger, or are you talking to yourself in a more destructive way than you would talk to a complete stranger? Take time every day to listen to your inner dialogue and consciously try to speak to yourself with respect. Like any habit, how you speak to yourself is unconscious, and it will take some conscious awareness to discover exactly what that inner dialogue consists of. But if you can learn to speak to yourself as you would speak to someone you love, your entire life can change for the better.

TODAY, observe your language patterns—both what you say out loud and the self-talk in your head (we'll get into even more about self-talk later in this book). And write down the words you're using on a piece of paper. Do you use the same words over and over? Are they negative or positive? When you think about alcohol, do you feel sorry for yourself and tell yourself you are not able to drink? Or do you feel excited about the challenge and tell yourself you don't *have* to drink—and don't have to wake up with another hangover? How are you treating yourself internally? Are the things you are saying to yourself generally helpful or hurtful? Will they help make these 30 days a more pleasant experience? Don't judge yourself for using negative language. Instead, think of some ways you can turn your language around and make it more positive. Make it a fun exercise.

| DAY 2 JOURNAL QUESTIONS

Remember, all the wisdom you seek is actually inside you; the most important words in this Experiment are the ones you tell yourself. Take some time and answer these questions in here or a separate journal (most effective), a voice memo to yourself, or simply by speaking the answers out loud for only you to hear.

1. *Language Patterns*

Observe your language patterns—both what you say out loud and the self-talk in your head. Write down the words you're using with yourself.

Extra credit: Carry a piece of paper (or the notes app on your phone) with you and notice every time you start to feel upset during the day. Stop and notice what you just said to yourself in your head. Jot those things down. Would you say that in that tone to someone you love? Even to a stranger?

_____

_____

_____

_____

_____

_____

_____

_____

_____

_____

_____

_____

_____

_____

_____

_____

_____

_____

_____

_____

2. *Change Your Words. Change Your Experience.*

Do you believe that how you talk (especially to yourself) can actually change your experiences? Anchor this by writing down a time this has happened. Notice how powerful this can be.

_____

_____

_____

_____

_____

_____

_____

_____

_____

_____

_____

_____

_____

_____

_____

_____

_____

_____

_____

_____

_____

_____

_____

_____

_____

_____

_____

_____

3. *Choose Better Words*

Make a list of things you can say (to yourself and others) over the next 28 days that will influence how this experiment feels for you.

Note: These must be things you actually believe. Otherwise, you risk increasing the cognitive dissonance in your mind.

_____

_____

_____

_____

_____

_____

_____

_____

_____

_____

_____

_____

_____

_____

_____

_____

_____

_____

_____

_____

_____

_____

_____

_____

_____

_____

_____

_____

Day 2 Reflections from alcoholexperiment.com

"My mind-set has definitely changed. Everyone around me is still drinking, and waking up with a hangover. This morning when I woke up I found myself wondering, 'Why would they do that to themselves? Why?' Then I remembered, 'Oh, yeah, I used to do that to myself, too.' It was so strange truly not being able to comprehend why people would purposefully ingest poison knowing that they would wake up feeling like shit!"   —CARL

"I'm feeling great without alcohol! New things have opened up for me—some simple things like planting a little garden, trying a different grocery store, exercising more. I've already lost weight, and I never have to worry about how much I'll embarrass myself while drinking. I feel more present with my children and am not forgetting as much, or having to constantly remind myself of things I said I'd do with them."   —ARLETTA

"I feel a change happening inside me, and I feel confident in myself again, or maybe for the first time. I feel like there is hope for the future and that there is so much to learn and ways in which I can grow and simply experience being human."   —MORGAN

❙ DAY 3 ❙

Why We Think We Like to Drink

*True happiness comes from gaining insight and growing
into your best possible self. Otherwise all you're having
is immediate gratification pleasure—which is fleeting
and doesn't grow you as a person.*
—KAREN SALMANSOHN

Clearly, we must like drinking. Otherwise we wouldn't do it, right? At least, in the beginning we liked it. Right now, you might be struggling with how much you actually hate the aftereffects. But there's no denying that the first drink feels good. Before we can unpack all the complicated pieces of the alcohol puzzle, it's important to understand what's actually happening in the brain when we drink.

So, I'm out with my friends, and I order a glass of wine. I've had a hard day at work, and I'm looking forward to relaxing and laughing with people I love. That first glass makes me feel giggly, and there's a little rush of euphoria that makes me feel good, maybe for the first time all day. What's happening is that the wine artificially stimulates the area of my brain called the nucleus accumbens, or the pleasure center. The chemicals responsible for euphoria are endorphins, the same chemicals responsible for the good feelings when you exercise.

I DOPAMINE AND SEROTONIN

Two main chemicals work in the pleasure center: dopamine, which is responsible for desire and craving; and serotonin, which is responsible for the feelings of satiety and inhibition. In a healthy brain, there is a delicate balance between the two. But alcohol throws off that balance, and so as I'm drinking that glass of wine lots of dopamine gets dumped into my system, making me want more of what gave me pleasure (the alcohol). Since the pleasure center has been artificially stimulated by an outside substance, my brain seeks to regain the correct balance. So it sends out a chemical downer, called dynorphin. This actually suppresses my feelings of euphoria, and as the effects of the first glass start to wear off, my sense of well-being actually falls *below* where it was when I started drinking. That means I'm *lower* than when I got off work after a hard day. Bummer.

The dopamine is still working, though, and makes me crave more of what made me feel good. So I order another glass of wine. And the cycle starts all over again. An unwanted effect is that in order to combat the depressant effects of alcohol, my body counteracts the alcohol by releasing things like adrenaline and cortisol. You may have heard of cortisol—it is also known as the "stress hormone." So now in my body's attempt to maintain homeostasis and combat the alcohol, I am lower than when I started. In other words, I now have to cross an even bigger gap to get above that baseline of pleasure. And that's miserable. Even worse, though, is that the alcohol is starting to affect other areas of my brain. My senses are being numbed, and my brain is actually slowing down. Eventually, I might slur my speech. Perhaps my vision blurs. I feel detached from reality. I convince myself that this is a welcome break from the real world.

The Cycle Continues

The drinking cycle continues, and I get more and more drunk. What was at first a nice tipsy feeling is now completely out of control. But I don't care because my brain isn't processing the long-term meanings and implications of my behavior. Eventually, if I'm drinking a lot, it's been slowed down so much that I have to work hard to walk straight on my way to the restroom.

My brain receptors have become numb, and my senses don't relay the information as well, and so memories aren't formed. I don't completely recall the embarrassing things I say or do while I'm drunk. I don't feel the pain I'm trying to escape. The stress from the workday fades away for a little while. But the stress remains when I sober up, and it's compounded by the hangover I'm suffering from. The embarrassing photos show up on Facebook. And my best friend won't talk to me because I pissed her off so badly . . . somehow . . . I'm not really sure what happened.

If you're reading this book, you know what I'm talking about. The initial rush doesn't last. The more drunk you get, the more you regret it when you sober up. It's a downward spiral. And if you're like me, you blame yourself. *Why can't I get it together? Why am I so weak? What's wrong with me?*

TODAY, realize that the cycle has nothing to do with you being strong or weak. It has nothing to do with you being a good or bad person. It's a chemical chain reaction that happens to everyone. Although we all feel the effects slightly differently based on our age, weight, sex, and environment, the biological reactions are the same.

▌DAY 3 JOURNAL QUESTIONS

Remember, all the wisdom you seek is actually inside you; the most important words in this Experiment are the ones you tell yourself. Take some time and answer these questions in here or a separate journal (most effective), a voice memo to yourself, or simply by speaking the answers out loud for only you to hear.

1. *Brain Chemicals*

Reflect on the teaching about what is happening inside your brain. Just write what comes to mind. How does this make you feel? What was most surprising about today's lesson? How can you use this knowledge going forward?

_____

_____

_____

_____

_____

_____

_____

_____

_____

_____

_____

_____

_____

_____

_____

_____

_____

_____

_____

_____

_____

_____

_____

_____

_____

2. *Not Your Fault*

Can you begin to see that your brain, in relation to an addictive substance, has actually been doing exactly what it is supposed to do? Feel that. You've truly been doing the best you can with the tools you have. Alcohol just might not be the best tool, at least not all the time. How does it feel to know that there is nothing wrong with you? Reflect on the knowledge that you are whole, not broken, despite what you may have believed. How does that make you feel?

_____

_____

_____

_____

_____

_____

_____

_____

_____

_____

_____

_____

_____

_____

_____

_____

_____

_____

_____

_____

_____

_____

_____

Day 3 Reflections from alcoholexperiment.com

"This is my third day and already I feel like I slept better. I woke up happy that I finally committed myself mentally. It is a shift I have a hard time explaining or putting my finger on. I am embracing the idea that I do not need to hit rock bottom. It is hard to break that way of thinking, but I believe in my heart now that it is true. I can quit right now, feel better right now, and not drink again. It is that simple. An a-ha moment!"   —MONICA

"I had a situation last night that would typically send me straight to the bottle or a six-pack of beer. I won."   —BRADY

"This is the first Saturday in as long as I can remember when I haven't woken up hungover and miserable. I am anxious, which feels like a craving, but I recognize that it is because I have so much time on my hands. What shall I do? I'm going to need to get some hobbies!"   —PENNY

||| ACT #2 |||

Alcohol and Sleep

| AWARENESS

When I started researching this book, I sent out a survey asking people what their biggest fears were about giving up alcohol. I was surprised to see sleep come up high on the list. It's a huge fear for people that they won't be able to fall asleep or they won't be able to stay asleep. Let's name this belief:

"I need alcohol to sleep."

If you're struggling with this belief, you're definitely not alone. One of my favorite authors, William Porter, who wrote *Alcohol Explained*, is well versed in alcohol's effects on sleep, and he explains this topic brilliantly. So let's dig into this belief a little deeper.

| CLARITY

I'm not sure how much the media is responsible for this particular belief. There's not a lot of insomnia portrayed in the movies or on TV. However, if you've ever had a bout of sleeplessness, you know how disconcerting it can be. Sleep is critical to our mental and physical well-being. And when you can't sleep, you'll do anything to be able to fall asleep. Lack of sleep has been linked to serious health problems, including cancer, heart disease, type 2 diabetes, infections, and obesity. It also affects alertness, mood, and physical strength. This is because your body repairs itself while you sleep. It's also a time when your mind digests what happened during the day. It assimilates the information and often comes up with solutions to problems. So when you wake up, you feel better physically and mentally. That means if you've experienced alcohol helping you sleep, then this belief takes hold very quickly.

Regular, high-quality sleep is essential to our well-being. So let's look at how sleep actually works. There are two levels of sleep: rapid eye movement (REM) sleep and deep sleep, or slow-wave sleep. Every night, you go through several cycles of both levels. First, you dip into REM sleep, when you're a bit restless and your eyes are literally darting back and forth inside your eyelids (which is where the name comes from). This is light sleep, but it's crucial to your good health. Scientists don't actually know why REM is so important, but they've done studies where rats were deprived of REM sleep and it killed them in just a few weeks. Once you cycle out of REM, you go into a deeper level of slow-wave sleep. That's when the body does the repair work that needs to happen to keep you healthy. When you're getting a good night's sleep, you go through six or seven cycles of both REM and deep sleep.

Now, what happens when alcohol is introduced into the equation? Alcohol is a chemical depressant, so it reduces neural activity in the brain. Normally, your brain releases a variety of chemicals and hormones at different times to help bring you back to homeostasis. As you already know, homeostasis is the delicate balance where all the systems in your body are working correctly. When you drink, you're introducing a foreign chemical. And in order to reach homeostasis, your brain has to release powerful counter-chemicals and stress hormones.

So the cycle looks like this:

You have a drink, and you stimulate your pleasure center while the blood alcohol is rising. But as time goes on and the alcohol levels start to go down, your brain knows there's a depressant in your system. So it releases stimulants (adrenaline and cortisol) to bring you back up into homeostasis. Unfortunately, the depressant alcohol wears off before the stimulants do, and you're left with an overstimulated brain for hours after the drinks have worn off. It's as if you drank alcohol and a triple espresso at the same time. The alcohol wears off, but the espresso is still affecting you hours later.

The alcohol is disrupting your sleep schedule. After you drink, you go into a deep sleep for the first five hours or so. That might seem great, but you don't get into REM sleep. And you need both. So while your body is trying to process all the chemicals in your body, your cycles are completely thrown out of whack. You wind up with only one or two cycles of REM sleep instead of the six or seven you actually need.

After those first five hours, you wake up and can't get back to sleep. Many people wake up at three or four in the morning and fret about everything they can think of. The worry and regret creep in, and the negative thoughts take over the brain. All this is happening because you're overstimulated and your body chemistry is completely out of balance. Here's the thing—any amount of alcohol will disrupt your sleep. It doesn't matter if you have one drink or you go on a margarita binge-fest. You're not going to sleep well. If you do this night after night, the lack of quality sleep cycles will begin to take its toll.

And there's another big problem. When you start getting ready for bed without alcohol in your system, your body releases its own chemicals to quiet you down and prepare you for sleep. But when you drink regularly, you train your brain to utilize the artificial depressants in the alcohol to do that job. So that means you're relying on alcohol to put you to sleep. But you still aren't rested, because your natural sleep rhythms are out of whack.

So what does this mean for you during this experiment? It means that for the first two to five nights of not drinking, your body may still be expecting those artificial depressants. Your brain might be confused during those early days, and you could have trouble falling asleep. The worst thing you can do at that point is to have a drink to help you sleep. It might seem like the right thing to do, but it will actually set your progress back. The good news is most people find they're sleeping better than ever after the fifth night. You've given your brain time to readjust itself and get the chemical release balanced again. And once this happens, for the first time in years, or maybe decades, you will start getting the rest that your body so desperately needs. This is great news!

While you're waiting for your brain to readjust, you can try a few tricks to help you get to sleep. First, avoid caffeinated drinks after about noon. Caffeine can affect the body for up to 10 hours. So you want it all out of your system by the time you're ready to hit the sack. The other trick is to get a bit of exercise. When you get your body moving, you'll actually find you sleep much better than if you're at rest all day long. You don't have to do anything extreme. You can simply take a walk in the fresh air and get your blood moving.

If you've been drinking for a long time, you may not even notice the daily fatigue you're experiencing because of disrupted sleep patterns. You might think it's because you're "getting older." Maybe you're always tired and you tell yourself, "That's just how I am." We are so overworked and undernourished that fatigue has become completely normal. Let me give you some good news: Once you stop drinking and get your sleep regulated, that fatigue and brain fog often disappear completely. You'll feel better than you have in ages! That's your reward. But you have to get through those first few days and give your body a chance to fix itself.

▌ TURNAROUND

The opposite of "*I need alcohol to sleep*" is "*I don't need alcohol to sleep.*" Come up with as many ways as you can that the opposite is as true as or truer than the original belief.

❙ DAY 4 ❙

Dealing with Discomfort

When you decide to give up alcohol, you might experience some discomfort. I am not talking about severe physical addiction here. If you've been drinking heavily for a long time, your body and mind may have become physically dependent to the point where you have severe withdrawal symptoms, such as delirium tremens or hallucinations. If that's the case, you need to get medical help. You may even need to be hospitalized for a while. When I say "discomfort," I'm talking about the physical symptoms that occur while your body is healing itself. I'm also talking about the psychological and emotional discomfort that comes up because you're giving up something you believe you need.

It takes time, up to a week or longer, for your body to rebalance after you stop drinking. While that's happening, you're probably going to feel uncomfortable. Because alcohol is physically addictive, there are withdrawal symptoms, which are different for different people. When I stopped drinking, I had headaches, anxiety, irritability, and weird nightmares that I accidentally had a drink. The first 10 days were the most intense, but the symptoms went on for about 30 days. Clearly, that's longer than the time it took for the chemical substance to clear out of my body. So, what gives? Why did it take so long? Shouldn't we feel better as soon as the alcohol is gone? Our bodies are more complicated than that, and there's an emotional side to withdrawal as well.

When researchers studied heroin addicts, they found that the severity of withdrawal could depend on the individual's access to the substance they were addicted to. For instance, if the person went to jail and suddenly had zero access to their drug of choice, the withdrawal symptoms weren't as severe as one might expect. But when that person was released years later, and they suddenly had access again, the withdrawal symptoms came back. How weird is that? How is it possible to go through withdrawal years after ingesting a substance? This demonstrates how physical and emotional withdrawals are intertwined. Each affects the other, and our subconscious can easily keep things buried for a long time and then allow them to resurface later.

| CHANGING YOUR MIND-SET

What helped me get through this initial period of physical withdrawal was flipping my mind-set. Instead of seeing the headaches and anxiety as punishment for an addiction that I should have been able to control, I chose to see them as signs that my amazing body was healing itself. I was willing to be sick and put up with the discomfort to make my body whole again. I knew I had been treating it poorly. So I decided to treat it with kindness and give it whatever time it needed to heal.

If you're not feeling your best right now, cut yourself some slack. Imagine if your child was feeling sick. Would you yell at her for being a "bad person" or tell her she was "getting what she deserved"? Of course not! You'd let her rest on the couch, eat chicken soup, and maybe watch some cartoons. You'd tell her to let her body do its job. Give yourself the same courtesy.

The Emotional Aspects

As you probably know, there's more to withdrawal than physical discomfort. There's an emotional side as well. And both sides are all tangled up with each other. It's almost like as soon as you get a handle on one, the other falls to pieces and you're so tempted to give up this experiment and crack open a beer. I get it! On the emotional side, you might feel sad, angry, or resentful. After all, you're giving up something you believe you enjoy. Your subconscious believes you need alcohol to loosen up, relax, have fun with your friends, or handle stress. When you take that coping mechanism away without dealing with these subconscious beliefs, there will be consequences in the form of emotional distress and cravings.

That is why I'm calling these 30 days an "experiment." You're simply testing the waters to see how you might feel if you weren't drinking. Your subconscious mind isn't necessarily going to like that, but it's better than laying down the law and saying, "No more alcohol ever!" That kind of ultimatum can result in a full-on emotional mutiny.

Throughout the course of this experiment, you're going to explore those subconscious beliefs of yours. One day at a time, you're going to read a little bit about different ideas that might make you question what you once thought was true. By the time you reach the end of this book, in fact, you might decide that you never need or even want another drink. And your subconscious will totally go along with it. That's called spontaneous sobriety, and it happens all the time. It happened to me. When your conscious and subconscious minds are in harmony and desire the same thing, there's no cognitive dissonance. And when that happens, there's no struggle. You have no cravings and no desire to go back.

Getting Curious

But that's later. For right now, simply realize that your feelings and physical symptoms are real. Take the time to feel them. Honor them.

Appreciate what your body is trying to tell you. And do not give in to the temptation to use alcohol to numb them. These symptoms are temporary. They will go away in time.

So what can you do in the meantime? How do you handle the emotional discomfort and strong desire to give in?

My solution was to get curious about my own behavior. Anytime I had a strong urge to drink, I sat with it and went deep into what was going on. I became an internal reporter. I asked myself questions all the time to find out what I was feeling exactly and what was actually causing me to feel that way. Sometimes I felt like I was missing out because I was with a group of friends who were all drinking. Other times I'd had a hard day at work and felt like I needed a drink to calm my nerves. Other times I felt like I'd been good for so long that I "deserved" to have a drink as a reward.

TODAY, instead of trying to ignore or overcome your discomfort by having a drink, ask yourself, "Why do I want to drink *right now*? What is it that I think alcohol will do to make this moment better?" And then ask yourself, "Is that true?" If you're completely objective and honest, you might surprise yourself with your answers.

Do this little exercise first. Write down your answers, or record yourself in a video diary or voice memo. By doing this, you're observing the symptoms as something separate from you. You're giving yourself perspective—and a little bit of time for the feelings to subside. And remember that your body is amazing. It's taking care of you right now by getting rid of all the toxins it's had to deal with for a long time. Yes, you might not feel your best for a bit. But when the process is complete, your body will feel better than ever.

And consider the online social challenge at alcoholexperiment .com; you can find thousands of others who are also doing this experiment. Sharing your insights with others in a safe, judgment-free environment is incredibly powerful.

▌DAY 4 JOURNAL QUESTIONS

Remember, all the wisdom you seek is actually inside you; the most important words in this Experiment are the ones you tell yourself. Take some time and answer these questions in here or a separate journal (most effective), a voice memo to yourself, or simply by speaking the answers out loud for only you to hear.

1. *Discomfort So Far*

Even the worst feelings fade with time. Today, you can memorialize any discomfort you've experienced to help you become more mindful in the future. Take a minute and write about all of the ways you have felt physically uncomfortable in these first days of the Experiment. Be as specific as possible.

_____

_____

_____

_____

_____

_____

_____

_____

_____

_____

_____

_____

_____

_____

_____

_____

_____

_____

_____

_____

_____

_____

_____

_____

2. *Temptations So Far?*

What, specifically, has tempted you to drink? What reasons have you given yourself to consider giving in? Become very mindful and outline below both your triggers and your brain's logic as it tries to convince you to drink.

_____

_____

_____

_____

_____

_____

_____

_____

_____

_____

_____

_____

_____

_____

_____

_____

_____

_____

_____

_____

_____

_____

_____

_____

_____

Day 4 Reflections from alcoholexperiment.com

"Good days but bad nights. Woke up at 3 a.m. not feeling the best but definitely not hungover. And a bit of a headache this morning. I spent the day thinking about all the holidays and times with my kids I don't remember. Yesterday it dawned on me how much time alcohol has stolen from me. Yes, I let it. But the reading today very much reinforced that. I am generally happy. Still thankful!"   —ROBYN

"I have been having such strange dreams, I feel such a physical difference. I didn't realize alcohol takes so long to get out of your system, so even though I binge-drink once or twice a week, I was feeling so crappy because I was never alcohol-free. I had constant headaches, fatigue, bloating, nausea. I am learning so much!"   —GEORGE

"Didn't expect the physical symptoms to be so real. Glad I understand why I am having them. Still better than being hungover. Need to be gentle on myself and others through this. Can't wait to sleep again!"   —HECTOR

❙ DAY 5 ❙

What Are Cravings, Really?

Knowledge renders belief obsolete.
—NANA JANE

I've found there are two kinds of cravings you have to contend with at different times: physical cravings and emotional cravings. Physical symptoms such as anxiety, restlessness, and the inability to sleep show up while the alcohol is still in your system. We know they're cravings because they go away if you give in and have a drink. It can take up to a week for alcohol to completely leave your system, so that's about how long you can expect those physical cravings to last. After that point, you're most likely looking at mental or emotional cravings. (Fortunately, you probably know exactly the last time you had a drink. When people try to get over a sugar addiction, they sometimes consume sugar without even knowing it because it's hidden in so many food products!)

Psychological or emotional cravings can be much harder to handle simply because they are triggered by certain circumstances that your subconscious knows (from experience) may be helped by having a drink. You've reached the point in your relationship with alcohol that it's taking more than it's giving, and you feel like you want to cut back or stop. That's a conscious decision you've made. But if your subconscious mind still believes that alcohol is key to relaxation and that you have to drink to have a good time with your friends, then those psychological cravings will creep in—sometimes years after you've had any alcohol. Your desires originate from your subconscious mind. And a craving is a desire.

CRAVINGS AND STRESS

For example, if you used to handle work stress by drinking, like I did, then every time you experience work stress, you'll likely trigger a psychological craving for alcohol. You've already wired your brain to do this. It's a learned response. Your subconscious believes drinking reduces stress, even though science has proven that alcohol actually increases stress over time. And even though you've made the conscious decision not to drink, your subconscious didn't get the memo. So it sends up a desire—a craving.

If your cravings are triggered by stress, you have to find another way to reduce that stress. Studies have shown over and over that exercise is a great way to do that. Once those endorphins get released, the stress and cravings subside. Mindfulness and meditation are other great ways to reduce stress. Don't worry, you don't have to shave your head and move to Tibet. There are all kinds of forms of meditation—all you're really doing is exercising your brain.

The Internal Battle

So you have this battle going on inside you. Your conscious and subconscious are fighting it out over whether you want a drink. It's frustrating. It's confusing. And it's tempting to try to ignore the craving or exert your willpower over it. But that rarely works. Science tells us that the more we try to repress a thought or ignore something, the harder it is to escape. It's much better to be completely present and mindful during a craving. Notice how you feel and what thoughts are running through your head when you separate yourself and become an observer watching this weird battle between your conscious and subconscious. Detach yourself from the outcome and you're less likely to give in.

I like to visualize my subconscious mind as a child riding in the backseat of a car. Suddenly the child decides he or she wants an ice cream cone and won't let it go. Children are the best salespeople in the world because they don't give up. They don't take no for an answer. They'll keep attacking the problem in a different way over and over until they get what they want.

"Can I have an ice cream, Mom?"

"That ice cream sure looks good!"

"Look! A gas station. Don't you need gas, Mom? I bet they have ice cream inside."

"What's your favorite ice cream, Mom? I like chocolate!"

"So, when are we getting ice cream? Now or after dinner?"

"You know what would make Dad happy? A surprise ice cream!"

If children think there's even the slightest chance that they'll get what they desire, they will keep pestering you. Even if you don't have kids, you've been a kid. So you know what I'm talking about, right? The only way to get children to give up is to get rid of the desire, which means either distracting them or making them understand that there is NO WAY they are getting an ice cream.

Distraction

This is how you deal with cravings, too. You can distract yourself with a book, a walk, or a dinner date. You can also substitute something that will satisfy the desire without giving in to the craving. If you need to hold a glass in your hand at a networking event, fill it with tonic water or soda. Often that's enough to satisfy your subconscious child.

But what if distraction doesn't work and you still have that craving? That means your little darling believes there's a chance you'll give in. We all know how that works with kids and ice cream, right? If you give in once, the next time they'll be even MORE relentless. It will be even harder to get them to stop nagging you. All the kid cares about is getting the ice cream, and they won't stop until they truly believe there's no way it's going to happen. Relying on willpower to resist a craving is like arguing with a child using grown-up logic.

"Sorry, honey, we don't have time to stop for ice cream . . ."

"It will spoil your dinner . . ."

"We don't have the money . . ."

"You don't need an ice cream . . ."

What kid is going to fall for that stuff? They'll come up with a counterargument every time. And they will outlast you! Eventually, they'll wear you down.

Here's something cool about your subconscious—it can produce strong desires, but it can't make you take action. It's your conscious mind that decides whether to give in.

You Have a Choice!

The more times you don't give in to your subconscious, the faster it will get the message next time. No means no. Be the parent. When your subconscious understands that you don't go back on your word, then it will believe you when you say, "Not today, honey. Maybe next week we'll get an ice cream, but for today we're going to skip it."

A good friend of mine told me about using a key phrase that got her kids to stop nagging. She said she would go into "duck mode," which meant she let whatever the child was saying roll off her like water off a duck's back. When she said, "duck mode," her kids knew there was no way they were going to get what they wanted. This is because she had never once gone into duck mode and then given in. She had taught them that duck mode meant business and that there was simply no point in arguing any longer. Because of her dedication to the tool, her kids truly believed that once she had gone into duck mode, it was in their best interest to be quiet. They knew there was no longer anything they could say that would make a difference. And so peace was restored. In my analogy of the child in the backseat of a car, the driver (your conscious mind) is in control, and the child (your subconscious mind) believes it. You can come up with a key phrase of your own—whatever works for you.

TODAY, anytime you start to crave a drink, visualize your craving as an incessant child. And then instead of getting angry or frustrated, use whatever technique gets the child to believe you're serious about your commitment. Distraction or duck mode—whatever works is great!

▌DAY 5 JOURNAL QUESTIONS

Remember, all the wisdom you seek is actually inside you; the most important words in this Experiment are the ones you tell yourself. Take some time and answer these questions in here or a separate journal (most effective), a voice memo to yourself, or simply by speaking the answers out loud for only you to hear.

1. *Describe Your Cravings*

How, exactly, do your cravings feel? Be really specific: How do you feel physically? How do you feel emotionally? Go into as much detail as possible and remember not to judge your craving. Just experience and describe it.

_____

_____

_____

_____

_____

_____

_____

_____

_____

_____

_____

_____

_____

_____

_____

_____

_____

_____

_____

_____

_____

_____

_____

_____

_____

_____

_____

_____

2. *The Stories Your Cravings Tell You*

We all have the little kid asking for ice cream inside of us. What does your "little kid" say to get you to give in to a drink? Some of my stories were: "I'll never feel good again without alcohol," "I won't be able to overcome this so why even try?," and "This is too hard, so what is the point?" What are yours? Write down all that come to mind.

_____

_____

_____

_____

_____

_____

_____

_____

_____

_____

_____

_____

_____

_____

_____

_____

_____

_____

_____

_____

_____

_____

_____

_____

_____

3. *Are These Stories True?*

Now take a minute to ask yourself if these stories are true. Who would you be without these stories? What would life feel like without these stories?

_____

_____

_____

_____

_____

_____

_____

_____

_____

_____

_____

_____

_____

_____

_____

_____

_____

_____

_____

_____

_____

_____

_____

_____

_____

_____

_____

_____

_____

Day 5 Reflections from alcoholexperiment.com

"Last night my husband had a bottle of wine in the fridge. Told him to go ahead, I didn't want any. . . . There was no craving, no thoughts of missing out."

—TAMMY

"I am feeling very accomplished. I went to a Mexican restaurant today and I did not order a beer or a margarita. . . . What?! That's huge for me! Most of my poor drinking habits are triggered in social situations, and so this was a small victory for me. I love going to see live music, and there is a concert coming up in less than a month and the idea of not having a drink there is daunting. I wonder . . . will I even have fun? OMG, I feel so ridiculous for even thinking this . . . but it's the truth. I am no longer going to lie or try to cover up my thoughts around drinking. I am just going to keep shining a light on them so that eventually they will have nowhere to hide and there will be nothing left for me to be afraid of."

—TRISH

"I've struggled with my spouse's drinking for years but realize I have a problem, too, and I need to focus on myself. I love waking up feeling great! I love not 'planning' around drinking. I feel good about not being part of the problem, which I was when drinking with my spouse. Really, how can I preach moderation or quitting when I'M not moderating or quitting?"

—PEGGY

❙ DAY 6 ❙

Why Willpower Doesn't Work for Long

If you don't sacrifice for what you want,
what you want becomes the sacrifice.
—ANONYMOUS

For our purposes we will specifically define *willpower* as using conscious mental energy or effort to stop doing something (like drinking) or start doing something (like exercise).

If you've ever tried to lose weight, stop gambling, or make your bed every day for a month, you've probably tried to harness willpower to get through it. Spending 30 days alcohol-free is no different. It's only 30 days, right? How hard could it be? Well, here's the deal with willpower—it's a finite and exhaustible resource. *Willpower* can also be defined as the ability to resist short-term temptations in order to meet long-term goals. Some people think it's a skill that can be honed and perfected. Or a muscle that can be built up and maintained. But it doesn't seem to work that way. New research shows it's more like an energy reserve, and when the reserve is low, there's not much you can do until you top it back up.

| WHY WILLPOWER FLUCTUATES

Mark Muraven, an associate professor of sociology at Case Western Reserve University, wanted to understand why he had lots of willpower at certain times but not others. He conducted an experiment to prove that willpower was more effective when conserved and that, when taxed, it could run out. Subjects, under the guise that they were participating in a taste-based experiment, were placed in a room with two bowls on a table. One bowl was full of fresh-baked cookies, and the other was full of radishes. Half the subjects were told to eat the cookies and ignore the radishes, and the other half were told to eat the radishes and ignore the cookies. (Bummer for them, right?)

After five minutes both groups were given a puzzle that appeared easy but did not actually have a solution. Because the puzzle was impossible, continuing to work on it required willpower. The subjects who had previously used willpower to ignore the cookies worked on the puzzle for 60 percent less time than the subjects who had not used any of their willpower reserves. And there was a drastic difference in attitudes. The radish-eaters were grumpy and frustrated, and even snapped at the researchers.

All Decisions Take Energy

Every decision you make requires you to expend a certain amount of energy, and that includes energy you might prefer to save up for exercising willpower. If you have a hard day at work, and you've had to make lots of decisions, your energy and willpower will both be lower. This is why it's easier to resist temptation early in the day, but by the time five o'clock rolls around, you just want a martini. It's exhausting exercising your willpower all day.

There's also something called the "what the hell" effect, which explains what happens when you abandon your quest for willpower, give in to temptation, and then, since you feel badly for giving in, throw caution to the wind and end up going overboard. You slip up and drink. Regret sets in, but since you've already had one drink, you think, "What the hell—I might as well get drunk."

No matter how much willpower you started the day with, by the time happy hour rolls around, it's pretty much gone. You might be able to muster up willpower for that evening, but what about when you get home? What about the next day? And the next?

What are you going to do? Lock yourself in a closet for the rest of your life?

Clearly, willpower is not the answer as long as your cognitive dissonance around drinking remains firmly embedded in your mind. As long as there are two competing ideas—to drink or not to drink—you will struggle and expend energy trying to resist those subconscious messages using your conscious logic. But once you resolve that dissonance and are of one mind about alcohol, there is no struggle. There's no decision to make. And willpower is no longer required. You can use it for something else, like saying no to that piece of chocolate cake. (Of course, you can use the ACT technique to take care of your chocolate cravings, too.)

TODAY, take out a small piece of paper or an index card and write down a few of the facts about alcohol that you now know to be true. *Alcohol actually increases stress in the body. When I go out with my friends, I'm happy with a tonic and lime. I don't need alcohol to have fun.* Then keep that card handy in your wallet or cell phone case. Whenever you feel yourself relying on willpower to get you through a situation, or you feel like you're about to give in, pull out the card and read it. Calming the dissonance in your mind will do more than trying to grit your way through the situation.

❚ DAY 6 JOURNAL QUESTIONS

Remember, all the wisdom you seek is actually inside you; the most important words in this Experiment are the ones you tell yourself. Take some time and answer these questions in here or a separate journal (most effective), a voice memo to yourself, or simply by speaking the answers out loud for only you to hear.

1. *Your Experience: Willpower*

When do you have the least amount of willpower? When you are tired, bored, lonely, hungry, angry? These times make it harder for us to handle cravings, and studies show we are more likely to give in in these moments. When are these times for you? Be specific; the more specific you are in writing these down, the more aware you will be when they crop up.

_____

_____

_____

_____

_____

_____

_____

_____

_____

_____

_____

_____

_____

_____

_____

_____

_____

_____

_____

_____

_____

_____

_____

_____

2. *Anchor in Your Learning*

Write down some of the things you've learned so far in this experiment. If you have doubts about them, write those down as well. By doing this you are changing your mind-set so that you will no longer have to rely on willpower.

_____

_____

_____

_____

_____

_____

_____

_____

_____

_____

_____

_____

_____

_____

_____

_____

_____

_____

_____

_____

_____

_____

_____

_____

_____

_____

Day 6 Reflections from alcoholexperiment.com

"I left work thinking I wanted—and needed—a drink. My boss has been a total jerk for a few days, and it is not like him to be like that. Anyway, it's very uncomfortable. I was able to resist the drink and ride it out. And I actually feel better. Alcohol does numb my brain so I quit obsessing about all of it. I may or may not talk to him about it tomorrow, but not drinking is really my first priority. It changes everything for me. I feel better, look better, am more clearheaded, less anxious, foggy, etc. I could go on and on. Thanks, everybody, and thanks, Annie." —CARL

"Two things are going really well (probably more, but these two are delighting me at the moment). 1. I'm waking up with so much more energy and I'm channeling it into all sorts of creative projects. 2. I feel my mood lifting a little more each day, and I was convinced I'd live the rest of my life under a cloud of depression and grumpiness. I'm welcoming back my silly, quirky, goofy self. I love that version of me! She makes me smile. (And God love my husband for hanging with the cranky, grumpy version for so long. He's smiling more these last few days, too.)" —CAMMIE

"For a while now, I have been somewhat grumpy about the cognitive dissonance. I gave up alcohol for a bit after finding out more about booze, but then started again. The problem was that with my new knowledge about alcohol, I really did not enjoy drinking. I hated the hangovers and the anxiety that followed. I was even mad that by knowing more about alcohol, my drinking 'hobby,' the thing that connected me with so many people in life, had been ruined for me—so I kept drinking. But this time is different. All that seems to have gone. There is clear blue sky in my head, not storm clouds. I can confidently say no to a drink. I know there are challenges ahead, but I am feeling positive about them." —JAMES

▎▎ ACT #3 ▎▎

Alcohol, Relaxation, and Stress Relief

▎ AWARENESS

If you're drinking to relax, like I used to do, you are not alone. Relaxation and stress relief are some of the main reasons people drink. After all, who can deny that a few drinks totally relaxes you and relieves everyday pressures, stress, and anxiety? There's a reason it's called "happy hour," right? You can't use willpower to grit your way through and ignore the idea that alcohol relaxes you. Let's name this belief:

"Alcohol relieves stress and helps me relax."

We watch people in movies and on TV and all around us drinking to relax. There's a reason that happy hour starts at five o'clock. Work stresses us out. Money stresses us out. Our relationships stress us out. And stress stresses us out—it's a major contributor to many deadly diseases. For most of us, the pressures and expectations of modern living seem out of control. And we're taught to simply drink our problems away instead of facing them head-on.

| CLARITY

So why do we believe this? When in our past have we observed and experienced alcohol taking the edge off stress and anxiety? We could start with our parents and relatives. When you were young, did your mom or dad come home after a long day and immediately pour a drink? It's been part of our culture since we were children. If not yours, what about your friends' parents? We certainly all watched TV shows and movies where the dad comes home and immediately grabs a beer from the fridge. Or the homicide detectives talk over the case at a local bar. As we grew older and went to college, partying was the natural way to blow off the stress from exams or a long day of lectures. We've seen people doing this in real life, and there are numerous movies whose whole story line revolves around a huge college drunkfest after final exams.

It's almost inevitable that we started mimicking what we observed. Everywhere we look, society is telling us that if we have to do something hard, we need a drink to cope with it. So it's pretty easy to see where this belief might have come from. Take a few minutes right now to write down some *specific instances* when you observed or experienced alcohol being relaxing. If your parents drank after work, what *exactly* did they drink? And how did they behave afterward? What specific movies or TV shows do you remember watching where a character drank to relax? Try to pinpoint how and when you started to believe that you need alcohol to relax.

Now let's look at some internal and external evidence to help you decide whether alcohol truly helps you relax. First of all, let's define *true relaxation*. What exactly are we trying to do with the stress and anxiety we may be experiencing in the moment? We're trying to get rid of it, right? True relaxation is the *absence* of stress and anxiety. It's not ignoring the stress or numbing it—real relaxation *removes it* completely. To get to that point, you must deal with the source of the stress—talk with your boss about a problem, rearrange your schedule to avoid a conflict, or whatever it is you need to do to remove the discomfort. You can't get that out of a bottle. A shot of tequila can't fix your marriage. It can only make you not worry about it for a little while.

It's true that you can equate that initial tipsy feeling with being relaxed. How long can you sustain it? Twenty minutes? An hour? Drinkers almost never feel relaxed for a full hour, because as the alcohol is metabolized, we actually feel more stress than we did when we started. Alcohol leaving the body makes us feel *worse*. So what do we do? Have another!

It's ironic that we drink to relax, because drinking actually adds stress to our lives. I'm not going to deny that alcohol definitely provides the illusion of relaxation, especially at first. But here's what's actually happening. That drink is simply numbing the senses and slowing the mind. For a short time, we truly don't care about our problems, and we feel relaxed. But we're not actually eliminating the problem or concern. Instead of solving the issue and removing it, we're actually postponing it and prolonging the pain.

Because we build a tolerance for alcohol, we need more and more of it to have the same effect, which introduces a host of other stress-inducing concerns. How much did I drink last night? Why is my wife angry with me? What embarrassing things did I do or say? How am I going to get up and go to work with this hangover? How can my bank account be overdrawn *again*? This cycle is the opposite of relaxation. It puts additional stress and strain on our health, finances, and relationships. And the more we use alcohol to numb our senses, the more alcohol we need, and the more stress we add to our lives. After a few years of regular drinking, the stress can truly become unbearable. Think about it like this: If alcohol truly relaxed us, wouldn't we need less of it over time? So why do we find we need more and more to reach the same level of relaxation? If we drink to relax on a daily basis, shouldn't it be easier, not harder, to get that relief?

Let's also take a look at the external evidence around this belief and what's actually happening neurologically when you drink. Your brain is a reactive mechanism. When you drink, it reacts to bring your body back into balance. Because alcohol is a natural depressant, your brain counteracts it by releasing stimulants, including adrenaline and cortisol. Guess what? Those are not only stimulants but also stress hormones. Cortisol is released in stressful situations and has been linked to a higher risk of infection, mood swings, high blood pressure, fat storage, and even premature aging. (Talk about added stress!) Adrenaline is linked to your fight-or-flight response, which is great if you're being chased by a lion. But in large amounts, adrenaline is also linked to insomnia, nervousness, and lower levels of immunity.

Here's where the bad news gets worse. Remember that alcohol takes about a week to completely leave your body. So if you're a regular drinker, you are in a constant state of withdrawal. Which means you have consistently elevated levels of cortisol and adrenaline. Which means you're always stressed on a physiological level. Add on the everyday stressors of work, health, and relationships, and it's no wonder you want to escape for a little while! One drink and that anesthetic takes over, decreasing your senses and slowing your brain function. The more you drink, the less you feel. And if you drink until you pass out, you get to feel absolutely nothing for a short time.

But guess what? As soon as you sober up, all those stressors will remain. And then some. You made things worse. And the longer you drink to "relax," the more the problems will pile up. And you'll become less and less capable of handling everyday complications.

Scientists studied this phenomenon with two groups of mice. One group was given alcohol over a 30-day period, and the other was not. At the end of the 30 days, they were put through extraordinarily stressful situations and their responses were measured. The mice that had consumed alcohol had a much harder time dealing with all the external stressors presented to them. The same was true for me. When I was drinking regularly, even the most mundane problems overwhelmed me. But once alcohol was no longer affecting my internal systems, I was able to handle them without a problem. I know life isn't always easy. But when you drink, you're limiting your ability to cope. Everything you do feels so much more difficult.

So what do you think? Does alcohol *really* relax you? Does it actually help you deal with stress and anxiety? Or is it simply numbing you out so you can ignore it for a little while? Understanding the root cause of your stress and removing it completely is the only way to enjoy true relaxation.

▌ TURNAROUND

The opposite of *"alcohol relieves stress and helps me relax"* is *"alcohol does not relieve stress and help me relax"* or *"alcohol adds stress to my life."* Come up with as many ways as you can that the opposite is as true as or truer than the original belief.

❚ DAY 7 ❚

Your Experiment and Your Friends

Whenever you find yourself on the side of the majority,
it is time to reform (or pause and reflect).
—MARK TWAIN

You've been working on this experiment for a week now. Congratulations! How do you feel?

❚ ARE PEOPLE STARTING TO NOTICE?

At this point, some of your friends might be noticing that something about you has changed. Maybe you've been out with them and turned down a drink. Or maybe they've noticed a change in your behavior or even your physical appearance.

Sooner or later, you're going to have to tell someone about what you're doing. And sometimes your friends won't understand why you've decided to spend 30 days alcohol-free. Not only that, but they may even keep offering you drinks right through the challenge. They may say, "C'mon, it's just one. Don't be such a loser."

When people want to quit smoking, everyone around them is supportive and thinks it's great. And a friend wouldn't even think of offering a cigarette to a friend in that situation. So what makes alcohol different?

We're Often Hesitant to Tell Our Friends

You might be a little hesitant to tell even your friends, and I believe there's a pretty good reason for that. I think the crux of the problem is that we treat alcohol differently than we do any other addictive substance. For example, we don't have "cigarette-aholics" or "heroin-ism," but we do have "alcoholics" and "alcoholism." When we say "cigarette addiction" or "heroin addiction," we're talking about the addiction, not the people themselves. But the word *alcoholic* defines a person. The word itself blames the person rather than the substance.

For some reason in our culture, a heroin addict is someone to be pitied because they've been overpowered by an addictive substance. But an alcoholic is someone who was weak and unable to control themselves around something as innocent as a glass of beer. And it's no wonder we do this. According to certain statistics, 87 percent of people over 18 have drank alcohol at some point.[1] That's a huge number. And I think the only way we can justify to ourselves that so many people drink is to simply not talk about the fact that alcohol is addictive, just like heroin and tobacco are.

As a Society, We Don't Seem to Realize That Alcohol Is Addictive

We don't talk about the fact that when we party on a Friday night and end up puking, that physical reaction is our body's way of saving our life because we literally poisoned ourselves.

And so the language that's developed around alcohol, and the attitude of blaming the person instead of the substance, has created this huge taboo against talking about it at all. We treat every other substance that's bad for us differently than we treat alcohol. I might be chatting with my friend in front of a big box of doughnuts and say, "Mmmm, this is a really good doughnut! But I'll only have half because all the fat and sugar isn't good for me."

But what if the entire conversation changed? What if the question about drinking a bit less became a wellness conversation, like stopping smoking or eating less sugar? What if we could talk about alcohol in the same way we talk about eating a few less doughnuts? Can you imagine what our society might look like if there was no stigma, no fear of the label *alcoholic* and we could truly have a wellness conversation around our drinking? I know I would have looked at my drinking much earlier, certainly before it became truly a problem, if it were not such a loaded topic. The great news? Just by participating in The Alcohol Experiment, you are part of a global movement to do just that! To look at our drinking well before the point of disaster. That's amazing! I am so proud of us.

No one ever says, "Mmmm, this is a good chardonnay! But I'm just going to have one glass because I worry about the breast cancer and the liver damage." That doesn't happen. We have successfully separated alcohol out from other toxic substances. We even say "alcohol and drugs," as if alcohol weren't also a drug, in spite of the fact that alcohol kills more people every year than prescription and illegal drugs combined.[2] In fact, according to two independent studies about what is the most dangerous drug, alcohol won the prize.[3]

So, I think this societal attitude is why people treat you differently when you quit smoking or cut down on sugar. Because when you tell your friend that you're not drinking, there's an automatic implied judgment. Because that friend probably feels like they drink about the same amount as you. And if you think you're drinking too much, then you must also think *they* are drinking too much. Whether it's true doesn't matter. And guess what? They probably have some internal conflict around their own drinking, so the fact that you are *not* drinking is painful for them.

Perspective Change

When I was drinking a lot, I couldn't comprehend why anyone would choose not to drink. Why on earth not? What was the big deal? It didn't make sense to me. Looking back on those days now, I can see that deep down inside I knew I was treating my body badly. And when

I was confronted with friends who'd made the decision to *stop* treating their bodies badly, it made me feel like they were strong and I was weak. I didn't like that.

And there's another reason your friends may try to sabotage your efforts. They don't want to lose you! One of the most fundamental parts of being human is that we crave community and interaction with other people. And we've given alcohol this magical power to make us all into fun-loving, laid-back party animals. I thought that without alcohol I wouldn't be any fun. I believed that alcohol was the glue that held some of my friendships together.

When I decided alcohol no longer had a place in my life, it set me apart. And humans don't like to be apart. So your friends may feel like you will ostracize them or you won't want to spend time with them anymore. Nobody wants that!

Is It Fear? Are They Afraid of Their Own Drinking?

If your friends aren't being supportive, realize it's probably out of fear. They're afraid you're judging them. Deep down, they know that maybe they shouldn't want to drink as much as they do. They may be afraid you won't want to spend time with them anymore. And they may be afraid that they might be an alcoholic. When people question their drinking, they might actually be wondering, *Am I an alcoholic?* And the implications of that seem horrific.

Alcoholism has been defined as a lifelong disease for which there is no cure. Alcoholics must completely abstain from drinking forever. They have to label themselves as alcoholics for the rest of their lives, even if they manage to stay sober. Alcoholism is portrayed as a never-ending fight for control. A fight that, if people lose, could cost them their marriage, their job, their children, or even their life. That is so scary! No one wants to think about that when all they're trying to do is unwind after a long day at work.

TODAY, plan how you can bring up the subject with those close to you so you can keep your fun, friendly relationship with them. Here are a few ideas for how to talk to your friends without alienating them:

Keep it light and joking: "I'm overdoing it on iced tea! Ha-ha."

Be self-deprecating (but not too much; you are doing an amazing thing and don't need to be apologetic): "I drank enough last month to last for the next 30 days, so I'm taking a break."

Let it lie. The truth is, the less you make of it, the less they will make of it. Sometimes we assume people are judging our behaviors when in reality people are mostly thinking about themselves. If you shrug it off like it's no big deal, they will also. I love to simply say, "I'm good, thanks. . . . By the way, I've been meaning to ask you, how have you been lately? What's new in your life?" This not only turns down a drink but also often kicks off a great conversation.

▌DAY 7 JOURNAL QUESTIONS

Remember, all the wisdom you seek is actually inside you; the most important words in this Experiment are the ones you tell yourself. Take some time and answer these questions in here or a separate journal (most effective), a voice memo to yourself, or simply by speaking the answers out loud for only you to hear.

1. *Telling Your Friends and Family*

Jot down some ideas about how to talk to your friends and family about The Alcohol Experiment. Write anything that comes to mind, then use what feels best when you have conversations with your friends and family. If you've already had these conversations, write down what worked and reflect on what didn't. Sometimes these conversations take trial and error—that's okay!

_____

_____

_____

_____

_____

_____

_____

_____

_____

_____

_____

_____

_____

_____

_____

_____

_____

_____

_____

_____

_____

_____

_____

_____

2. *Drinking as a Wellness Conversation (Instead of an Addiction Conversation)*

Reflect on the reading: How does it make you feel to think of drinking less as a wellness conversation instead of an addiction conversation? What would it be like if taking a break from drinking were celebrated in the same way as someone stopping smoking cigarettes? What do you think about the fact that society treats alcohol differently than other drugs? Take a moment to feel proud that by taking part in this experiment, you are part of the movement to make the question around drinking less an easier one for anyone to ask.

_____

_____

_____

_____

_____

_____

_____

_____

_____

_____

_____

_____

_____

_____

_____

_____

_____

_____

_____

_____

_____

Day 7 Reflections from alcoholexperiment.com

"I can't believe I am here at Day 7. Feeling more positive and having more belief and confidence in myself. You don't realize what alcohol steals from you until you get it back. Stay strong, everyone!"   —MATTHEW

"It doesn't matter what others think of my not drinking—this is my journey. But socially I am more comfortable now. Knowing I had a problem and just rode along enjoying the buzz, not paying attention to what I was doing to my body, really makes me sad. But on the other hand, it keeps me alcohol-free knowing I can't have one because it would start all over again. It is quite freeing to put this addiction behind me and cut the ties that alcohol once had on me."   —TOMMY

"I'm loving this! Thank you so much, Annie, for the resource! So far I'm on Day 7, and it's been pretty easy. I think when you're changing your mind about something, you have to mentally ingest as much supportive information as possible. As for the reasons I give people I don't know very well (or feel I'll be judged by), I prefer to say that alcohol was making me depressed, so I decided to stop to feel better. It's definitely the truth! And no one can argue that alcohol isn't a depressant. This way, I feel empowered instead of disempowered by my choice. I don't choose to be labeled as an 'addict' or 'alcoholic.' If I had to find another reason to give people to remain neutral and free from judgment, I would just say that alcohol was making me feel sick, and it didn't agree with my body. That's definitely the truth!"   —ZOE

| DAY 8 |

How Alcohol Affects Your Senses

All our knowledge begins with the senses.
—IMMANUEL KANT

Your five senses are how your brain collects information about what's going on inside and outside your body. If there's a fire nearby, your brain needs to be able to smell the smoke, feel the heat, and hear the crackle to make decisions. It also needs to see the fire to sort out whether you've got a dangerous threat (like a nearby explosion) or you're enjoying a nice, relaxing campfire. Your senses are amazing tools.

So what happens to those tools when we drink? They are dulled and become much less effective communicators. Worse, our brains process the information more slowly. It's kind of like a video that takes forever to buffer and play on your computer. There's a lag. It might be inconvenient and cause you to say something embarrassing. Or that lag might be deadly and cause you to drive your car into oncoming traffic. Unfortunately, there's no way to know how bad the lag is until it's too late.

| WHAT HAPPENS IN THE BRAIN

Alcohol depresses the central nervous system and slows down your neurotransmitters, which are the chemicals responsible for moving information back and forth between your body and your brain. When your brain can't process the information as quickly as usual, your senses are affected. They're sitting there staring at that "buffer bar," saying, "Come on . . . come on . . . why is this taking so long?"

You know how sometimes a video never fully loads on your computer? Your brain can do that, too. That's when you pass out. But before you get to that stage, you'll notice your senses dulling. Blurred vision, slurred speech, numbness in your fingers and toes—sound familiar? Have you ever wondered why people talk louder when they're drunk? It's because their sense of hearing is impaired. Even your sense of touch is affected, as your ability to perceive pain decreases. That may seem like a good thing if you have chronic back pain, but it's not so great when you fall down and break your arm—but you can't feel it until you've done even more damage.

An Early-Warning System

Our senses keep us safe. They alert us to big dangers but also give us smaller hints when something doesn't feel quite right. In addition to being an early-warning system, they also help us experience pleasure and happiness. Did you know that one of the most arousing scents for men is pumpkin pie? Seriously, it's an aphrodisiac (which may or may not explain the popularity of pumpkin spice lattes).

Memories: One of Life's Most Precious Gifts

Our memories are also connected to our senses. When we drink, we're dulling those senses of pleasure and robbing ourselves of wonderful happy experiences. And we're robbing ourselves of the memories we should be storing. One of the reasons you don't remember the party last night is because you didn't get that sensual information stored away. Your senses were too dull and slow to store away the experience of laughing and joking with your friends, or of that first kiss you've been waiting for. Is it worth not remembering your child's birthday party because you just had to have a few glasses of wine to get through it? One of my biggest regrets is my son's third birthday party. We had this incredible party, and even looking at the photos I can't remember it. I had made sangria early and drank quite a bit of it, and no matter how hard I try to remember anything, that day is gone. The funny thing is that no one could even tell how much I was drinking, but the memories are just not there. And to this day it breaks my heart that I missed such an important day. When I think about how many things I've missed that I don't even know that I've missed—because they weren't as evident as a birthday party—I realize how much alcohol has stolen from me.

Too often, we take our senses for granted and don't realize how much we'd miss them if they went away. Keeping your senses sharp not only keeps you safe, but it also helps you enjoy life experiences more and remember them later.

TODAY, take some time to focus on each sense individually. Look around you. What do you see that's beautiful? The smile on your spouse's face? The trees? The sky? Appreciate the fact that you can hear the birds and the ocean, as well as oncoming traffic. How does that coffee smell this morning? And the fresh-baked bread you had with lunch, how did that taste? Run your hands through the grass. How does it feel? Prickly? Or soft and lush? Your senses are what make you feel alive. Treat them with respect.

▌ DAY 8 JOURNAL QUESTIONS

Remember, all the wisdom you seek is actually inside you; the most important words in this Experiment are the ones you tell yourself. Take some time and answer these questions in here or a separate journal (most effective), a voice memo to yourself, or simply by speaking the answers out loud for only you to hear.

1. *Your Incredible Senses*

Think about your senses. Can you imagine what it would be like if you lost even one? Consider and journal about each sense and the impact that alcohol has on each. Blurring your vision, numbing your taste buds, impacting your sense of smell and hearing, and diminishing your ability to feel. Our senses are how we experience life. Have you taken them for granted?

_____

_____

_____

_____

_____

_____

_____

_____

_____

_____

_____

_____

_____

_____

_____

_____

_____

_____

_____

_____

_____

_____

_____

2. *Is It Worth It?*

Understanding the impact alcohol has on our senses, ask yourself why you may have wanted to diminish them or your experience of life. And be honest, there is no wrong answer, just a reflection for you and your journey.

_____

_____

_____

_____

_____

_____

_____

_____

_____

_____

_____

_____

_____

_____

_____

_____

_____

_____

_____

_____

_____

_____

_____

_____

_____

Day 8 Reflections from alcoholexperiment.com

"This lesson reminds me of something my yoga teacher once said: that a body in balance craves what will keep it in balance, whereas a body out of balance will crave what keeps it out of balance. Never thought to apply this to alcohol before. I'm so amazed at how I could convince myself that drinking was no big deal while at the same time knowing that I needed to quit. And now I see how it has contributed to my lifelong low-grade depression, something I thought I was born with and I'd just have to live with. For the first time in my adult life, I'm hopeful that I will finally know what it's like to live with joy. I've been seeing glimpses of that since I quit the sauce, and I like it!"

—PAMELA

"I am learning so much from this experiment. Right now I can't even imagine putting alcohol into my body again. I can see how it has dulled my senses and caused me much grief and anxiety. I find myself looking back at all the things I missed by not being fully present and the mistakes I made due to alcohol. I'm trying not to dwell on the mistakes but use them as a catalyst to move forward."

—FRANCES

"I feel so alive. I was suffering from slight depression but never went to the doctor for any medication. Now I realize the slight depressive feeling I was having every day was the effects of the alcohol. I don't have it anymore, and everything seems sharper and crisper. Coffee smells better, tastes better, and gives me that clean energy in the morning that I could never quite reach after a night of drinking! Also I don't lie awake and worry about my children, money, my health, etc. . . . Everything that I wanted alcohol to give me, sobriety has given me."

—BILL

❙ DAY 9 ❙

The Power of Self-Talk

I AM. Two of the most powerful words;
for what you put after them shapes your reality.
—GARY HENSEL

If you've ever tried to make a change in your life or start a new habit, you know how easily negative thinking and self-talk can defeat your best intentions. You can start the day strong and full of optimism. But as the day wears on, the voice inside your head can get louder and more insistent until it becomes easier to give in. Sometimes it can feel like there's a constant loop of negativity playing in your head, over and over, louder and louder. It's possible you've been experiencing this your whole life in lots of different ways. The good news is that you can change it. The better news is it's not difficult, though it might take some time and practice.

❙ AWARENESS IS KEY

Let's talk about becoming aware of your self-talk. Recognizing what you're telling yourself is the first step. And one way to become deeply aware of how you're talking to yourself is to imagine that the voice inside you that's chattering it up is actually another person. Imagine they're sitting in the chair next to you and just listen objectively. Let them chatter on for a while. Would you ever let a real person talk to you like that? Would you sit and listen to all those negative stories? And would you humor them as they went on and on and on? Of course not. You would never in a million years let somebody sit next to you and never shut up about everything that's wrong with you. Once you personify that voice in your head as an actual individual, you realize how intense and incessant it is. Simply by becoming aware of this self-talk, you have unlocked the door to changing it.

Research shows that most of our thinking is recycled from the day before. In fact, up to 80 percent of your thoughts from today were probably also thoughts you had yesterday. We often give in to what our inner voice is saying simply because it's so repetitious. And repetition masks itself as truth. When something becomes familiar to us, like a thought pattern, we believe it because it's familiar. This is how advertising works. The more often you see an ad on TV or in a magazine, the more likely you are to believe its claims. So whatever you're telling yourself over and over again, eventually you're going to start believing it. Even if it's blatantly not true.

Self-Talk and Cravings

During this experiment, you might be doing a lot of self-talk. I actually want you to recognize two different types. You have the self-talk that is conniving, that will do anything to convince you to pick up a drink. This type of self-talk involves both justifications and comparisons. We'll repeatedly tell ourselves that we need the alcohol, that we won't be okay without it, that we won't be able to sleep without it, and that just one won't hurt. It's also easy to justify our own drinking when we compare our behavior to other people's. If you're a regular drinker, you might say, "Well, at least I'm never fall-down drunk," or "At least I'm not as bad as so-and-so." If you're a binge-drinker, you might say, "Well, at least I don't drink every night." Notice if you're making these kinds of comparisons. Some other self-talk you might be hearing in your head includes things such as:

"This is too hard."

"This has already been too difficult."

"I'm not going to be successful, so I might as well give up now."

All these things are just stories that you tell yourself. And because you repeat them so often, you don't even hear them anymore. You just accept them as true. So you have to stop and hear them again by becoming aware of what you're telling yourself. That way you can make a conscious decision about whether they're actually true. Some people who've been through this process find it helpful to personify the repetitive voice. They call it the Wine Witch or the Alcohol Monster. When you see the voice as something that's not you, it's easier to see through its manipulation.

It's Not Really You

Here's how to recognize that the voice is not really you:

- It tells repetitive stories.
- It has a single aim—to get you to drink.
- It is one-sided and manipulative.

You are stronger than the voice. And it will quickly weaken when you recognize it for what it is and put some distance between you and it. Give it some space. It's very noisy, I get that. But its bark is worse than its bite. It has no actual power over you. It's that little child in the backseat of the car who is desperate for an ice cream. She's not going to give in easily, but ultimately you're in charge.

Self-Talk and Self-Worth

The other type of self-talk, which is possibly more insidious, is the constant negative dialogue we have in our own minds toward ourselves. This is when we beat ourselves up and are harder on ourselves than we would ever be on another human. Here's the thing—you did not create yourself. Think about that for a minute. You are here. You are breathing. But you did not *choose* to be here breathing. You didn't create your beating heart or your hair color or anything else about you. And because of that, you have no right to treat yourself badly. No right. That's the most important thing to realize. Anytime you catch yourself in negative self-talk or beating yourself up, take out a notebook or your phone and write down what you're saying. Write the exact words. Then read them out loud. Would you ever say that to a child or your mother or a good friend? If not, then *stop saying it to yourself!*

You owe it to the universe or God or whoever you believe created you to treat yourself nicely! It's not enough to just repeat a positive mantra a few times a day. When you can talk to yourself like you would talk to your own child or another loved one, you will find that your whole life will shift direction. I'm not talking about now and then. I'm talking about all that repetitive chatter going on in your brain—use words and tones that you would use with that loved one. All the time.

Becoming aware of how you speak to yourself is the first step. The second step is actually changing how you speak to yourself. Most people think this is difficult, because they've been beating themselves up for so long that it's become a habit. And you can't "get rid" of a habit easily, because it's a neurological connection in your brain. It's an unconscious loop that repeats itself over and over. By definition a habit happens without thinking. It's unconscious behavior. Once you wake yourself up and become aware of the habit, you have to make a conscious decision to change it. And to do that, you have to rewire the neurological connections in your brain with new behaviors. It does take effort, but it's completely worth it!

The Power of Gratitude

What helped me get out of the habit of negative self-talk was gratitude. I consciously bring to mind everything I'm grateful for, even the dumbest little things. If I'm writing in my journal, I might notice the pen and think, *I'm thankful that I can write. I'm grateful that I can read and convey my thoughts on paper. Oh look, there's the sky—the clouds are beautiful and I love how they look against the blue. I'm so grateful that I'm alive and I can see and appreciate nature's beauty.* In addition to running through this exercise whenever you become aware of negative self-talk, you can also pick a time every day to stop and think over the past 24 hours and find three to five things you're grateful for.

Here's the kicker: You're probably not going to feel grateful. You'll probably feel cheesy at first. You might think, *I don't feel grateful; I feel angry at myself, which is why I was giving myself such a hard time about my behavior.* It doesn't matter if you feel it. It works anyway. You're suggesting to your subconscious that there's a different pattern it can use, there's a different way to talk to yourself. You're rewiring your brain to look for the positive in everything, and that changes your habit. Trust that you are making changes in your brain, even if you don't feel the results at first. Studies have shown that this simple gratitude exercise can improve your overall happiness in all areas of your life. And I can say that in my experience, that's absolutely true. But it takes practice and patience. So, be nice to yourself, okay?

TODAY, let's do a writing exercise to help you become aware of your negative self-talk. This is adapted for our purposes from Byron Katie's process of questioning our thinking called The Work (thework.com). Let's expose your repetitive stories for what they are and diffuse them in your subconscious. Your feelings are preceded by subconscious beliefs. So whenever you start to feel anxious or bad, you can work backward to uncover the belief that's causing the feeling. Once you know the belief, you can use the simple strategy below to help let it go.

Step 1: Identify that you are not feeling your best and use that as a signal to listen to the voice inside your head. What are you thinking right now? What are the thoughts going through your mind? What are the exact words and phrases you used? Write them all down.

Step 2: Ask yourself what are the beliefs or stories underlying these thoughts?

Step 3: Instead of trying to combat the stories or beliefs directly, be sneaky and just ask yourself how they make you feel.

Step 4: Look at the situation and ask yourself how you would feel without those thoughts. Imagine how the moment would feel if you couldn't tell yourself those stories or have those beliefs. What if they just disappeared from your mind? How would you feel? What would be different?

Here's an example:

1. What are you feeling and thinking?

"I'm feeling anxious. My chest is tight and I have a sort of tingling running through me. My muscles are tight. These feelings give me pause, so I back up and listen to my thoughts or self-talk. I might hear, 'I am never going to get ahead at work—I need a beer.' Or 'My kids are out of control. I can't believe I haven't figured out how to get them to behave. Is it five o'clock yet? I can't wait to open that bottle of wine I bought this morning.' Or 'Everyone else seems so much happier than I do. What's wrong with me? I'll pour myself this drink, and that will help.'"

2. What stories and beliefs are underlying the thought that I need a drink?

"I believe a drink would make me feel better right now because I think alcohol will help me relax and deal with the stressors in my life."

"I want to numb these uncomfortable feelings, and I know alcohol can do that."

3. How do these stories and beliefs make me feel? Specifically, you might consider how the thought "I need a drink" feels in the context of doing this experiment and the fact you are not drinking right now.

"I feel uncomfortable and upset. I feel deprived. I feel weak when I think I need to have a drink to help me relax. I know that the facts say I won't actually relax. I feel like giving in now will actually make me feel worse."

4. How would you feel without these thoughts? What if you simply couldn't think that you need a drink—how would you be feeling?

It might sound like this: "I'm in a challenging situation, and, yes, there are difficulties, but they aren't compounded by this sense of struggle over drinking."

Or this: "My mind is free to focus on ways to feel better that don't involve alcohol."

There's a huge level of stress and anxiety you're building up here because you're feeling this inner conflict of wanting something you've decided that for now you are not going to have. When you become aware of these conflicting emotions (I want a drink / I'm taking a break from drinking), an amazing thing happens. Your subconscious mind identifies these feelings as painful and naturally lets them go. It's like when you're a toddler and an adult says, "Don't touch that stove. It's hot!" At first you don't know what those words mean, so you have to touch it. You have no reason not to. But once you touch the stove and burn yourself, you're never going to touch it on purpose again. It hurts! That lesson becomes deeply ingrained in your subconscious and you never have to think about not touching a hot stove again. It's the same phenomenon that happens when you simply ask yourself the question, "How do I feel when I believe this story?" When you believe that you need alcohol to relax, but you're not allowing yourself to drink—or when you believe you need alcohol to have a good time, and you're not allowing yourself to drink—how does that feel?

This exercise works because it reveals to your subconscious mind how painful certain stories and beliefs are. Your subconscious says, "Oh, those feelings are painful," and this miraculous thing happens: Your subconscious mind naturally lets go of the belief because it identifies the belief as painful. We aren't always aware of our self-talk, and that is why emotions, even the negative ones, are such a gift. Emotions are the signal that something in our thinking is causing stress. Your job is simply to listen to your thoughts, identify the thoughts causing you stress, and question them. If this works for you and you want to know more about this amazing technique, I highly recommend Byron Katie's book *Loving What Is*.

DAY 9 JOURNAL QUESTIONS

Remember, all the wisdom you seek is actually inside you; the most important words in this Experiment are the ones you tell yourself. Take some time and answer these questions in here or a separate journal (most effective), a voice memo to yourself, or simply by speaking the answers out loud for only you to hear.

1. *Identify Your Inner Dialogue*

Take a minute to think about what you regularly say to yourself. Write it down. If you can't think of anything, wait until the next time you feel anxious or uncomfortable. Use this as a signal to stop and listen to what you are saying inside your head. What are the exact words and phrases you used?

_____

_____

_____

_____

_____

_____

_____

_____

_____

_____

_____

_____

_____

_____

_____

_____

_____

_____

_____

_____

_____

_____

_____

2. *Question Your Inner Dialogue*

Now that you have a list of things you say to yourself, ask yourself the following questions and write down your responses: 1) Would I say this to someone I love? A child? A friend? Would I even say this to a stranger? 2) How does this make me feel? 3) How does this make me behave?

_____

_____

_____

_____

_____

_____

_____

_____

_____

_____

_____

_____

_____

_____

_____

_____

_____

_____

_____

_____

_____

_____

_____

_____

_____

3. *You Have the Power*

This is such an enlightening exercise. And you truly have the power to change how you talk to you! Take a moment to appreciate the awareness you've brought to your Inner Voice, even if you've realized some of the things you've been saying to yourself are painful. Now you can change them! Write down a list of new things to begin to say to yourself. Make sure you actually believe them (it doesn't do you any good to tell yourself "I'm amazing" if you don't actually believe it!). And then reflect on how it would make you feel and behave if you said these new things to yourself regularly.

_____

_____

_____

_____

_____

_____

_____

_____

_____

_____

_____

_____

_____

_____

_____

_____

_____

_____

_____

_____

Day 9 Reflections from alcoholexperiment.com

"I went out with two girlfriends for dinner last night. We all drank water. There was a moment when we were having a great laugh over something and I had the best a-ha moment mid-laugh! I can absolutely have a great time without booze. I was giddy with happiness over this realization. Slept really well again last night."   —GEORGIA

"Realizing a belief can cause discomfort and that I can change that simply by asking myself honest questions is so empowering. We don't realize how we are programmed by commercialism and advertising. We want to believe that we know what's best for ourselves, but to realize that some of our habits, thoughts, beliefs, or routines aren't actually our own ideas, but rather repetitive messages we take on as fact and live our lives by, is very humbling. Taking back our own thoughts, ideas, and beliefs has helped make me feel whole again."   —RODNEY

"Took a couple of sips of wine with dinner and decided that it wasn't that good, and I got a flash of what my evenings looked like just a couple of weeks ago: too much wine, flushed cheeks, tired, trying not to weave when I get up (don't think I was fooling the hubby), just falling into bed or falling asleep in front of the TV. Zoned out—not connecting. But tonight I threw the wine down the drain after the first couple of sips! Gone. Feels great. I look forward to a good night's sleep and another day tomorrow where I feel rested and relaxed. Also, it's empowering to think about being AF [alcohol-free] during stressful times at work—gives me confidence!"   —MARIA

||| ACT #4 |||

Alcohol, Our Culture, and Society

| AWARENESS

We all have an evolutionary need to fit in with a group. It's a survival mechanism. We even have something called mirror neurons in our brains. If we see someone yawn, stretch, or scratch their nose, we're likely to do the same thing. Humans evolved to fit in with others. Think about it. When a prisoner has the harshest punishment inflicted, it's solitary confinement. Being separated from the group is the worst thing we can think of to punish a criminal. Let's name this belief:

"If I don't drink, I won't be part of the group."

So it makes total sense that to fit in with an alcohol-obsessed society, we must be drinkers. But let's break that down so you can decide whether that's something you want to continue.

| CLARITY

It's pretty easy to figure out where this belief comes from. We all observe evidence of this every single day. Our cultural conditioning practically demands that we drink. We see alcohol all around us, even at church and school functions. Every baby shower, birthday party, wedding, and funeral has some form of alcohol available. All our friends, family members, and authority figures drink. Therefore we should drink, too, just to be considered "normal."

The same attitude used to be true of cigarettes. Do you remember? People smoked because it was just the thing to do. Everyone smoked. Doctors even recommended their favorite brands. That was the reality at one point. Of course, we now know that smoking is dangerous and never should have been encouraged in the first place. And only after many decades of pressure has smoking become "denormalized." Now, smokers are shunned in restaurants, public buildings, and social events. They are forced to go outside to smoke.

Don't think the alcohol industry doesn't know this. It spends billions of dollars each year in the United States alone on advertising to make sure we get the message loud and clear. Cool people drink. Funny people drink. Sexy people drink. And now, thanks to a new trend in alcohol marketing, fit people drink. That's right, the newest trend is to associate drinking with good health. Yoga studios have wine tastings. Low-carb beer brands spend millions on Super Bowl commercials with hard-body athletes. And articles circulate on the internet about how this wine or that spirit can prevent everything from cancer to Alzheimer's disease. So according to the media, if you want to be cool, funny, sexy, and fit, you'd better be a drinker.

We've also experienced that feeling of fitting in when we drink with our friends, right? It's fun. We feel cool, at least for a little while. Whether we're pounding beers at a baseball game or sipping champagne at a classical music festival, it doesn't matter. When our friends are gathered around us, we're all drinking and having a great time. We fit in. The advertising works so well because it mimics our everyday behavior. Or maybe we behave the way we do because the advertising works so well. Either way, order another round—it's halftime! Never mind the consequences in a few hours or the next morning. Never mind the arguments with your spouse or the lost memories or the raging hangover. You've got to be part of the crowd.

So, yes, you probably drink to fit in. And yes, it's a cultural phenomenon. Society's view of nondrinkers is that they're boring. They're buzzkills. They aren't any fun to be around. I find this hilarious now because I'm still the life of the party, even without a drink in my hand. The truth is, the funny people are funny whether they're drinking or not. And the lame people aren't any more interesting just because they're loaded. But the mind is a powerful thing. And since we believe drinkers are more fun, they seem to be. And so we drink, even when we might not want to. And we pressure others to drink, mostly to justify our own choices.

When I wrote *This Naked Mind*, over 7,000 people volunteered to read it and give their feedback. I was shocked to hear that so many of them thought they were alone in their struggle to control their alcohol consumption. They all thought they were the only ones struggling. They thought if they questioned how much they were drinking, people would make fun of them or cast them out of their circle of friends. So they kept the problem hidden, often even from themselves. One of the main reasons people say that they can "take it or leave it" is because they've never tried to leave it.

Once I was honest about my drinking, suddenly others felt like it was okay to question their drinking, too. They worried about the effects on their health and their families but were too afraid to talk about it. In the years since I wrote that book, I've discovered that the people who defend drinking the loudest are often the most worried about how much they drink. They desperately want to have the same amount of fun while drinking less, but they just don't see how it's possible. The cultural conditioning is that strong.

I also want us to ask, What kind of culture are we creating by choosing to be a part of it? It's not popular to talk about, but there is a lot of evidence that an alcohol-saturated culture is actually a culture of violence. According to published studies, in 86 percent of homicide cases, the perpetrator was drinking at the time of the murder. Or what about domestic violence? Fifty-seven percent of the men involved in marital violence were drinking. Seventy-five percent of cases in which a child died from abuse involved alcohol. There's a hotline in the UK that children can call to have a bedtime story read to them if their parents are too drunk to do it. How heartbreaking is that? As a new mother of a baby girl, I'm horrified to hear the alcohol-related statistics for sexual assault. Sixty percent of sexual offenders were drinking at the time of the offense, and sexual assault is at an all-time high. In fact, if you look at the rise in alcohol consumption and the rise in violent crime, they track each other pretty closely. As drinking rates rise, so do the cultural ramifications. Is that the kind of culture we truly want to fit into?

I know it sounds like I want to wipe alcohol off the planet, but that's not the case. What I want is for us, as a culture, to be more mindful of the consequences and think carefully about what we're choosing to promote as normal. Because you're part of this experiment, you have a unique opportunity to be a mindful observer and decide for yourself. Consider whether you can enjoy life and have just as much fun with your friends if you're NOT drinking.

| TURNAROUND

The opposite of "*If I don't drink, I won't be part of the group*" is "*If I don't drink, I will still be part of the group*" or "*If I drink, I won't be part of the group.*" Come up with as many ways as you can that the opposites are as true as or truer in your life than the original beliefs.

▌FITTING IN DURING THE EXPERIMENT

You might be worried that if you stop drinking, you'll lose all your friends, even if it's only for this 30-day experiment. This can be especially challenging if you believe you'll be boring without the alcohol. Since you're not making any immediate decisions about the rest of your life, let's talk about how to get through this experiment while keeping your friendships intact.

1. **Don't preach.** Nobody wants to hear all your research into the dangers of alcohol. They already know most of it, trust me. And at this point, they don't want to be harassed about it. I became an anti-alcohol evangelist at first, and people pitied my husband for having to put up with me. If people ask you about the experiment, give them a brief summary to answer their questions. And maybe point them to this book. Staying low-key will do more good than making them feel like you're judging them. If they want to make a change with their own drinking, they're already judging themselves.

2. **Be a positive example.** Show your friends that you can have just as much fun without drinking (and without talking about it all the time). Let them see for themselves that you simply don't want to drink right now, and that's okay. Again, your friends might feel that by not drinking, you are judging their behavior. Even though this isn't true, they may still think it. So don't isolate them. Be as friendly as ever. Let them know you are doing this for you, and don't try to force the idea on them.

3. **Be creative.** You don't have to tell anyone you're not drinking for 30 days. If you're worried about how your friends will react, don't say anything. It's a personal decision, so keep it to yourself for now. There are lots of ways to explain why you might not

be drinking on a particular evening. Here are some of my favorites from our community:

"I can't tonight; I'm driving."

"I overdid it last night, so I'm taking the night off."

"I'm on a detox that doesn't allow alcohol."

"I'm watching my weight."

"I'm trying to cut back."

"I'm doing an alcohol-free challenge."

"I don't feel like it tonight."

"I have an important meeting tomorrow, so I want to keep a clear head."

If you do decide to continue this 30-day experiment for 60 days, 90 days, or indefinitely, you will eventually want to tell your friends what's going on. And chances are that many of them won't get it. They won't understand. But that doesn't mean they will stop being friends with you. It can take time, but eventually most of them will accept your decision. Keep it all about you, not them. This is a change you've made for yourself. Make sure they know you aren't going to impose your new beliefs on them. Here are some of the phrases I've used:

"I realized I'm happier when I'm not drinking."

"I'm on a health kick, and giving up booze is part of it."

"I decided alcohol was no longer doing me any favors."

"These days I feel better when I don't drink."

"I was no longer having fun with alcohol."

Also be aware that your own attitudes can affect how others in your group treat you. Notice if you're feeling smug or judging your friends for their alcohol consumption. Examine your own treatment of nondrinkers in the past. Do you have some of the same assumptions that you're afraid people will place on you? Also notice the actual reactions you receive from your friends. Your fears may be completely unfounded, after all. Your decision not to drink may be a total nonissue.

Mindful observation is the key to deciding this belief. Can you have as much (or more) fun and fit in with your friends without alcohol? The answer for me is absolutely yes! I'm betting you'll come to the same conclusion. But don't take my word for it. Test it out yourself.

❚ DAY 10 ❚

Dealing with Sugar Cravings

Be gentle with yourself, you're doing the best you can!
—ANONYMOUS

It might surprise you to learn that you may experience heightened sugar cravings during this challenge. This can happen for a couple of reasons. First, most alcoholic drinks contain more than alcohol; in fact, they contain quite a bit of sugar. So your brain is accustomed to the sugar rush from your drink of choice, which will create an intense craving for sugar. Second, both sugar and alcohol create a similar kind of response in the brain.

Let's dig in to why. When the brain perceives something as being important to survival, it produces a chemical called dopamine in response. Dopamine is also called the learning molecule because it is signaled when the brain wants us to repeat the behavior or learn. It is used for reinforcement. A good example of this is the fact that sex is vital for the survival of the species, and so sex produces high levels of dopamine in the brain. Addictive substances cause the brain to flood with dopamine. That is true for alcohol and for sugar, which is also addictive. The dopamine is triggered by the substance, in this case, rather than by something important for survival, but the flood of dopamine tricks the brain into believing that alcohol is vital for survival. Just think—because of the flood of dopamine, your brain is learning that alcohol is important for your very survival. No wonder it's so addictive!

Now, sugar has this same effect. Eating sugar produces huge levels of dopamine. In fact, some studies say that the brain reacts in a similar way to sugar as to substances such as cocaine and heroin. This again is for survival; sugar is incredibly calorie-dense and is an immediate source of energy. If you are trying not to starve, this is a very good thing. However, today it is not necessary and leads to an overconsumption of sugar. When you take a break from alcohol, the loss of a dopamine response causes the brain to seek out the high levels of dopamine in other forms, and sugar is one of the most readily available substitutes. Finally, you may be accustomed to using alcohol as a treat or reward. If you say things like, "I had a hard day and I need a drink" or "I need a drink to relax," you're probably associating alcohol with a treat. But since you're not drinking right now, your brain searches for another way to get that treat or reward, and a very common way to do that is with sugar.

So, you might think you're craving sugar when what you actually want is a treat or reward. Maybe a night out with friends, a movie, or a massage would give you the same feeling of getting a treat, without all the sugar.

At first, I made sure to be gentle with myself. Shaming yourself for any behavior from drinking to eating too much sugar is counterproductive to lasting change and self-acceptance. When I stopped drinking, I knew that I was already accomplishing something amazing by taking a break from booze, and worrying about my sugar intake seemed like a lot to take on at the same time. When I was drinking regularly, I was consuming close to two bottles of wine per day. A bottle of red wine is about 600 to 800 calories, so just by cutting out the drinking, I was saving myself over 1,000 calories. For someone drinking the equivalent amount in beer or mixed drinks, the calorie count is much higher.

I was so happy and proud of myself that I consciously allowed myself to indulge in other areas. I kept gummy bears and fruity candy on hand for those times when I needed an extra boost. I didn't feel the need to eat a lot of baked goods or ice cream, so I bypassed those. Something in the math worked in my favor because I lost 13 pounds in the first 30 days. This is *not* to say that you will have the same experience. You might lose weight; you might not. But you should feel proud of yourself for sticking with the experiment. Indulging in a little extra sugar worked to keep the alcohol cravings at bay and keep me from feeling deprived. This wasn't a long-term strategy or anything (I never carry gummy bears around with me now). It was a way to treat myself gently.

Allowing myself the extra sugar worked for me. However, if you don't want to go that route, here are some ways you can keep the sugar cravings at bay.

1. **Elevate your heart rate.** Exercise naturally boosts serotonin, the happiness hormone. I highly recommend exercising as much as possible during this challenge to help you purge your system of toxins and reduce the cravings naturally. Exercise also reduces stress and lets you get a handle on your emotions in a healthy way without resorting to alcohol to numb away anything you don't want to deal with.

2. **Eat fruit when you feel the need for sugar.** The fiber and fructose (natural sugar) in fruit will keep you satisfied longer than a piece of candy or other processed sweets will.

3. **Drink lots of water.** When you're thinking about sugar, you're often dehydrated and actually craving water. You can add lemon or lime slices and maybe a bit of stevia (a natural sugar substitute) to give a nice flavor to plain water. Your sweet tooth gets satisfied and you're hydrated as well.

4. **Keep your blood sugar stable.** Eating several small meals with

protein throughout the day will stabilize your blood sugar. Protein and fat take longer to digest, which helps keep your energy levels even. In addition, protein breaks down into amino acids, which are responsible for a whole host of processes, including healthy brain function. One amino acid that you need to feel good is GABA (gamma-aminobutyric acid). When you feel low, it's often because you don't have enough protein in your system to produce amino acids. Alcohol produces GABA in excess. So when you take the alcohol away, you're going to need to replace that amino acid at healthy levels. Eating enough protein will do the job. I have noticed a direct correlation between how much protein I eat and my anxiety levels throughout the day. Eventually, I was able to wean myself off my depression medication, which was great. But eating protein was also a key component to keeping my moods and energy levels stable.

5. **Consume naturally fermented food and drinks.** Wait, fermented? Aren't we trying to get away from fermented drinks? Yes, we are, but these contain such a tiny level of alcohol that they shouldn't cause a problem. And there are so many health benefits to fermented foods. Foods like sauerkraut, kimchi, kefir, and kombucha are fermented naturally and contain live cultures (probiotics). Studies have shown that eating fermented foods is one of the best ways to reduce cravings for sugar and processed foods. Be aware that cooking kills off the good stuff. So canned sauerkraut or processed and sugar-laden yogurt isn't going to work. You need to buy naturally fermented foods that require refrigeration to keep the cultures alive.

| BABY STEPS

There's definitely a temptation to do everything at once. You might be thinking, *Oh, well, I'm taking a break from alcohol, so I might as well quit sugar, start meditating, and run five miles every day. I'm going to be the best version of me!* While that's a noble thought, it rarely works in the long term. Once you start down the path to self-improvement, it's natural to want to pile on the good habits and become a brand-new person. But studies show that this is a recipe for failure. Take baby steps and be gentle with yourself. Focus on this one goal of eliminating alcohol for 30 days, and then you can revisit your other goals next month. Because the beautiful thing is that once you tackle this cornerstone habit and reduce or eliminate your alcohol intake, you'll begin to implement a whole host of other habits almost by default. I'm a different person. I exercise regularly, including my weekly tae kwon do practice and my daily mindfulness practice. And I started a business. All these changes stemmed from changing my drinking. I didn't know it at the time, but making that big change caused a positive ripple effect across so many aspects of my life.

TODAY, make a plan for how you're going to tackle sugar cravings whenever they come up. If you're going to let yourself indulge in sugary foods during the experiment, what choices will you make? Do you have them in your pantry at the moment? If not, you might want to consider stocking up. If you plan to exercise, what will you do exactly? How can you prevent those cravings from showing up in the first place?

| DAY 10 JOURNAL QUESTIONS

Remember, all the wisdom you seek is actually inside you; the most important words in this Experiment are the ones you tell yourself. Take some time and answer these questions in here or a separate journal (most effective), a voice memo to yourself, or simply by speaking the answers out loud for only you to hear.

1. *Sugar and Your Experiment*

What is your plan for handling sugar cravings? Have you been dealing with this already? Are you planning to let yourself indulge or will you try to avoid extra sugar? What alternative choices will you make? Do you have alternatives in your pantry at the moment? (If not, you might want to consider stocking up.)

_____

_____

_____

_____

_____

_____

_____

_____

_____

_____

_____

_____

_____

_____

_____

_____

_____

_____

_____

_____

_____

_____

_____

2. *Baby Steps*

Reflect on the concept of baby steps instead of trying to do everything at once. What have you tended toward? Do you try and do it all and then beat yourself up when you don't get it all right? Or are you gentle with yourself, taking baby steps toward your goal? How would you like to be in the future?

_____
_____
_____
_____
_____
_____
_____
_____
_____
_____
_____
_____
_____
_____
_____
_____
_____
_____
_____
_____
_____
_____
_____
_____

Day 10 Reflections from alcoholexperiment.com

"I know I'm one of those people who can overdo it with the self-improvement tasks, so I'm trying to be okay with an imperfect diet that includes some comfort foods while I get through the first 30 days of not drinking and get used to being someone who doesn't drink. Quitting alcohol is hard enough. I'm choosing to be okay with pasta and dessert for now as long as I'm also eating more nutrient-dense foods, too." —LEIGH

"I have found that cutting out drinking has given me more time and energy to put in place healthy habits that have only been thoughts before. I'm being careful to start out slow but consistent. I'm not craving sugar so much as that 'treat,' which has been a bit of a struggle to satisfy. I find that my appetite has increased, so I've started eating smaller meals more often. Also, I'm craving carbs more! Does that have something to do with alcohol? I would expect so. Just being mindful about that, too. And yes, *gentle* is the word for this experiment . . . in every way!" —ROSS

❚ DAY 11 ❚

The Alcohol Culture Is Shifting

Don't be afraid of being different.
Be afraid of being the same as everyone else.
−ANONYMOUS

Drinking has become so prevalent, so pervasive in our culture, that it's difficult to escape its influence. But there's an amazingly vibrant minority of people who are taking a step back and thinking about that status quo. They've found they are participating in something that isn't much fun anymore, and they're choosing to pause and reflect. The result is an entire culture shift around alcohol.

I first noticed the shift in some of the super-athletes and people who are deeply involved in the fitness and health world. They realized that while they were eating all-organic food, exercising, and doing yoga, they were also drinking a known toxin in excessive amounts. People are waking up, and they're starting to question that behavior.

❚ YOUNG PEOPLE ARE DRINKING LESS

The idea that drinking alcohol might not be such a great idea is becoming more prevalent among young people as well. Young people today are drinking much less than their counterparts were 10 years ago. This change is motivated in part by a desire for better health and to buck their parents' drinking trend. I've heard people say that alcohol is their "parents' drug," and so these young people are choosing not to drink. According to a recent poll, 66 percent of adults under 24 years old in America don't feel that alcohol is important to their life.

If you contrast that with older people, the opposite is true. Drinking among older generations, especially women, is going up. In fact, according to a recent study, there was a whopping 107 percent increase in alcohol use disorder (AUD) among adults 65 and over, and an 82 percent increase in AUD among those 45 to 65 years old.[1] So, a very intelligent, mindful minority believe that alcohol is less important to their social life than it was to their parents'. In fact, the study says that 41 percent of Gen Y drinkers think alcohol is less important to their own life than it was to their parents' lives. I believe social media has contributed to this new attitude, too. When your entire life is documented on Instagram and Snapchat, you don't want to be caught drunk or passed out. Seeing videos of their friends' behavior can also be a deterrent.

I CUTTING BACK IS A GLOBAL PHENOMENON

Drinking less is not only a local phenomenon; it's global. In the UK, a fifth of British adults under 25 don't drink at all. And that number has been drastically increasing, according to the UK's Office for National Statistics. According to the National Drug Strategy Household Survey in Australia, the percentage of teenagers drinking there was cut in half in 2016. And weekly risky drinking among 18- to-24-year-olds dropped from 32 to 22 percent between 2010 and 2013. The declines are happening across the board—in both sexes and in all sorts of socioeconomic strata, and in both urban and rural areas. Similar studies have come out in Canada and Sweden.

A UK program called Dry January, in which people stop drinking alcohol for the month, has expanded globally over the years. In 2017, 5 million people signed up to do Dry January. According to research by the Public Health England, 67 percent of people will cut back their drinking over the rest of the year after participating in Dry January. And 8 percent of those people will stop drinking completely because they feel so good.

Other exciting things show evidence of this trend toward less alcohol consumption. The first alcohol-free bars are opening in major cities like London and New York City. The first nonalcoholic spirit, called Seedlip, has come out. And there's an alcohol-free rave movement called Daybreaker, in which people gather to watch the sun rise and have a massive dance party.

You might be surprised to learn that some of the most successful entrepreneurs, musicians, authors, and actors don't drink. This list includes Warren Buffett, Tony Robbins, Tobey Maguire, Stephen King, Daniel Radcliffe, Tyra Banks, Natalie Portman, Jada Pinkett Smith, Bradley Cooper, Larry Ellison, Christina Ricci, Bruce Willis, Eric Clapton, Jim Carrey, David Beckham, Jennifer Lopez, Ben Affleck, Eminem, David Murdock, Tim McGraw, Keith Urban, Joe Manganiello, and Gerard Butler.

There's also a culture of start-up entrepreneurs who are no longer drinking. Entrepreneurship comes with intense amounts of stress, as men and women work themselves around the clock to achieve success. Many extremely successful entrepreneurs have identified alcohol abstinence as their keystone habit. It's the one thing that allows everything else to fall into place. Suddenly it's cool to be a nondrinker.

You're in good company when you choose to take a break from alcohol. You're actually part of an amazing, vibrant, and healthy culture shift.

TODAY, keep your eyes open and see if you can catch people not drinking. Notice how many people are choosing iced tea, water, or soda over alcohol. And realize you're not alone.

| DAY 11 JOURNAL QUESTIONS

Remember, all the wisdom you seek is actually inside you; the most important words in this Experiment are the ones you tell yourself. Take some time and answer these questions in here or a separate journal (most effective), a voice memo to yourself, or simply by speaking the answers out loud for only you to hear.

1. *Culture Shift*

How does it make you feel to hear about the culture shift when it comes to drinking? Excited? Empowered? Reflect on your thoughts about this shift.

_____

_____

_____

_____

_____

_____

_____

_____

_____

_____

_____

_____

_____

_____

_____

_____

_____

_____

_____

_____

_____

_____

_____

_____

_____

2. *What If?*

Imagine that you grew up in a world where alcohol was less accepted in society than it is today. (After all, alcohol is the only drug on the planet you have to justify *not* taking!) Imagine that there was no peer pressure to drink when you were younger, or in your life today. Imagine that it was just as accepted to not drink as it was *to* drink. Imagine it was simply seen as a preference rather than an obligation. How do you think that would have changed your relationship with alcohol? Imagine future generations: What would it look like for them if we could change the culture now? How might the future look different in that case?

_____

_____

_____

_____

_____

_____

_____

_____

_____

_____

_____

_____

_____

_____

_____

_____

_____

_____

_____

_____

Day 11 Reflections from alcoholexperiment.com

"I'm so incredibly grateful for The Alcohol Experiment. I can't imagine going back. Looking back at the moments lost and mistakes made is incredibly hard but hugely rewarding. Even though I considered myself a functioning drinker, I don't think I was really fooling anyone. I'm sure I have said and done things that have hurt those around me over the years. It's a hard pill to swallow, but I will use it as a building block of my new sober life. I feel as if I've experienced a rebirth of sorts. I will forgive myself and move forward."　—PATRICK

"I have been plagued with depression for years, which only got worse with alcohol when sober and the false reality that I could only be happy when drinking. I have been asking myself where have I gone? I've felt lost and detached from myself. I've lost my interests, passions, and drive. Like Annie said, children are the happiest people and they don't drink. I would often reflect back to myself as a child and wonder where I had gone. Now that I understand alcohol was contributing to this, I am experiencing all these emotions again and loving life for the first time in a long time."　—MILLIE

||| ACT #5 |||

Alcohol and Happiness

| AWARENESS

For so many of us, alcohol has been central to so many meaningful and fun events in our lives that we blend the two together without thinking. Holidays, birthdays, weddings—celebrations of all kinds practically require alcohol in some form or another. So it's no wonder we feel like alcohol makes us happy. It seems like it's always there when we're having fun. Let's name this belief:

"Alcohol makes me happy."

| CLARITY

Where did this belief come from? We've been conditioned to believe that drinking makes us happy. We see people on TV, in movies, and all around us smiling and laughing while drinking. How can we help but smile as the gang shouts, "Norm!" or Carrie Bradshaw polishes off another cosmo with her best friends?

We've also experienced this belief in our own lives. When we drink, we think we feel happier because our filters are removed. Isn't it interesting that every time we've been in a fun social setting there was alcohol involved? These experiences cemented your belief, and alcohol became deeply intertwined with happiness. We feel free to express ourselves without boundaries. We think we're funnier and the life of the party, at least for a little while.

So is it true? Does alcohol really make you happy?

Let's start by defining what *happiness* means to you. Does it mean something fleeting and temporary, like a fun evening out? Or is it something more? Take some time to think about this. Write down some situations that describe happiness for you. Then ask yourself, Did you always need alcohol to be happy? When you were a kid, did you need a six-pack before every Little League game? Or did you and your girlfriends play hopscotch with real scotch? The average four-year-old laughs hundreds of times a day, no alcohol required. Think back and recall the years before you started drinking. Remember those friendships and activities that brought you joy.

Okay, now let's talk about how much time you actually spend drinking. I know for me, I would get off work around 6:00 p.m. and I'd probably drink until 10:00 or 11:00. Then I'd go to bed. I can remember feeling relieved for the first half hour of the evening, happy that my stressful day was over. But I don't remember feeling overly happy and joyous for the other four hours. I do remember waking up around 3:00 every morning and fretting for at least an hour over what I'd done—worrying about what I might have said or what I might not remember the next day. I remember dreading the morning hangover. Can I say that the few hours of drinking offered enough happiness to overcome the dread and keep me going for the whole next day? No, I can't. For me, it wasn't worth it.

The pursuit of happiness is so ingrained into human existence that no matter how happy we are, we're constantly on the hunt for more. When we see others laughing and enjoying themselves, we naturally want what they have. If they have a beer in their hand, we want one, too. If they're drinking champagne toasts at midnight, we want to do it, too. Whether it's a party, a sporting event, or a concert, did the alcohol actually cause the fun? Or were you in a happy environment and the alcohol wasn't actually the key component?

Happiness is at the very heart of advertising, especially alcohol advertising. But there's no balance in advertising. Alcohol actually causes far more unhappiness than happiness. It slows our minds and chemically depresses us. The ads never show the unhappiness that alcohol causes.

You don't see the middle-of-the-night anxiety or tears because we've again broken our promises to ourselves.

You don't see the drunken fights where people who love each other are now screaming at each other like they are mortal enemies.

You don't see the morning-after neglect that children suffer because their parents have painful hangovers and can't get out of bed.

You don't see the emotional, physical, and sexual abuse.

You don't see the drunk driver's face after they cause a fatal accident.

You don't see the husband taking his own life because he's lost everything—his family, his job, his money, his home, his self-respect.

You don't see the arguments and fistfights.

You don't see the violent crimes.

You don't see the unwanted pregnancies.

In short, you don't see the sheer and unrelenting misery that alcohol can cause.

Drinking doesn't just make the drinker unhappy. It makes the people around them unhappy, too. How many times does a spouse have to put up with their partner coming home drunk and starting a fight before they decide to leave? How many jobs does a drinker have to go through before they lose their family's home? How long will a girlfriend put up with mediocre sex and frequent hangovers before she decides she can do better? The damage alcohol does in our society is so widespread; we all have a story about alcohol and how it has destroyed someone we know.

And the children. Alcohol's effect on children is heartbreaking. Their whole world revolves around their parents. Their minds, bodies, and beliefs are tied to their parents' behavior. They model what they see and hear. Do they hear people at the bar laughing at their mom's jokes? Or do they hear her sharp tone with them when she gets home, the alcohol is wearing off, and her anger is flaring? Do they see groups of friends enjoying an evening concert? Or do they only see the hangover in the morning? What about when it gets really bad? Leading to emotional or even physical abuse? And children of alcoholics are up to four times more likely to develop alcohol addiction later in life.[1] It's a terrible cycle all based on the false belief that drinking makes us happy.

But maybe you think I'm being extreme here. Maybe you've never gone to such extremes, and that postwork drink is a harmless habit that seems to make you happy. But here's the question: Does it actually make you happier overall? It's true, there's a bit of a rush when alcohol first enters your system. Alcohol is an interesting substance because it is both a stimulant and a depressant. Alcohol acts as a temporary stimulant just after it enters your system while your blood alcohol content (BAC) is rising. A rising BAC affects the parts of the brain responsible for elation and excitement. But after only 20 to 30 minutes, your BAC starts to fall and the depressive effects take over, and people report feeling uneasy, sad, lonely, restless, and generally unhappy.

Since the rush doesn't last, and you end up feeling worse than you did before that first drink because of a falling BAC, you need another hit to keep the BAC rising. But that initial nice tipsy feeling never comes back in quite the same way, no matter how many drinks you consume. You drink more and more to get that rush back. But the more alcohol you consume, the duller your senses become. Your perceptions change and you can no longer assess how drunk you are. It's possible to keep the BAC rising for four hours or so. But once your BAC crosses a certain threshold (0.05 or 0.06), the alcohol becomes a downer, even if your BAC continues to rise. What's more is that the longer you keep drinking, the longer it's going to take for your BAC to come back down. And that means 10 or more *hours* of feeling uneasy, anxious, upset, and even depressed. How fun is that?

Look at it logically. If a little alcohol makes you happy, shouldn't a lot of alcohol make you happier? So how come the more you drink, the less you feel that euphoria? The more you drink, the more likely you'll do or say something embarrassing. The more you drink, the more likely you'll feel terrible in the morning. How can that possibly be defined as happiness?

But we all see friends and families giggling, joking, and enjoying themselves while drinking. Have you ever stopped to consider that maybe they'd be enjoying themselves as much (if not more) without the drinks? Maybe it's the occasion and not the alcohol providing the happiness. It's hard to separate the occasion from the drink, though, because drinking is completely intertwined with every social event we attend.

Yet, when I look back now, it's almost a joke how much happier I am without drinking! I can finally truly enjoy social occasions for what they are—a chance to hang out with my friends and have a good time. Whether they're drinking or not doesn't affect my own enjoyment. Only after alcohol has completely left your system can you fully realize that, yes, you can feel joy and happiness and incredible energy levels on a consistent basis.

When Does the Fun Begin?

Let's consider this from a different angle. Think back to the last good time you had fun drinking. Maybe it was last night. Maybe it was a few hours ago. Think about when, exactly, the fun began. At what point did you start to feel good about the experience? Because I usually drank after work, my fun began the minute I'd walk out of my office. It was like I could finally breathe. The workday was done. I could relax. I'd already be feeling good just anticipating spending the next few hours doing something fun. I'd reach for my first glass of wine with a smile on my face. For me, these feelings began 15 to 20 minutes or so before I even took my first sip. The anticipation of having the rest of the evening in front of me made me feel good.

The same thing happens with the Friday effect. It's Friday night.

You've got the whole weekend ahead of you, and you're feeling good. Naturally, you celebrate with a few beers down at the pub with your mates. Ordering that first round gets you into the weekend mood, right? But the cheering and excitement and fun happen well before any alcohol has had time to take effect in your body. You don't even have the drink in front of you yet.

So ask yourself, "When does the fun actually begin?" Is it when you're drinking? Or is it the anticipation beforehand that kicks things off? Could the fun actually be coming from the connection you have to the people and places you frequent when you drink? Also ask yourself, "How do I define *fun*?" What does that mean for you, and how does alcohol make things fun? How does it make you happy?

True connection and pleasure come from consciously experiencing a moment in time. You have to be present and aware of what's happening around you for it to register as happiness in your brain. But alcohol's chemical effect on your mind is the exact opposite of being present and aware. Alcohol numbs your physical and emotional experience. It makes you less and less aware as the night goes on until you can't even remember what happened the next morning.

| TURNAROUND

The opposite of *"alcohol makes me happy"* is *"alcohol makes me sad"* or *"alcohol doesn't make me happy."* Come up with as many ways as you can that the opposite is as true as or truer in your life than the original belief.

Try the Happiness Exercise

The world's leading happiness researcher, Barbara Fredrickson, says the 10 most positive emotions that combine to create the emotion we call happiness are joy, gratitude, serenity, interest, hope, pride, amusement, inspiration, awe, and love. I want you to take the time to do this short happiness exercise because it will completely shift your subconscious feelings about alcohol in a truly profound way. Please write your answers down on paper, because writing cements your thoughts to your subconscious.

Consider each of these emotions, one at a time. Take the first one, joy. Write down all the ways alcohol increases joy in your life. Take as much time as you need. Then write down all the ways alcohol robs you of joy in your life. Think about your reality now—not what life used to be like or what you hope it will be in the future. Right now. How does alcohol add joy? How does it take joy away? Then go on to gratitude. Ask yourself the same questions. And follow that with the next emotion, continuing until you've covered all 10: joy, gratitude, serenity, interest, hope, pride, amusement, inspiration, awe, and love.

This exercise will give you an incredible perspective on how much joy you're truly receiving from alcohol, and how much you're losing. Research has shown that only 10 percent of our overall happiness depends on external things, whether that's a new car, a relationship, or alcohol. Things don't make us happy. Ninety percent depends on our internal environment. How relaxed are we? How confident? How peaceful? You have the power to make changes that will truly make you happy. And that's great news, because while we can't always change our outer environment, we can absolutely influence what's going on internally.

DAY 12

Your Incredible Body and Brain

*Take care of your incredible body. It is the most amazing thing
you own, and it is the only place you truly have to live.*
—ANONYMOUS

Today I want to take a minute to celebrate the incredible miracle that
is you! Most of us don't take the time to think about how amazing our
bodies and our brains are. Think about all the incredible physical and
mental feats we can perform. Our brains are more powerful than
supercomputers; in fact, we created supercomputers. We've developed
cures for diseases. We've even propelled ourselves off this planet and
onto the moon. Is there anything we can't do if we put our minds to
it? Our minds are powerful, and since we don't fully understand their
power, they can sometimes work against us.

We've already discussed your mind's incredible ability to hinder
your growth and progress. But it's so important to understand, that I
want to go into more detail here. Neuropsychologists have shown that
we actually create what we anticipate. When we anticipate something
negative, it becomes reality. And so, for example, if you anticipate that
giving up drinking is going to be difficult, that you're going to be deprived and not have any fun, then that becomes your reality. Some
people call this the placebo effect, and it's absolutely real. There was
an interesting study done in which people were exposed to poison ivy.
Doctors rubbed poison ivy on one arm of each participant and told

them that it was actually a plain leaf. Then they rubbed a plain leaf on each participant's other arm and told them that it was poison ivy. All but two people experienced an allergic reaction to the plain leaf and did not react at all to the actual poison ivy.

If somebody brushes up against poison ivy in nature, they will have a reaction. There is a physical reaction that happens when those chemical compounds come in contact with the skin—you get an itchy rash. Yet if your brain *believes* that nothing should happen, then nothing happens.

If your brain is strong enough to overcome a reaction to exposure to the chemical compound in poison ivy, it's also strong enough to ensure you are miserable at a party if you've decided you will be miserable without drinking.

THE HEALING PHARMACY WITHIN

Your brain and body's function is to ensure you survive and thrive. Consider that for a moment. This amazing living computer is not meant to ingest large amounts of alcohol every single day. If it were, it would have been built into our physiology. Instead, we have an infinite, incredible pharmacy within us. We deliver all the right emotions and chemicals that we need to live a healthy and balanced life, in the right doses, at the right times. Consider the fight-or-flight response. If you're being attacked by a bear in the wilderness, your body responds to help you escape that bear. Your heart starts beating faster, you become lighter on your feet. Parents have been able to pick up very heavy objects that have landed on their children because our bodies can release chemicals that make us 10, 20, even 30 times stronger than normal if we need to be in an extreme moment.

Our bodies and our brains can do such incredible stuff, and so often we overlook it. We don't even consider how intricate and powerful we are. There's a lot of talk these days about loving ourselves, and certainly we need to love ourselves. But we confuse loving ourselves with thinking that we're beautiful, sexy, talented, or good at all these external things. In my opinion, that is not truly loving ourselves.

When you have a child, you love that child not because of their behavior but simply because they exist. You want to feed that child good food and take care of their body because you want them to be healthy. We need to love ourselves as we love our children. Loving yourself includes getting to know yourself, accepting yourself, and making a conscious decision not to take your health for granted. You are the person you will be spending the most time with for the rest of your life, so stop judging yourself and take a minute to appreciate the true, miraculous nature of this body and mind that you've been given. We need to care for ourselves out of love and compassion, remembering that we were created whole, complete with everything we need to not only survive but thrive. We must take care of our bodies to accomplish what we set out to do in the world. We love our bodies out of gratitude, because they keep us alive and healthy, and because they house our personalities—the very essence of who we are.

Some of the most impressive people in the world don't drink. Not because they've had a problem with it, but simply because they naturally don't want to put alcohol into their bodies. Comedic actor Jim Carrey once said, "I'm very serious about no alcohol, no drugs. Life is too beautiful."

TODAY, take some time to appreciate how amazing your body is. Give it a great big *thank-you* for keeping you alive.

▌ DAY 12 JOURNAL QUESTIONS

Remember, all the wisdom you seek is actually inside you; the most important words in this Experiment are the ones you tell yourself. Take some time and answer these questions in here or a separate journal (most effective), a voice memo to yourself, or simply by speaking the answers out loud for only you to hear.

1. *A Letter to Your Body*

Take some time and write a sincere thank-you letter to your incredible body. It might feel cheesy, but trust me, it will be worth your time. This exercise will give you precious awareness and insight for your future decisions. It is powerful.

_____

_____

_____

_____

_____

_____

_____

_____

_____

_____

_____

_____

_____

_____

_____

_____

_____

_____

_____

_____

_____

_____

_____

_____

_____

_____

2. A Letter from Your Body

Imagine that you are your body. You exist simply to keep the spirit of you alive. Your intention is to function in the best possible way—maintaining balance, purging toxins, and striving for longevity. As your body, what would you ask of the part of yourself that has the power of choice in how the body is treated?

_____

_____

_____

_____

_____

_____

_____

_____

_____

_____

_____

_____

_____

_____

_____

_____

_____

_____

_____

_____

_____

_____

_____

_____

Day 12 Reflections from alcoholexperiment.com

"I have never really considered how lucky I am to have the body I do. I should really be filled with joy and gratitude for the 48 years my body has gotten me through . . . with very few complaints. I've never thanked it, appreciated it, given it unconditional love. And yet it keeps doing its best for me every minute. A thankless, never-ending job that hasn't been easy. . . . The booze, cigarettes, lack of sleep, physical exertion, stress, etc., over the years . . . and yet the body comes out swinging every day to do its best for me. I have completely taken my body for granted. I've only pummeled it and criticized it my whole life. That is just so sad. I treat my body worse that I would ever treat someone I hate. Let me be grateful for this body I've been given and appreciate it every day by being conscious of how I treat it and what I put in it."   —PRISCILLA

"I'm just starting to get a glimpse of how wondrous and unlimited life could be if I wasn't groveling around in the mud every day with alcohol and hangovers. And that, then, leads me to realize how much precious time—and life—I've wasted in the last 35 years."   —JONATHAN

||| ACT #6 |||

Is Alcohol Healthy in Moderation?

| AWARENESS

We all know that drinking too much is bad for us. You know, in a very general, fuzzy sort of way. But science! We've all seen so many reports and studies that prove it's healthy for us in moderation, right? Beer lowers our risk for heart disease, right? Red wine is good for my heart, and it also has the ability to improve cholesterol, fight free-radical damage, help manage diabetes, fight obesity, and prevent cognitive decline. Doesn't it?

Let's name this belief:

"Alcohol is healthy in moderation."

Yeah, let's dig into this one.

| CLARITY

It makes total sense that you believe alcohol is good for your health when you take into account the hundreds of articles you've probably seen promoting this research. It's no accident that many drinkers can quote scientific studies and comparative mortality rates between drinkers and nondrinkers.

It's easy to convince yourself that there may be some truth to these articles because you haven't experienced the opposite and because it makes us feel better about our choices. After all, if you've never had a heart attack or stroke, who's to say the three bottles of wine you drink every night aren't contributing to that? You don't have Alzheimer's. So it's possible your alcohol consumption has something to do with that. Antioxidants are good for us. So the wine you drink with antioxidants must be good for you, too. Our brains are excellent at rationalizing. And the alcohol industry counts on that when they promote this kind of pseudoscientific reporting.

The fact is, there are a handful of studies claiming that alcohol is good for you. Some of them were even funded by the alcohol industry itself. And there are thousands of studies that prove the exact opposite. The difference is that the positive studies get far more attention than the negative ones. Why do you suppose that is?

First of all, people share information based on something called social currency. If I think an article will raise people's opinion of me, then I'll share it. If the post makes me look funny, smart, or righteously outraged, I'm much more likely to send it along to all my friends. Our friends hang around us because we all think and believe more or less the same things. So if I drink, and I believe it's healthy, there's a good chance my friends do, too. And we all want our beliefs confirmed by science. So I may share an article about alcohol lowering cholesterol so that all of us can feel better about our drinking habits.

Secondly, there's a marketing concept that familiarity breeds belief. The more often you hear or see something, the more likely you are to believe it. (Which explains a lot of what goes on in politics.) So every time you see a health benefit touted in a social media post or blog article, it reinforces your belief that alcohol is healthy in moderation.

Economics come into play here, too. Journalists make money by writing popular articles that get attention. They live and die by their likes, clicks, and engagement. The more readers who see an article, the more advertising is sold, and the more value those journalists bring to their news or online organization. Telling people that drinking is healthy gets clicks. And these days it doesn't seem to matter if the information is taken out of context or even completely fabricated.

We believe alcohol is healthy in moderation because our friends tell us, the media tells us, and scientific studies tell us it's true. We've heard it so many times it's become "common knowledge."

So, is drinking really healthy for us? Since thousands upon thousands of studies typically aren't reported on, let's look at the most obvious evidence we can find. How about vomiting? That's normal, right? If we drink too much, we throw up. If you think about the mechanics of vomit, it's actually pretty miraculous. Our bodies have an automatic rejection reflex if we ingest anything that's harmful to us. We don't die, because our bodies know better. Unfortunately, alcohol is an anesthetic and numbs our gag reflex, which means we don't vomit as soon as we should, given how much we've consumed. So the poison takes effect and we get hangovers.

Sometimes we even come to believe that worshiping the porcelain throne is a badge of honor. Look at me! I'm working today even though I'm super-hungover. I'm so tough. Give me a prize. The internal evidence is staring you right in the face as it pours out of you in rivers. And it's gross! How can something your body reacts to so negatively be good for you?

Let's also look more closely at the popularly cited evidence to support the idea that alcohol is good for us. We've all heard about the health benefits of resveratrol and antioxidants in wine. There are ways to get those same antioxidants without addictive and life-destroying effects, but let's say for the sake of argument that we think the research shows alcohol is good for our hearts. Diving in more deeply, there's more evidence that shows the opposite. There are scientists who study scientific studies. They pull together all the data on the participants and they analyze the findings until they come up with their own conclusions. A study published in the *British Medical Journal* looked at this idea that alcohol is heart-healthy.[1] It analyzed the drinking habits and cardiovascular health of over a quarter of a million people and concluded "that a reduction in alcohol consumption, even for light to moderate drinkers, is beneficial for cardiovascular health." Huh.

But wait—don't drinkers live longer than nondrinkers? One wildly popular study, the Holahan study,[2] has been widely publicized in mainstream news outlets like CBS News,[3] *Time*,[4] and even *Medical News Today*.[5] Its creator, Charles J. Holahan, claims that people who drink live longer than abstainers. I think it's worth taking the time to analyze this study a bit so you can see where this social belief comes from.

The study took 1,824 people ages 55 to 65 and then looked at how many were alive 20 years later. Of them, 1,479 were drinkers and 345 were not. They found that a higher percentage of nondrinkers had died during the period of the study. So, they found a correlation between drinking and death. Correlation is not causation. They did not measure or account for the cause of death at all, so we have no idea how these people died. If you look more deeply into the study, you'll find that they say the abstainers were more likely to have had prior problems with alcohol, which is why they didn't drink. Interesting. It also goes on to say that they were more likely to be obese and smoke cigarettes.

Come on! We're saying that drinkers live longer based on a study of only 345 people who had prior alcohol problems *and* were obese smokers? Really? Think about that for a second. Are you willing to risk your health based on such a small, skewed sample?

According to the World Health Organization, "alcohol can damage nearly every organ and system in the body. Its use contributes to more than 60 diseases and conditions."[6] The WHO also reports that alcohol has surpassed AIDS as the leading risk factor for death among males between the ages of 15 and 59.[7] And a groundbreaking and incredibly comprehensive global study came out in 2018 stating that there is in fact no safe level of drinking; even a single drink, even on occasion, is detrimental to your health.[8]

In a study of the harmful effects of 20 different drugs, alcohol came in as the most dangerous drug.[9] It's more harmful than heroin or crack cocaine when you look at the "ratio between toxicological threshold [or how much it will take to kill you] and estimated human intake."[10]

The International Agency for Research on Cancer declared alcohol a carcinogen in 1988. Not only is alcohol pure ethanol, which is extremely toxic, but it can contain at least 15 other carcinogenic compounds, including arsenic, formaldehyde, and lead.

We've also known alcohol causes cancer for 30 years, and yet it's news to most drinkers. No matter how little or what type of alcohol you're drinking, you're increasing your risk of cancer of the breast, mouth, throat, rectum, liver, esophagus, and other organs. Cancer Research UK says, "There is no safe limit for alcohol when it comes to cancer." Why don't we know this? People just don't talk about such things.

The term "drink responsibly" came from the alcohol industry itself. It wants you to feel good about your drinking, think that you're being socially responsible. Never mind that you're probably killing yourself. I know this is depressing. It should make you angry. But the good news is that any reduction in alcohol consumption lowers your risk for cancer. The fact that you're reading this book and taking a break is helping your body heal itself.

It's incredible to me that in our society more attention is given to the side effects of even the most benign prescription drugs, which must all be listed individually in the advertisement, yet there is no disclaimer in alcohol ads. Fortunately, you can decide for yourself. Now that you know some of the risks and the ways that science gets reported, take some time to think about what you're truly doing to yourself. Is it worth the risk?

▌ TURNAROUND

The opposite of *"alcohol is healthy in moderation"* is *"alcohol is not healthy in moderation."* Come up with as many ways as you can that the opposite is as true as or truer in your life than the original belief.

A Personal Note about Moderation (or Mindful Drinking):

It might seem confusing that on the one hand I am telling you that alcohol can be harmful to your body and on the other I am going to end this experiment by giving you tools to help you moderate if that's what you choose. You might be asking: How are you saying alcohol is addictive while also allowing space for moderation? I understand how this might be confusing, but here's the reality: We are human beings and adults. And no matter what I or anyone else says, we will make our own decisions. We value our freedom of choice, and we knowingly do risky things all the time; most of us make the choice to get into our cars and drive every single day, even though we know how many car accidents there are.

So often we drink because someone shoves a beer into our hand, or because everyone else is, or because we've gotten in the habit. I invite you to instead become fully aware and then decide consciously what to do. A friend of mine called her drinking habit "accidental drinking." She never thought much about it, it was just what she did! She still drinks, but she doesn't do it "accidentally" anymore. She mindfully considers her drinking; she decided that it is better to be fully informed about alcohol than to leave her relationship with it unexamined and accidentally get addicted and screw her life up—which was the direction she was headed with her "accidental drinking."

I am not here to tell anyone what they should or shouldn't do. And the truth is that fear and horror stories rarely persuade people to change. I am not presenting this information to scare anyone but to give you tools to move forward in whatever direction is right for you, with a foundation of knowledge and awareness. That is the crux of The Alcohol Experiment: my intention is to help you better understand the way alcohol interacts with your body and mind so you can make decisions about how and if you want the substance in your life from a very conscious, open-eyed, and aware place.

I believe that we owe it to ourselves, our families, and the world to become mindful in our collective relationship with alcohol. Ultimatums to stop drinking, fear tactics, and judgments are not going to effect lasting change. Instead, my hope is to educate and give you the power to decide, because I believe that if we approached alcohol fully aware, we would drastically reduce the harm and misery alcohol causes to our society and ourselves.

| DAY 13 |

Let's Talk About Sex

All my senses are awakened. Sex is more fantastic than ever!
—CARRIE (ALCOHOL EXPERIMENT PARTICIPANT)

Yes, I am going there. Why? Because this was a major barrier for me. I was convinced that I needed a few glasses of wine to "get in the mood," and I was terrified of sober sex. I'll tell you all about my personal experience, but first let's have a look at what the science says.

| SAFE SEX

Let's get safe sex out of the way before we dig into the juicier stuff. The truth is that sex is not much fun if it results in unwanted pregnancy or STDs. Studies show that women are more likely to sleep with someone they don't feel comfortable with and less likely to use a condom after they've been drinking. And men are more likely to misinterpret a woman's interest, which can lead to all sorts of unwanted situations and consequences.

Alcohol, Testosterone, and Libido

Drinking reduces testosterone levels in both men[1] and women. We've probably all heard of (or been in) situations where a man can't perform because he drank too much. This is why. In one study done on rats, their testicles decreased by 50 percent when they were fed a steady diet of ethanol. And yes, ethanol is the same thing that is in both your gas tank and that bottle of tequila. A reduction in testosterone for men means some pretty unpleasant side effects, like shrinking testicles, breast enlargement, fatigue, lowered libido, decreased sperm production, and, of course, erectile dysfunction.

In women, low testosterone can be responsible for some pretty unsexy side effects, including hair loss, weight gain, fatigue, disrupted sleep, depression, and anxiety. But that's not the worst of it. Reduced testosterone in women is also responsible for decreased libido and a condition called anorgasmia, which is the *inability to have orgasms!* Now that's no fun!

Reduced testosterone is not the only way that alcohol affects libido. As the amount of alcohol in the body increases, the brain's ability is impaired and less able to sense sexual stimulation. Further, as a depressant, alcohol affects libido by interfering with the parts of the nervous system that are essential for arousal and orgasm, including circulation, respiration, and the sensitivity of nerve endings. According to the Mayo Clinic, alcohol is a common cause of erectile dysfunction. This is for two reasons. First, dehydration can lead to an increase in the hormone that is associated with erectile dysfunction: angiotensin. Dehydration also causes a decrease in blood volume, which makes it more difficult to both get and maintain an erection. Alcohol also causes circulatory issues, which means that no matter how much a man wants sex, alcohol can make it physically impossible to sustain, or even get, an erection.[2]

The bottom line, no matter whether you are a man or a woman, is that while alcohol may lessen your inhibitions to fall into bed, it will decrease your ability to become and stay aroused. Not to mention your enjoyment. Which leads me to . . .

Sober Sex Is Truly Better Sex

Yes, I know you might find that hard to believe. I surveyed hundreds of people who have taken part in The Alcohol Experiment, and the truth is . . . sober sex is better sex! Your brain is receiving the full impact and unimpeded information from your senses—and wow. I had no idea sex could feel that good. When I was drinking, I rarely remembered it the next day, and I certainly don't remember having the level of pure physical enjoyment that sex now brings. And all the science backs this up! You are literally more in touch with your body when you aren't drinking and more present to the experience. The signals your nerves send are stronger without alcohol—meaning not only are orgasms stronger, but also it is easier to have one (or many)!

But you don't have to take my word for it. Here are some recent posts in The Alcohol Experiment community about sober sex:

"My second day AF I had the best sex of my life. I've been sold on being AF from that point on."   —Tracy

"Sober sex is the best! It had been so long since I'd had sex sober that I forgot how much I really enjoyed it."   —Kelly

"Completely agree on sober sex being better. So much easier and quicker to umm . . . you know . . . I'll just say it, orgasm! LOL. Finally feel like sex doesn't have to be a chore with the husband, but actually look forward to it now."   —Kim

"Right!? Sober sex is one of my main motivations for staying sober. Things in the bedroom have gotten fun again."   —Lori

And the best part? You get to find all this out for yourself!

| HOW TO GET IN THE MOOD

Yet it's true that alcohol does lower our inhibitions. While this leads to all sorts of unpleasant things—like sleeping with someone you just met, or don't really like—it can also be difficult to get in the mood if you aren't used to sex without drinking. Here are a few things you can do to get in the mood.

It may sound obvious, but wait until you get to know someone enough that you trust them enough to want to have sex. This is another huge benefit of sober sex; the people we have sex with are actually people we like and want to have sex with!

Sexy massage is an amazing way to calm your nerves and get in the mood. It awakens all the senses, sends relaxing signals throughout the body and brain, and allows you to get into the moment and the mood. Not to get too personal, but I recommend warm oil and candlelight.

Communicate. Again, this may be a no-brainer, but it's amazing how little we actually communicate during sex. Let your partner know what you want and what you like. Talk through any anxieties you have. Open, honest communication is truly sexy.

Don't wait to be in the mood. This is one of the biggest barriers to sober sex. Women especially often get in the mood after they are being touched, after that nice massage, during a couple's bath. If you wait until you're in the mood, not only will you create more fear around sober sex, but you will also reinforce your beliefs that alcohol is vital to sex. The truth is that nothing can influence our subconscious mind like our own experiences, and by showing up and giving yourself the experience of sober sex, you can easily (and enjoyably!) prove to yourself that everything I am saying is true.

The great thing is that by doing it a few times your body will remember what it is made for, and, like everything else, you will decouple the belief that alcohol is necessary for sex. Realizing you don't need alcohol to have sex can be a major aphrodisiac.

▍DAY 13 JOURNAL QUESTIONS

Remember, all the wisdom you seek is actually inside you; the most important words in this Experiment are the ones you tell yourself. Take some time and answer these questions in here or a separate journal (most effective), a voice memo to yourself, or simply by speaking the answers out loud for only you to hear.

1. *Sober Sex*

When you think about sex without alcohol, how do you feel? Describe your feelings in detail. And be honest; there is no wrong answer. It is so important and helpful to get your feelings (and fears) down on paper.

_____

_____

_____

_____

_____

_____

_____

_____

_____

_____

_____

_____

_____

_____

_____

_____

_____

_____

_____

_____

_____

_____

_____

_____

2. *Let's Find a Turnaround!*

When thinking about sober sex, come up with at least three things you have either enjoyed already or are looking forward to about sober sex. Perhaps it's how much more your senses will feel without the numbing effect of alcohol. Or maybe it's the butterflies you will have when your nerves aren't dulled. Allow yourself to dream and get excited (innuendo intended!). The better we feel now, the easier we attract this new and exciting reality into our lives.

_____
_____
_____
_____
_____
_____
_____
_____
_____
_____
_____
_____
_____
_____
_____
_____
_____
_____
_____
_____
_____
_____

Day 13 Reflections from alcoholexperiment.com

"The sex thing was a huge issue for me. I'd spent most of my life using alcohol to get in the mood. I avoided it as long as I could, but you can only do that so long. Then I found that I was even initiating at times. Like in the morning or early afternoon—which for me made those first nondrinking sexual moments much easier and more enjoyable. They didn't trigger me to drink. And I am happy to report that it gets so much better. You start feeling so much more."   —MEG

"Wow! I'm smiling and thinking about how I will feel when I have sober sex. I really won't know till it happens. And I swear I'll be true to myself and not fake anything. That may end up being a good OR bad thing with my husband. I don't know."   —JK

"Better sex? How awesome! I have been fortunate to have an amazing love/ sex partner for 43 years! The sex was always good. How much better might it have been without the anesthesia of alcohol? WOW! That's a sexy thought in itself, no regret involved."   —CAZZ

"Biggest milestone yet! Spent a week at my mountain house and went to the 'Saloon' Friday night. I'm known as a big wine-drinking party girl there among my friends. Didn't catch too much flack. My husband always complained that when I drank, he couldn't get me to go home. Well . . . stone-cold sober for the first time with my old buds and he still couldn't get me to leave! I had more fun than ever! And surprisingly the sex *was* amazing! Thank you, thank you, thank you, Annie!"   —ERIN

❙ DAY 14 ❙

Staying Mindful in the Midst of Chaos

In the midst of movement and chaos, keep stillness inside of you.
—DEEPAK CHOPRA

You've probably figured it out by now. This whole experiment is about mindfulness and becoming aware of ideas, thoughts, and actions that used to happen without your conscious knowledge or approval. It's easy to feel weak or hopeless when we keep having urges and desires to drink, especially if we give in to them. At this point in the experiment, awareness is the actual goal, not total abstinence.

Want to hear some good news? Becoming aware of your urges, even if you give in to them, can have a positive effect on how you respond to those urges days or weeks from now. When you stay present and mindful during a craving, you might be able to resist it in the moment. But even if you don't, you are still helping yourself in the long run.

Numerous studies show that when you try to repress or ignore an urge, you're actually making it worse. You're making it stronger. So, instead of running from it, turn around and face it head-on. Dive in and roll around in it. Become aware of all the feelings and emotions and physical sensations you're having during the craving. What is happening in your mind and in your body? I like to use a technique called Surfing the Urge. This technique was developed by Sarah Bowen, PhD, and Gordon Alan Marlatt, PhD, research scientists at the Addictive Behaviors Research Center at the University of Washington. Originally designed for studying smoking addiction, it works well for any cravings or urges.

Bowen and Marlatt gave a group of smokers a new package of their favorite cigarettes. Then they asked the smokers not to smoke for 12 hours before the study. By the time the group came in for the study, they were desperate for those cigarettes. Instead of giving in to the cravings right away, the researchers asked them to sit and do some very specific things. Look at the package of unopened cigarettes. Then wait a few minutes, being mindful of how they felt. Open the cellophane. Wait a few minutes and notice how they felt. Smell the cigarettes. Wait. Take one cigarette out and hold it. Wait. Take out a lighter. Wait. Light the lighter but not the cigarette. Wait. You get the point. The participants were present and mindful of their thoughts and feelings during each step of a process they would normally perform unconsciously.

▎DISRUPT THE CYCLE

Neurologically, you're physically disrupting the craving cycle in your brain. It is possible to separate yourself from your addiction. And the more often you do it, the easier it becomes and the less tightly the addiction will grip you. And it works even if you give in! Those smokers all had that cigarette at the end of the study. They satisfied their cravings, which might look like a failure. In the following 24 hours, there was no real difference in their smoking behavior. But by 48 hours later, those smokers had cut back their cigarette consumption by 37 percent. It happened naturally and without struggle. They no longer lit up the second they felt the urge. And over time, it had a positive effect on how well they were able to resist those cravings.

TODAY, think of your craving as a wave. It builds and builds, applying more and more pressure, until it peaks. Then it gradually subsides until it disappears for a while. Similar to how the size and severity of an ocean wave depend on the weather and other environmental circumstances, your cravings will depend on the stress levels and other factors in your life. Sometimes your "crave wave" will be small and manageable. Other times it will seem like it's crashing down on you, and you're powerless to resist the undertow. No matter how powerful the urge, mindfulness is the key.

At whatever point you notice a craving, ask yourself these questions:

What was I thinking right before the craving started? What was I feeling? What was my emotional state?

What am I thinking and feeling right now? How does my body feel physically? Am I nervous, sweaty, or anxious?

Are these thoughts and feelings true?

Would I feel better not thinking these thoughts?

Don't try to stop thinking them; just ask the question. You're tickling your subconscious, that's all.

As a detached observer, you might find the next craving is a little less intense. Or you might find you can resist it for an hour, long enough to distract yourself with something fun. I'm not suggesting you should give in to the cravings, especially during the experiment. I am suggesting that even if you do have a drink, this technique is worthwhile, because the positive effects on your brain and behavior build up over time.

DAY 14 JOURNAL QUESTIONS

Remember, all the wisdom you seek is actually inside you; the most important words in this Experiment are the ones you tell yourself. Take some time and answer these questions in here or a separate journal (most effective), a voice memo to yourself, or simply by speaking the answers out loud for only you to hear.

1. *Mindful Cravings*

At whatever point you notice a craving, journal through these questions:

What was I thinking right before the craving started?

What was I feeling physically?

What was my emotional state?

_____

_____

_____

_____

_____

_____

_____

_____

_____

_____

_____

_____

_____

_____

_____

_____

_____

_____

_____

_____

_____

_____

_____

_____

2. *Uncovering Judgment*

What judgments and condemnations (of yourself) come up when you are craving? Do you judge yourself as weak? Broken? Different? Write down all the judgments and just get them out of your head and onto paper.

_____

_____

_____

_____

_____

_____

_____

_____

_____

_____

_____

_____

_____

_____

_____

_____

_____

_____

_____

_____

_____

_____

_____

_____

_____

3. *Discovering Truth*

Have a look at each point on your list of judgments and ask yourself: *Is this true? Or are there other reasons for my cravings (perhaps how alcohol works in the brain, or maybe you were just tired)?* Write until you find a place of acceptance and compassion for your craving brain rather than judgment and condemnation.

_____

_____

_____

_____

_____

_____

_____

_____

_____

_____

_____

_____

_____

_____

_____

_____

_____

_____

_____

_____

_____

_____

_____

_____

_____

_____

Day 14 Reflections from alcoholexperiment.com

"I used to drink because I was stressed. Since I've stopped drinking and already learned other coping tools like meditation, I hardly feel stressed anymore. Drinking causes the stress, but I just couldn't see it until I removed it from my life."

—AARON

"One of the reasons I'm doing this is because when my daughter asked me not to get a beer at a soccer game, I did anyway. I chose a drink over her earnest request. I even brought her up to the bar with me. I justified it to her as something I needed to relax. Immediately after getting the beer, the game started again and I took the beer to my seat. I realized I didn't even want it. I just wanted to drink with my friends at halftime. I bought it to fit in, to get that feeling of being the fun drinker. It was eye-opening. Now I tell her all the time that I'm not drinking anymore because she suggested it, and what a great idea that was. She's so proud, but more than that she's seeing that she matters more to me than a drink."

—MELISSA

"I am discovering that my use of alcohol is directly related to my uncomfortable feelings. I am essentially trying to escape myself and quiet down the chatter in my head. Somewhere along the line I learned that emotions shouldn't be tolerated, which is a lie. I am working on identifying my thoughts and emotions and then questioning their validity. I am trying to uncover what the real issue is behind my emotions. More often than not, it is a feeling of low self-worth and not being/doing enough, not being deserving of love unless I perform. I am getting so tired of this story. I have dragged this story around most of my life and I am ready to put it back on the shelf."

—EMILY

||| ACT #7 |||

Alcohol and Parenting
(a.k.a. Mommy Juice)

| AWARENESS

I remember so many times when I told my kids, "No, you can't have a sip. That is 'mommy juice.'" In fact, it's become such a well-used term that wine marketers have actually branded a line of wines "Mommy Juice." Both my husband and I were absolutely convinced that alcohol was a vital and necessary part of parenting. I remember getting him a Father's Day card one year that said "It's not drinking alone if the kids are home."

Let's name this belief:

"I need a drink to handle my kids."

But whether you're a parent or not, this section is incredibly powerful because what we're actually talking about is stress. Drinking to relieve intense stress. Parenting happens to be one form of stress that millions of people share, and the alcohol industry has latched on to that and targets parents, especially moms, as a market segment. So, if you're not a parent, read this through anyway and substitute your stressors. Maybe you're a college student trying to get through a rigorous semester. Maybe you have a high-pressure career. Whatever that stress is for you, the same addictive processes are happening in your brain.

Before we dive into deconstructing this belief, I want to tell you a story I learned from Allen Carr. He's an addiction expert who specializes in helping people quit smoking. He talks about a deadly meat-eating plant from the islands of the South Pacific called a pitcher plant. If you're an insect flying through the jungle and you catch a whiff of its amazing-smelling nectar, you are instantly attracted. You fly in closer, perch inside the rim, and start to drink. It's so tasty, and you're so focused on drinking, that you don't notice the gradual slope under your feet. And you begin to slide down toward the center of the plant. But you've got wings. You can fly out anytime. Just a couple more sips and you'll be off. The nectar is intoxicating—why not enjoy it? You deserve it, after all. Like all drinkers, you think you're totally in control and can leave at any time. But the slope gets steeper and steeper, and the darkness closes in around you. You try to stop drinking and fly away, but it's too late. The pitcher plant has you completely in its grasp. Eventually you stop drinking long enough to look down and make out a pool of dead bodies floating in the liquid. You're not drinking nectar—you're drinking the juice of other dead creatures. You are the drink.

As disgusting as that story is, it illustrates a point that we don't talk about enough. Alcohol is addictive, not only to some people—to *all* people. And we need to understand that something as innocent as having a glass of wine to get through making dinner for the kids can end up becoming a huge problem. The only way to get out of the trap is to avoid it altogether. And the only way to do that is to understand that alcohol is, indeed, a trap. Oftentimes addiction takes hold when we use a substance to relieve stress. And in our society today, there aren't many things more stressful than parenting, especially when the kids are young.

| CLARITY

Do you believe you need to drink to handle being a parent? I totally did. I thought I was relaxed and more present with kids. I thought if I had a glass of wine, I could play their games longer. Where did this come from? If you start paying attention, you'll see the messages all around you. The alcohol industry has targeted parents in a major way—everything from TV commercials to movies to social media memes. You can't scroll through Facebook for 15 seconds without seeing a post about alcohol and drinking to get through the day. We are telling ourselves this lie that we need to drink to deal with the kids. Here are some of the placards I've seen recently:

This margarita tastes like I don't even have kids.

The most expensive part of having kids is all the wine you have to drink.

Motherhood: Powered by love. Fueled by coffee. Sustained by wine.

Wine: The Duct Tape of Parenting.

Mom's happy meal: a Xanax and bottle of wine.

Dear children, You whine. I wine.

Homework: Turning parents into day-drinkers.

Alcohol branding has gotten out of control, with wines like Mad Housewife, Mommy's Time Out, and Mommy Juice. Marketers are actually targeting stressed-out moms with a substance that's only going to make things worse. Humorous Facebook pages and websites, such as Mommy Needs Vodka and Hurrah for Gin, are growing in popularity. This segment of the industry has seen a 25 percent surge in sales, which is huge growth. Parents are getting the message loud and clear—it's socially acceptable to drink away your stress.

The message is always presented as funny. But it's not. More than 40 percent of mothers say they drink to deal with parenting stress, and 30 percent say they've witnessed another mother drinking excessively on a playdate. As I write this, my heart breaks thinking about two women who emailed me in desperation because if they don't stop drinking, the court system is going to take away their children. These are smart, successful women. They volunteer, they have powerful careers, they help out with the PTA—and they are in big trouble. One of them received a DUI with her kids in the car. I know one mom who woke up from a blackout, and the last thing she could remember was being on a playdate with her toddler. She had *no idea* how she got home or how she had gotten her child into his crib for nap time. Talk about scary!

Parents are becoming so addicted to alcohol that they risk losing their kids. And we're making jokes about it.

As heartbreaking as that is for the parents, it's even worse for the children who have to witness their parents' embarrassing and dangerous behavior. It's worse for those little boys and girls who have to leave their parents and navigate a strange new world on their own, all because their mom or dad couldn't get it together.

This is harsh, I know. And I want you to understand that it's NOT FUNNY.

I also want you to know that it's not your fault. If you're a parent and you drink, you are in the pitcher plant. You probably feel like you can fly out, and it's not a big deal. But make no mistake: You are sliding down into the pool of decay. But once you understand what's happening in your brain when you drink to relieve stress, it's easier to resolve the cognitive dissonance around drinking and kids. And once you do that, you'll be able to push off and fly away from the temptation.

So let's look at the internal evidence first. Are you okay with how much you're drinking as a parent? I know I wasn't. I justified it. I made jokes about it, like the memes we see on social media. But I knew deep down it wasn't right. I can remember thinking, *How would we drive the kids to the hospital if we had to? We're both drunk.* I've heard countless stories of people who grew up with parents who drink. They were all so embarrassed by their loved ones' behavior that they swore they'd never be like that. Yet they come to me truly not knowing how they've become their parents. They're repeating the exact same behavior they witnessed as kids, and they feel powerless to stop it.

The statistics on alcohol and child abuse are tragic. But maybe you're not that bad. Maybe you only have a drink or two every now and then when the kids are particularly challenging. Children are incredibly perceptive. When you say, "Hang on, honey—I'll play with you as soon as I get a beer," they pick up on the subtle message that the drink is more important than they are. What words are you using with your kids, and what messages are you sending them? I can remember my own son telling me he didn't like it when my lips turned purple. That was a sign to him that I was changing into someone he didn't like, someone who was only half there. Children report that when their parents are drinking, it's like they aren't really there. They're distracted and only half paying attention.

We tell our kids that this is "Mommy's juice" and to do as we say, not as we do. But it's human nature to want what we can't have. So by withholding this magical liquid from our kids, they are being trained to want it more. Studies show that children who grow up seeing their parents drunk are three times more likely to have problems with alcohol and drugs. They have more eating disorders. And they're four times more likely to suffer from depression. Some parents offer sips of alcohol to their kids to prevent the "forbidden allure" of something for grown-ups. But research is showing that these same kids are actually *more* likely to drink as adults. We're subconsciously conditioning our own children to believe that they cannot handle life without alcohol. Is that true? Is that what you want for them?

How will our children believe us when we tell them about the dangers of alcohol if we're drinking ourselves? When they're eventually told that it's addictive and can rob you of your memories and health, they're going to worry about us. Or they won't believe the facts because Mom and Dad wouldn't drink if it was really dangerous. I remember learning about how cigarettes cause cancer and being terrified for my parents and the people I cared about who smoked.

Each of these ACT technique chapters are trying to undo some subconscious belief you adopted growing up. Are you unknowingly setting your own kids up to have the same misguided beliefs about alcohol?

Okay, let's talk about the external evidence and what's actually happening in your body. When I first started drinking, it was a fun social experience. But over time, it turned into something I felt I desperately needed, especially after my second son was born. It was a stressful time in my life when I was traveling for work every other week. I felt guilty because I wasn't home. And when I was home, my husband worked long into the night after the kids were in bed. Wine was more than just a fun way to relax; it became my friend and ally. It wasn't something I wanted. It was something I thought I *needed*.

Here's the thing—it wasn't my fault. And if you're in the same boat, it's not your fault, either. Your body is trying to help you survive. Dr. Kevin McCauley has spent his career studying the brain science behind addiction, and he talks about something called the hedonic system. It's the part of our brain that pursues pleasure as a means of survival. Remember that your brain is *always* seeking survival above everything else, right? And interestingly, intense stress can be seen by your brain as a serious threat.

Here's how it works: Your hedonic system runs off a baseline reading. In times of severe stress, that baseline goes up and things that used to be pleasurable, like taking a walk or reading a book, don't cut it anymore and you need something more to lower your stress levels. And that means you're more likely to reach for alcohol or another addictive substance to relieve the stress. By drinking to relieve stress, from parenting or anything else, you've literally rewired your brain to believe that's the only way you can survive it. You're stuck in the pitcher plant. People will say, "Just stop drinking, for heaven's sake. You're about to lose your kids!" But it's not that simple. Your evolutionary mind now overrides your common sense. Survival trumps all, and your brain equates alcohol with survival. You literally cannot resist when it gets to this point. Your brain tells you that you actually *need it to survive.*

Throughout history and in all parts of the world, people handle parenting just fine without alcohol. So, we're not born with this need to drink to handle stress. We're *conditioned over time* to believe it. All the jokes and social media memes we read and share are sending the message loud and clear. Our own parents might have perpetuated the message. We're telling ourselves we can't handle it. We're not resilient enough. We're weak. When we do that, we're giving away our power to alcohol.

But before you come down on yourself (like I know I did), please remember we are all doing the best we can, and making the best decisions we know how to make with the information we have. Until you read this chapter, maybe the only information you had was a funny joke you heard or your own experience that dealing with the kids is easier when you drink. But now you know the truth. You've been fed false information. You've been tricked into thinking that alcohol makes life simpler, when in fact it's the opposite.

You now have new information.

You understand what's happening with your hedonic system.

You are aware of what your drinking is doing to your kids.

And you are making a great new choice. As you take this 30-day break from alcohol, you have the opportunity to become more mindful and to decide whether you want to go in a different direction. So do the best you can with this new information.

▌ TURNAROUND

The opposite of "*I need a drink to handle my kids*" or "*I am a better parent when I drink*" is "*I don't need a drink to handle my kids*" or "*I am a worse parent when I drink.*" Come up with as many ways as you can that the opposite is as true as or truer in your life than the original belief.

▌DAY 15 ▌

Social Life and Dating

Be bold, be brave enough to be your true self.
—QUEEN LATIFAH

▌ SOCIAL SKILLS

Look, social skills are exactly that—skills. You need to learn and practice them to get good at them. So many of us start drinking at a young age, and we never develop the skills to feel confident talking in social settings with new people or going on a date without alcohol. We don't crack bad jokes and learn how to recover. We don't get shot down and move on. We don't experience heartbreak without the numbing effects of a drink to make us feel better. It takes practice. If we were all perfect at everything from the moment we're born, what would be the point? Life is all about experimentation and growth.

The good news is that it's never too late to learn how to interact socially with confidence, even if you'd prefer to be home alone with a book. But don't put pressure on yourself. Don't expect that you'll find your soul mate right out of the gate. Give yourself the gift of making mistakes without judgment. It's okay to dance silly and be expressive while you're sober. People like it. They admire it, and they wish they could do it. The best part is you'll remember it later. If it was a good experience, you'll cherish the memory. If it was a bad experience, you can learn from it and grow your social skill set.

Small talk can be stressful. And no matter how extroverted you are, walking into a room full of strangers is often nerve racking. It's a common human experience, and very natural, to feel uncomfortable meeting and socializing with new people. It is believed that this mechanism of initial discomfort around strangers helped protect us when we lived in a more tribal society. It ensured we were cautious as we got to know others and would not say or do anything that would lead to discord among tribes. Alcohol seems to provide the perfect solution, but with all sorts of icky consequences. So instead of alcohol, here's an easy way to engage people in conversation without feeling awkward—ask questions! Seriously, the question mark is the introvert's best friend. Get the other person talking and you won't have to do all the work. How was their day? What did they do for lunch? What job would they have if they didn't have to make money? What hobbies do they enjoy? Where did they grow up? How many siblings do they have? Where did their grandparents grow up? It goes on and on. You could spend an entire evening without having to talk about yourself at all. Of course, whoever you are talking to is probably going to ask you questions, too. But it's so much more comfortable to answer a direct question than it is to come up with awkward small talk. And the truth is that being genuinely curious about others is both fun and rewarding.

DATING WITHOUT DRINKING

If you're single, you might be thinking there's no way you'll be able to meet people or go out on dates during this experiment. Maybe you rely on alcohol to make you funnier or feel more attractive. Maybe drinking is the only way you have enough courage to go out and talk to strangers in social situations. Or maybe you feel like no one could ever be attracted to you without the wit and charm you think comes from a bottle.

So maybe during this experiment you practice caring for yourself a bit more. Look in the mirror. What qualities do you like the most? Do you have a killer set of biceps? Are your ankles shapely? Or do you have an amazing smile that can light up a room? Focus on what you love about yourself, and others will be drawn to you. We think loving ourselves means thinking our bodies are sexy or thinking we are smart enough, good enough, etc., when really we should be learning to love ourselves as we love our children. Because they exist. Love your body because it keeps you alive. Take care of it because it is what takes care of you. Treat it tenderly because you care for it like you would a child. You don't love your kids because they are attractive enough. You love them because they are your kids. Again, we didn't create ourselves, so what right do we have to treat ourselves so badly?

Make Your Own Dating Rules

Next, let's examine this assumption: *Drinking is the only way I have enough courage to go out and talk to strangers.* Okay, the first thing to know about yourself is whether you are an introvert or an extrovert. Some people just aren't wired to hit the party circuit and hook up with people they don't know. Our culture idolizes the extroverts, the people who crave social interaction. But a full 50 percent of people are actually introverts. They would much prefer to interact with one or two friends in a low-key setting. If that's you, great! Don't force yourself to be something you're not. I'm not suggesting you can't ever meet new people or go out on first dates. I'm saying you can do it in a way that feels more comfortable. If you have to have alcohol to meet people, maybe you need a different approach. Instead of going to big, boozy parties with loud music, try taking up a hobby and joining a club full of people interested in the same things. Maybe you join a rock-climbing gym or a country club where you can sign up to meet people on the golf course. Who made the rule that a first date is always "meeting for a drink"? You can make up your own rules. A date could be taking a class together, or volunteering together, or having coffee on a Sunday morning. Be unconventional. It's cool!

Alcohol and Attraction

I feel more attractive once I am buzzed. I can let loose and stop focusing on my flaws. Guess what? Even though you might feel more attractive, the opposite is happening. It's easy to believe alcohol is helping because your inhibitions are lowered and other drunk people around you have dulled their senses with alcohol, too. But if 100 people are drinking heavily, 80 of them wish they could enjoy themselves with less booze. This might surprise you, but when people are looking for a partner, they find minimal alcohol consumption much more attractive. Even when I was drinking I tended to respect nondrinkers and felt they would make better partners and parents. I secretly thought it was so badass when someone said, "I don't drink." A pretty girl or a hot guy who has self-confidence without drinking? Superattractive.

TODAY, think about an alternative way to meet new people. One that's comfortable and easy. Or if you're already in a committed relationship, think about how you can take your partner out on a date where alcohol doesn't enter into the equation. Could you go on a midday bike ride and picnic? Could you find a lake and go swimming at midnight? Get yourself outside the usual "dinner, drinks, and a movie" date mode and surprise yourself! If you're in different surroundings, engaging in different activities, there's a chance you won't even think about adding alcohol to the mix. And anytime you catch yourself feeling awkward, ask a question. That's sure to take the pressure off and get the conversation flowing again.

I DAY 15 JOURNAL QUESTIONS

Remember, all the wisdom you seek is actually inside you; the most important words in this Experiment are the ones you tell yourself. Take some time and answer these questions in here or a separate journal (most effective), a voice memo to yourself, or simply by speaking the answers out loud for only you to hear.

1. *Meeting New People*

Are you afraid to meet new people or socialize without a drink? Why? What do you think will happen? Be specific and detail your fears.

_____

_____

_____

_____

_____

_____

_____

_____

_____

_____

_____

_____

_____

_____

_____

_____

_____

_____

_____

_____

_____

_____

_____

_____

_____

_____

_____

_____

2. *Exploring Your Fears*

How does what you've written above make you feel? Don't judge if your feelings are right or wrong, just notice how they all make you feel.

_____

_____

_____

_____

_____

_____

_____

_____

_____

_____

_____

_____

_____

_____

_____

_____

_____

_____

_____

_____

_____

_____

_____

_____

_____

_____

_____

3. *Is It True?*

Look at all your thoughts and fears again, and ask yourself: Are they true? Can you be absolutely 100 percent certain they are true?

_____

_____

_____

_____

_____

_____

_____

_____

_____

_____

_____

_____

_____

_____

_____

_____

_____

_____

_____

_____

_____

_____

_____

_____

_____

_____

_____

_____

4. *Are You Willing to Find Out?*

What are you willing to experiment with and be curious about in order to discover the truth? Are you willing to go on a date sober? Or to a sales conference? Or a happy hour? Whatever you decide, go into the experience with 100 percent curiosity and zero expectations. Journal about your experience.

_____

_____

_____

_____

_____

_____

_____

_____

_____

_____

_____

_____

_____

_____

_____

_____

_____

_____

_____

_____

_____

_____

_____

_____

_____

Day 15 Reflections from alcoholexperiment.com

"Day 15 and going strong. I have been lucky so far in that I have not been in a social situation where I have to make small talk with strangers. That will change soon, and it will be very interesting to see how I respond, because in the past I have always used alcohol to feel comfortable." —JOYCE

"Day 15 AF. Feeling good and I'm finally sleeping through the night now. I'm no longer having physical cravings for alcohol, but sometimes still have what I call 'routine cravings,' which is when I perform a task that I used to associate with alcohol (such as watching TV or movies or just relaxing on the patio in the evenings). During these moments it just feels like something is missing, but I'm not missing alcohol at all, or its negative effects, and look forward to creating a new routine for myself AF." —RUSSELL

"I can recall wanting to get my drink on before meeting a new person so that talkative, personable me could feel comfortable to come out and play. Sober me, overthinking me, quiet me didn't seem like someone a new person would like. Drinking did feel like a way to get out of my head and be able to talk and to meet and to drop all the judgmental stuff that goes on in my head sober. What happened, though, I can see now, is there was a loss of connection to the other person. The connection I felt was more illusion than reality. I was so concerned with being personable, I forgot to be real. Drinking allowed me to chat up my first husband at a bar. If I was sober, I would have never even wanted to get to know him. He would have bored me to tears. I divorced him after five years. But can I really say not marrying him would have made my life better? We have a great daughter. I learned about myself. Maybe I can say this: Had I not been drinking, not chatting up a boy I would have never otherwise chatted up or been attracted to, I may have saved myself years of grief. I can now appreciate raw, uncomfortable, sober weird-feeling moments that have not been smoothed over by the easy-breezy flow of alcohol. Is the awkward moment something to embrace instead of fear? Yes, I think it is." —ALEXIS

| DAY 16 |

The Power of Belief

Beliefs have the power to create and the power to destroy.
Human beings have the awesome ability to take any experience
of their lives and create a meaning that disempowers them
or one that can literally save their lives.
—TONY ROBBINS

You've heard this before, and you'll hear it again: Your mind is incredibly powerful. It can be a staunch ally or your worst enemy, depending on how you use it. The good news is that once you learn how the mind works, you can take control and use its power to change anything in your life. If you believe that you're going to be miserable without a drink in your hand at a social occasion, sporting event, concert, or even home alone, you will be. If you believe you're going to be lonely, you will be. If you believe you're going to be bored, you will be. If you believe this experiment is miserable, it will be.

I'm not asking you to counter these beliefs. Simply thinking, *I believe I will be happy without alcohol*, isn't enough. That's using willpower, and we all know that willpower doesn't last in the long term. Worse, your brain knows you're lying to it. You have to actually *believe* what you're telling yourself. So, how do you make that happen? Can you actually install new beliefs like you're installing software on your computer? Absolutely! When you start to question your beliefs, you create space in your mind for new beliefs to be installed.

| CONDITIONING

Let's talk about conditioning for a moment. Neuropsychologists agree that we spend our lifetimes being conditioned. We're teaching our brains what to expect in any circumstance. Whether what we expect actually happens doesn't matter, because we will manufacture circumstances that deliver exactly what we expect. This phenomenon has been studied over and over again. As we just learned, if you expect to be miserable, you will be. If you expect that going alcohol-free for 30 days won't be that big of a deal, it won't be. The ACT technique is designed to help decondition you—to change your beliefs and what you expect. Once you shake the foundations of those conditioned beliefs, you can start to move forward without being hindered by unhelpful and unhealthy beliefs.

A major fear for people before they start The Alcohol Experiment is that they won't be able to do it. They don't believe it will be possible to stop drinking, even for a short time, because of whatever their circumstance is. They don't believe it will be possible to be alcohol-free and happy at the same time. Or alcohol-free and relaxed at the same time. That's a completely understandable fear, but it's based on a false belief. Once you start to see other people being successful, you start to believe you can be successful, too. This is what's so great about The Alcohol Experiment community. You get to see other people who are alcohol-free and happy. They're making it. And you can, too.

Confirmation Bias

So you know you're being conditioned to believe certain things and expect certain things in life. But you also help cement those beliefs into your mind with something called confirmation bias. Have you ever tried to look something up online and stopped looking once you found an article or a website that confirmed what you thought? Take dietary fat, for instance. There are plenty of studies and articles and forums out there that claim fat is bad for you. There are just as many that claim the exact opposite. So which do you believe? You believe what you've been conditioned to believe, unless you're consciously trying to change that conditioning.

Confirmation bias doesn't only happen when we're surfing the net or browsing social media. When drinking becomes uncomfortable for us, we develop cognitive dissonance. The mind is uncomfortable because we're wrestling with two conflicting ideas—alcohol relaxes us versus alcohol is making us miserable. That dissonance is incredibly painful, so the brain looks for ways to ease the pain. How? By looking for confirmation one way or the other. Maybe we share social media posts about the benefits of red wine. That confirms wine is good for us, and so the dissonance is eased. Maybe we put funny plaques on the wall, like "Gone drinking. Will return when I can't remember why I started." What that does is make us feel better because it's funny, but subconsciously it also makes us feel weak because it's confirming our belief that we need alcohol to deal with our lives.

Recently, I've noticed more and more slogans that are supposed to be funny but really aren't. "I'm not addicted to wine. We're just in a very committed relationship." And "A day without wine is like . . . just kidding, I have no idea." These plaques are for sale for women to put up in their kitchens. The truth is that we're justifying an addiction. We're using confirmation bias to justify heavier and heavier amounts of drinking.

Visualization

Now you know the ways you reinforce your beliefs. What are some ways you can go about breaking and reconstructing them? One of my favorite ways is to use visualization. I know that might sound a little woo-woo, but stick with me here. Numerous studies show that the mind can't tell the difference between a real memory and a powerfully visualized memory. One strong visualization to try is to picture yourself going out and having a great time without alcohol.

When I first gave up drinking I would visualize the entire evening. I'd imagine myself going out for the evening with some friends. I would imagine the restaurant we were going to. I'd imagine ordering a big steak dinner and, instead of the usual bottle of wine, visualize ordering a tonic and lime. And then I'd visualize myself laughing and laughing and having a great time. It worked! The brain can't tell the difference, because when it has colorful, vivid, convincing pictures, it essentially tries to make those pictures a reality. So those visualizations are actually affecting your future reality. How cool is that?

One mistake people make is to think about and visualize what we *don't want*. But the mind doesn't necessarily understand the word *don't*—you get whatever you think about. Which, in this case, is the opposite of what you do want. So if you imagine, *I don't want to just sit there being miserable*, but you're thinking of yourself sitting there miserable, that's what your brain works from. It tries to make that scenario a reality. But if you think of yourself going out and having a great time, your brain tries to make *that* scenario a reality.

Just saying it out loud doesn't work. You have to visualize all the nuances—the entire scene. And be as specific as you possibly can when you visualize. Mentally rehearse what you're wearing, what you're thinking, and what you're saying. Take the time to sit for five or six minutes, set a timer, close your eyes, and go through the visualization. And don't worry and think, *What if this doesn't work?* Try it. Be as specific as possible.

If you want to boost the effects even further, add emotions to your visualization. How will you *feel* going out to dinner and ordering an iced tea? *I'm going to feel amazing. I'll feel so in control of myself and so proud that I'm having so much fun without alcohol.* Then try to feel the feelings in the moment while you're visualizing. Get that excited feeling in your chest. Feel the tingling in your hands. Put that big smile on your face. The more emotions you visualize, the more powerful your visualizations will be.

TODAY, think of the next stressful thing you're going to go through when you might be tempted to give in and have a drink.

Maybe it's going out with your friends. Maybe it's just surviving another stressful day at work. Then go through the visualization exercise above and visualize the experience exactly how *you want it to go*. Make some notes about the visualization in your journal. Then after the event, come back and write down what actually happened. Did you get what you expected? Did your visualization come true?

▌ DAY 16 JOURNAL QUESTIONS

Remember, all the wisdom you seek is actually inside you; the most important words in this Experiment are the ones you tell yourself. Take some time and answer these questions in here or a separate journal (most effective), a voice memo to yourself, or simply by speaking the answers out loud for only you to hear.

1. *Visualization*

Think of the next time you might be tempted to drink. Think of it in detail and then spend some time writing down your vision of the experience exactly as you want it to go.

_____

_____

_____

_____

_____

_____

_____

_____

_____

_____

_____

_____

_____

_____

_____

_____

_____

_____

_____

_____

_____

_____

_____

_____

2. *Reflection*

Return to your journal after the event or situation that you visualized above and write down exactly what happened. Was it what you expected? Did your visualization come true?

_____

_____

_____

_____

_____

_____

_____

_____

_____

_____

_____

_____

_____

_____

_____

_____

_____

_____

_____

_____

_____

_____

_____

_____

Day 16 Reflections from alcoholexperiment.com

"Wow, I'm so stoked! This is the longest I've been alcohol-free in probably a year and a half. I'm thrilled to have broken the cycle and to be creating new healthy habits and altering my neural pathways. My husband discreetly had a few drinks last night. I could smell it on him. He was respectful and was not obvious or drunk. The best thing is, I didn't desire to join him. I didn't even ask or bring it up. I'm too content with the changes I've made for myself and the future to fall back into the bottle."   —CAMI

"Day 16 and I'm so proud of myself. I feel alive and present in this wonderful life! Keep going—it gets better!"   —REGINA

"I used visualization and made it through my first event AF. Turning down wine/beer was easier than I thought. At the same time, I do struggle thinking about how I'll get through this summer. I waffle between thinking my problem is 'not that bad' and yet I have tried to stop drinking four times in the past five years. It may not be 'that bad,' but I'm uncomfortable with it and I want more out of life. I know that overall, it's not going to enhance my health in the long run. I definitely have my good and bad days, only about 16 AF now. I really would love for this to be my last attempt. I cannot wait until being AF is automatic and as easy as being a nonsmoker. I keep reminding myself I kicked the cigs. Here's to the day when to drink/not drink isn't even an issue because I just don't care that I don't drink!"   —BAILEY

||| ACT #8 |||

Alcohol Is My Friend

| AWARENESS

"Alcohol helps when I am feeling lonely."

Many people feel like they're less lonely when they drink. It's like even if their friends don't understand them, "Uncle Jack" (Jack Daniel's whiskey) and "Old Grand-Dad" (bourbon whiskey) totally get them. It seems to keep loneliness away. I know this was true for me.

| CLARITY

You probably do feel less alone when you drink. And at some point, you might have had a bad day and decided to try drinking alone. There's no one watching you when you drink by yourself, so you can drink a lot quickly. You don't have a social situation to slow you down. So your blood alcohol content rises fast and you feel that quick hit of happiness right away. It feels euphoric for that first 30 minutes or so.

Naturally, when you've experienced this firsthand, the belief that alcohol fights off loneliness settles into your subconscious and makes itself at home. And when you drink to overcome pain, the alcohol actually has a more pronounced effect, because it is a numbing agent, than when you drink for pleasure. So what's actually going on?

That first feeling of euphoria takes away any discomfort you were feeling earlier—the very discomfort that made you decide to have that drink. And you probably feel pretty good being alone, maybe for the first time in a long time. For most people, being alone isn't fun. It's awkward and uncomfortable. But when you add alcohol, suddenly it's great. So of course you feel like it's the booze that's fighting off the loneliness. It's nothing more than a chemical concoction, yet you can even start to develop a friendlike relationship with it. It's not that alcohol is your friend, it's that you feel the pain of loneliness less when you're drinking.

Let me ask you some questions, though. Since you started drinking alone, has your life become more or less solitary? In my experience, I looked forward to drinking, and when I was drinking alone, I could do it pretty much whenever I wanted. One woman told me she knew something needed to change when she started looking forward to her evening glass of wine even more than her kids coming home from school.

Has your life become more social or less social since you started drinking alone? It's normal for people to start avoiding social situations, even ones where they used to drink with their friends, because they figure out they can drink as much as they want at home with no one judging them. And they don't even have to deal with people—bonus! Soon you might find reasons to excuse yourself from any social situation so you can drink alone.

Are you closer to or further away from the people you love? Your children. Your partner. I thought my drinking brought me closer to my partner because I could unwind around him. But over the years, as I increased my drinking, I often found myself in bed with a glass of wine when he was downstairs watching TV. The alcohol actually drove us apart.

Is drinking the only social activity your friends seem to do these days? You might be feeling lonely because alcohol is the only shared experience you have anymore. I remember when I stopped drinking, a dear lifelong friend I'd known since kindergarten stopped coming over to hang out. It was a long time before I finally found out that she didn't think we'd have anything to talk about or do if we weren't drinking margaritas together. This took me by surprise. I had no idea she felt like that. I'd known her for over 30 years, and we'd only been drinking together for the past 10. Even though we had a huge shared history, she had this overwhelming fear because recently we had only alcohol in common. She was worried that it would be awkward. I told her that every new experience without alcohol took a little while to get used to and asked her to come over. If it was awkward or uncomfortable, well, at least we'd get a good laugh out of it.

She came over for the first time in two years. And we had the best time together! We talked about our families and politics and religion. We laughed until our stomachs hurt. We had so much fun connecting with each other that we completely forgot about the movie and hike we had planned. And now we're closer than we've ever been. All because we showed up and connected to each other. That was something that alcohol had been stealing from us all along, and we didn't even know it.

Let's look at the external evidence for a minute. There are actual physiological reasons that alcohol robs us of our ability to connect with other people. Alcohol slows down the speed your neurons fire in your brain. This means you think more slowly. You take longer to respond. And the longer the alcohol is in your system, the harder you have to concentrate just to speak at all. You don't retain much of what's happening around you. So you retreat further and further into yourself. Alcohol blurs the edges around what's actually going on. You also become emotionally withdrawn.

Here's something to try during this experiment. Go out with a bunch of your friends while they're drinking (and you're not). Then try to have a real heart-to-heart conversation with them. You'll find it's nearly impossible to get them to take you seriously. You can see it in their eyes that they're not entirely present. They're distracted.

Maybe they're too quick to laugh or respond, like they're trying too hard. If this behavior surprises you, realize you never noticed it before because you were drinking, too. You were also withdrawn into your own little world. I didn't notice any of this until I stopped drinking. How can two people form a true and lasting connection when they're both worried about falling off their chairs? You have to have other times when you're not drinking with your friends if you want to experience a true connection and dispel any feelings of loneliness.

Real human connection comes from being vulnerable. Researcher Brené Brown has centered her life's work on this idea. Think about it. When people seem completely put together and perfect, do you want to connect with them? Probably not. You might want to be like them, but you don't want to reach out and talk to them. That comes only when a person is vulnerable and shows their flaws as well as their strengths. Yet we try to pretend we're perfect all the time. We think if we pretend we're GREAT, then people will want to be friends with us. But it's only when we admit that we are hurt or disappointed—when we're NOT perfect—that people connect and our loneliness subsides. Even if you and your best friend experience a drunken moment of weeping—and a confessional "I love you, man!"—chances are pretty good that neither of you will remember it in the morning. Alcohol makes you think you're connecting, when you're really withdrawn.

If we truly want to combat loneliness, we need to be courageous enough to be raw and real. We need to talk about our struggles. The more I show up with my real stories, the more people come back with their own real stories. We're all struggling together. The more we pretend we have it all together, the more we push other people away. Drinking Annie was pretty good at small talk and making the jokes, but she wasn't great at making lasting connections. In fact, despite the perceived closeness and the fact that we poured out all our drunken secrets to one another, the people I drank with most were not people I felt I could call on if I was having a hard time. As alcohol steals our ability to connect, the more alone we become. It masquerades as our best friend, and all our relationships become superficial. No one is truly themselves after even a few drinks, and we lose the ability to be truly vulnerable. We lose our chance for real, true relationships.

As my drinking progressed, I found that it isolated me more and more. The more embarrassed I became about my struggle, the more worried I was about people judging me, and the more I wanted to be alone with the bottle. Drinking often starts out as a social activity, but then it becomes something that we do alone and sometimes even in secret, driving us further and further away from true human connection.

TURNAROUND

The opposite of *"alcohol is my friend"* is *"alcohol is not my friend"* or *"alcohol is my enemy."* Come up with as many ways as you can that the opposite is as true as or truer in your life than the original belief.

❚ DAY 17 ❚

Relieving Boredom Without Drinking

Boredom leads to creativity.
Imagination is more important than knowledge.
−ALBERT EINSTEIN

If drinking used to be a major activity for you, this experiment might leave you with more time on your hands than you thought it would. That is a great thing! Yet you might feel a bit bored, so let's explore that emotion today. Interestingly, boredom is one of the top reasons that people go back to drinking. It's important to get a handle on this uncomfortable emotion so it can't undermine your experiment.

Boredom can be a loaded topic, especially when it involves other people. There's a lot of implied guilt and blame involved, as you'll soon discover. The common belief among regular drinkers is that alcohol relieves their boredom and makes boring people easier to tolerate. But when you get right down to it, what is boredom? We might define it as a disinterest in the world around us or even in our own thoughts. It's like saying our lives are not enough for us. That being alive is not enough; we need something else. The concept of boredom is nothing new. References to it appeared in ancient Pompeii as early as the first century AD. I imagine it's probably been around since humans first existed.

Boredom is an incredibly uncomfortable state for many people. Scientists studied this by putting people in a room for 15 minutes to be alone with their thoughts. The only other item in the room was a device they could push to give themselves an electric shock. Eighty percent of the people decided to shock themselves and cause pain rather than sit and be bored. One person actually shocked himself 180 times! We brush boredom off as this trivial thing that we should be able to simply snap out of, but researchers are finding that it's not trivial at all, and there are some fascinating connections between boredom and addiction to substances like alcohol.

When we're young, we're taught to feel guilty about being bored. I remember my dad telling me that boredom doesn't exist and it was all in my head. In school, children are often told to stop complaining or that they're weak-willed and unimaginative if they're bored. Some parents say, "Only boring people get bored," or "If you're bored, I'll give you something to do!" (Of course, that thing is always unpleasant, like cleaning your room or taking out the trash.) And over time, we learn to be ashamed of this state of boredom.

So we have this feeling that we don't know what to do about, and our parents, teachers, and other authority figures tell us we shouldn't be feeling it. That sets us up for classic cognitive dissonance. We feel bad or embarrassed that we're bored, so we seek out ways to change our state of mind. Some people eat. Some people mindlessly scan social media. And many of us reach for a drink. For a short time, alcohol numbs the boredom and the guilt we feel about being bored in the first place.

Back in 1986, psychologists at the University of Oregon developed a test to study boredom. It's called the Boredom Proneness Scale, and you can actually take it online. It's not surprising that people who are easily bored are more prone to addiction. Teenagers who report being easily bored are 50 percent more likely to try drinking, illegal drugs, or smoking. Think back for a moment. Have you always been prone to boredom? Or did you have creative activities to engage in? What were they? How did you handle boredom before you started drinking?

It's important to understand that boredom isn't always a bad thing. I read a study where doctors put participants inside an MRI machine.

When they reported feeling bored, there was a 5 percent drop in their overall brain activity. But there were huge increases in activity in certain areas, specifically the parts of the brain that recall autobiographical facts, the part that seeks self-knowledge, and the creative center where hypothetical situations are invented. All those creative parts of the brain were much more active, even though the overall activity was lower. Interesting, isn't it? Boredom may well be responsible for all the great works of art and literature, your favorite movies, and technological innovations. Albert Einstein was a notoriously bored person. Legend has it that his famous theory of relativity came about when he was particularly bored in an algebra class and was imagining that he could escape by being faster than a beam of light. What amazing things do you have inside you that are waiting to be shared with the world?

Some people believe that true bliss and contentment actually happen on the other side of boredom. They believe that boredom is a sublime emotion, something to be savored and appreciated. In fact, researchers are urging parents not to fill their kids' summer schedules with activity. They suggest setting kids up in situations where they will be bored in order to foster their ability to be still in their emotions. Children need to develop the ability to pay attention to the little things that bring lasting joy. It's a skill we're robbing our children of by providing constant on-demand entertainment.

Of course, beyond a certain point, boredom becomes unhealthy. Studies show that when people (and animals) are bored too long, they can actually go insane. When you're drunk, you aren't capable of feeling boredom because you've numbed your senses and emotions. Boredom is your brain telling you it needs to be stimulated. So think of some ways to do that.

My favorite ways to relieve boredom involve activities where I'm striving to reach a goal. Since my husband and I started tae kwon do, we're always working to improve our skills and move from white belt through the colored belts; eventually we hope to earn our black belts. Sustained growth and achievement is built right in. Happiness is often found in areas of growth. Maybe you want to write a novel and you can check off the chapters as they're completed. Even something as simple as walking can give you a sense of achievement. Try a GPS app to track your daily miles as you walk the distance it would take to make it to Rome. Celebrate with a big Italian dinner party when you reach virtual Rome.

When you're drunk, everything feels the same. Whether you're eating a nice dinner, you're at a concert, or you're home watching Netflix, it's all the same numb, fuzzy feeling. Every single experience you have feels exactly the same. After I gave up drinking, I saw that life has so much variety to offer, and we need all our senses intact in order to experience it. When we take the time to appreciate it, life without alcohol is the opposite of boring.

And what about the belief that drinking makes other people more interesting? My answer to that is to ask why you're with those people in the first place. I certainly understand needing to be at a business or networking function where you don't want to be. And I did my fair share of drinking to deal with people I had no interest in. But when I did that, I robbed myself of the ability to form true connections with people who might be worth getting to know if I gave them a chance. When you drink to make someone else more interesting, you're the one getting cheated. You're poisoning yourself just so you can be around someone you don't want to be around in the first place. I've found that if I pay attention, I can usually find something worth knowing about everyone. And if I really can't stand someone, I can politely excuse myself and go find someone else to talk to. I don't need a drink to do that.

So what do you think? While it's true that alcohol does temporarily relieve boredom by slowing down your brain, it also numbs your ability to experience and appreciate the things that bring you joy. Given what you now know about the creative centers in your brain lighting up during periods of boredom, are you more likely to put up with those uncomfortable emotions to see what's on the other side? Imagine what might emerge!

TODAY, remember that boredom has a purpose. Turning it off robs you and the world of something beautiful and important that only you can offer. Try, just for now, to sit with your boredom. Let it wash over you. Allow the discomfort. And see what happens.

Then make a list of all the activities you'd like to try someday. Don't hold yourself back or put anything off-limits. Want to go sky-diving or drive race cars? Add them to the list. Want to quit your job and start your own business? Great! How about taking up ballroom dancing or shipwreck diving? Spend some creative energy making up a long, wild list. Then start thinking about which activity you want to do first and go do it! Even if all you do is research it a little on the internet, it's a start.

You have something amazing inside you that's just waiting to be created. Boredom is your brain crying out for stimulation. You simply need a healthy kind of stimulation.

▌ DAY 17 JOURNAL QUESTIONS

Remember, all the wisdom you seek is actually inside you; the most important words in this Experiment are the ones you tell yourself. Take some time and answer these questions in here or a separate journal (most effective), a voice memo to yourself, or simply by speaking the answers out loud for only you to hear.

1. *Reflection*

Reflect on today's lesson and in your own words talk about the benefits of boredom.

_____

_____

_____

_____

_____

_____

_____

_____

_____

_____

_____

_____

_____

_____

_____

_____

_____

_____

_____

_____

_____

_____

_____

_____

_____

2. *Your Anti-Boredom List*

Spend a few minutes making a list of all the activities you'd like to try someday. Don't hold yourself back or put anything off-limits. Spend some creative energy writing a list that excites you.

_____

_____

_____

_____

_____

_____

_____

_____

_____

_____

_____

_____

_____

_____

_____

_____

_____

_____

_____

_____

_____

_____

_____

_____

_____

_____

Day 17 Reflections from alcoholexperiment.com

"I can relate to the boredom. Boredom has always been with me and I always answered with, 'Hey, a beer sounds good!' or 'Let's get a little wine,' or 'How about a cocktail?' I felt a lot of tension last night, I think due to my unanswered boredom. My wife was having her wine and I was drinking water, which was not a problem. The tension was coming from boredom. I didn't know it at the time, but it makes perfect sense now. . . . This is an excellent learning adventure! There is some discomfort, there is some pain, but seeing my old lifelong friend Al Cohol being exposed for the backstabbing, toxic, miserable substance that he really is, that is refreshing, exciting, hopeful, and motivating. I can't wait to keep living this life!" —TIM

"I found that alcohol was keeping me unfocused and scattered and afraid to tackle the things I want to do. I am coming out of that fog. All I want now is to push myself in ways that I never have before. Alcohol for me was a lot about fear and lack of confidence, and this is starting to change. I feel great today." —BRYCE

"Woke up this morning feeing euphoric. Couldn't wait to start the day. I can't remember the last time I felt this good for more than a day at a time. There have been so, so many years of wine-filled evenings leaving me exhausted and disappointed. I used to be a morning person, optimistic and energetic, but in the last few years I've become down and blue and lethargic—struggling to get through the dull day until 7:00 p.m. when I can have that first glass. I really think I lost myself in the blur. The last 17 days have been a revelation. I think the old me is on his way back." —JULIAN

❚ DAY 18 ❚

Why Tolerance Is Literally a Buzzkill

Happiness is not a matter of intensity
but of balance and order and rhythm and harmony.
–THOMAS MERTON

❚ THE SCIENCE BEHIND TOLERANCE

Do you believe that a high alcohol tolerance is a good thing? I used to. People would make fun of me and say I was a "cheap date" because I got drunk so quickly. I didn't like that, so I consciously tried to increase my tolerance so I could keep up with my coworkers. Other people consider high tolerance a bad thing and consciously try to decrease their tolerance so they can get drunk faster and not have to spend so much money for the same buzz.

Alcohol tolerance is your body's way of trying to regulate itself in the midst of confusing signals and chaos. Let's look at the brain science, so you can see what's actually going on when you consume alcohol. Your brain has what's called a "pleasure circuit," and it's made up of the prefrontal cortex, the nucleus accumbens, and the ventral tegmental area (VTA). Alcohol affects your prefrontal cortex and makes you feel less inhibited. It gives you a temporary feeling of pleasure. Unfortunately, the more impaired your prefrontal cortex becomes, the less you're able to say no to that next drink. You're also less able to resist the dumb things you think about doing or saying. An impaired prefrontal cortex is why people drive when they shouldn't. You've damaged the part of your brain responsible for good judgment. After all, that's what your inhibitions are.

As the alcohol hits your system, the VTA stimulates dopamine release. Dopamine helps you feel pleasure. One of the main areas of your brain that actually registers enjoyment is the nucleus accumbens. It's not surprising that addictive substances stimulate these areas of the brain more effectively than everyday pleasures, such as taking a walk with your dog, watching a movie, or enjoying a good meal. In fact, addictive substances stimulate pleasure chemicals far beyond normal levels. That might sound great at first, but remember that your body is always trying to protect you by maintaining homeostasis. It wants to keep you in balance.

After drinking, your inhibitions are low and your pleasure chemicals are unnaturally high. A part of your brain realizes that no good can come of that, if left unchecked. So, as I explained earlier, it releases a counter-chemical called dynorphin. When you've got too many pleasurable endorphins racing through your system, your brain releases a sedative. Dynorphin counteracts the endorphins.

Now, if your brain had to do this only once, it might be okay. You feel high for a little while, cue the dynorphin, then you come back down and that's the end of it. Unfortunately, we all want to keep that happy-go-lucky feeling, and our inhibitions are lowered. So as soon as we feel ourselves coming back down, we order another drink. The alcohol brings you back up, but not as high as you were previously. Your brain says, "Uh-oh," and releases even more dynorphin to bring you back down. This time, you go even lower than earlier. You bring yourself back up with another drink, and your brain reacts with another hit of dynorphin. As you become more and more numb, the endorphins don't work as well, and you never rise to the same level you were at just one drink ago.

The cycle looks like this:

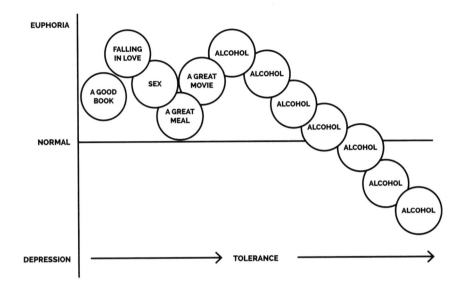

Each subsequent drink brings you lower and lower until you fall well below the baseline of happiness you started with. This is why happy drunks often wind up crying at the end of the night.

It's a neurological fact that the more alcohol you consume, the lower your pleasure dips until you are much worse off than you were when you started. Does that sound like fun to you?

Decreased Tolerance for Fun

There's even worse news, though, because your brain is smart. When drinking for fun becomes a habit, like hitting happy hour every day after work, it can predict exactly when and how much dynorphin it needs to release. So it prereleases the stuff! It takes proactive measures to protect your life. This is how tolerance builds up. You need more alcohol to even feel that first release of endorphins because your brain has already released the countermeasure. Bummer.

When your pleasure levels are artificially stimulated on a consistent basis, your brain gets used to it. And soon, you find you can no longer enjoy normal, everyday activities that used to make you happy.

Spending time with your kids, walking your dog, painting, playing games—none of that offers enough pleasure anymore. Your fun becomes entirely dependent on a substance that your brain has to work hard to keep from killing you.

Dynorphin affects the pleasure you get from *everything*. That means when you build a tolerance for alcohol, you're also building a tolerance for sex, and laughter, and ice cream! Anything you used to find pleasing doesn't do it for you anymore. You have to return to using alcohol (or whatever your drug of choice is) in higher and higher quantities until you become more and more focused on your next drink. Eventually, everyday pleasures don't even register anymore. That IS a big deal.

What you're doing is building a tolerance to fun, a boredom threshold for life. And the worst part is, you might not even notice it's happening. I remember feeling like if I couldn't drink than what was the point. Although I used to enjoy all sorts of things, I now couldn't imagine enjoying myself without a drink. What was that? How could it be that nothing was enjoyable without a drink? How did it get that way? This is how. Little by little alcohol replaced anything fun and meaningful I used to enjoy.

TODAY, think back to a year or so, or maybe even farther if you've been drinking regularly for a long time. What activities did you used to enjoy? What did you like to do when you were younger? Baseball? Swimming? Skiing? Try to think about when you last engaged in that activity and had fun. Who was with you? Were you laughing? How did you feel physically? How did you feel emotionally? What was it that made you love that activity? If you haven't done it in a long time, what made you stop?

The goal here isn't necessarily for you to pick up an old hobby. I want you to notice whether your tolerance for alcohol has also rendered other activities and people less meaningful or enjoyable. Let your subconscious mind mull it over for a while. Is it worth abandoning everything you think is fun and pleasurable in life for a few fleeting moments of artificial fun? You now know what's happening in your brain chemically. It's not like you can simply decide to have more fun with alcohol in your system. Your brain *will* counteract the alcohol. It's trying to save your life. Maybe all the extra calories, hangovers, and regret just aren't worth it. You get to decide.

❙ DAY 18 JOURNAL QUESTIONS

Remember, all the wisdom you seek is actually inside you; the most important words in this Experiment are the ones you tell yourself. Take some time and answer these questions in here or a separate journal (most effective), a voice memo to yourself, or simply by speaking the answers out loud for only you to hear.

1. *What Has Tolerance Cost You?*

When I was drinking every day, I couldn't imagine even enjoying dinner without a drink in hand. Think back on your life and list the activities that you used to enjoy that you no longer think will be enjoyable without a drink.

_____

_____

_____

_____

_____

_____

_____

_____

_____

_____

_____

_____

_____

_____

_____

_____

_____

_____

_____

_____

_____

_____

_____

2. *Could It Be Tolerance?*

I realize it may be hard to see that the things you think are only fun with alcohol (happy hour, sporting events, sales meetings, first dates) might actually be *more fun* if alcohol is not in the picture. But try that concept on for a minute: Take what you learned in today's reading and tell yourself why these activities might actually be more fun without a drink.

_____

_____

_____

_____

_____

_____

_____

_____

_____

_____

_____

_____

_____

_____

_____

_____

_____

_____

_____

_____

_____

_____

_____

_____

Day 18 Reflections from alcoholexperiment.com

"My husband came home after being away for a week, and he commented on the amount of weight I'd lost. I've been eating more than ever. I'm crediting this to not drinking! I really hadn't noticed. I've been busy. He said I looked better, too. Not that I want to define myself by what others say, but this was definitely motivation to continue."

—MIA

"My greatest passions in life are reading, creativity—writing poems and drawing, having fun adventures with my friends in the bush, and being dramatic with my friends and sisters. We always make up funny skits and have a laugh. I was on the phone with my sister last night reminiscing, and I told her that we'd had so much fun without booze when we were younger. We were just free and in the moment. If we could be that way then, we can do it now. What a profound realization."

—TERRI

❚ DAY 19 ❚

Dealing with Depression

Stars can't shine without darkness.
–ANONYMOUS

Often it feels like depression and alcohol are linked in this chicken-and-egg scenario. Which comes first? Alcohol itself is labeled as a depressant, meaning it suppresses your arousal levels and reduces excitability. It's capable of causing both sadness and depression, as well as making a sad situation worse. I've personally struggled with anxiety and depression since I was young, and I was officially diagnosed with clinical depression almost two decades ago. So, as you might imagine, I'm particularly interested in this area of research.

When you use alcohol to numb your sadness, you're also numbing anything that makes you feel happy. And that only worsens your depression. It's kind of like when you get a shot of novocaine at the dentist. You may only need work done on one tooth, but the chemical in the shot affects the whole side of your face. So on one side of the chicken-and-egg scenario, alcohol does chemically cause depression.

On the other side, depression can actually lead to an alcohol addiction. In my case, I can remember being filled with anxiety and depression from a young age. Your experience may be different, but I used to look outside myself for something I was missing that would make me happy—a boyfriend, a husband, a career, a house, a child. As I achieved these things one by one, I would still feel this sadness and emptiness. So I'd become obsessed with the next thing I was missing. Eventually, I had it all—I had a marriage and a family, I was at the top of my profession, I had a beautiful house in Colorado. I couldn't think of a single thing I needed to make me happy. Yet I was depressed. And that's when my drinking became a real problem. I was already a daily drinker, but it wasn't until I no longer had anything external to obsess over that I turned to alcohol to numb my pain. Even though I was on three different prescribed depression medications, nothing solved the problem.

In a way, I believe my alcohol addiction saved my life because it forced me to turn inward and figure out what was actually going on. It forced me to finally face my depression head-on. In that moment, I began a painful, terrifying, life-affirming journey inside to know myself and accept myself just as I am, sadness and all. And I have to confess, I felt so much guilt about being sad given my amazing external circumstances.

▌ WHAT MATTERS

Whether your depression came first, or your alcohol is causing it, doesn't matter. What matters is that the feelings are there and that you want to feel differently. And at least for me, I wanted to have a box to put those feelings into. A reason for them. Once I stopped drinking, my mind kept seeking a reason for my feelings of sadness. And the only thing that had changed was that I no longer drank. So that's what my brain latched on to. Little thoughts came into my head: *You weren't this sad when you drank. It's not fair that you've cut out such a powerful tool. Maybe just one glass of wine would make you feel better. It's the abstinence that's making you feel sad.* Of course, I knew these thoughts weren't true, especially later, when I applied the ACT technique to them. But that didn't stop the thoughts from being there. And when we're depressed, we obsess. We blow the thoughts up and make them true inside our heads until the thoughts become a compulsion.

So I became obsessed with research. And my research proved to me definitively that self-medicating with alcohol is a terrible idea! It leads to neurochemical addiction, and it prolonged my bouts of depression because I never had to come face-to-face with my pain. I was never forced to address the real issues. When I looked back through the lens of the ACT technique, I remembered that I was far more depressed when I was drinking than I ever was without the alcohol. My brain was trying to trick me, and I just had to remember the truth.

Finding My Truth

It took work and effort for me to unpack all these emotions and try to understand them. It took a lot of patience with myself to accept that some feelings just exist and there's no reason for them. It took a lot of acceptance to love myself, sadness and all. None of that was possible when I was self-medicating with alcohol. I was too numb to make the effort. And my life now is so much better and I have much less anxiety, fear, and depression than at any other time in my life. I'm no longer on medication, and I have the tools to handle the occasional low periods when they come along.

Depression is incredibly complex. And every person experiences it differently. One thing that I know to be true, though, is that alcohol doesn't help. It only masks the problem and makes it worse.

TODAY, realize that alcohol could be either the chicken or the egg. In fact, it could be both at the same time. Now that you've been alcohol-free for a little while, it can be tempting to buy into the idea that if you're sad or depressed, it's because you're no longer drinking. I know that was true for me. But think clearly for a bit. Apply the ACT technique to this. Were you this sad before you started drinking heavily? Did alcohol actually make you happier? Or did it just numb the pain for a while? Now that you've removed the alcohol, are these feelings new? Or were they present before? There's no right or wrong answer. I only ask that you be honest with yourself. Shine a light in the dark places where you hide secrets from yourself. That's where you'll find the truth.

I DAY 19 JOURNAL QUESTIONS

Remember, all the wisdom you seek is actually inside you; the most important words in this Experiment are the ones you tell yourself. Take some time and answer these questions in here or a separate journal (most effective), a voice memo to yourself, or simply by speaking the answers out loud for only you to hear.

1. *Defining Happiness*

Sometimes we strive for something without considering what it actually means to us. Take a moment and in your own words define happiness. What, specifically, does true happiness look like to you in your life?

_____

_____

_____

_____

_____

_____

_____

_____

_____

_____

_____

_____

_____

_____

_____

_____

_____

_____

_____

_____

_____

_____

_____

_____

_____

2. Remembering Happiness

Take a moment to reflect: When was the last time you felt really, truly happy? Reflecting on alcohol, has it made you happier or has it just numbed the pain?

_____

_____

_____

_____

_____

_____

_____

_____

_____

_____

_____

_____

_____

_____

_____

_____

_____

_____

_____

_____

_____

_____

_____

_____

_____

3. *Put Alcohol to the Test*

Consider alcohol, and think about this honestly: Did alcohol truly make you happier? Did it add to the things that you feel make up happiness in your life? Or did it just scratch the itch of craving and temporarily numb pain? Explore this question in detail and be honest; this is an experiment. You are gathering data. There are no wrong answers here, only information.

_____

_____

_____

_____

_____

_____

_____

_____

_____

_____

_____

_____

_____

_____

_____

_____

_____

_____

_____

_____

_____

_____

_____

_____

_____

Day 19 Reflections from alcoholexperiment.com

"This has been such a great experience. I never could have imagined how life changing this has been for me. Now that the alcohol is gone, I have clarity and peace every day. Yes, there are stormy thoughts and emotions, but they have always been there. The alcohol just numbed them temporarily. Dealing with them without alcohol makes me see how manageable they are. They are just fleeting thoughts, nothing more. So good to have me in control again!"

—JORDAN

"Depression is such an important issue to talk about. My father suffered from depression, and no one ever talked about it. I feel like there was so much shame about the topic—like you are not allowed to have depression. I am finally trying to heal this part of my life and not numb out. There is no shame in depression; it can in many ways be a gift. I am learning how to breathe through it and acknowledge pain without letting it take over. Thank you to everyone who writes comments and reads. You all have been so important to me!"

—JOY

❚ DAY 20 ❚

Our Headline Culture and the Science of Sharing

The problem with the internet
is that it can be difficult to confirm authenticity.
—ABRAHAM LINCOLN

Okay, obviously Abraham Lincoln didn't say that; he was long dead before the internet came into existence. But I think that little joke makes the point that it is difficult to confirm what is true online. We all like to stay informed and feel smart, yet we're all extremely busy, so we don't often take the time to confirm what we see or read online. We live in this headline-driven culture where we're constantly scrolling through headlines, whether it's on social media or the bottom third of a news show. We don't have a lot of time to digest and analyze the millions of pieces of information we're bombarded with each day. So we read the headlines and trust that the actual news story, article, or video is true. After all, it's the news. It has to be fact-checked, right? Wrong. In this age of the 24-7-365 news cycle, there's simply no time to check stories for accuracy. Twenty years ago, there was time between when a story broke and when it was actually reported. Even if it was only a few hours, that was enough time to corroborate stories and double-check statistics. Journalists prided themselves on accuracy and a lack of bias.

But these days the media is required to pump out new information as fast as it can, regardless of the truth. The internet is a content beast that's never satisfied. We can't feed it fast enough. And if an organization does get called out for a mistake, they can easily change it with a few clicks. They don't have to print a correction in the next day's paper or give an embarrassing on-air apology. Besides that, our culture's collective attention span is so short that even the most scandalous misrepresentations are quickly forgotten.

And let's not forget about clickbait and fake-news websites designed to look legitimate at first glance. These are driven by money and greed. The more clicks a story gets, the more money the site makes from advertisers. The writers know this, so they manufacture headlines designed to make you curious or angry so you click the link. Chances are you know good and well that the article is clickbait, but you go ahead and check it out anyway because the headline is so compelling or infuriating. Of course, it doesn't matter what the headline says, because the body of the article (which most people probably won't read) goes on to explain that the headline wasn't true—so that makes it okay in their eyes.

SOCIAL CURRENCY

So we're exposed to news stories and content that may or may not be even remotely accurate. But it doesn't matter because we don't have time to read past the headlines anyway. And then what happens? How do such blatantly false articles get shared across the internet and go viral? The science of sharing says that people share content that gives them social currency. That means we share things that we think will make us look good in other people's eyes. As we've discussed, anything that confirms our own personal biases or makes us look smart or hip or funny—that's what gets shared. Anything that makes us feel bad or uncomfortable gets ignored. Consequently, positive articles about alcohol are shared far more often than ones about its negative effects on our lives.

What does any of this have to do with drinking? It comes down to conditioning. We see all these headlines about the benefits of alcohol. They get shared over and over again because they confirm our beliefs and make us feel good about our behavior. If we're drinking more than we want to and we see a headline that says red wine contributes to heart health, great! We have a reason to feel good about our wine habit. And we'll probably share that post. But how *accurate* is that article or video? Does drinking red wine *really* help your heart? Or are there chemicals *in* red wine that *might* help? And might you get those chemicals a safer way, like from a nice green salad? Who knows? Few people will actually dig down into the article or the actual research to find out. They'll only read the headline and keep on drinking, even though there is overwhelming evidence pointing to the *negative* effects of alcohol on the heart. Remember that repetition mimics truth. So the more often we see a headline about red wine and heart health, the more likely we'll believe it and repeat it to others.

Another example is a study that came out about dementia and alcohol. At first glance, it seemed to be saying that if you were a moderate to heavy drinker, then you were more likely to live longer and have better brain function. One headline read, "Moderate to heavy drinkers are more likely to live to 85 without developing dementia."[1] Let's dissect that for a minute, shall we? First of all, if you're scanning headlines, you probably digest only the first half of the headline, meaning you'll think that heavy drinking helps you live longer—which is absolutely not true. Even if you read the entire headline, you'll still think heavy drinking is good for your cognitive health—which is ironic because there's actually a condition called alcohol-induced dementia. But most people don't know that, and they're not going to dig into the article or read the research to get to the bottom of that headline. I did that because the headline didn't jibe with what I know about alcohol's effect on our health. Not only was the article seriously flawed, but also the study itself was questionable, and the caveats at the end basically negated the entire thing. But the news cherry-picked certain pieces of information and pulled them out of context to match their bias that drinking is good for you.

Funded by the Alcohol Industry

Many of the studies on the health benefits of alcohol are actually paid for by the alcohol industry. That might seem ridiculous, but it happens all the time. The industry is getting ready to spend in the neighborhood of $100 million on a new round of research studies. One can only imagine how skewed those studies are going to be. Yet if the results show a positive health benefit in any way, news articles will be written and people will share them—netting the industry a far greater return on their investment. They need to keep people happy about their drinking, or it's all over. So any little correlation between alcohol and good health, no matter how tenuous or sketchy, helps them keep you addicted and sell more booze.

You might think that marketing and advertising don't work on you. But the facts say they do. Oddly, they work even better on your subconscious beliefs *because* you don't think the ads are having an effect. You believe you're immune to advertising, so you don't put up walls against it. You don't question the validity of the claims. And because you don't actively question things, the pro-alcohol messages seep right into your brain, where they can keep on conditioning you to consume greater and greater amounts. And all those viral videos, social media articles, memes, and funny drinking quips your friends share with you? That's *all* advertising! It's all conditioning. And we let it into our minds without hesitation.

TODAY, think about what you're letting into your mind. Do you even question the truth anymore? Does it matter that headlines are deliberately misleading you just to get a click and make a few cents? And examine your own social media sharing behavior. Do you find yourself scanning headlines and sharing them without actually reading and understanding the article? Does that bother you? What (if anything) would you like to do about it?

| DAY 20 JOURNAL QUESTIONS

Remember, all the wisdom you seek is actually inside you; the most important words in this Experiment are the ones you tell yourself. Take some time and answer these questions in here or a separate journal (most effective), a voice memo to yourself, or simply by speaking the answers out loud for only you to hear.

1. *Be the Gatekeeper*

Consider all the sources of information that you come across in a day. Journal about their validity. Have you taken time to question the information that comes your way to find out what is really true?

_____

_____

_____

_____

_____

_____

_____

_____

_____

_____

_____

_____

_____

_____

_____

_____

_____

_____

_____

_____

_____

_____

_____

_____

_____

2. *Your Social Sharing*

Examine your own social sharing behavior. Do you find yourself scanning headlines and sharing without actually reading and understanding the article? Does that bother you? Write about what (if anything) you would like to change going forward.

_____

_____

_____

_____

_____

_____

_____

_____

_____

_____

_____

_____

_____

_____

_____

_____

_____

_____

_____

_____

_____

_____

_____

_____

_____

_____

Day 20 Reflections from alcoholexperiment.com

"Alcohol is the new cigarette. My parents both smoked and typically had highballs after a long day. It was the sophisticated, intelligent lifestyle. Both , my parents died of lung cancer. Today we know that smoking is harmful to anyone's health—it is highly addictive and very difficult to quit once you are hooked. Very few people smoke casually. Smoking is considered unwise, and people who refuse to quit or can't quit are thought of as being addicted and unable to overcome this problem, as opposed to being 'cool,' which may have been what they thought smoking was when they started.

"Years from now we may be saying the same things about alcohol. We may be recognizing that although some people can manage having a drink once a month or on a special occasion, this is by far the exception not the rule. Perhaps we will be recognizing that so many lives have been lost and/ or negatively impacted by alcohol. I am beyond grateful for this program and the learning we are all receiving and applying to our lives."   —MANNY

"I feel great! I've gone from feeling very sleepy, falling asleep for naps in the day and crashing hard in the evening, to having an abundance of energy. I've crossed some threshold. I have been healing, and my newfound energy is a good sign. The tricky thing is that I've felt my craving for a drink more intensely. I think it's because I'm forgetting how horrible it makes me feel. So I remind myself of the hangovers, the self-loathing, and the wasted days. I know my cycle with it. One or two drinks here and there will spiral downward to a bottle a night. I don't want to go back there, so I'm going to continue to move forward! It's getting better all the time! The scale has started to budge. I'm wanting to get out and move after work, get exercise. I'm journaling, doing some real therapy, and dealing with past hurts. Finally! This is totally the way to go."   —SUNNY

❚ DAY 21 ❚

Hey, Good Lookin'!

Make the most of yourself, for that is all there is of you.
—RALPH WALDO EMERSON

You want to look 10 or 20 years older? Alcohol can help! Sure, when you're drunk, you don't care as much about how you look. But the effects alcohol has on your physical appearance are hard to deny, and they last way longer than the average hangover.

❚ ALCOHOL MAKES YOU FAT

You might be surprised to learn that alcohol is more quickly stored as fat than excess calories from sugar, carbohydrates, or protein—or even from fat itself. Alcohol has 7 calories per gram (fat, for example, has 9 calories per gram), but alcohol does not require as much time or effort for digestion; it is quickly absorbed. Not only does alcohol provide a dense source of calories—which is quickly stored as fat—but because alcohol is poison to the liver, the liver prioritizes processing alcohol over digesting other foods (and all other tasks) and stores it as fat.

Alcohol contributes to weight gain in a few other ways. First is the effect alcohol has on blood sugar. Alcohol can actually contribute to dangerously low blood sugar levels. This is important to know because low blood sugar can make us feel bad (uneasy, tired, restless, and anxious) and also because low blood sugar can be dangerous—especially to diabetics.

When it comes to weight gain, low blood sugar caused by alcohol can lead to an overconsumption of calorie-rich foods. It works like this: When your blood sugar begins to go down and you don't have alcohol in your system, your liver kicks in and turns stored carbohydrates into glucose (a form of sugar) to send into your bloodstream. But when you take a drink, your body doesn't rebalance your system in this way; instead the liver turns all its attention to purging alcohol from the system as quickly as possible. Since alcohol is poisonous to the human body, again the liver will put all other processes on hold, including balancing blood sugar, as it works to detoxify the alcohol.

This is one of the reasons you feel hungry during a bout of drinking. Since your liver is focused on detoxifying alcohol, it does not process the food you are eating or the energy you have stored in your muscles into fuel for the body. You feel hungry even if you've just eaten. This leads to the late-night snacking of high-calorie foods that you would never consider eating while sober. When I was in college, we would do a 3:00 a.m. run to Taco Bell after a night of drinking, and when I lived London, it was a midnight kebab. Even if you do a late-night food run, you probably wake up ravenous the day after having a few too many. This is because your liver is often occupied for many hours with processing the alcohol—and protecting your body. At the same time, your blood sugar levels continue to drop and hunger sets in.

If your liver is still undertaking the monumental task of ridding the body of alcohol, your blood sugar can continue to drop even when you are eating foods that are high in sugar and carbohydrates. In short, not only is alcohol itself empty calories, but the very process the body goes through to rid itself of the alcohol often leads to a massive overconsumption of calories.

Finally, when you're drinking at dinner, your inhibitions are lowered. So, of course, you order a big dessert at the end of your meal. Your normal eating routines are just not as important as drinking, eating, and socializing with your friends. Granted, all these things can happen even without alcohol in the mix. But when your inhibitions are lowered, you're more likely to throw caution to the wind and keep eating.

ALCOHOL AFFECTS YOUR SLEEP

We've already talked about how your sleep is disrupted after drinking. They don't call it "beauty sleep" for nothing. Wine always helped me go to sleep more easily. But then I'd wake up around 3:00 a.m. as my body tried to process the alcohol, and my system was out of whack from drinking. Then I'd lie awake beating myself up for overindulging and promising to be better the next day. Over time, that lack of regular, restful sleep starts to make you look pale and strung-out.

ALCOHOL MAKES YOU LOOK OLDER

Alcohol speeds up the aging process because of a premature loss of collagen and elasticity in the skin. Your face looks red and swollen because alcohol actually widens the blood vessels that bring blood to the face. This is because alcohol is what is called a vasodilator, which literally means expanding blood vessels. The real bummer about this is that over time, blood vessels get bigger and bigger. This can lead to permanent redness or blotchiness. It also leads to a loss of skin tone. All that expanding also encourages broken capillaries, or blood vessels that burst, especially around the nose and face.

Alcohol is a major source of dehydration. That doesn't only affect your internal organs. Your skin is the largest organ you have. Instead of being smooth, soft, and supple, your skin will wrinkle and become cracked and scaly. When you look in the mirror and don't recognize the face staring back, it's not your imagination. You truly do look different.

Your hair and nails are also affected. Alcohol contributes to brittle hair, split ends, and cracked nails. Speaking of hair, alcohol can actually cause you to lose your hair. This is because alcohol causes a zinc deficiency in the body, which leads to hair loss.[1]

Bloating is another big problem. When your body becomes dehydrated, it's deprived of fluid and electrolytes. Your body will counteract this by retaining the water it already has. Your gut starts to bloat. Your feet, hands, and face may also swell and become puffy. And your weight will go up.

One of the big signs that I had a big night was purple lips and teeth. I could see it the next morning, and over time my teeth became quite stained. It's not pretty. And if all that isn't enough, alcohol makes you smell bad. According to the Institute of Alcohol Studies, up to 10 percent of alcohol consumed leaves your body through your sweat, breath, and urine. That detoxification process smells horrific.

TODAY, take another selfie. Notice the difference in just three weeks from your before photo. Impressive, right? At the end of the experiment, we'll take another selfie and you will see how it keeps getting better and better. If even a few weeks without alcohol makes a visible difference you might ask yourself if alcohol is really doing you any favors.

▍ DAY 21 JOURNAL QUESTIONS

Remember, all the wisdom you seek is actually inside you; the most important words in this Experiment are the ones you tell yourself. Take some time and answer these questions in here or a separate journal (most effective), a voice memo to yourself, or simply by speaking the answers out loud for only you to hear.

1. *Mirror, Mirror . . .*

Have a look in the mirror. Look back on your starting selfie. What changes have you noticed already? Has even a few weeks without alcohol made a visible difference?

_____

_____

_____

_____

_____

_____

_____

_____

_____

_____

_____

_____

_____

_____

_____

_____

_____

_____

_____

_____

_____

_____

_____

_____

2. 3-Week Check-In

What about how you feel? Take a moment to write a three-week check-in. How do you feel? What has happened that is a surprise? Anything you didn't expect?

_____

_____

_____

_____

_____

_____

_____

_____

_____

_____

_____

_____

_____

_____

_____

_____

_____

_____

_____

_____

_____

_____

_____

_____

_____

3. *Honesty Day!*

Be honest with yourself: What are the places where you know that alcohol has been taking a toll on how you look. Is it in your skin? Or your belly? Was it making you puffy? Or tired around the eyes? Reflect, be truthful, and even get a bit vain about what alcohol had been costing you in terms of your physical appearance.

_____

_____

_____

_____

_____

_____

_____

_____

_____

_____

_____

_____

_____

_____

_____

_____

_____

_____

_____

_____

_____

_____

_____

_____

Day 21 Reflections from alcoholexperiment.com

"I took a selfie about a month before I started the AE. I looked dead in the eyes, red, watery eyes, no hair, no makeup . . . just bloated and dead. I took one yesterday while working a booth at a flea market. I had been up since 3:00-ish a.m., and the photo still looked better than a selfie I took mid-afternoon in my drinking phase."

—MELANIE

"Day 21 on the AE—I am fat and tired and achy and unfit. I am also happy that I can say I have genuinely started to change some of that. I am proud that I have finally found a way to say, 'I don't drink'—so simple and so powerful. Now I can see the possibilities opening before me for changing how I eat, being able to start to do some sort of exercise, and feeling less like an old lady. I am actively trying to improve my situation rather than losing those thoughts in the fogginess of alcohol misuse. It's dawning on me that it is down to me to take care of this body I am in, before it is unable to take care of me—that's not anyone else's job! I do feel weary today, but I made myself go out for that walk to the shop with my husband, rather than sitting at home or going by car. Tomorrow, I have decided, will be day one using the exercise bike we have in the study—it has been waiting patiently for me to remember it is there!"

—NICOLE

"I'm amazed at how people are telling me how good I look with only three weeks AF. And I feel even better. I'm going out to dinner and events and really not even giving a drink a second thought."

—CORA

▌DAY 22 ▌

Drinking Due to Unmet Needs

Human happiness and human satisfaction
must ultimately come from within oneself.
—DALAI LAMA

In 1943, Abraham Maslow published his now famous "hierarchy of needs" (illustrated on the next page). He was interested in human motivation and what made people behave the way they do. He proposed that people must meet their lower needs first before they will be motivated to move up to fulfill their needs at the next level. If a caveman was starving, and there was a bison on the next ridge, he'd forgo the need for safety, pick up the nearest rock or stick, and go hunt down that beast for supper. Once we have our physiological needs met (food, water, shelter, etc.), we can move up to meet our need of safety. Imagine you're in an abusive relationship. Can you see how you might meet the need for safety by getting so drunk that you black out and forget about how bad your life is?

▌FILLING OUR OWN NEEDS

Human beings haven't changed much over the past several thousand years, but our surroundings have changed dramatically! If we drink in social situations, it may be filling the need for safety because we feel safer when we fit in with the crowd. If we're working at a soul-sucking job we hate, and we drink to deal with that stress, it could be filling a need for security. You're trading the stress of an unfulfilling job for the security of a regular paycheck and benefits. And the bottle is how you're able to cope.

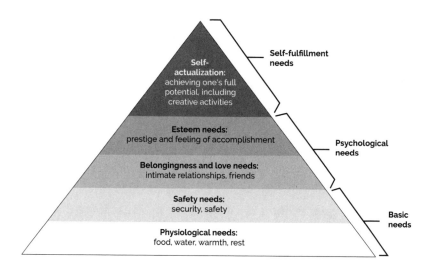

The Need for Connection

Connection and belonging are other often unmet needs. We used to live in tribal societies and extended families where human connection happened naturally. These days we're encouraged to be independent. We isolate ourselves at home and at work. We commute alone, even if we're surrounded by people on a crowded subway. We plug into our mobile devices and ignore the world, connecting with our friends virtually while our true human need for connection goes unmet. But drinking is something we can come together as a group and partake in. Social media and technology can give us a false sense of connection. But it's not the same physical, electric connection we get from being engaged in conversation with another human in the same room. We can't touch someone's arm to console them on Facebook. We can't smell someone's intoxicating perfume on Instagram. We can't taste that succulent cherry pie on Snapchat. Our senses are what make us human. A computer can take in digital information and decide how to react. We are not computers. We need that sensual input to feel alive.

We also have a human need for love and esteem, especially from ourselves. When we spend all day beating ourselves up for being stupid, weak, fat, clumsy, or whatever, it creates some pretty intense trauma. The old saying "Sticks and stones may break my bones, but words will never hurt me" is so wrong. Words do hurt, especially when they come from ourselves. So we drink to numb that pain and quiet the internal voice that's saying we're not good enough or we haven't done enough with our day. We have a need to care for ourselves, and we do that by indulging in an activity that we think will make us feel good—like drinking, shopping, gambling, or bingeing on chocolate.

It may seem overwhelming at first to think about the fact that you may be drinking to fulfill unmet needs. But shining a light on the possibility is a start. Becoming aware of the fact that there may be unmet needs in your life will often be enough to lead you down the path to answers. Just asking the questions below will lead you to answers.

TODAY, ask yourself . . .

"What are the possible unmet needs in my life right now?"

"How was I using alcohol to fill a need?"

"How could I fill that need in a healthier way?"

| DAY 22 JOURNAL QUESTIONS

Remember, all the wisdom you seek is actually inside you; the most important words in this Experiment are the ones you tell yourself. Take some time and answer these questions in here or a separate journal (most effective), a voice memo to yourself, or simply by speaking the answers out loud for only you to hear.

1. *My Unmet Needs*

Take some time and consider, what are the possible unmet needs in my life right now?

_____

_____

_____

_____

_____

_____

_____

_____

_____

_____

_____

_____

_____

_____

_____

_____

_____

_____

_____

_____

_____

_____

_____

_____

_____

_____

_____

2. *How Has Alcohol Been the Answer*

Reflect on how you may have been using alcohol as a stop-gap in order to meet your needs.

_____

_____

_____

_____

_____

_____

_____

_____

_____

_____

_____

_____

_____

_____

_____

_____

_____

_____

_____

_____

_____

_____

_____

_____

_____

_____

3. *Consciously Choosing*

Now that you have this awareness, how can you consciously choose to meet your needs? How can you fulfill your needs in healthier ways? What new vehicles or tools can you introduce in your life to ensure your needs are met?

_____

_____

_____

_____

_____

_____

_____

_____

_____

_____

_____

_____

_____

_____

_____

_____

_____

_____

_____

_____

_____

_____

_____

Day 22 Reflections from alcoholexperiment.com

"Very grateful to Annie Grace for sharing her story. I would feel worthless in the throes of a hangover, anxiety-ridden, and just so awful. I'm so thankful to be AF 22 days and no longer experiencing that pain. I'm really feeling confident that I can remain AF. Life is so much better without alcohol in it. I can't imagine why I'd want to go back to drinking."   —ELI

"It's Sunday morning here in Perth, Australia. My kids spent the night at Nanna's house. Just 22 days ago, my husband and I would be extremely hung-over today having a night off from kids. Today we're about to go for a run! After spending a night with friends watching a roller derby game, instead of hitting the after-party, we went home and watched a movie together! A movie I will actually remember because I didn't fall asleep watching it half cut! I'm having a great weekend!"   —MEGAN

"Over 3 weeks! On Day 16 I said I was going to post a daily gratitude. Well, I didn't follow through with that. I've been so busy! So here are a few grati-tudes to get me caught up:

Day 16: No wine-stained lips.

Day 17: Grateful for my fur-ever friends. Love my puppies!

Day 18: A husband who is supporting me on this journey.

Day 19: Grateful that I live in a beautiful place, river, mountains, blue skies!

Day 20: Wow! I haven't fallen off my bike after drinking! Grateful that I never did any serious harm to myself while drinking!

Day 21: Grateful that my body lets me run 5 miles.

Day 22: Haven't blacked out in 22 days! Love that I now go to bed, read, sleep, and get up clearheaded!"   —HANNAH

||| ACT #9 |||

Alcohol and Sadness

| AWARENESS

"I drink when I'm sad. It takes the edge off."

Many people believe alcohol not only helps them have a good time with their friends but also relieves the physical feelings of sadness. They feel better while they're drinking. Let's name this belief:

"Alcohol relieves my sadness."

| CLARITY

It's pretty obvious where this belief comes from. We've all observed people in our lives and in the media feeling good with a drink in their hands. Movies and TV shows are constantly equating drinking with happiness. But we've also watched the sad drunks crying their eyes out in public after a night of heavy drinking.

I know for me, the feelings of sadness that were already present only got worse after I'd had a few drinks. So what gives? Which one is it? Does drinking make you happy or sad? Alcohol does give us a little reprieve from our feelings, but not for long. If you've ever had a drink to help you escape from sadness, you know it never lasts. To find out if alcohol makes us happy or sad, we have to understand what's going on in our bodies chemically.

Can you think of a time when this happened for you? Maybe you started out feeling great, but as the evening progressed, you ended up weepy or just bummed out. There's a physiological explanation for this. You're definitely not imagining it. This effect is related to something called the biphasic response to alcohol. We touched on it earlier when we talked about blood alcohol content (BAC). How can alcohol make us feel good for a little while and ultimately be a depressant?

Biphasic means there are two phases happening when alcohol enters the body: The BAC rises and then it falls. Depending on when you last ate, one drink can raise your BAC for between 30 and 60 minutes. My friends and I used to skip eating just so we could feel tipsy faster. Maybe you've done the same thing. But sooner or later, your BAC starts to fall, and you don't feel as happy. So what do you do? You have another drink to keep the stimulating effects going.

While that uptick is happening, you feel excited, relaxed, and maybe a bit numb because the alcohol is artificially stimulating your pleasure center. Then, inevitably, the downturn happens, and alcohol's true nature as a depressant comes into play. You become anxious, depressed, sad, or weepy. Maybe you get sleepy. Your body is compensating for the endorphins by releasing counter-chemicals. It wants you to come back down. And down you come, until you start to feel really bad.

The BAC falls slower than it rises, though, so you feel bad longer than you felt good. The negative feelings start when the BAC starts falling or gets high enough that it reaches 0.05 to 0.06. Many people don't notice the increasing negativity, though, because they sleep off the effects, and only notice the next morning when they feel terrible. And because your body starts to feel miserable at a BAC of 0.05 to 0.06, even if you could tolerate that much alcohol, you can't keep the good feelings going all night long—either because of a falling BAC or because you've reached such a high BAC that you WILL inevitably feel sad and depressed. You can't help it. It's chemical. One of the things that disguises this phenomenon is the fact that we mainly drink in the evening. Your BAC continues to rise for a few hours and then the miserable falling of your BAC occurs during your sleep. Sure, it interrupts your sleep patterns, but other than that, you are not aware of the sad feelings that the alcohol causes during the long decline in your BAC.

When I was 17, I was diagnosed with a major depressive disorder. It came and went. I took all sorts of medications and was always in some counselor's office. Sometimes I wanted to sleep all day. Other times, I couldn't sleep at all. The most serious bout I had was after my youngest son was born. It was a terrible time, and my drinking escalated because I didn't want to feel that sadness. What I didn't know then was that I was actually making things so much worse. At one point, I was taking three antidepressant medications and a sleeping pill. None of those mix with alcohol! But I was desperate for relief, so I drank anyway. Which meant I was dangerously combining pharmaceuticals with alcohol and probably rendering those medications completely ineffective.

Tragically, there's a strong link between alcohol and suicide. In fact, drinking is the most common factor with all suicides. More than one-third of victims were drinking prior to death. And statistics show that people who are dependent on alcohol are 120 times more likely to die by suicide—120 times! That's because alcohol causes depression and makes us act impulsively. It's heartbreaking, and so many people have had suicide touch their lives in one way or another. A dear friend of mine took his own life.

When you're using alcohol to self-medicate and escape pain, drinking takes on a dark side. Maybe you're trying to forget some childhood trauma, or you have postpartum depression, like I did. Whatever the reason, your pain is real. And no one is blaming you for wanting to get rid of it. But the problem is that the chemicals you're using to self-medicate are making things worse. And the more you use alcohol to try to take away the bad feelings, the more of it you need to reach the same temporary relief. And the worse you feel. The depression not only doesn't go away; it can actually escalate.

And what's so wrong with feeling sad occasionally anyway? We're conditioned to believe that we should never experience discomfort. But why is that exactly? TV commercials make it clear that we shouldn't tolerate feeling bad. Any time we have the slightest inkling of a negative feeling, we should numb it, medicate it, or run away from it.

But in reality, that is just not true. Nothing incredible has ever happened that didn't have at least a little pain, sadness, or discomfort. Consider the birth of a child, or even those awkward first dates. These things are not entirely comfortable, yet they are some of the most profoundly joyous occasions. Heck, there is an entire period in our history dedicated to the sadness of one man (and the genius that came from it)—Picasso's Blue Period.

Trying to get rid of all sadness, all discomfort, is contrary to the principles of how the universe works. Consider what a seed must do to become a tree. Two things. First, it must cease to be a seed by changing and breaking out of its shell; both very intense things. And second, it must go down, grow roots *before* it grows up and becomes a tree. Sadness is natural and normal. It is something we can learn from. When we tell ourselves it is wrong to feel sad, as I did for many years, we compound the feeling of sadness with a feeling of something being wrong with us, of guilt. It's okay to feel all our emotions— nothing is wrong with us. And imagine what we might learn or create if we allow ourselves (like Picasso did) to feel. Along with painting, so much great poetry and literature has been produced by artists exploring and being present with feelings like sadness. Feelings that we've been taught by society and advertising are somehow "bad." I have to wonder how can any feeling be "bad," especially one that produces so much beauty?

Once I figured out how to reverse my unconscious conditioning and stopped drinking, I was able to work with a naturopathic doctor on actually curing my depression. Over the course of several years, I put practices into my life like mindfulness, healthy, protein-rich meals, and regular exercise—all of which combined to make me happier than I'd ever been. And I was able to get off all three of my antidepressant and antianxiety medications. But not before I spent many times lying on the floor of my closet crying and feeling like my family would be better off without me in it. I had those thoughts. I had those times. I felt worthless.

All that seems completely foreign to me now, though. And it's terrifying to think what I might have done given the close link between alcohol and suicide. If you're in this place now, if you're self-medicating with alcohol and hoping it will make things better, consider what's actually happening in your bloodstream. Think hard about the fact that no matter how much you drink, you will come down, and the depressive effects will take hold. Depression lies to us, and alcohol makes those lies believable. So when life drags you backward with hardship and sadness, it simply means that you're getting ready to launch forward into something great! Out of the pain and sadness, you can find the courage and strength to truly heal yourself instead of masking the symptoms with alcohol's temporary lift.

Something great is waiting for you. I know it!

| TURNAROUND

The opposite of *"alcohol relieves my sadness"* is *"alcohol doesn't relieve my sadness"* or *"alcohol makes me sad."* Come up with as many ways as you can that the opposite is as true as or truer than the original belief.

❙ DAY 23 ❙

Alcohol's Effect on Your Health

It is not the strongest of the species that survive,
nor the most intelligent, but the one most responsive to change.
—CHARLES DARWIN

Have you ever thought about how amazing your body is? Think about its ability to survive challenges and overcome illness. It's an unbelievably complex organism that is both hard as nails and delicate at the same time. Something as tiny as a germ can send it reeling for weeks. Yet you can abuse it for years and it will still keep you alive. We take our bodies for granted so often and don't give ourselves the love and attention we need to truly thrive. The truth is, the better we take care of our bodies, the better they will take care of us.

You probably know that drinking is bad for your health in general. But you may not be aware how harmful it truly is. Our culture tries to soothe its own guilt over drinking by finding obscure ways to say it's healthy. There may be certain chemicals in a glass of red wine that are beneficial, but the overall damage that wine can cause far outweighs the benefits. If you want to dive deep into the science behind all the ways alcohol can harm your health, you might want to check out my first book, *This Naked Mind*. For now, though, let's go through the basics. The information below was compiled from a variety of studies, but the primary source is the US Department of Health and Human Services.

▎YOUR BRAIN

Alcohol slows the pace of communication between neurotransmitters, the chemical messengers that transmit messages between different parts of your brain and body. It interrupts your brain's pathways, literally reducing the speed of delivery of information between parts of your brain and body by slowing down your brain's neural highways. It slows communications from your senses, deadening them and decreasing your responsiveness.

Your cerebellum, limbic system, and cerebral cortex are most vulnerable to alcohol. Your cerebellum is responsible for motor coordination, memory, and emotional response. Your limbic system monitors your memories and emotions. And your cerebral cortex manages activity, including planning, social interaction, problem solving, and learning. It comes as no surprise that alcohol hinders motor coordination. After all, being tipsy or unable to walk a straight line is a classic indicator of alcohol use. But did you know that alcohol robs you of your natural ability to manage your emotions? This is why alcohol causes unhappiness and irritability, and why some drinkers describe their binges as either crying jags or fits of rage.

What is more terrifying is that, over time, the artificial stimulation your brain receives from drinking makes you neurologically unable to experience the pleasure you once did from everyday activities, such as seeing a friend, reading a book, or even having sex. Alcohol interferes with your ability to behave, think, and interact socially. Drinking impedes your natural capacity to remember, learn, and solve problems.

Just one bout of heavy drinking, meaning five drinks in two hours for men or four drinks in two hours for women, can cause permanent alterations in your nerve cells and reduce the size of your individual brain cells. Toxins released by your liver and passed into your brain during alcohol metabolism are responsible for poor sleep, mood imbalance, personality changes (like violence or weeping), anxiety, depression, and a shortened attention span, and they can result in coma and death.

▌YOUR HEART

Your heart beats over 100,000 times per day to carry 2,000 gallons of blood through your body. That's a big job. Alcohol weakens the heart muscle so that it sags and stretches, making it impossible to continue contracting effectively. When your heart can no longer contract efficiently, you are unable to transport enough oxygen to your organs and tissues, so your body is no longer nourished appropriately.

Drinking large amounts in one sitting, even on rare occasions, can affect the electrical system that regulates your heartbeat. Your heart may not beat hard enough, which can cause your blood to pool and clots to form. The opposite can also happen. Your heart can beat too fast, which doesn't allow for the chambers to fill with blood. In turn, an insufficient amount of oxygen pumps out to your body. As a result, binge-drinking raises your likelihood of having a stroke by 39 percent.

Your blood vessels are stretchy, like elastic, so that they can transport blood without putting too much pressure on your heart. Drinking alcohol releases stress hormones that constrict your blood vessels, elevate your blood pressure, and cause hypertension, in which the blood vessels lose that elasticity.

▌YOUR LIVER

Two million Americans suffer from alcohol-related liver disease, making it a leading cause of illness and death. Your liver stores nutrients and energy and produces enzymes that stave off disease and rid your body of dangerous substances, including alcohol. When your liver metabolizes alcohol, it creates toxins, which are actually more dangerous than the alcohol itself. Alcohol damages liver cells by causing inflammation, and it weakens your body's natural defenses. Liver inflammation disrupts your metabolism, which impacts the function of other organs.

Further, inflammation can cause liver scar tissue to build up. Simultaneously, your liver function suffers because alcohol alters the natural chemicals in the liver needed to break down and remove scar tissue.

Drinking also causes steatosis, or "fatty liver." Fat buildup on your liver makes it harder for the liver to operate. Eventually fibrosis (some scar tissue) becomes cirrhosis (much more scar tissue). Cirrhosis prevents the liver from performing critical functions, including managing infections, absorbing nutrients, and removing toxins from the blood. This can result in liver cancer and type 2 diabetes. Twenty-five percent of heavy drinkers will develop cirrhosis.

| YOUR IMMUNE SYSTEM

Germs surround us, making our immune system our most important tool for fighting off disease. Our skin is the first line of defense against infection and disease. But if germs do make it into the body, we have two systems that provide defense: the innate system, which fends off first-time germ exposure, and the adaptive system, which retains information about prior germ invasions and promptly defeats repeat attackers. Alcohol suppresses both systems.

Our immune system uses small proteins called cytokines to send out chemical messages about infection in a kind of early-alert system. Alcohol disrupts the production of cytokines. When working correctly, cytokines alert our immune system to intruders, and our immune system responds with white blood cells that attack, surrounding and swallowing harmful bacteria. Alcohol impairs both functions, leaving us more susceptible to pneumonia, tuberculosis, and other diseases. Further studies link alcohol to an increased susceptibility to HIV, not only increasing our chances of contracting HIV but also impacting how rapidly the disease develops once contracted.

| ALCOHOL AND CANCER

Occasional drinking couldn't possibly cause cancer, could it? Yes, apparently it does. In a meta-analysis of 222 studies across 92,000 light drinkers and 60,000 nondrinkers with cancer, light drinking was associated with higher risks for many types of cancers, including breast cancer. A seven-year study of 1.2 million middle-aged women highlights the direct and terrifying link between drinking and cancer. According to this study, alcohol increased the chance of developing cancers of the breast, mouth, throat, rectum, liver, and esophagus.

The most frightening revelation is that the cancer risk increases no matter how little women drank. According to the National Cancer Institute, the risk of breast cancer was higher across all levels of alcohol intake. According to Cancer Research UK, "There's no 'safe' limit for alcohol when it comes to cancer." It also doesn't matter what type of alcohol you drink. It's the alcohol itself that leads to the damage, regardless of whether you imbibe beer, wine, or hard liquor.

Although many of us are not aware of the relationship between alcohol and cancer, it should not come as a surprise. Again, alcohol was officially declared a carcinogen in 1988. Alcohol itself, ethanol, is a known carcinogen, and alcoholic beverages can contain at least fifteen other carcinogenic compounds, including arsenic, formaldehyde, and lead.

Alcohol causes or contributes to cancer in different ways. When your liver breaks down alcohol, it produces a toxic chemical called acetaldehyde. Acetaldehyde damages your cells, rendering them incapable of repair and making them more vulnerable to cancer. Cirrhosis also leads to cancer. Alcohol increases some hormones, including estrogen, contributing to a breast cancer risk. It also causes cancer by damaging DNA and stopping our cells from repairing this damage.

In summary, any level of alcohol consumption increases the risk of developing an alcohol-related cancer. This is a discouraging message, I know.

The good news is that even though there is no safe level of drinking when it comes to cancer, studies show that a reduction in intake—or even better, stopping altogether—lowers your cancer risk.

ALCOHOL AND DEATH

You probably already know that you can die from alcohol poisoning by drinking too much alcohol in one sitting. What you may not know is that an alcohol overdose can also occur from a continual infusion of alcohol into the bloodstream over time, resulting in death that does not correlate with a single binge. Early death from alcohol steals more than 2.4 million hours of human life per year in the United States. According to the Centers for Disease Control and Prevention, alcoholism reduces life expectancy by 10 to 12 years.

This information may lead you to ask what level of alcohol use is safe. According to the most up-to-date research (2018), there is no risk-free level of alcohol consumption. In fact, alcohol use is the leading risk factor among people 15 to 49 years old, and the seventh leading risk factor for death among all ages. The most recent, and most comprehensive, study says that "the level of consumption that minimizes health loss is zero."[1] Considering how many people drink every day, this is a sobering fact indeed.

TODAY, give your body a big thank-you! And decide whether that glass of wine or pitcher of beer is worth all the health risks you now know about. Once you learn the risks, you can't unlearn them.

DAY 23 JOURNAL QUESTIONS

Remember, all the wisdom you seek is actually inside you; the most important words in this Experiment are the ones you tell yourself. Take some time and answer these questions in here or a separate journal (most effective), a voice memo to yourself, or simply by speaking the answers out loud for only you to hear.

1. *In Your Own Words*

Today's only journal reflection is for you to tell yourself what you learned in this chapter. Anchor it in. I know it might feel like you're just repeating what you just read, but it is vital for the subconscious to truly understand, and for your actual desire to have a drink to change. Simply write down what you learned about alcohol and your health, in your own words. Go into as much detail as possible and don't underestimate the power of this seemingly simple exercise.

_____

_____

_____

_____

_____

_____

_____

_____

_____

_____

_____

_____

_____

_____

_____

_____

_____

_____

_____

_____

_____

_____

_____

_____

Day 23 Reflections from alcoholexperiment.com

"So interesting that health was the topic of today's reading—I went to the doctor today, and my blood pressure was in the ideal range (it was 118/66). When I was drinking, my BP was borderline high or outright high and my previous doctor wanted me on blood pressure meds. I have also lost three pounds in the 25 days I've been free from alcohol."   —MIRANDA

"When I was drinking, I didn't want to know the harmful effects of alcohol. I wouldn't read or listen to any reports about it. I knew it wasn't good for me—especially since I am a cancer survivor—but I wasn't ready or willing to give it up. Now I want to know all the negative effects. I want to know the truth. It reinforces my desire to remain AF."   —RUSTY

"I'm still seeing drinkers as crazy people! I can't believe how much damage alcohol has caused my body and am stunned that some of it contains formaldehyde, arsenic, and lead! How does the drinks industry get away with it? I just don't get it anymore."   —GAIL

||| ACT #10 |||

Alcohol and Anger

| AWARENESS

People tell me all the time that when they give up alcohol, everyone and everything seems to get on their nerves. For no reason at all, they want to lash out at people. They're frustrated, impatient, and angry, and they don't get why that's the case. This is a real phenomenon, and I want you to understand where it comes from, so you won't use it as a reason to keep drinking. Let's name this belief:

"Drinking helps me keep my cool."

| CLARITY

It's pretty simple to understand where this belief comes from because if you've ever tried to stop drinking in the past, you know that you do get short-tempered. It happens. And we've certainly witnessed people in movies and on TV getting angry whenever the character gives up any addictive substance, such as alcohol, cigarettes, or even sugar. It's easy to conclude that if quitting alcohol makes you angry, then drinking must help with anger. We assume the alcohol must provide some sort of calming effect. Let's dig deeper into this one.

You've been without alcohol in your system for a little while now, and you might be feeling on edge or short-tempered with people around you. It's not that you're always like this and the alcohol was calming you down. It's quite the opposite. You're experiencing withdrawal symptoms as the alcohol leaves your system. You've experienced this before, though you may not have realized it. Think back on a few times when you were short with people. Maybe these were moments of extreme anger or even violence, but you definitely regret your behavior. You weren't yourself. Take a moment to remember two or three of those episodes. And notice where alcohol fit into the picture. Most likely, those bouts of anger occurred a few hours to a few days after your last drink. Is that true for you? It's because, again, the alcohol was leaving your system.

There's a well-documented link between aggression and alcohol consumption. Drinking is involved in about 75 percent of all child abuse deaths[1] and half of all violent crimes. On college campuses, 95 percent of all violent crimes and 90 percent of sexual assaults involve alcohol.[2] Why? What is it about alcohol that fuels all this anger and aggression? The biggest reason is that alcohol gives you tunnel vision. It narrows your focus so you can't or won't see extenuating circumstances. You're unable to accept any alternative points of view. Let's say you leave a sporting event and your team lost. Bummer. But you've been drinking and you're upset about it. As you're walking out of the crowded arena, someone in the opposing team's jersey bumps into you. Your perception is that he shoved you on purpose. He did it to rub it in—his team won and yours lost. Since your team lost, you lost. You're a loser! Had you been sober when that happened, you might have simply said, "Oh, sorry. It sure is crowded in here." When you're drunk, you lose your reasoning power, and you're far more likely to react with aggression. You lose the power to read social cues and behave appropriately. That simple bump could easily turn into a fistfight right there in the hallway.

Chemically, as your blood alcohol content is falling, you experience a surge in stressors and stress hormones, such as adrenaline and cortisol. Adrenaline in particular is the hormone involved in the fight-or-flight response. When you're drinking, you're far more likely to choose the fight option. Aggression just seems like the right decision. And remember, alcohol also affects the prefrontal cortex, which is responsible for helping us make good decisions. It's your brain's command center. The alcohol lulls that part of your brain to sleep, so you're less able to resist unwise behavior (like drunk-texting your ex at two in the morning).

In addition to the physical changes happening in your body and brain, there are social ramifications linking aggression and alcohol. Because so many people drink, we all understand what happens. We all know drinking makes us more aggressive and edgy. So we're more likely to forgive someone who snaps at their kid or gets into a fight when they've been drinking. We all know how a hangover feels, so we're more likely to cut our friend some slack when they're short-tempered. Because we can always "blame it on the alcohol," we're more likely to give in to our more aggressive impulses.

So why do these feelings continue after we are no longer consuming alcohol? Remember that it takes about a week for the chemicals to stop affecting your body and brain. It takes time for the toxins to completely leave your system. That withdrawal process doesn't feel good. It's only natural that you're on edge for a while. Give yourself a break. Be gentle and let the cleansing happen. It might be a good time to take a few days away by yourself so you don't have to worry about hurting the ones you love.

There's something you should know about anger itself. You may not realize it, but anger is actually a secondary emotion. It shows up to mask another emotion, usually hurt or worry. If your children are misbehaving in a restaurant and you get angry at them, you might be feeling worried about what the other patrons are thinking. Or you might be hurt that they're not listening to you. You are probably afraid that your child's misbehaving is an indication that you are somehow failing as a parent. It's an insecurity. Either way, you react with anger to cover up what you're actually feeling. Anger, unlike pain or fear, is a socially acceptable emotion. Everyone gets it, especially other parents who've been there themselves.

Once you're aware of this phenomenon, it's fascinating to catch yourself getting angry and then trying to figure out your feelings. You can use your anger as a sort of warning light to explore what you're feeling, rather than masking it with more alcohol. It takes courage, but you can step out of the moment and say, "Okay. I'm angry with the kids right now. What is it I'm afraid of? I'm scared that I'm screwing up as a parent. What if they never listen to me again? What if I can't ever get them to behave? If I were a better parent, and not focused on my work so much, they would behave better." That's a lot of negativity. It's also a lot of weight to carry as a parent. Just being aware of it, though, can help you be kinder to yourself. Emotions can be powerful, but most of the time they're not pointing to something that is truly wrong.

The temptation is to go have a drink to chill out and handle the anger. But you know that's not going to solve anything. In fact, things will get worse. So here's a great way to handle your anger without alcohol—change your physical state. Your mind and your body work together to create all emotions, especially anger. If you disrupt that pattern by changing something physically, you can break anger's hold on you. Something as simple as a cold shower or getting some exercise works wonders. Screaming into a pillow at the top of your lungs can work great. Do some push-ups or jumping jacks or play with the dog. Get active!

Another tool you can use to defuse anger is to consciously try to get even more angry. I know that sounds weird, but when I tried this, it was like a miracle. Let's say there's an anger scale from 1 to 10. First, evaluate where you are. Maybe you're annoyed and feel like you're at level 6. Your teeth are clenched. The adrenaline is surging, and your blood is pounding in your ears. Okay. Try to make yourself even more angry. Try to level-up to 9 or 10. Don't be surprised if you find yourself laughing. Because anger is a secondary emotion, it falls apart when you try to use it as a primary emotion. If you are "trying" to be angry, it doesn't actually work. The feeling just goes away.

Finally, using mindfulness as a tool can help as you try to cope with frustrating circumstances and everyday anger. You don't have to sit and meditate on a cushion for 30 minutes every day. Although if you want to, go for it! Mindfulness means becoming aware of your thoughts and feelings, consciously noticing when you're upset and thinking about what's behind that. When practiced regularly, mindfulness gives you a little bit of space in your brain from the time you're triggered and when you actually get angry. Even a fraction of a second is enough to help you get a handle on things before you react badly. In that little bit of space, you can put the other tools into action.

It's important to realize that the irritability and stress you feel as the alcohol is leaving your system is temporary. I'm not saying you'll never get angry or lose your temper ever again. But the additional edgy feeling will subside.

❙ TURNAROUND

The opposite of "*drinking helps me keep my cool*" is "*drinking helps me lose my cool*" or "*alcohol makes me angry and irritable.*" Come up with as many ways as you can that the opposite is as true as or truer than the original belief.

| DAY 24 |

Are Addictive Personalities Real?

Change your thoughts and you change your world.
—NORMAN VINCENT PEALE

Before we talk about addictive personalities, let's agree on a definition of addiction. For simplicity, and our purpose today, we can say that addiction is nothing more than doing something on a regular basis that we don't want to do. Notice that there's a conflict or disagreement in that sentence. We're doing it. But we don't want to be doing it. There's cognitive dissonance. Because the conflict is happening inside our minds, it's understandable that we might think an addictive personality is to blame.

While it's true that some people fall into the addiction cycle quickly and others never become dependent on alcohol, it's dangerous to use this term to describe people. Why? Because it puts the blame squarely on the shoulders of the individual. It makes them solely responsible for their addictive behavior—even though it's the *substance* that's addictive. The way alcohol reacts chemically with our bodies is how we become addicted. There are a whole host of factors involved, like age, weight, environment, culture, and, yes, even personality. But the same personality traits that might contribute to an addiction can also be the way out.

| THE WAY IN IS THE WAY OUT

Take my case: I'm decisive. I have a strong will. I take commitments seriously. All those traits likely caused me to become addicted to alcohol. I was strongly committed to my decision to drink. However, once I decided to stop drinking, I was equally strong-willed and committed. The way in was also the way out. My father is the same way. He makes up his mind once and sticks with it. When he was drinking, that meant he had no cognitive dissonance around alcohol. He liked to drink, so he did. And those same traits made it easy for him to stop when the time came. Once he realized alcohol wasn't making him happy anymore, he just stopped without any problem.

Take someone who goes along with the crowd and is easily influenced by others, as another example. Environment plays a huge part in whether they become addicted to alcohol. If they hang out with heavy drinkers, chances are they'll become one, too. In that case, their best hope might be to find a new crowd to hang out with or at least one person who inspires them to enjoy activities without drinking. Same personality trait, two completely different outcomes.

The idea of an addictive personality leaves the drinker with little hope. They might feel like, "Oh well, this is the personality I was born with. Might as well make the most of being a drunk!" When in fact that person may have everything they need to overcome their addiction if they were able to take a different perspective.

As a society, we revere alcohol. We love it. And we turn a blind eye to all the harm it causes. So, by labeling a person as having an addictive personality, we're letting alcohol off the hook as the problem. It also lets us off the hook. Other people might have a problem, but we're fine. This can even lead to overconfidence with drinking and make us more reckless. How many times have you seen someone drive home from a party when they should have called a cab? Chances are that their last words as they headed out the door were "I'm fine." Let's hope they were.

TODAY, think about whether you've considered yourself to have an addictive personality. Have you blamed yourself for that downward spiral and let alcohol off the hook for its part in the equation? Write down a list of your top three positive and negative personality traits, and be honest. No one is going to see this but you. Then, for each one, think about how that trait could lead you deeper into addiction AND how it could lead you out of your drinking cycle. Don't judge yourself. Don't try to do anything with what you're writing. Just introduce a new idea and let your subconscious mind mull it over for a while.

▌ DAY 24 JOURNAL QUESTIONS

Remember, all the wisdom you seek is actually inside you; the most important words in this Experiment are the ones you tell yourself. Take some time and answer these questions in here or a separate journal (most effective), a voice memo to yourself, or simply by speaking the answers out loud for only you to hear.

1. *Your "Addictive Personality"*

Have you considered yourself to have an addictive personality? Have you blamed yourself for that downward spiral and let alcohol off the hook for its part in the equation? How has that felt to you? How do you feel now with your newfound knowledge?

_____

_____

_____

_____

_____

_____

_____

_____

_____

_____

_____

_____

_____

_____

_____

_____

_____

_____

_____

_____

_____

_____

_____

_____

_____

_____

2. *The Best and Worst of Your Personality*

Make a list and be honest. Write down a list of your top three positive and top three negative personality traits.

_____

_____

_____

_____

_____

_____

_____

_____

_____

_____

_____

_____

_____

_____

_____

_____

_____

_____

_____

_____

_____

_____

_____

_____

_____

_____

_____

3. *Now Consider*

For each trait you just listed, consider how that trait could lead you deeper into drinking more than you intended. And now consider how *the very same personality trait* could lead you out of the drinking cycle.

_____

_____

_____

_____

_____

_____

_____

_____

_____

_____

_____

_____

_____

_____

_____

_____

_____

_____

_____

_____

_____

_____

_____

_____

_____

_____

_____

Day 24 Reflections from alcoholexperiment.com

"Well this is hard for me. I don't like to think of my negative personality characteristics, because I don't want to own them. I am strong—like many others in this experiment; I like to do things myself. (Control issues?) I am loyal, kind, and forgiving, which has led me to forgive myself each morning and start each day fresh (only to drink again that night). It is so good for me to forgive myself, but I find myself wondering what I'll do once the 30 days are up!"
—LINDSAY

"I can totally see why the traits I have can work for or against addiction, I can either spiral downward or climb upward. I say 'climb,' which implies effort in this experience, but I have really not put forth much effort except to open my mind to This Naked Mind. I feel now that my opened mind was ready and happy to receive this new info and way of thinking."
—MARLEY

"It is interesting that the same personality traits that can lead to the spiral down into addiction can also be helpful in finding the way out. One thing that is sticking with me is the fact that the only thing we have any control over is ourselves—we can only change our own thoughts, behaviors, and wishes. We cannot change anyone else."
—BESS

❙ DAY 25 ❙

Setbacks and the Way Forward

You never fail until you stop trying.
—ALBERT EINSTEIN

Occasionally I get messages from people who have used my book *This Naked Mind* to stop drinking and then, after a little while, have started again. Sometimes it's triggered by a traumatic event, like a death in the family. Sometimes it creeps up on them slowly. They figure they can handle themselves for one night, but then one night of drinking turns into a week and then into a month. At some point, they recognize they're no longer in control.

If you make a decision to stop drinking beyond this 30-day experiment and you end up slipping, it's important that you relax and don't beat yourself up. It doesn't mean that you're an "incurable addict" or a bad person. And it certainly doesn't mean that you're beyond hope. All it means is that you're human. People get to the end of the 30-day experiment and they're full of excitement. They feel empowered, like a light came on in their brains and they can suddenly see the truth. But we all live in the real world, and the real world is full of pro-drinking messages. Alcohol advertising is everywhere. Our friends might pressure us to drink, even though they know we don't want to. You might think you're immune to this kind of pressure, but it's relentless.

▌ YOUR PERSPECTIVE IS FOREVER CHANGED

The beautiful thing is that by reading the daily lessons and going through the exercises, you've learned a skill. You understand cognitive dissonance and how to resolve it without resorting to numbing out. You have the tools and you know how to use them! That's such good news.

When I first started to question my drinking, it took almost a year of education and exploration before I finally resolved my dissonance for good. And for all I know, I may have to do it again in the future. At the moment, I feel like I'll never touch another drink. I just don't have a desire for it anymore. But I'm well aware that no one is immune, and the desire could come back. I doubt it will, but if it does, I know what to do.

Reframe Mistakes as Necessary Experience

I live in Colorado, and we get a lot of snow in the winter. Driving on snow takes special skill. You need to turn on your four-wheel drive. You need to slow down and allow extra time to get to your destination. But sure as anything, when the first snowfall of the season hits, people drive like idiots! Because they've forgotten what it feels like to lose control of their vehicle, even for a few seconds. Cars and trucks slide off the road, and the night sky is lit up with red and blue lights from police cars trying to rescue stranded motorists. It's like everyone gets amnesia between April and October. Once the next snowfall comes, we remember. We're more cautious. We learn from our mistakes.

Regaining control of your drinking might take a few tries. You might feel like you've got a handle on it, and then suddenly you're right back where you started. Don't blame yourself or beat yourself up. Forgive yourself and learn from the experience. Go back to your lists from Day 1 and say, "Okay, what needs to happen from here so I can regain control?"

I believe it gets easier every time you do it, because your subconscious mind has more control over your behavior than the alcohol does. Every time you go back and repeat the abstinence period, you are subconsciously reinforcing your desire to stay in control. When your subconscious and your conscious mind are in harmony, YOU are back in the driver's seat.

TODAY, remember that as long as you're alive, you'll never run out of chances to regain control of your life. The only way to fail at this is to give up and stop trying.

I DAY 25 JOURNAL QUESTIONS

Remember, all the wisdom you seek is actually inside you; the most important words in this Experiment are the ones you tell yourself. Take some time and answer these questions in here or a separate journal (most effective), a voice memo to yourself, or simply by speaking the answers out loud for only you to hear.

1. *Consider "Failure"*

Think about the concept, that the only way to fail at this is to stop trying. That as long as you approach setbacks with compassion and understanding and a renewed desire to find your personal freedom, there is no failure. What does this mean to you? What commitments are you willing to make to yourself to ensure that your "failures" become stepping-stones toward where you truly want to be?

_____

_____

_____

_____

_____

_____

_____

_____

_____

_____

_____

_____

_____

_____

_____

_____

_____

_____

_____

_____

_____

2. A Letter to Your Past Self

Take some time and write a letter to your past self, the self that was nervous just before Day 1 of *The Alcohol Experiment*. Talk about how you feel today, what your biggest a-ha moments have been, and what your hopes are for the future. Tell yourself anything you wish you would have known before you started. Be honest, there are no "right" or "wrong" things to say.

Day 25 Reflections from alcoholexperiment.com

"It is amazing how fast the time has gone—25 days is just amazing to me. I did have two slips, and really took stock in what my triggers are. I am so grateful to learn so much about myself, and proud that I can be in charge of my decisions. I continue to work on self-love every day, and I do have a lot of work to do. However, I truly believe the alcohol moves me right back to self-loathing. There is nothing fun about drinking for me. That didn't take long to realize. I see it more of a habitual ritual, which has to change for me to truly love myself and be my best me."
—KATHLEEN

"Going alcohol-free is the tip of the iceberg to so many other life-changing, positive ways! Freedom! I had no idea this process would start a reinvention of my life."
—LAURA

"After 25 days on the program, I couldn't be happier! Last night I went out with my wife, children, grandchildren, and in-laws for dinner. Wore my favorite pants that I haven't been able to fit into for 10 years! I looked better and felt great, and when asked what I wanted to drink, I just said I would have a Coke!

"My daughter said, 'You look great, Dad!' That made me feel even better!

"People were drinking all around me, as it was a licensed venue, but I felt very strong, almost superior, and did not for one moment feel like an alcoholic drink.

"In the past, I may have felt pressured to have a drink, but I just don't care what other people think anymore. In the past, if I didn't have a drink (or not much), I would have a drink when I got home. Last night came home, had an ice cream and herbal tea, watched some TV, went to bed, slept well, and woke up early to go to the gym. That's my new life! Thanks, Annie!"
—DARBY

| DAY 26 **|**

Liberation vs. Fixation

Freedom is realizing you have a choice.
—T. F. HODGE

Sometimes it's hard to tell when alcohol is actually running the show. We tend to rationalize and feel like we're drinking in moderation, when in fact we're no longer in control of our actions. So I came up with a scale called Liberation vs. Fixation to help me figure out whether I was in control. Liberation is when I can take the substance or leave it. I'm in control, and I will have a great time whether I choose to drink. Fixation is when the cravings and addiction have taken hold and I am losing my power over my own choices. Here are the clues that can help you decide where you are in terms of moderation.

One of the most painful things for us as humans is to feel powerless. Ironically, we give away our power to alcohol without even realizing it is happening. Today's ideas will help you recognize where you are inadvertently giving up your power to booze so that you can consciously decide to take it back.

Liberation is being offered a beer and truly feeling like you could take it or leave it. Fixation is *waiting* to be offered a beer. It's walking into a party and wondering *when* someone will offer you a beer.

Liberation involves no internal dialogue. There's no "other voice" in your head arguing with you. Fixation is talking with yourself about whether you should have a drink, if you will feel bad in the morning—

there's a nonstop chatter about the substance. That chatter focuses your mind on the drink, making you want the substance even more.

Liberation means you can have one drink and not give it another thought. You're perfectly content. Fixation means you're thinking about your next drink, often before the one in your hand is even finished.

Liberation does not come with a jonesing for the substance after it leaves your system. Fixation often means withdrawal symptoms and cravings begin as soon as the substance begins to fade away. Someone who can handle themselves around chocolate can have just a bite. But someone addicted to chocolate has to finish the whole bar that's in front of them, and then strategizes how to get more.

Liberation puts the focus on the people and the environment. There's little or no focus on the substance. Fixation puts the focus on the drink, not the party, even if that focus is how *not* to drink.

Liberation lets you be around the substance without a problem. Fixation means you can't have it in the house without temptation.

Liberation is rational. You can decide not to drink because you have to get up early in the morning. Fixation is irrational. Even though you have that early meeting, you still want to drink.

None of these ideas are universally true for every person. They are simply guidelines to give you perspective as to where you truly are in terms of moderation. If you find yourself fixating on alcohol and having internal conversations about it, then you're probably heading down that slippery slope and might want to be extra careful.

TODAY, define what *moderation* means to you. If you're aiming to be moderate in your drinking going forward, it's important to decide exactly what that means. Does it mean two drinks a week? Or two drinks a month? Or one drink every other weekend? Keep going and determine how you want to feel as you moderate. How much of a hangover is too much? Is it okay if you have a slight headache, but not okay if you're puking the next day? If you don't define what *moderate* means, you won't have any way of knowing when you've gone too far.

In reality, you're going to want to define this as you go. Before you go to that party, decide you're going to have one drink and then stop. Before you head to that networking event, decide you're going to drink ginger ale instead of alcohol. And if you're going to drink whatever you want and not feel guilty about it, fine. But make that decision *before* you start drinking. And stick to the not-feeling-guilty part.

DAY 26 JOURNAL QUESTIONS

Remember, all the wisdom you seek is actually inside you; the most important words in this Experiment are the ones you tell yourself. Take some time and answer these questions in here or a separate journal (most effective), a voice memo to yourself, or simply by speaking the answers out loud for only you to hear.

1. *Liberation vs. Fixation*

Consider the day's teaching in your own life and write honestly about what your relationship with alcohol was before this experiment. Were you truly liberated in your choices, or were you fixated on alcohol to a point where your choices did not feel entirely like your own?

_____

_____

_____

_____

_____

_____

_____

_____

_____

_____

_____

_____

_____

_____

_____

_____

_____

_____

_____

_____

_____

_____

_____

_____

_____

2. Your Future

Based on the idea of Liberation versus Fixation, brainstorm at least three instances in your future that you will use as guideposts to determine if you are truly liberated or if you are fixated on drinking. Feel free to use examples from the chapter, and if you come up with more than three that is even better! And remember, you don't necessarily have to be drinking to be fixated on alcohol. I've known sober people who are still, years later, fixated on alcohol. The goal here is to become hyper-aware of when and where you are fixated so that you can do the mental work (employ the ACT technique) to liberate yourself from your fixated thinking.

_____

_____

_____

_____

_____

_____

_____

_____

_____

_____

_____

_____

_____

_____

_____

_____

_____

_____

_____

Day 26 Reflections from alcoholexperiment.com

"I have come to the realization that I will never be a moderate drinker and I don't want to go back to the obsession that is fixation. When I hit Day 30, no way do I even want to think about trying to moderate. It won't happen and I will be back in hell in no time. No thanks!" —HILLARY

"I love moderation. I was in that group that was prevented from changing by the thought I could never have a drink again. I am using awareness and positive self-talk now to decide for myself when I want a drink. Not just drinking out of habit and social circumstance." —PATRICIA

"I was definitely fixated on alcohol. It really occupied my thoughts for the past few years, if I'm honest about it. Learning skills in this experiment has been invaluable to me moving forward. The Alcohol Experiment has taught me how to change how I think about alcohol. I'm starting to venture out more and more, and as I do, I always visualize how the night is going to go while I'm getting ready. I throw on some good music while sipping a nonalcoholic beer and see the night play out in my mind; how I want it to play out, how it will play out. I find practicing visualization gives me a little pep in my step, a bit of confidence. It's like I've been here before and I already know the ending. I chose it. It's frickin' happening. I'm really digging feeling this good." —ETHAN

Is Alcohol Really Poisonous and Addictive?

How you think about a problem
is more important than the problem itself.
—NORMAN VINCENT PEALE

Wow! You are nearly there. I am proud of you. I hope you are proud of yourself! Today I want to conduct a bit of a review and summarize a lot of what I've said about the nature of alcohol and how your body neurologically and physiologically reacts to it.

It's interesting that our culture has completely obscured the fact that alcohol is poison to our bodies. Not only that, but it's an addictive poison. Before you decide whether you believe those two statements, please take a minute to read the facts. Take off the blinders about whatever you *feel* alcohol to be, and let's look at the actual chemical composition of this controversial liquid.

Before we discuss alcohol as an additive substance, let's talk about what addiction actually is. It's nothing more than an up-and-down cycle. You consume something (sugar, drugs, alcohol—doesn't matter) and you feel better temporarily. Then the feeling goes away. You want that feeling back, so you consume the same substance again. But this time it doesn't feel quite as good as your subconscious mind remembers, so you need a little bit more. Then the effects wear off, and you consume it again. It's literally a high-and-low cycle that keeps you coming back to whatever substance you subconsciously believe makes you feel better.

I A CLOSER LOOK AT THE CYCLE

Now let's review how that happens with alcohol. Please understand, these are the chemical facts about how alcohol works in your brain and body. This isn't my opinion; it's fact.

There are four types of alcohol: methyl, propyl, butyl, and ethanol. If you consume even tiny amounts of the first three types, you'll either go blind or die. They are extremely toxic. Ethanol is the only type of alcohol humans can consume without dying. However, it's still so toxic that if you take even just a sip or two of pure ethanol, you will instantly vomit the poison out of your body. Ethanol is a general anesthetic. If you inject two or three milliliters of ethanol per kilogram of body weight, you will anesthetize the human body. That means you'll go completely unconscious. Ethanol was used as a general anesthetic in Mexico, London, and Germany in the 1929–31 era, but was abandoned because of its toxicity.[1]

When we drink, we're consuming pure ethanol in tiny amounts. A strong beer is about 6 percent alcohol by volume. Wine is generally 12 to 16 percent alcohol by volume. Even hard liquor is only 40 percent alcohol, and people usually add mixers, which dilute the percentage even more. We're masking the poisonous ethanol with a lot of other stuff that makes the drinking taste better. But the anesthetic effects remain.

Anesthetic and Depressant

In addition to being an anesthetic, alcohol is a depressant. It depresses your feelings and your nervous system. Depending on how much pure alcohol you consume, you might pass out completely or just feel nicely numb for a while. But our brains react to stimuli, and they are designed to maintain balance, or homeostasis. That means if you consume something that's an anesthetic and a depressant, it's automatically going to try to counteract those things with stimulants like cortisol and adrenaline. These stimulants leave you feeling anxious and uneasy. So you reach for that next drink to take away that uneasy feeling, and the brain fights back with even more of its own chemical stimulants. And the cycle starts.

Let's say you had a hard day at work and you just want a drink. Happy hour it is! You head to your favorite watering hole and have a drink. Within a short time, everything slows down. The alcohol's natural depressants dull your senses, and you subconsciously interpret that as relaxation. You feel better, for about 20 to 30 minutes. Then it's time for your brain to kick into action and regain balance. There are depressants in your system, so your brain releases more stimulants to bring you back up. The problem is those stimulants make you even more uneasy and anxious than you were to start with. Well, one drink was good, so two must be better, right?

You have another drink in an effort to counteract the chemicals your brain released in an effort to counteract the alcohol. Confused? So is your body! It releases more stimulating stress hormones to battle that second drink. Back and forth. Depressants. Stimulants. Depressants. Stimulants. This cycle might continue on and on until you pass out from the sheer amount of poisonous ethanol in your system. And thank goodness, because blacking out gives your body a chance to metabolize the poison and detoxify your blood as best as it can.

The Downward Cycle

Here's the interesting part, though. Every time you take another drink to counteract the stress hormones, you return to a level that's *below* where you were just 30 minutes earlier. Imagine a "feel good" scale from 1 to 10, with 10 being you feel amazing. Then imagine you head into happy hour at about a 6. It's been a hard day, but you got through it, and you know a drink will get you to a 9 or 10. After your brain counteracts that first drink, the second one might bounce you back up to only a 7 or 8. Then your brain will bring you back down. And you might try to bounce back, but this third time you make it to only a 5—lower than you started off the night.

Chemically, you're fighting a losing battle. Or maybe it's actually a winning battle because your brain will do everything in its power to keep you from actually dying.

So why don't we recognize alcohol as an addictive substance like cocaine or heroin? It's the same high-low cycle in our bodies. So what's the deal? I think it has to do with time. Drugs like heroin are metabolized quickly, especially if they are injected directly into the bloodstream. It doesn't take long for numbing and that high to take effect. And it's easier to see that the next hit needs to be more powerful than the last to get you to the same high. But alcohol is different. It enters the bloodstream more slowly. We only notice that the drink makes us feel better because that's what happens first. We don't notice the slow decline as those stimulant hormones take effect. We pay attention only to the climb, not the fall. So our subconscious minds learn that alcohol lessens the anxiety and stress. We *believe* that alcohol makes us feel better. But an addiction cycle is actually taking place because we find ourselves on this roller-coaster ride. Until you look at the entire cycle consciously, it's difficult to see what's actually happening on a chemical level.

Alcohol is addictive because you wind up *worse off* after each drink.

And you mistakenly believe that another drink will bring you back up.

It's the problem and the solution at the same time. It's the chicken and the egg.

It's a cycle. And you can break it if you choose.

What happens when you allow the cycle to continue? You build up a tolerance to the poison. Tolerance is your body's way of protecting itself any way it can. Your body is smart. It learns. And it prepares to fight the battle ahead. If you normally drink four glasses of wine a night, your body has learned that, and your brain measures out the necessary counter-chemicals for a normal night of drinking. So, if you decide you're going to have just one, your body has already unleashed the countermeasures for much more than that. Which means you don't get the same effect from one glass. You need more to get the same numbing effect. It takes four or five glasses before you even feel it. Because, guess what, your body anticipated those four glasses and gave you exactly what you needed to stay in homeostasis. It outsmarted you. And over time, you're going to need more and more alcohol to reach the same levels you used to get with just one glass. The dangerous part there, of course, is that the poison builds up. And once you get to a certain percentage of alcohol in your body, the anesthetic kicks in and you pass out. Or you die.

Detoxing from Alcohol Is Even More Toxic

Here's the kicker. In order for your body to process and get rid of the alcohol, it has to create the chemical acetaldehyde. The amount of acetaldehyde that is released into your body from just one unit of alcohol would never be allowed in any food because it would be deemed too toxic. Acetaldehyde is actually *more toxic* than the alcohol itself! So, we drink. We build tolerance. To get the same feeling of relief from everyday stress, we need to drink more. We produce higher and higher levels of acetaldehyde to process the alcohol. And we don't even realize how much poison is circulating in our bodies at any given time.

How much is too much? At what point can our bodies no longer keep up?

Think about that for a minute.

Hangovers, self-loathing, and regret are all unfortunate side effects of too much alcohol. But the chemical reality of drinking is downright *terrifying*! Once we consciously realize what we're *actually* putting into our bodies—ethanol and acetaldehyde—we can't go back to blissful ignorance. Now that you know what happens and why alcohol is addictive, you can't unknow it. By bringing this information into our conscious minds, we can finally see that the benefit we think we're getting from alcohol is actually relieving a symptom that alcohol caused to begin with.

TODAY, take a few minutes to write a thank-you note to your body. Thank it for taking such good care of you so far. Tell it you understand now. You get it. You know that alcohol is actually a poisonous chemical called ethanol. And you finally get that your body has to produce an even more poisonous substance, acetaldehyde, to process and get rid of the ethanol. Explain your current understanding of the addiction cycle to your body.

Now that you consciously understand what's happening, you get to make a conscious decision about your drinking habits.

▌ DAY 27 JOURNAL QUESTIONS

Remember, all the wisdom you seek is actually inside you; the most important words in this Experiment are the ones you tell yourself. Take some time and answer these questions in here or a separate journal (most effective), a voice memo to yourself, or simply by speaking the answers out loud for only you to hear.

1. *My New Knowledge*

Write out the big things you have learned in this lesson about alcohol. What has been surprising? What did you kinda know before and now know for sure?

_____

_____

_____

_____

_____

_____

_____

_____

_____

_____

_____

_____

_____

_____

_____

_____

_____

_____

_____

_____

_____

_____

_____

_____

_____

_____

_____

2. *How This Knowledge Makes Me Feel*

Consider how everything you've just written (and learned) makes you feel. Writing specifically about how you feel helps you both process your feelings around new information and cement the concepts in your mind. Remember as you are writing that all of your feelings are valid. Just allow yourself to become aware of them.

_____

_____

_____

_____

_____

_____

_____

_____

_____

_____

_____

_____

_____

_____

_____

_____

_____

_____

_____

_____

_____

_____

_____

_____

_____

_____

_____

_____

_____

Day 27 Reflections from alcoholexperiment.com

"My biggest lesson so far is this. Alcohol is an addictive poison . . . period. Whether I just have one drink or 10, any amount of alcohol is a poison to my body. Learning this fact has been life changing for me. I used to believe that since I was a moderate drinker, I was not harming my body by drinking a glass or two of wine daily. I now know the truth and I see alcohol for what it is—POISON!"   —MIKE

"Wow, I am amazed at how far I've come! Looking at everything I thought was a problem on Day 5 and how many of those things have been resolved, or are in the process of being resolved, is so empowering and inspiring. I'm moving on and moving forward, and if I stick at it, I will be successful. There is hope. There is always hope."   —GEORGIA

"Woke up this morning and felt so good laying there. I looked back on how miserable I used to feel when the alarm went off every day and wondered how I was going to get through the day. Now I feel well rested and ready to start my day. This program is amazing. I'm a little disappointed that it is ending soon. Off to the gym. Here's to an AF day."   —NATASHA

‖ DAY 28 ‖

The Truth About Moderation

Don't bother just to be better than others.
Try to be better than yourself.
—WILLIAM FAULKNER

We're coming to the end of this experiment, and you're going to have to decide what to do next. Will you stay alcohol-free for another 30 days? Or 60 days? Or indefinitely? Or will you decide to carry on as before but become more mindful of your behavior?

Before we go any further, I want to congratulate you for making it this far! Whether you sailed through without a single drink or gave in a time or two, you are not the same person you were when you began the experiment. You have new information and you get to make new decisions. I also want to make it clear that this is your decision, and there are no wrong answers. And guess what? You get to change your mind anytime you want to. That's your right and prerogative as a human being.

That said, let's talk about moderation for a bit. I do believe moderation is possible. Either alcohol just isn't important to a person because they have not developed an emotional or physical addiction and can truly take it or leave it. Or they are willing to put in the effort to pay attention and moderate how they drink. This means constant vigilance and regular assessment. And it means being willing to make changes whenever they become necessary. I know a gentleman who drinks 17 units of alcohol every Friday night. He doesn't drink any other night of the week. And he's been doing this without fail since 2002. So, yes, it is possible.

▌ THE POWER OF DECISION

But there is incredible power in making a decision. Once you've truly made a decision about something in your whole body and mind, there is no Plan B. There's no turning back. And that's a good thing because it lets you escape the "maybe" trap. Instead of running around in circles your whole life thinking, *Maybe I'll drink tonight . . . no, I shouldn't . . . but sure, I can moderate for a while . . . but, oh, things seem to be getting out of control . . . so is it time to cut back again?* Let's face it, that's exhausting. When you make a decision that you're not a drinker anymore, that's it. You're free from the hamster wheel. Alcohol no longer has a hold over you because you are of one mind. Your conscious and subconscious want the same thing. How cool is that?

The key for me was changing my perspective from "I don't get to drink" to "I could, but I don't want to." What I personally wanted for myself was for alcohol to become irrelevant in my life. A total nonissue. And that's where my own experiments led me. Because I made the decision that I no longer wanted to put that stuff in my body, moderation was no longer even a decision I had to make. Of course, it took a journey to get to that point. But once I got there, I've never looked back.

The ins and outs of moderation are complex both physically and psychologically. So before you make a decision to moderate, consider these ideas.

1. **Moderation means you're always making decisions.** What should I drink? How much is too much? Should I have this next

drink? Research shows that any decision, small or large, takes energy. Decisions make you tired, which in turn makes you grumpy and exhausted. And if you thought moderation was tough when you're in a good mood, when you're tired and cranky from the effort of moderation, it becomes next to impossible. Making one big decision with all your mind, body, and spirit liberates you from the hundreds of daily decisions around alcohol that sap your energy.

2. **Moderation doesn't make sense from a physiological perspective.** Alcohol creates a thirst for itself. We've already covered how this substance is neurochemically addictive. It artificially stimulates the pleasure centers in your brain, and you release counter-chemicals to depress that stimulation. As the alcohol leaves your system, your mood plunges further than it was before you started drinking. And you naturally want more of it to get back up to that beginning threshold of pleasure. Moderation means you're constantly going through this cycle and fighting with lower and lower levels of pleasure. The effect of one drink is to want another drink. Can you see the difficulties that moderation poses physiologically?

3. **Alcohol impairs your ability to stick with your intentions.** We know drinkers make bad decisions, right? I can remember making simple rules about my moderation, like I was going to have two glasses of wine and then stop. Yet I would inevitably wake up in the morning feeling horrible about not only breaking my commitment, but also about not being able to remember how many glasses I actually did have. I hated myself for failing at moderation. The truth is that even a single drink impairs your prefrontal cortex, which is where you make decisions. So the biological deck is stacked against moderation because just one drink can damage your decision-making power.

4. **Alcohol makes you thirsty.** It's a diuretic and dehydrates you. So that next drink becomes even more enticing, simply because your body is craving liquid. And since you're also craving more alcohol (see reason no. 2, above), it only makes sense to satisfy that thirst with more alcohol.

5. **Alcohol numbs your response to normal stimuli.** Over time, the regular production of dynorphin in your brain suppresses your ability to enjoy everyday activities. And eventually, you lose interest in anything but drinking. So if your plans for moderation are even remotely regular, drinking once a week or having one glass a night, you can fall into this trap. What starts out as a "reasonable amount" of alcohol soon becomes not enough. And you're right back on that hamster wheel of addiction. This, of course, is tolerance, and tolerance is one of the main criteria for alcohol use disorder.

6. **Alcohol increases cravings but not pleasure.** By releasing dopamine into your system, your brain is increasing the desire for alcohol. Dopamine causes a want, a craving. Then by releasing dynorphin, your brain is decreasing the pleasure you get from that drink you want so badly. Over time, you *want* to drink more and more, but you actually *like it* less and less. So moderation leads you down this slippery slope that's all about chemicals, and not about your personal strength or willpower.

TODAY, put the idea of moderation under the microscope of the ACT technique. With everything you now know, do you still believe moderation is a good idea? Do you believe it's even possible to enjoy moderation? And if you do decide to moderate, can you remain open to the possibility that it might turn out to be less than you hoped for?

▌ DAY 28 JOURNAL QUESTIONS

Remember, all the wisdom you seek is actually inside you; the most important words in this Experiment are the ones you tell yourself. Take some time and answer these questions in here or a separate journal (most effective), a voice memo to yourself, or simply by speaking the answers out loud for only you to hear.

1. *Your Key Takeaways*

What are the most important things you learned from today's reading? With everything you now know, do you still believe moderation is a good idea? (Again, there is no wrong answer, this is about figuring out what is right for you!)

_____

_____

_____

_____

_____

_____

_____

_____

_____

_____

_____

_____

_____

_____

_____

_____

_____

_____

_____

_____

_____

_____

_____

_____

_____

_____

_____

_____

_____

_____

2. Mindful Drinking in Your Future

Define what exactly mindful drinking means to you. If you aim to drink in moderation, with both eyes wide open, it is important to decide exactly what that means for you. How much do you plan to drink at a time? How often? What situations will you allow yourself to drink in? How will you measure success? Just begin a rough plan today, it doesn't have to be perfect. Because if you don't take time to define what you want and what success is for you, then you won't know if you are hitting your goals.

_____

_____

_____

_____

_____

_____

_____

_____

_____

_____

_____

_____

_____

_____

_____

_____

_____

_____

_____

_____

_____

Day 28 Reflections from alcoholexperiment.com

"For the first time, I feel like I have the tools to control my drinking, which at this point is looking more and more like quitting altogether. I just don't see the point of starting again, even in moderation—at least not for me. I can truly say that I see no benefits. I'm a little apprehensive about life AF. I plan on returning to the lessons and rereading *This Naked Mind* for support. Mainly, I'll be reminding myself of the fantastic difference between my former dynorphin-filled, low-energy self, who had lost confidence in herself, and the self of late, who has regained energy and hope and revels in each day met without a hangover or cloudy head. One who feels much more able and capable to deal with the challenges in her life."   —CHERI

"I've tried moderation *so* many times and besides being exhausting, I hated being a slave to alcohol. I'm not going to sacrifice the freeing feeling I'm experiencing on Day 28 just for a buzz. I know I'd be re-addicted in no time. I'm turning 59 tomorrow and I've been drinking for 44 years! I have such a hard time believing I'm still alive. And lastly, I do not miss all the self-hatred and shame alcohol fed me."   —CORBIN

"I drank an entire bottle of wine last night. Not part of an 'experiment' but just a decision to have one glass that led to four glasses. Snapped at my husband over something I don't remember. My daughter told me I had 'wine breath' and didn't want to kiss me good night. I fell asleep alone. Woke up at 4:00 a.m. sweaty and heart racing and looking for water and so disappointed in myself. So the lesson today about moderation is a good one for me. I know I can go to a restaurant and only have one glass with dinner, but I can't have an open wine bottle in my home. I keep learning this same lesson. Over and over again. This is not the life I want for myself, and I have the power to change it. My kids are 10 (twins) and they are watching and learning from me. They deserve better—a better mom and a better example. My husband deserves better from me. And I deserve better from myself—need to take better care of myself, and feelings of self-loathing post-drink are soooo damaging. I am better not drinking. I know this to be true. I am the best version of myself when I am AF. My outlook is healthier and better, my mood is enhanced, I am more present, I am more hopeful. I am just more. Moderation is not for me."   —VICTORIA

▌DAY 29 ▐

Tough Love

The golden opportunity you are seeking is in yourself.
It is not in your environment. It is not in luck, or chance,
or the help of others. It is in yourself alone.
—ORISON SWETT MARDEN

As we are in the last two days of this experiment, it's time for some tough love. Please know today's lesson is written with love and compassion. At the end of the day, the key to unlocking how you handle alcohol is on the inside. You are the only one who can make the change. The choice is yours. No one else can do it for you. And you have a unique opportunity right now to take complete responsibility for your actions going forward.

We spend so much time thinking, *I would drink less if my life weren't so stressful.* Or *If my husband hadn't left me, I wouldn't be drinking so much.* Or *If my kids were nicer to me . . .* Or *Maybe when the kids are out of the house . . .* There's always a reason or an excuse for drinking too much. The truth is, this train runs only one way— forward. Based on your personal physiology and the addictive nature of alcohol, things are only going to get worse over time. You'll build up a tolerance and need more and more alcohol to deal with the cravings. You'll drink more and more. Look at your friends and relatives who choose to drink. Are they drinking more or less than they did five years ago? Depending on their age, they might be drinking less than they did back in the booze-soaked college days. But in general, what has been the progression during normal post-college adulthood?

Hopefully, this experiment has taught you to be mindful about your drinking habits. It has given you the power to look at behavior from a different perspective. If you go back to mindless drinking, you could be headed somewhere you don't want to go. Self-medicating with alcohol is not a long-term answer to anything. In fact, it's the opposite. It only *increases* stress, depression, and anxiety. If you've got real-world problems, drinking is only going to mask them in the short term and make things worse in the long term.

I consider myself lucky to have started looking at my drinking when I was still in control of the situation. After the first or second time I drank in the morning, I took a step back and started to make some life-altering decisions. The longer you delay making changes, the harder it will be. Your brain will become accustomed to the alcohol. Remember that dopamine is one of the feel-good chemicals your brain releases to experience satisfaction and pleasure. Alcohol destroys dopamine receptors over time, which means you'll have a harder time getting pleasure from everyday activities like playing with your kids or going to the movies with friends.

The longer you're on the train, the harder it is to get off. So ask yourself, Where are you headed? What does your future look like if you don't make a change? What's life going to be like for you a year after this experiment? How about in 5 years? Or 10? Whatever alcohol is costing you now, it's going to cost more in the future.

▌ REMEMBER YOUR WHY

Think back to why you started this experiment in the first place. You wanted to shift, to pivot, to make space for a better tomorrow. And you may even be searching for your true purpose in this world. How are you meant to give back? And how can you ever do that if you're not your best self? You've come so far in the past few weeks. Really, you are amazing. And you owe it to yourself to put some thought and intention into how you want to go forward from here. How do you want your life to go?

Does it make you sad or bummed out to say, *I'm never going to drink again*? That's the case for so many drinkers. They have lots of memories of drinking with their friends or having wine with their spouses, and it's sad to set an ultimatum to *never, ever* touch alcohol again. You might get to that point, and that's great. But ultimatums like *I'm never going to drink again* set you up for failure. It's like going on a diet and saying, *I'm never going to have chocolate again as long as I live*. Never is a long time! So instead of that, try setting some non-negotiables for your life. These are promises you make to yourself that allow you to make conscious decisions about your drinking. But if you cross over a certain line, then you return to a longer period of abstinence.

It's important that you don't consider this a punishment for screwing up. It's simply a line in the sand that you're drawing for yourself. It actually gives you *more* control over your own behavior than if you leave your drinking up to chance. One of my own non-negotiables was about memories. *I'm never going to get so drunk that I black out and forget things. I'm not going to sacrifice my memories of family vacations or social gatherings because I'm drinking too much*. Or *I'm never going to drink so much that I puke the next morning*. Before you return to drinking, reflect on your drinking days. At what point did you go too far? Draw your line in the sand and stick to it. If those behaviors start creeping back into your life, return to this experiment and try it for 60 days or 90 days. It doesn't matter how many times you catch yourself and return to abstinence. What matters is that you catch yourself sooner and sooner every time. And that you reflect after each episode whether it's worth it to return to drinking. It might be. But you also might start to notice that it's not fun anymore. You might decide you're tired of going around and around with the whole alcohol game. That's okay, too. You can always return to abstinence. And eventually, you might decide to stay there.

Gaining Control

It's impossible to make these kinds of decisions when you don't have full control. When you're in the grips of a craving, something primal comes over you, and a neurological need takes precedence over your conscious desire to do better. So you need to set your non-negotiable line in the sand right after a period of sobriety, like this 30-day experiment. You are in full control of your faculties, and you can make rational decisions without cravings or emotional addictions influencing you. When you make a firm decision about something, it's SO much easier! You don't have to go around and around in your brain wondering if you should stay sober for a while. You know the exact point you need to do it. Then you just do it, and get your life back on an even keel.

When people successfully complete a period of sobriety, they feel so confident and happy. They know they can handle anything that comes their way. They finally have control over their drinking habits. It breaks my heart to see these same people completely blindsided when they find themselves reverting to their same old behavior patterns. They don't see it coming. And worse, they are so cruel to themselves when it happens. Their self-esteem completely disappears. If they could physically beat themselves up, they would.

PLEASE don't let this happen to you. As long as you realize you could slide backward at any time, you will remain vigilant. Use the tools I've given you in this chapter to monitor what's happening in your life. And make the decision that you want freedom and control over alcohol MORE than you want to drink, which means that quitting forever is always a possibility if necessary. Don't beat yourself up if you find yourself backsliding. Learn from your mistakes and move forward again. If you allow it, you can get stronger every time you come back.

I also want to reframe your definition of *success*. When I worked in the corporate world, we often celebrated even a 5 percent increase in sales or a 10 percent decrease in costs. If you made a 10 percent reduction in how many calories you ate each day or a 20 percent improvement in how many times you went to the gym, that would be huge! Yet for some reason we have this idea that we're either 100 percent perfect or we're failures when it comes to alcohol. Let's look at it a different way:

- If you normally drink every night, then by making it 30 days without a drink, you've made an 8.2 percent reduction in your drinking in the last year. Congratulations! That is huge.
- If you made it through this experiment but slipped up one day, you've got a 97 percent success rate! If you slipped up five days, you are still at an 84 percent success rate—that is massive!

I love it when people start to look at their drinking in this way. By celebrating the wins, instead of the blips, we start to see real positive changes. It puts a smile on my face when I go from getting sad emails from people who can't get past Day 1 to excited emails from people who report they now have a 70 percent alcohol-free rating for the month. This reframing can change everything.

TODAY, realize that real change starts with making commitments and start defining some non-negotiables—the lines in the sand that you *will not cross*. And if you do cross the line, you have a huge warning light flashing red and saying, "WHOA! Wait a second. You're heading someplace you don't want to go!" Crossing your line in the sand is your signal to step back and take another break. Maybe you need another 30-day reset. Or maybe you need to go back and read your journal entries. What are your non-negotiables? And what will happen if you do happen to break one of them? Take some time to write these down and commit to them.

❙ DAY 29 JOURNAL QUESTIONS

Remember, all the wisdom you seek is actually inside you; the most important words in this Experiment are the ones you tell yourself. Take some time and answer these questions in here or a separate journal (most effective), a voice memo to yourself, or simply by speaking the answers out loud for only you to hear.

1. *Where Is Your Train Headed?*

Now it is time for you to be truly honest with yourself. There is no downside; the only things that result from honest reflection are awareness and motivation for change. You are not *losing* anything through complete honesty. You can still *always* make your own decisions. You will just be making them from an empowered, knowledgeable place. Today, considering the train analogy and understanding that over time you become more tolerant to alcohol (while enjoying it less), where was your "alcohol train" headed before this experiment? If you don't commit to changing your relationship with alcohol going forward, what will your life look like in a year from now? Five years? Ten?

_____
_____
_____
_____
_____
_____
_____
_____
_____
_____
_____
_____
_____
_____
_____
_____
_____
_____

2. *Asking a New Question*

Reflect on this new question: "How do I live my happiest, best life?" instead of the old question "Do I have to stop drinking?" Can you accept that living alcohol-free might be a tool to living your happiest, best life? If you determine that living alcohol-free is a tool you need in your life, can you envision making peace with that decision knowing that it is contributing to your happiest, best life? Write whatever comes to mind as you consider this idea.

_____

_____

_____

_____

_____

_____

_____

_____

_____

_____

_____

_____

_____

_____

_____

_____

_____

_____

_____

_____

_____

_____

3. *Write a Letter to Your Future Self*

Take a few minutes to imagine yourself in five or ten years. Think about what you will look like, where you will be, who you will be with. What you will like and dislike. Think compassionately about this self of the future and imagine how your choices today will determine the quality of life for this very special you of tomorrow. Take some time to write a letter to your future self. Write your hopes, fears, and dreams with love and compassion.

_____

_____

_____

_____

_____

_____

_____

_____

_____

_____

_____

_____

_____

_____

_____

_____

_____

_____

_____

_____

_____

_____

Day 29 Reflections from alcoholexperiment.com

"Feeling vibrant energy working its way into all parts of my life from being 29 days booze-free has inspired me to continue on my path of abstaining. I am working on health and fitness goals and to start drinking again would be counterproductive. I am also looking for a new job, so I am putting my energy toward things that are priorities. These positive actions will get me out of the booze grave I dug myself into. I now know that daily intention is part of my journey. I know from experience that when I do things mindlessly, they spiral out of control. I hurt the people that I love. I hurt myself and am unkind to myself. I know that old way of doing things leads to deep despair."

—PHILLIP

"Maintaining my clearheaded, energetic self is more important than alcohol. Experiencing life and situations honestly is more important than alcohol. Facing my fears AF, working through problems and roadblocks, and discovering new things in life and new things about myself are all more important than alcohol. Alcohol is just a substance than seemingly offers temporary relief at best. At worst, it has robbed me of living my best life for too long. No more—I am in control of my life now."   —MELINDA

"I have decided to remove alcohol completely from my life. Should the time come when it returns, it must never again become anything but an insignificant trifle to be picked up briefly and put back down again in its place. It will never again supplant time with friends and family, genuine connection, and joy; it will never again dominate my conscious (and subconscious) thoughts and intentions."   —BENJAMIN

"This has been so enlightening. I am so grateful to Annie and all the energy she has put into this program. It has worked for me in that my relationship with alcohol has changed. I see it for what it is. I don't know if I will give up alcohol altogether, but this is a process for me, and I know I have the tools now to deal with my non-negotiables. Thank you, Annie Grace, for your hard-won wisdom and your generosity in sharing it with the world. This is a revolution."   —SUSAN

❙ DAY 30 ❙

What's Next?

❙ FIRST, CONGRATULATIONS! YOU DID IT!

Completing this 30-day experiment is a big accomplishment, and you should be proud. No matter where you go from here, you will never lose this time of learning, self-reflection, and empowerment. And while you may not realize the enormity of your accomplishment, I promise you that powerful shifts have happened. You have embarked on a path of awareness, and you will naturally and effortlessly be more mindful of your drinking in the future. What happens next will depend on where you fall on the spectrum of drinkers. Everyone is different, and your results from this experiment may surprise you.

It's possible that you found the past 30 days difficult and still feel emotionally dependent on alcohol. If that's the case, you may want to check out the resources at thisnakedmind.com.

It's also possible that . . .

You feel amazing and want to continue alcohol-free for the next few weeks, just to see how it goes.

You feel amazing and never want to drink again.

You feel amazing and would like to return to more moderate, mindful drinking.

However you feel is perfect. Remember, this was an experiment, not a life sentence. And the whole purpose of these past 30 days was to get mindful and present around what alcohol is and how it affects the human body and mind. You've done that. Which means you succeeded.

There is often a big fear around returning to drinking after a period of abstinence, like during this experiment. People wonder whether they can really do it, or whether they will ruin all the work they've put into themselves over the weeks or months. They are afraid to trust themselves to go back to drinking. It's always possible that you could head down that slippery slope toward out-of-control drinking at some point. And my goal is to help you recognize that downward trend as soon as possible. The sooner you recognize what's happening, the sooner you can stop yourself and reverse the trend.

No matter what you're feeling right now, I want to offer you a few different ideas to give you some additional insight into where you are right now and what you might truly want. Again, these ideas have no right or wrong. There's no judgment around them. Whatever you decide is good. But you have a unique opportunity at this moment. You've completely purged alcohol from your system, and you have the chance to objectively observe what *actually* happens when you drink. If you tried these strategies at the beginning of the experiment, you'd get different results because you'd have remnants of alcohol in your system. So take this opportunity to become a reporter and actually study the facts and your behavior before making any decisions about your future.

Strategy 1: Get Drunk for Science

Before I dive into this strategy, please know that I *do not recommend you do this* unless you've decided to go back to drinking. If you are planning to take a longer break, great! That's awesome. This is not required, but I *highly* suggest you do it before you pick up your next drink mindlessly.

When we drift back into drinking, we immediately reprogram our unconscious because we often drift back into it either during a celebration or when we are stressed. In each of those situations, you deliver a strong subconscious message to your brain. If you drink for celebration, chances are that you are in a situation where it is going to be fun *anyway*, like a birthday party or that vacation you've been planning. So when you have a drink and you do have fun, you've delivered a powerful message to the subconscious that alcohol is fun.

When we slip back into drinking for stress, the same thing happens: the alcohol seems to work because alcohol will numb your brain and therefore any uncomfortable feelings you have for a limited time (20 to 30 minutes for one drink). Yet in that 20 to 30 minutes you've delivered a powerful message to your subconscious that alcohol is great to relieve stress.

I recommend that if you decide to go back to drinking, you do it mindfully with this strategy. The strategy will show you exactly how alcohol truly makes you feel, which allows you to make a mindful decision about it.

But again, do this only if and when you decide to drink again. It is not recommended if you've already decided to continue your experiment.

Now, we know that going out and drinking with friends or having a beer at a concert is fun, right? But is it the alcohol? Or is simply being with your friends and enjoying some great music the fun part? The only way you can know for sure is to separate the two, which means drinking alone. There's an exercise I've used to figure this out. Basically, you need to remove all the external sources of stimulation from your environment. Anything like TV, music, or friends will distract you from the actual feelings you're getting from the alcohol.

Here's what to do: Get drunk alone with a video camera and be mindful about how you're feeling during the whole experience. You'll want to record your thoughts and sensations around the first drink you consume. And then you'll want to continue recording your feelings as you continue to the next drink and beyond. You're basically getting drunk for science! Your own personal science. To help you decide whether you want to continue on this path.

When you have your first drink, notice how long it takes to get that tipsy feeling. Tell the video camera exactly what you're feeling. What sensations are you experiencing? Is there any anxiety? And notice how long that feeling lasts. When I did this experiment, my video went something like, "Okay, this feels interesting. I'm a little tingly. I'm not necessarily with it right now, but my brain has stopped running a million miles an hour, and that's kind of a nice feeling." Whatever you notice is fine. No one is going to watch this video but you.

Then wait at least an hour. See how it feels to come off that first drink and then objectively ask yourself if you feel better or worse an hour later. Just sit and be mindful of how you're feeling and what thoughts might be running through your head. Then you can talk to the video camera again and say something like, "Okay, that tipsy feeling is pretty much worn off now. And I'm starting to feel a little bit uneasy. I really want that next drink." The one-hour delay is important because it takes that long for your body to fully metabolize one drink, and you want to record how it feels to come off the first one. And how badly do you want to pour the next one? You might be fine, or you might be surprised how much you want it.

I drank an entire bottle of wine during my video experience, and it was one of the most enlightening things I've ever done, because I wanted to know all the stages. Record yourself in 15-minute intervals. Set a timer, turn on the camera for 5 minutes or so, and talk about how you're feeling. Talk about any conclusions you've drawn so far. Tell stories. Is this fun? Are you enjoying yourself? Are you feeling more or less stress than before you started? You could even prepare some questions that you want to answer on camera ahead of time. But talking about anything is fine because you're going to watch the video the next day and make some observations. How do you look around the eyes as the video progresses? How is your voice? How is your skin tone? How is your demeanor? Is that person in the video who you want to be? Maybe yes. Maybe no.

I did this myself after about 40 days alcohol-free. Now this is *important*—you need to be at least 30 days alcohol-free in order for this experiment to have the impact it should. Here's why—it takes at least 30 days for your body and brain to rebalance from drinking, and if you are less than 30 days AF, you may be experiencing some type of benefit as alcohol addresses any of the withdrawal symptoms (both physical and psychological) that your prior alcohol intake created. This means drinking will feel better than it would normally because of the deficit and imbalance your prior drinking caused.

If you decide to do the experiment, do it alone, do it mindfully, follow all the rules, stay safe, and be sure to film it. It was one of the most powerful things I've done in terms of truly opening my eyes about alcohol. I couldn't even watch the video for years, but I knew without a doubt that when I decoupled alcohol from both "scratching the itch" of my withdrawal symptoms and from the natural pleasures of life (friends, going out, etc.), there was no joy for me in alcohol alone. You can watch my experiment video as part of the online social challenge at alcoholexperiment.com.

If you have not yet signed up for the online social challenge, you can sign up to watch just the experiment video at alcoholexperiment .com/drunkforscience.

Strategy 2: Non-Negotiables and Lengthening

After you watch your video the next day, you might decide that you do want to return to moderate drinking. Here's a strategy for keeping yourself objective and honest about whether you're truly in control moving forward. Go back and refresh your memory on your non-negotiables. These are your lines in the sand that you will not cross without some sort of consequence. If you haven't set yours yet, you can go back to the beginning of the experiment and refresh your memory on your big WHY. Why was it important for you to undertake this experiment? Base your non-negotiables on what's important to you.

For me, it was my memories of my children growing up. It's such a finite, precious time, and my memories were getting fuzzier and fuzzier. In fact, it breaks my heart that I can't remember my son's third birthday. Even though I wasn't blackout drunk or anything, I have memory gaps. So I set a non-negotiable that if I couldn't remember something after a night of drinking, then I had crossed a line and it was time to do something about it.

Another non-negotiable for me was drinking as self-medication. If I simply "had to have a drink" because I was stressed out for some reason, that was not okay. I was totally committed to finding other healthy ways to deal with stress and uncomfortable emotions. I couldn't keep going back to the bottle every time I had a bad day or things were tough, because I knew where that train was headed, and I did not want to be on it when it crashed. Before I started drinking, I used to run or read a book to handle negative emotions. I knew without a shadow of a doubt that alcohol was making things worse.

The "lengthening" strategy is a great tool because you never have to give up drinking forever. You simply give it up for longer and longer periods each time you cross your line in the sand. For example, if I had just come off a 30-day abstinence period and broke one of my non-negotiables, then I would immediately start a 60-day break. And the next time it happened, I'd start a 90-day break. And so on. Even if I wound up giving myself a three-year break, it's not "forever"—so my brain has an easier time accepting it.

The trick is setting up the non-negotiables and the consequences ahead of time, when you've been alcohol-free for a while. This way, you're not punishing yourself for "being bad" in the past. All you're doing is objectively setting boundaries for the future, just like any responsible person would with a potentially dangerous substance. YOU are in control of the entire situation, not the alcohol.

The end result is that you keep pushing out your time frames longer and longer whenever you cross a line in the sand. A friend of mine used this strategy and eventually lengthened her experiments to be a year without drinking. After a year she no longer saw any point to drinking again. If you ask her, she won't say she's quit alcohol forever. She simply says, "Not right now. I just don't feel like it." Alcohol has become truly small and irrelevant in her life without her ever having to make a painful decision. This is because no matter how long she lengthened her experiments, she knew she could always go back at the end of the abstinence period *if she wanted to.* After a year, she no longer wants to! How amazing is that? It's freeing to know you're in control.

Strategy 3: Understand That *Maybe* Means *Yes*

If you're coming off the experiment and you're at all concerned about backsliding, it's important to go forward mindfully. It's tempting to leave your options open. *Well, I'm done with the challenge. Maybe I'll have a drink tonight at dinner.* Or *Maybe I'll have a few margaritas while I'm on vacation. Maybe* almost always means *yes.* If you don't make a decision ahead of time, you're going to end up drinking. That might be fine, or it might not. But by not making a conscious decision, you're giving up a little bit of control, and you haven't even had a sip yet. It doesn't matter whether you decide to drink that evening—just realize that it's the decision that matters.

Before you go out with your friends . . .

Before you head to your favorite watering hole after work . . .

Before that big holiday party . . .

Make your decision. Will you be having a drink? Visualize it. Imagine how great that iced tea will taste with dinner. Or imagine yourself easily saying, "No, thanks," to that second glass of wine. Once you've made a decision, it's easier to stick to it. If it's a "maybe," then 99 percent of the time it's going to be a "yes."

What's Next?

What's next is entirely up to you. But in my experience, once you start drinking again, you can quickly regret that decision because you start to realize you're not actually in control. I've seen it hundreds of times. Someone finishes a 30-day challenge, and they think they're fine. They'll have one or two nights of moderate drinking, and then before they know it, they're right back where they started. They thought they were in control, but it's a slippery slope. It's kind of like the kids' game Chutes and Ladders, where you try to get to the end of a long, winding track. You get to skip ahead by climbing up ladders, but one long chute can put you back at the beginning. You'll be moving along nicely, thinking you're about to win the game, when—*bam*! You land on a chute that slides you back several levels. There are two options at that point. Get angry, blame yourself, flip the game board over, and go grab a drink. Or you can just laugh at yourself, realize you need to start that forward progress over again, and know in your heart that you can make up that lost ground.

No one sets out to screw up their life with alcohol. There's never a conscious intention to drink to the point of giving yourself a deadly disease. You aren't even consciously aware of when your drinking became something more than you intended or when you unknowingly gave your power over to alcohol. Circumstances line up just right and—*bam*!—your marriage is over. Or you lose your kids. Or you get fired from your job. The good news is that unlike a game of chance, you do have some control over your own behavior. And you have a choice to *learn* from your setbacks.

I made a promise to myself a long time ago to never beat myself up over slipups or mistakes. Instead, I promised to treat them as learning experiences and a chance to move forward with new resolve. You have the same opportunity. Setbacks are part of being human, whether it's with drinking or gambling or being a good parent. We all have good days and bad days. The point is to learn from the bad days so you have fewer and fewer of them in the future.

TODAY is Day 30. If you've decided to stop drinking indefinitely, great! Kudos to you. If you've decided you want to keep drinking and feel you can do so more mindfully, great! Whatever decision you make is good. You can always change your mind. You are the boss. And the social challenge at alcoholexperiment.com is available if you want accountability in achieving your goals. And if you need more resources for this incredible journey you've begun, please visit me at thisnaked-mind.com.

▌ DAY 30 JOURNAL QUESTIONS

Remember, all the wisdom you seek is actually inside you; the most important words in this Experiment are the ones you tell yourself. Take some time and answer these questions in here or a separate journal (most effective), a voice memo to yourself, or simply by speaking the answers out loud for only you to hear.

1. *Getting Drunk for Science*

Reflect on the idea presented in this chapter. If you haven't joined the online community at alcoholexperiment.com, consider visiting alcoholexperiment.com/drunkforscience to watch the video of my personal experience "getting drunk for science." Then decide if you plan to do your own. If yes, write down your exact plans (following all the suggested instructions). If not, journal about why not.

_____

_____

_____

_____

_____

_____

_____

_____

_____

_____

_____

_____

_____

_____

_____

_____

_____

_____

_____

_____

_____

_____

_____

2. *Your Non-Negotiables*

What are your non-negotiables? What are the "lines in the sand" that you will not cross? Write specifically about those things that are more important in your life than alcohol. What will you not sacrifice any longer for the sake of a drink? Reflect on your past, write about where you *never* want to be again. Take your time and come up with a solid list of non-negotiables.

_____

_____

_____

_____

_____

_____

_____

_____

_____

_____

_____

_____

_____

_____

_____

_____

_____

_____

_____

_____

_____

_____

3. *Your Lengthening Strategy*

Consider the "lengthening" strategy outlined in today's reading. Do you plan on using this strategy as you go back into mindful drinking? What initial length are you committing to? How long will you commit to if you break any of your non-negotiables during that time? How will you ensure that from this moment forward, you—and not the alcohol—are in control? Detail out a plan that feels great to you and that you are excited about.

_____

_____

_____

_____

_____

_____

_____

_____

_____

_____

_____

_____

_____

_____

_____

_____

_____

_____

_____

_____

_____

_____

Day 30 Reflections from alcoholexperiment.com

"30 days ago I was in utter despair. I was afraid but also sick of being addicted and ready to make the changes I seriously needed. My before-and-after pictures tell a huge story. I am astonished at the changes! In this month I have also fixed up other parts of my life. I am now getting somewhere that I like and I have goals. I have my zest for life again and my creativity back. I know in my heart that I will succeed. I now believe in myself and only want to be a happy woman who loves and respects herself and others. This is what coming home feels like. Thank you, Annie, for this gift."

—BRIANNA

"If you really want something, you can achieve it. I tried so many times (thinking I wanted it badly), but I wasn't ready—I didn't want it enough. This time I did, and I'm sure that was the key to a successful 30 days, and will be the key to my future success. Sure, it's hard, but you can do it if the mind is clear on what you want! Unlike some, I can't trust myself to go back to drinking moderately, so for me this is the end of a very rough, abusive relationship. Thank you, Annie. I'm so glad I found this, so glad I participated, and so proud I have come this far."

—BECKY

"Thank you. Just thank you. Here's to mindfulness. Here's to friends and family and fun. Here's to everything in its place. Here's to being present. Here's everything I've gotten in touch with over the last 30 days. Thank you."

—SAMUEL

"Thank you a thousand times, Annie, for creating this experiment. It's the best, most educational, and compassionate alcohol program I've ever come across. Your enthusiasm has been contagious for me. I can see clearly now that alcohol is disguised poison and never, ever delivers what it promises. Thank you to everyone who did the experiment, too, for all your honesty—you definitely contributed to my being able to complete the 30 days. Wow. I'm going to do the experiment again now."

—VINCE

One Final Word

Before you close this book, I want to say how amazing I think you are. I know I've said it before, but I mean it. Simply by reading through this book with me day by day, you've done something to be proud of. I hope you take a few minutes to appreciate yourself for doing this experiment.

My good friend Alex told me recently how he became an expert marksman and target shooter, and I wanted to include the story here because it illustrates a great point. When he was young and learning how to shoot, the range instructor put him about a foot away from the target. He was so close, there was no way he could miss. It was a guaranteed success for him. Then the instructor moved the target a little farther back, and Alex shot from that distance for a while. Again, there was almost no way he could miss. Over time, the target was moved farther and farther away, but Alex kept hitting it. He became an expert quickly because he built his skill on success. His confidence grew as he hit the target over and over again, and when it moved back just a little bit, that confidence kept his hand steady.

Most people learn to get better by failing and trying to correct the mistakes. That instructor could have started Alex at a respectable beginner distance away from the target and helped him make corrections. But building on failure is so hard. Every miss is a chance to tell ourselves that we can't do it.

Now some people might say, "Well, it was easy to have success when he was only a foot from the target." And that's exactly the point. When you're a beginner at anything, including sobriety, the task is supposed to be easy. If it's too difficult, you'll give up and believe you can't do it. But when you build on a foundation of success, the next step becomes achievable. You don't expect to run a marathon without first running a mile. You don't test for a black belt before you get a yellow one. You don't learn to read before you know the alphabet. What good does it do to start a beginner on a target that's 100 feet away? They're going to miss and lose confidence. They might even give up before they've had the chance to develop the muscles and skill needed to succeed. What a shame.

I designed The Alcohol Experiment to be easy and without pressure because I wanted you to experience success. And you did. Even if you only made it one day, you succeeded! Even if you didn't make it a single day but you learned something about yourself, you succeeded!

The goal was never to get you to stop drinking, but simply to experiment and take an introspective look at your relationship with alcohol. There was no way you could fail.

How cool is that?

YOU ARE A SUCCESS!

At the end of the day, this is your journey.

My wish for you now is that you take that success and let it be a foundation for whatever you choose to do moving forward. The target for you is a decision you make about alcohol and your life, and you want to make it *easy*. If you decide to go another 30 days without drinking—if that's easy for you—great. If you decide moderation is your thing and you're going to skip that second glass of wine, just for tonight, cool. You can do it.

You're already successful, so make your next steps easy. You don't have to set yourself up for failure by deciding to quit forever, if that's going to be hard. In fact, I don't say that I've quit alcohol forever. I know if I did, my brain would rebel and I might be tempted to have a drink. I like to say that I drink as much as I want, whenever I want. And the reality is that by knowing and reminding myself of the truth about alcohol, I haven't wanted a drink in years. Take it in steps you know you can achieve. And then move the target back as your confidence grows. It's your life. You get to decide.

When most people decide to quit drinking, they think they have to make it a lifelong commitment. That means that if they *ever* have a drink *in their entire life*, they've failed. That's a lot of pressure! But if they decide, *I'm not going to drink for today*—or *this week*, or *this month*, or even *this year*—it's much easier to handle.

Your brain is amazing, and you can program it to do what you want by repeatedly succeeding. If you make the target too hard to hit, you'll consistently fail. When that happens, your brain gets the message that you're a failure. And you start to believe it! When you believe you're a failure when it comes to alcohol, that belief makes your life SO difficult. Train your brain to believe you're successful instead, and you can do anything you decide to do.

Make the smallest possible decision that you know you can succeed at. All you have to do is show up, hit the easy target, and congratulate yourself on a big win.

You have all the tools you need to succeed with this book. If you'd like more support and resources, I invite you to join me and thousands of other people from around the world at alcoholexperiment.com.

You're already a success. You got this!

With all the love in my heart,
Annie

Acknowledgments

First, thank you to my incredible Naked Mind team—you amaze me every single day.

My brilliant agent, Margaret Riley King, whose vision has given my work the ability to travel the globe.

Charles Sailor for the introductions and conversations and encouragement that helped make all this possible.

Linda Sivertsen for taking the time to listen and seeing something worth talking about.

Mom and Dad—thank you for raising me to see things differently and giving me the courage and confidence to go after the vision in my head.

To Byron Katie, whose work has helped shape my inner life and, more importantly, my inner peace.

Brené Brown, whose work encourages me to be vulnerable and brave the wilderness.

Glennon Doyle, whose truth telling I am inspired and encouraged by.

Dan Harris, whose work inspired me to explore mindfulness, which opened up an entirely different aspect to my life and my work.

Rob Bell, whose faith and ability to talk about grace keep me grounded and hopeful.

Jay Pathak, your words continuously shape the direction of my life.

Thad A. Polk, whose research in the field of the brain and addiction is of vital importance.

Julie Ann Eason, whose talent in writing has made this book what it is today.

The entire amazing team at Avery, who have worked so hard to bring this important book into the world.

Most important, to every person who is inspired to ask the question "Is alcohol really making me happy?" and who is courageous in seeking an answer.

Appendix

▍HOST THE ALCOHOL EXPERIMENT IN YOUR COMMUNITY!

Are you looking to bring The Alcohol Experiment into your workplace, gym, family, church, college, or other community group? Awesome! I'm happy to hear that. I believe that everyone should have the opportunity to take a break from alcohol, examine their beliefs around this substance, and take control of their future.

I also believe the true power of The Alcohol Experiment is strengthened and extended when done within the space and support of a group. That's why I offer private communities our Live Alcohol Experiments, and why we're outlining how you can host your very own Alcohol Experiment.

Below you'll find everything you need to get started.

What you'll need:

- A start and end date
- A primary form of communication with your participants: text, email, online social group, Slack, or any other type of messaging app
- A way to make copies of reading questions and worksheets for the group
- Your meeting format (see below)

- Set meeting dates and locations (I recommend publishing all meeting times and locations for the whole experiment in advance)
- Some extra copies of *The Alcohol Experiment*, in case someone doesn't have one or needs one at a discussion meeting
- A charity of your choice and a way to collect donations. (Some people have hosted an Alcohol Experiment for a cause, which is a great idea!)

I recommend meeting no fewer than four times during your 30-day Alcohol Experiment. If you can meet more, great! Establish a day, time, and place that works best for everyone who is a part of your group. Make sure you get the names and contact information for everyone in your group, as you'll want to keep in touch during the days you don't meet. Everyday support is a crucial part of The Alcohol Experiment. Start an email chain, group chat, or Facebook group where all the members can come and share what they're learning each day, talk about their successes and struggles, and ask questions if they need to. This is also a space to put reminders about your weekly face-to-face meet-ups.

Suggested Meeting format:

Please note that everything below is optional. Make this yours! Maybe you want to bring in some fun mocktails. Maybe you want to alternate moderators. Have fun, enjoy the experiment, and adapt it to you and your group!

- Meetings should last one to two hours.
- Read The Alcohol Experiment Manifesto to open:
  - It's YOUR body . . . it's YOUR mind . . . it's YOUR choice. During The Alcohol Experiment, you'll make a choice to go

30 days without alcohol, just to see how you feel. You'll become a detached reporter, researching the facts, writing down your observations, and possibly drawing new conclusions. This is an exciting experiment, not a punishment. You're not weak-willed for questioning your drinking. There's no judgment or labeling here. You have a unique opportunity to remember how to enjoy life without alcohol. And with this unconventional approach, I'm willing to bet you'll enjoy the process.

- Read group guidelines. (Feel free to make these your own! These are simply suggestions):

  - We see a world where everyone who questions their drinking is supported and applauded, not made to feel shame or embarrassment. A world where asking if life would be better with less booze is treated the same as quitting smoking, giving up sugar, or cutting back on coffee.

  - Our mission is to allow anyone to experiment with the role of alcohol in their life by taking a 30-day alcohol-free challenge.

  - We support all paths on this journey and above all else, respect the fact that your relationship with alcohol is an individual path.

  - While we aim to provide anecdotal and scientific education, we will never judge an individual's decision in regards to their own drinking.

  - We ask that you be respectful and supportive of others, even if their path is different from your own.

- Each person goes around and introduces themselves.

- Moderator asks if anyone has any milestones they want to share.

- Moderator begins discussion questions. Participants can answer when they feel comfortable.

- One note on moderating: Depending on the group and how well everyone knows one another, it can be really handy to have a story or personal experience to share for each of the discussion questions. Prepare these ahead of time and you can jump-start the conversation!

- Intro meeting: Before the month begins, outline meeting rules and read the introduction of the book. Discuss what an ACT is and try a few examples.

- If you're meeting four times (not including the intro meeting), you should break up the discussion into these chunks:

  - Meeting 1: Discussion of Days 1–7

  - Meeting 2: Discussion of Days 8–14

  - Meeting 3: Discussion of Days 15–22

  - Meeting 4: Discussion of Days 23–30

Discussion questions

Meeting 1: Days 1–7

What's your why?

Have you tried getting curious? How did it work?

Which alcohol facts stand out most to you?

What have you shared with your friends and loved ones about this experiment? How did you do it?

In any remaining time, try the ACT technique as a group or allow for free discussion.

Meeting 2: Days 8–14

Did you do the negative self-talk writing exercise? What surprised you the most?

Are you avoiding sugar or indulging? Did you try some of the practical steps in the book?

How does it make you feel to be part of the cultural shift?

What does loving yourself mean to you?

In any remaining time, try the ACT technique as a group or allow for free discussion.

Meeting 3: Days 15–22

How are your social skills now that you're not drinking? What are you working on?

How have you been building a boredom threshold for life? How has your view on boredom changed?

How have you been questioning the truth about alcohol advertising?

What are the possible unmet needs in your life right now?

In any remaining time, try the ACT technique as a group or allow for free discussion.

Meeting 4: Days 23–30

What did you already know about alcohol's effects on the body? What did you learn?

Have you considered yourself someone who has an addictive personality? Why or why not?

How do you define moderation?

What are your non-negotiables?

What are your biggest takeaways from The Alcohol Experiment and what's next for you on this journey?

In any remaining time, try the ACT technique as a group or allow for free discussion.

At the last meeting, define what next steps are. Will there be an online social group where everyone can keep in contact as they continue on this journey? Will you continue to meet once a month going forward? Will you do another Alcohol Experiment next month? It's entirely up to you. I highly recommend keeping in contact with everyone in the group and planning a future meetup at some point to check in. I also recommend repeating The Alcohol Experiment as frequently as you're able and to invite more people to join you!

Important Note & Additional Resources:

If you have someone in your group who seems to need a bit more help, you can send them to thisnakedmind.com to explore all of our more intensive coaching programs. And if there is ever anyone you are concerned about, please advise them to seek medical attention.

ACT TECHNIQUE WORKSHEET

When you complete ACT with a belief or story that is keeping you stuck or causing you pain, that belief lets go of you both logically, and far more powerfully, emotionally. This means that through this process the story or belief stops causing you pain and stress.

Complete this worksheet for any belief or story that is not helpful to you or is holding you back. It doesn't have to be specific to alcohol—it works for anything!

Step 1: Awareness

What is your belief or story? Name it and write it down.

_____

_____

_____

_____

What experiences and observations led you to form this belief? Where did it come from? You may need to think back on your life and even your childhood. List a few to get a good idea of where this belief originated for you.

_____

_____

_____

_____

Step 2: Clarity

Is this belief internally (inside yourself) true? When you pause and reflect on the belief, can you find areas inside you where it is not actually true?

_____

_____

_____

_____

Is this externally true? What external evidence can you find that supports or discredits this belief? For this part you may want to do some quick research or observations. Look around you and find evidence for this belief.

_____

_____

_____

_____

Step 3: Turnaround

State the opposite of the initial belief—in the same words. Then find as many reasons as you can that the opposite is as true as or truer than the original belief.

_____

_____

_____

_____

Decide if the initial belief is still true for you and if holding on to this belief is serving you. Ask yourself if there are any peaceful or stress-free reasons to keep the initial belief.

Notes

Day 7: Your Experiment and Your Friends

1. **87 percent of people:** "Alcohol Facts and Statistics," National Institute on Alcohol Abuse and Alcoholism, last modified June 2017, niaaa.nih.gov/alcohol-facts-and-statistics.

2. **alcohol kills more people:** Ibid.; "Overdose Death Rates," National Institute on Drug Abuse, last modified September 2017, drugabuse.gov/related-topics/trends-statistics/overdose-death-rates.

3. **the most dangerous drug:** Dirk W. Lachenmeier and Jürgen Rehm, "Comparative Risk Assessment of Alcohol, Tobacco, Cannabis and Other Illicit Drugs Using the Margin of Exposure Approach," *Scientific Reports* 5, no. 1 (January 30, 2015): 8126, doi:10.1038/srep08126.

Day 11: The Alcohol Culture Is Shifting

1. **107 percent increase in alcohol use disorder:** "Alcohol Abuse Soars for Older Americans," David Frank, *AARP Bulletin*, November 16, 2017, aarp.org/health/healthy-living/info-2017/alcohol-abuse-boomers-binge-drinking.html.

Act 5: Alcohol and Happiness

1. **children of alcoholics:** "A Family History of Alcoholism," National Institute on Alcohol Abuse and Alcoholism, NIH Publication No. 03–5340, reprinted June 2012.

Day 12: Your Incredible Body and Brain

1. **this idea that alcohol is heart-healthy:** "Association Between Alcohol and Cardiovascular Disease: Mendelian Randomisation Analysis Based on Individual Participants Data," BMJ, July 10, 2014, bmj.com/content/349/bmj.g4164.

2. **wildly popular study, the Holahan study:** "Late-Life Alcohol Consumption and 20-Year Mortality," Wiley Online Library, August 24, 2010, onlinelibrary.wiley .com/doi/pdf/10.1111/j.1530-0277.2010.01286.x.

3. **CBS news:** "Heavy Drinkers Outlive Non-Drinkers: Cheers to That!" CBS News, last modified August 31, 2010, cbsnews.com/news/heavy-drinkers-outlive -non-drinkers-cheers-to-that.

4. *Time*: "Why Do Heavy Drinkers Outlive Nondrinkers," *Time*, last modified August 31, 2010, content.time.com/time/magazine/article/0,9171,2017200,00 .html.

5. *Medical News Today*: "Why Do Moderate Drinkers Live Longer Than Abstainers," *Medical News Today*, August 30, 2010, medicalnewstoday.com/articles /199398.php.

6. **more than 60 diseases and conditions:** "Harmful Use of Alcohol," World Health Organization, last modified June 2009, who.int/nmh/publications /fact_sheet_alcohol_en.pdf.

7. **alcohol has surpassed AIDS:** "Global Status Report on Alcohol and Health," World Health Organization, 2011, who.int/substance_abuse/publications /global_alcohol_report/msbgsruprofiles.pdf.

8. **no safe level of drinking:** "Alcohol Use and Burden for 195 Countries and Territories, 1990–2016: A Systematic Analysis for the Global Burden of Disease Study 2016." *The Lancet*, August 23, 2018. Doi:10.1016/s0140-6736(18)31310-2.

9. **most dangerous drug:** "Drug Harms in the UK: A Multi-Criteria Decision Analysis," *The Lancet*, November 1, 2010, thelancet.com/journals/lancet/article /PIIS0140–6736(10)61462–6/abstract.

10. **toxicological threshold [or how much it will take to kill you]:** "Comparative Risk Assessment of Alcohol Tobacco Cannabis and Other Illicit Drugs Using the Margin of Exposure Approach," PubMed Central, National Library of Medicine National Institute of Health, January 30, 2015, ncbi.nlm.nih.gov/pmc /articles/PMC4311234.

Day 13: Let's Talk About Sex

1. **Drinking reduces testosterone levels:** Mary Ann Emanuele and Nicholas Emanuele, "Alcohol and the Male Reproductive System," National Institute on Alcohol Abuse and Alcoholism, accessed July 21, 2018, pubs.niaaa.nih.gov /publications/arh25–4/282–287.htm.

2. **alcohol affects libido:** Lizette Borreli, "Alcohol and Sex: What Is 'Whiskey Penis' and How Does It Affect the Male Libido?" Medical Daily, medicaldaily

.com/alcohol-and-sex-what-whiskey-penis-and-how-does-it-affect-male
-libido-357278.

Day 20: Our Headline Culture and the Science of Sharing

1. **"Moderate to heavy drinkers are more likely to live to 85 without developing dementia":** Gary Robbins, "Moderate to heavy drinkers are more likely to live to 85 without developing dementia," *San Diego Union-Tribune*, August 1, 2017, sandiegouniontribune.com/news/science/sd-20170801-story.html.

Day 21: Hey, Good Lookin'!

1. **alcohol causes a zinc deficiency in the body:** "Zinc Fact Sheet for Health Professionals," National Institutes of Health: Office of Dietary Supplements, last modified March 2, 2018, https://ods.od.nih.gov/factsheets/Zinc-HealthProfessional/.

Day 23: Alcohol's Effect on Your Health

1. **the level of consumption that minimizes health loss is zero:** "Alcohol Use and Burden for 195 Countries and Territories, 1990–2016."

ACT 10: Alcohol and Anger

1. **drinking is involved in about 75 percent of all child abuse deaths:** "The Impact of Alcohol Abuse on American Society," Alcoholics Victorious, alcoholicsvictorious.org/faq/impact.

2. **95 percent of all violent crimes and 90 percent of sexual assaults involve alcohol:** "Alcohol, Drugs and Crime," National Council on Alcoholism and Drug Dependence, Inc., last modified June 27, 2015, ncadd.org/about-addiction/alcohol-drugs-and-crime.

Day 27: Is Alcohol Really Poisonous and Addictive?

1. **Ethanol was used as a general anesthetic:** John W. Dundee, Martin Isaac, and Richard S. J. Clarke, "Use of Alcohol in Anesthesia," *Anesthesia and Analgesia* 48, no. 4 (July–August 1969): 665–69.

Also by
Annie Grace

AVERY